GODS, GENES,

and

CONSCIOUSNESS

Also by Paul Von Ward:
Dismantling the Pyramid
Our Solarian Legacy

GODS, GENES,

and

CONSCIOUSNESS

Nonhuman intervention in human history

HAMPTON ROADS
PUBLISHING COMPANY, INC.
for the evolving human spirit

PAUL VON WARD

Cover design by Marjoram Productions
Cover art © 2003 Picturequest/Digital Vision Ltd.

Hampton Roads Publishing Company, Inc.
1125 Stoney Ridge Road
Charlottesville, VA 22902

434-296-2772
fax: 434-296-5096
e-mail: hrpc@hrpub.com
www.hrpub.com

If you are unable to order this book from your local
bookseller, you may order directly from the publisher.
Call 1-800-766-8009, toll-free.

Library of Congress Cataloging-in-Publication Data

Von Ward, Paul, 1939-
  Gods, genes, and consciousness : nonhuman intervention in human
history / Paul Von Ward.
     p. cm.
  Includes bibliographical references (p.) and index.
  ISBN 1-57174-379-0 (5 1/2 x 8 1/2 tp : alk. paper)
  1. Gods--Miscellanea. 2. Human-alien encounters. 3. Consciousness--
Miscellanea. I. Title.
  BF1999.V657 2004
  001.942--dc22
                                             2004007651

10 9 8 7 6 5 4 3 2 1

Printed on acid-free paper in Canada

Dedication

For June and Rod Dugger,
and others like them,
who will not agree with all the conclusions herein,
but whose nurturing and loving support
for their successor generations
make possible humanity's continuing experimentation
with life and its exploration
of the farthest boundaries of our universe.

Table of Contents

Preface

"In the name of God, _____." The reader can fill the blank with any imaginable curse, blessing, praise, wish, prayer, epithet, or affirmation and be certain that it will be spoken somewhere in the world today.

An Arab says, "The Jews subverted Allah's order for the universe." A Jew says, "*YHVH* gave us this land." An American president reportedly tells an Arab and a Jew, "God instructed me to [act]." Are they all speaking of and to the same god? Whence these concepts of Allah/*YHVH*/God? How many other such gods have been identified throughout human history?

Moses (3,500 years ago) reported to the Hebrews that a god spoke to him from a burning bush and gave him commandments and books from a cloud of fire and smoke on the mountain. Saul (2,000 years ago) reported a voice spoke to him from the sky on the way to Damascus and set him on the path to define and organize the new religion of Christianity. Mohammed (1,400 years ago) reported that the Archangel Gabriel came in a vision and instructed him to start a new religion. Joseph Smith (1820s) reported that the angel Moroni showed him where the Book of Mormon was buried. A group of people in Chicago (early 1900s) channeled the *Urantia Book* that has stimulated a small religious movement. Charles Wise (1970s) reported that Jesus dictated a book to him to "set the record straight" on how he had been misrepresented for 2,000 years. Such communications from beings more advanced than humans have over time led to many religious movements, some more successful than others.[1]

The histories of these religions have been filled with hatred for nonbelievers and bloody struggles among groups of believers. The history revealed in this book suggests that the nature of their Advanced Being-instigated beliefs spawns and nurtures their internecine conflicts. Militants in every religion have continually persecuted heretics, converted "heathen" and "infidels" by the sword and economic inducements, and tried to control the minds of millions. On the other hand, many devotees have been inspired to produce great works and noteworthy service to humanity. A built-in set of conflicting institutional values has suppressed initiative and made people psychologically dependent and susceptible to manipulation by demagogues, and yet has simultaneously given comfort, hope, and joy.

In the last 50 years, thousands of humans have reported contact with extraterrestrials, or ETs (another name for Advanced Beings). Some say they have been raped by them, abducted and frightened, and even used as parents for hybrid children. Others say the ETs have enlightened them, providing new knowledge and insights useful to humanity. Some have appeared as physical beings, while others have been "energetic" or "light beings." There have been reports of valuable technology provided to humans by some of these ETs.

Thousands of people daily serve as channels for voices with messages no different in substance from world religions or the reports of those who have had contact with ETs. People pray to their angels, seek the advice of their spirit guides, and talk with discarnate beings in more dimensions than one can imagine. Some go out of body to meet them.

What is all this human communication with nonhuman entities? Why have some of these communications had such significant consequences for human history and others none?

Why have the beings themselves and the human reactions to them been so socially divisive? Just who are these disembodied voices and ethereal beings?

I call them ABs. The term AB, Advanced Being, refers to any category of nonhuman, conscious entities who may have been involved in human affairs. If you believe in one god, multiple gods, ETs, heavenly messengers, angels, spirit guides, a holy spirit, devils, ascended beings, spirit voices who speak through human channels, higher dimensional conscious entities, something you call your "higher self," or any similar phenomenon, you already agree that ABs exist. Have one or more of them affected your life? If the answer is yes, have you ever considered that other ABs may exist? Have you thought about the influence they could have had on other people's lives and in human history?

When using the term Advanced Beings, I do not mean to imply that they are more advanced than humans in all respects. This definition simply recognizes reports made by people over several millennia. After communication or contact with such beings, individuals have described them as having powers or technologies stronger or more advanced than our own. These powers may be like those of an angel who can appear and disappear instantaneously, or may involve the use of sophisticated technologies by flesh-and-blood ETs whose spacecraft exceed the current limits of human technology or scientific understanding.

An AB may have powers of communication unknown to humans and operate in realms not readily accessible to us. ABs may have the power to unilaterally decide when and how to speak to us, even to choose whether to respond when we ask them to talk with us. None of this means they are necessarily more intelligent or more morally and ethically developed than humans. It means only that they can decide when, as we might put it, to initiate a call or answer the phone. However, whether the ABs take the initiative or we ask them for advice, it would behoove us to test their views against our own knowledge and wisdom. After all, they can only offer their own limited perspectives on a still-evolving universe.

Looked at in this way, the question "Are we alone in the universe?" seems foolish. Scientists still seeking answers to this question mislead themselves if they only tune in on pulsars and distant stars. The answer lies under our feet and in our collective stories: Other conscious beings inhabit the universe, and we have never been alone. The proof lies in self-evident artifacts and human experience.

This, the most important story in human history, receives little attention by either academic or popular historians. The nature of the story explains why established scholars fear to investigate it. It calls into question their own and almost everyone else's mental state, raising the specter of self-delusion across all of humanity that has atrophied our emotional and intellectual development. What to do about the evidence for other intelligent beings in the universe lies at the center of a covert struggle for control of the structure of human consciousness.

Many scholars concerned about the challenges humans face attribute the most critical rift in consciousness to that between science and religion. For instance, philosopher Ken Wilber said in 1998, ". . . take into account that 90 percent of the world's population has a religious outlook based on some kind of mythology—God the Father and so on—and that the standard scientific view gives these myths as much credibility as they give the tooth fairy. . . . There's an enormous split between reason and meaning that must be healed."[2]

Healing humanity's psychosis will require more than Wilber suggests. A Faustian bargain between science and religion has created the current split in human consciousness. Both must first free themselves of their own blinders before they can be incorporated into a natural and holistic perspective that recognizes the "multiplicity and unity of the universe."[3]

The bifurcation in human consciousness is more like a species multiple personality disorder combined with a Tower of Babel syndrome. Human society, because of its misunderstandings about contacts with Advanced Beings over the millennia, has developed several incompatible subpersonalities. Some are neurotic, while others are psychotic, and they all babble in different languages.

It is no wonder the world situation is what it is today. A divided self is self-destructive, whether it's an individual, a society, or a species. With groups fighting among themselves, it is like a body whose essential organs are warring against each other. Severed from our history, we know not why we fight. Severed from our inherent humanity, we know not why we cannot find love. Severed from our natural world, we know not where to find inner tranquillity and universal peace.

This book introduces new concepts to describe these problems and make sense of them. It proposes a way to find common ground among the world's cultures, with their different ideas on gods and their relationship to humans. It holds that the truth is hidden in plain sight. Therefore, the Old Testament, the Vedas, the Greek myths, the Sumerian tablets, and other historical sources are analyzed without prejudgments as to their validity.

You will find that I have taken sacred texts and other ancient materials for the purposes of this book as *reliable references* to the existence of other beings and advanced technologies. To accept them only as fantasy or metaphor, we must first be able to demonstrate that they do not refer to actual events. Until we have proven their claims are false, we have no defensible justification for not interpreting them as plausible scenarios in our still-evolving knowledge.

This book explains why modern science and religion do not want to address the possibility that humans interact with many Advanced Beings. It shows how intelligent people have been conditioned to ignore or suppress a significant part of human history and current human experience. It exposes why governments refuse to reveal that they are just as interested in the subject as anyone and have collected much evidence that deserves to be shared with all of humanity.

A note to my friends of all religions. To some, this book will appear to be a denial of some beliefs you cherish most. My intent has not been to undermine your faith in the source of all life and the purposefulness of all beings. I share with you the awe and reverence we feel for the majesty of creation and the ineffable nature of its origins. I share with you the deepest respect for the integrity of all individuals and the responsibility each of us has to search for and live a deeper truth. I have faith that all beings are joined by a reality that transcends culture and place. It is my hope that this tentative offering of the results of my search can help us find the tie that truly binds.

Acknowledgments

It would be impossible to name all the people who have contributed to or influenced my thinking about this book. Writers like many of those quoted or referenced in the text have helped open my eyes to questions that I did not even know to ask. Conversations with a large number of people about their AB "experiences" have provided some of the answers. However, a few individuals must be thanked for their support during the times when the book was only a vision unfulfilled. Each provided friendship and assistance in specific ways that kept me going:

Joyce Shafer for support in the initial stages of research. Laara Lindo and Yasuhiko Kimura, then of the University of Science and Philosophy, for providing a forum and resources to try out the AB hypothesis on some of the brightest people on Earth. Frank DeMarco, Hampton Roads publisher, for trust and confidence in the project. The DuPont Library staff at the University of the South in Sewanee, Tennessee. Colleagues in the Institute of Noetic Sciences Chattanooga community for trial runs and friendly support. Margaret Donohue for comments on versions of text and publicity photo. Edward Carlos for critiques and sharing of experiences. Mark Preslar for reference materials on linguistics and language. Tom Jarrett for radio interviews and other support. The Stone Door Sivananda Yoga Center for reference materials and a forum for testing new ideas. Shelley Tanenbaum for introduction to PEER's work and added encouragement. Members of my Sunday "soiree" discussion group and others who "spurred" me on. Jan Gessler for much needed empathy and sensitive photography. And last but not least, Richard Leviton, Hampton Roads senior editor, whose skillful use of an editorial scalpel combined with probing questions and keen insight considerably raised the quality of the written text.

While all these people made invaluable contributions to my effort, only I am responsible for the final product. I apologize to them collectively and individually for any misuse I made of their advice and for the way I may have twisted their views to suit my own purposes.

Introduction

The preface linked the history of religions and their gods to the modern phenomenon of aliens and ETs. Expressing such a linkage did not result from a failure in the author's computer software. Substantial and tangible historical evidence suggests that humans *still* interact with the same sorts of ABs as our forebears did in the cradle of Western civilization—the birthplace of all the modern supernatural religions—and that the UFO cover-up has ancient roots.

When I started historical research on the concepts of God and the gods in the early stages of Western civilization, I thought I would be dealing with an era that was in the long-lost past. I wanted simply to understand what cultural factors might have been at the roots of the bloody antagonisms that have characterized the relationships among the great religions for the last 1,500 years. I had no idea that I would find such substantial evidence of AB intervention in human history and learn that it had continued, in different forms, since the time of the first *Homo sapiens*.

That discovery compelled me to assess the odds that myths and legends of the gods were based on actual involvement of physical ABs on Earth. I wanted to test whether credible evidence substantiated the Bible's account of multiple ABs (the Elohim) who had been involved in the origins of early humans (the Adamu). Several biblical references make this assertion and further state that the gods had walked and talked with humans and had "intercourse with the daughters of man." Most of the material in parts 3 and 4 in this book was gathered to test that AB-intervention hypothesis. As you will see from chapter 3 and later sections, there is enough direct and corroborating evidence to say that biblical references to ABs can be reasonably assumed to be based in fact.

When I recognized that the accounts of modern human encounters with ABs were in many ways similar to ancient stories recounted by societies around the world, I began to suspect that we were dealing with the same phenomenon. If we were, why is there such a concerted effort by governments and other institutions to cover up the reality of current AB activities? If people have always known about such beings, why make a big deal of it today?

Then it hit me: I had become so enmeshed in my own validation of the historicity of tangible ABs in the Mideast since the days of the Flood, and particularly during the period around the time of Jesus, that I had forgotten that most people today do not believe such beings existed. I had forgotten that modern religions, in contrast to early Indo-European cults, now considered their sacred texts to be metaphorical. They had decided somewhere along the way that the gods they worshipped were supernatural. That is, they lived beyond the natural universe and revealed themselves only to special groups.

Suddenly, I began to see something of the problem. Somewhere along the way, the founders of modern Judaism, Christianity, Islam, and all their offshoots had convinced their followers that a supernatural god had chosen them as its special representatives on Earth. They had further asserted that their god was the True Supreme God of the Universe. They went so far as to claim that their religion was the only valid channel for humanity to reconnect with that god.

The light bulb in my head began to glow more brightly. If for some reason believers were to realize that the roots of their religions lay in a period of actual AB-gods resident on Earth, each religion's claim to have found the "one true god" from among all the others would become suspect. The whole theology of their god having "chosen them" for a unique role in history might be seen as self-serving. And what if some of those gods were still around? What if they were to spill the beans so that just any human could know the true story?

Finally, the full light dawned on me. I saw why so much effort was expended to deny the UFO/ET "open secret." Something much deeper than just admitting that a few UFO sightings and some ET encounters might be real was at stake. By working the historical AB-intervention hypothesis from both ends, first from the Sumerian and Hebrew texts and then from twentieth-century UFO/ET reports, I saw the linkage. The "secret" was not the fact that ABs might be in Earth's space today, but that they had *always* been. And further, that historical fact had been denied and suppressed (lied about) to create religions based on false premises through which a few men would control human consciousness.

I recognized it would be very difficult to convince most people that Western history as we know it concealed such a secret, despite the evidence now in clear sight, without some link to the reality experienced by people today. That link is the threat posed by official recognition of UFO sightings and ET contacts.

If enough people were to begin to realize that the UFO/ET phenomenon was part of our ordinary reality, they would take the next step and realize that similar phenomena in history were also part of ordinary reality. They would see through the supernatural fiction of just two millennia of Indo-European history. The whole basis of privilege and authority on which modern power structures sit would be undermined. Their control of economic resources, including the financing of science and education (to maintain blinders on human consciousness), would be threatened. That is why the patrons[1] of supernaturalism, those who use it to manipulate divisions and wars to control the functioning of nation states, need to maintain the cover-up of the past and the present as long as possible.

This motivation explains why the fragmentation of human consciousness has been fostered and reinforced with controls over theology and science through the centuries. In order to make sure that the various human "subpersonalities" do not talk to each other and compare notes, one only needs to create diversions and foment conflict so that people do not have the energy to focus on long-term trends in society. Do not leave them time to imagine how things could be different. Using the Tower of Babel tactic, many languages and confused terminology within a single language prevent the development of a consensus for positive change. Thus, a few-decades-old UFO/ET cover-up is only a small part of the effort.

However, because it can open the lid of a Pandora's Box, confirmation of the cover-up would remove a linchpin of the power brokers' present strategy. Consequently, they fear something called the Disclosure Project. Several hundred current or former U.S. officials have formally indicated a willingness to tell the public all they know about the U.S. government's UFO-related activities, if Congress will release them from their secrecy oaths.[2] They include military and intelligence officers and others whose work put them in contact with UFOs, crash information, and reverse-engineering activities and exposed them to other life-forms. They collectively represent a "smoking gun" of the present-day cover-up of ABs, with the potential to destabilize all major institutions.

When Did the UFO/ET Cover-up Begin?

For the reader not already well versed in this issue, the following brief overview may be helpful. Although accounts of historical AB presence can be found in almost every culture, most people in the twentieth century had forgotten or misinterpreted them.

Beginning in the 1940s, many Americans learned that unidentified flying objects (UFOs) had been sighted in the skies over their country. According to some sources, the first downed UFO was in the San Diego area; the U.S. Navy reportedly retrieved it in 1941. During World War II, American and British fighter and bomber pilots in the skies over Europe reported strange lights (dubbed "foo fighters") buzzing their planes, sometimes causing their electronics to fail. The first 1947 sighting of "flying saucers" in Oregon was widely reported. In early July 1947, the U.S. military reported the crash of a UFO near Roswell, New Mexico. Although the story was quickly retracted, a number of civilian witnesses confirmed one or more crashes and reported that nonhuman beings, dead or alive, were in or close to a craft.

The U.S. government hastened to claim the initial military press release was describing a fallen weather balloon (since proven to be false). It threatened witnesses and engaged in a disinformation campaign with the aim of smearing the reputations of anyone publishing facts related to UFOs and extraterrestrials. Even so, citizen reports of strange objects in the skies continued to increase for five years. Early in this UFO era, the National Security Act was passed, and the Central Intelligence Agency was established. The U.S. Air Force started Project Blue Book to analyze sightings, finally suggesting most could be explained by natural phenomena, but admitting some could not.

On April 7, 1952, *Life* magazine ran a cover story on the accumulating evidence for visitors from outer space, a subject subsequently covered by more than 350 U.S. newspapers. Public interest peaked in July 1952 when on two consecutive Saturday nights (July 19 and 26) UFOs over Washington, D.C., were tracked by airport radar, observed by civilian pilots, chased by Air Force jets, and viewed by large numbers of visitors and residents in the D.C. area. President Harry Truman publicly demanded an explanation. The Air Force responded with obfuscation.

On the Tuesday following the sightings, the Pentagon held a press briefing on the UFO issue, attended by the largest number of journalists since World War II, with the obvious purpose of dampening the public's interest. Major General John Samford talked for almost an hour and a half, giving tidbits of history relating to UFOs from biblical times to the nineteenth century without seriously addressing the twentieth-century phenomenon.

He alluded to the theory of temperature inversion (that could affect radar images) and other natural explanations, spoke about the problem of definitions, and left the briefing room without answering the real question. Journalists duly reported on the temperature inversion theory (still unscientifically touted in a 1969 Air Force report), without mentioning that it could not account for the visual sightings by civilian and military pilots, and contributed wittingly or not to the official suppression effort. That event initiated over half a century of efforts by reporters and private researchers to make the full story public and a more powerful counter-effort by the government to censor it.

In an effort to divert attention from the evidence of UFO/ETs in Earth's airspace, the U.S. government in the 1960s started to promote the idea of a Search for Extraterrestrial Intelligence (SETI) that would focus on outer space. SETI development under NASA continued for two decades, being expanded in 1988 into a dual mode, but Congress withdrew funding from the program in 1993. With government encouragement, a private SETI Institute was set up to engage millions of citizens in a waiting mode, seeking a clear signal from some distant star. This made it easier for the government to distract citizens from real ABs.

Parallel with an increase in reported UFO sightings and ET contacts throughout the second half of the twentieth century, more Americans began to report contacts with angels and other beings from whom they received information, and sometimes assistance.[3] Echoing the government's method of dealing with the issue of nonhuman intelligence, Christian church leaders downplayed reports of angels and direct inspiration, asserting that God no longer works with humans in such a direct manner. The media treated the subject with no more respect, ignoring or relegating it to tabloid-style ridicule.

Given the opposition of the established institutions of government and religion to such channels of information, many who experienced ABs kept it to themselves or a few friends, unwilling to subject their information to ridicule and themselves to public ostracism. This meant AB reports would not be rationally and publicly analyzed to distinguish hard evidence from fantasy. As a result, most people assumed none of the reports should be taken seriously, which seems to be what officialdom intended. Experiencers doubted themselves.

However, by the 1990s the cat was out of the bag, and serious research was being published in books and periodicals, and professionals were meeting with experiencers. Many people were no longer ashamed to be identified with the encounters. Some of those books and reports are dealt with in the following chapters. A brief Internet search will bring the reader new to this subject up to date on developments.

The government denial has gone to the incredible point of even lying about having made an assessment of the UFO threat to national security (one it probably made in the 1950s). Such government-wide stonewalling and obvious cover-up have forced intelligent and responsible people in all walks of life to seek public disclosure of any evidence relating to other forms of conscious life and other-world communications.

Crisis of Confidence

Whether one believes any particular conspiracy theory or not, a majority of citizens have come to the view that officials often conspire to obscure or fudge the facts about things that would endanger their particular agendas. As for the issue of ABs, I believe a crisis of public confidence is brewing.[4] It is almost as if a state of collective schizophrenia were emerging, where "official reality" is incongruent with the lived experience of large groups of citizens. Private groups increasingly call for recognition of the obvious activity of unknown craft and alien beings and their inner communications with humans. The more they seek attention, the stronger the resistance of the government and scientific and religious institutions to admit the existence of any evidence. Still another factor adds to the complexity.

Beyond denying the three-dimensional existence of ABs, a powerful elite appears to want to keep ordinary individuals from learning to use innate inner senses to discover how they are being manipulated. They encourage suppression of research about inner ways of knowing by discrediting discoveries about the psychic powers of humans and their relationship to other dimensions, including nonphysical ABs.

Modern society seems, thus, to have reached an impasse between different epistemologies (ways of knowing) and between mutually exclusive cosmologies (theories of how the universe works). This impasse portends even deeper social divisions, conflicts that go beyond intellectual debates to a precipitous breakdown of civil society. Becoming more alienated intellectually and energetically, fearful groups on any side of the AB issue may begin to lash out at those holding views that undermine their own dogmas about what is "natural" or "divine."

I believe the process of a potential implosion of collective consciousness has already begun. The notion that humans are unique and alone in the universe is getting harder and harder to support. The crisis will arise, if we do not consciously prepare ourselves, when evidence of AB involvement in human affairs, indisputable even to most skeptics, becomes accepted by a critical mass of the public.

As the public evidence for other life-forms mounts, the issue of alien influence may become even more divisive than conflicts over race, immigration, religion, or abortion, with even more import for the future of humanity. I intuit that the key piece of evidence, from a scientific discovery or the initiatives of another intelligent species, which makes our connections with other beings universally self-evident, will likely appear soon. Before that knowledge dam bursts, it is imperative that a rational dialogue begin on to what extent humans have not been and are not alone. In a preventive mode, we need attempts now to develop a broad-based consensus about the tangible evidence and to consider its implications for individuals and institutions.

If we do not, the result could be a precipitous upheaval in the structures of power and authority in society, followed by a period of destructive social chaos before a new order can evolve. Fear of this potentiality also energizes the vested interests to resist any open discussion of these issues even more. I suspect they wish to hold out until they have enough control of social institutions (primarily those of defense, security, intelligence, and police systems) and the Earth's resources to weather "the awakening." If they can keep the lid on that long, no human freedom movement can overthrow them.

Overreaction Expected

I believe (perhaps too idealistically) that those institutions of control are fighting a losing battle. I sense that they, too, fear that possibility and will overreact to the present situation. Their short-term tactics of suppression will become simultaneously more aggressive and subtle.

If that sounds like a radical statement at this point (and I hope it turns out to be one), you may not consider it so by the time you finish this book. Too much is at stake for some groups among us to quietly open the archives. From self-interest, the authorities cannot reveal evidence that suggests ABs of various types have *always* been involved in human affairs. They cannot afford to have people come to understand how their forebears used that direct intervention to cause the fragmentation of human consciousness. This fragmentation has made it possible for a few people to gain effective control over nation-states and the profits from the labors of their citizens. The public that ignores this history cedes power to those who perpetuate the notion that "divine institutions" and "materialistic consumerism" represent the best we humans could have achieved.

Divide and Conquer

If I am correct about a possible overreaction, what can we expect to see? The tactic of "divide and conquer" has been the historical tool of groups who wish to control nations or empires. It can involve everything from formal wars to undeclared wars to terrorism, economic imperialism, cultural and religious conflicts, and fomenting class struggles. Possible forms of suppression can include greater censorship of scientific and professional channels, efforts to discredit alternative views, restricting free access to public media, and use of the criminal justice system to harass people with humanistic perspectives.

Continuing the Tower of Babel confusion of languages by manipulation of terms for ABs among disparate groups in society will impede efforts to compare the fragments of AB evidence. Another tactic that may be used to sow confusion is to treat anyone who reports contacts with other forms of consciousness as mentally ill. A third tactic marginalizes individuals who speak of their experience with ABs, by relegating their stories to the tabloids and ostracizing them from mainstream conferences or other public forums. The groups in question will keep everyone too preoccupied with needless mayhem to be able to see the larger agenda: control over the Earth's resources and manipulation of mass consciousness to maintain their self-arrogated power over human destiny.

A More Hopeful View

We are now in a stage of human development where we can exercise the choice to expand our conscious awareness instead of continuing the downward spiral of fragmentation. Recent developments have, for the first time in recorded history, provided a framework large enough to transform human consciousness. The last quarter of the twentieth century saw a fundamental change in the scope of human awareness, from a primarily Earth-centered perspective to recognition of a human role throughout the solar system (incorporated into Arthur C. Clarke's fictional *Rendezvous with Rama*).

The increasingly active international space program has quietly transformed the way almost everyone thinks about the human place in the web of life. With a functioning space station, Mars orbiters, Hubble telescope images, and growing numbers of newly discovered planets, more people think, "If the universe is that large and that complicated, some of these planets must have conscious life. We cannot be all alone. And some of them must be older and more advanced than humans." One logical extension of that thought is, "I wonder if they have ever visited our solar system?" Which leads to the question, "Have they ever interacted with humans?"

The proliferation of expansive images of the physical universe has been accompanied by increasing numbers of individuals opening themselves up to other conscious beings and other levels of consciousness. More people have come to recognize they also have the same kind of AB-sourced communication and insight that in the past led to the founding of new religions or persecution as false prophets and witches. Increasing numbers have to understand that they, too, can communicate directly with everything from a transcendent consciousness to specific intelligent beings in other dimensions.

As the number of AB voices available to us has grown exponentially, many humans are now beginning to realize that we have to turn to one another to compare the input from all these sources. Some have begun to be cautious about accepting any one message as the ultimate message, recognizing that any being from any part of the universe has its own perspective and its own agenda. People have started to recognize the responsibility we have to test ourselves and make wise choices about what to believe and what to act upon.

The current era is different from the past in two other respects. First, there is the rapid proliferation of the number of people experiencing or at least willing to talk about contacts or communications with nonhuman consciousness. Second is the proliferation of the number of sources (other entities interested in humans) reported. These sources include not only beings perceptible to ordinary human senses, but also nonmaterial beings. It is almost as if Earth has become a focus of cosmic attention. That may suggest we are *in extremis,* attracting others who want to help bail us out from our self-created mess. On the other hand we may have finally reached a level of potential maturation conducive to benefiting from outside help, like youths who reach a point where they are willing to accept advice from more mature adults.

Throughout this book, and particularly at the end, I point out opportunities for healing action. It is my hope that the kind of discussion this book stimulates will awaken people to serve as catalysts for greater openness and constructive change. I strongly believe that, as humans, we are potentially undaunted by the challenge of rediscovering our common roots with other intelligent beings and our universal purpose in being.

My Process

In the chapters to follow, I survey and sample the evidence for the AB intervention hypothesis from many fields of study. I describe the nature of that evidence, giving you references for further reading so that you can draw your own conclusions. In this investigation the most difficult challenge was not in finding relevant information. The challenge was one of overcoming implicit assumptions from my own mindset. I had to accept the possibility that all I had been taught in good schools and great universities had to be called into question.

I realized the answer to the question of whether other beings have intervened in human development is not nearly as elusive as the three existential questions over which other cosmologists pontificate ad nauseam. These questions (Whence the universe? What is the purpose of life? What awaits us after this life?) require answers beyond human experience. I had the advantage that if such an intervention has occurred, one should be able to discern evidence of its impact. I discovered that history has abundant evidence related to the AB issue.

I wondered: If an AB intervention had happened, what impact would it have had on human development? And why did modern humanity almost forget this aspect of its early history? I address these questions on the basis of current credible reports on AB contacts and the mass of historical materials readily available to a student willing to research.

Some may question the epistemology of this work, wishing to know definitively if I have used only academic research (previously documented findings), "channeled" all the material from some divine source, done all the primary research myself, or simply concocted a good story. The truth is that it represents all possible ways of knowing that I could possibly exploit.

I have used hard science and historical documentation from others where relevant research has already been done. I have accessed primary sources when available but given them my own interpretation. I have intuitively pieced together disparate bits of information from a variety of sources to draw some inferences that are, as far as I know, unique and that raise serious intellectual questions that deserve consideration. To be honest, some of the tentative conclusions came into my consciousness unbidden, from some source I have not been able to identify. But, this is the way all progress in human consciousness seems to work in what is evidently a multidimensional universe.

Hypotheses Used in My Approach

I trust this book will be seen as an antidote to the escape from self-responsibility and self-accountability of both supernatural religion and materialistic science. Although different from the history you read in school and in mainstream periodicals, it derives from information about our history now available to everyone. I urge you to suspend your judgment and read it with a view to testing the following tentative hypotheses against evidence you have.

• Universal consciousness manifests in various levels of beings throughout the living universe, with humans being local, direct manifestations of that consciousness.

- During *Homo sapiens*' natural path of development on Earth, Advanced Beings have interacted with and continue to interact with them in different ways.

- At one or more times in human history, nonterrestrial ABs have developed colonies on Earth and used their powers to influence human development.

- Human history has also been affected by Earth-wide cataclysms, and some survivors have received civilization-shaping technical assistance from ABs.

- A symbiotic relationship developed between those human survivors and the AB colonies and has influenced human development to the present time.

- As ABs deserted their Earth colonies, human separation anxiety resulted in magical thinking that retarded our intellectual and psychological maturation.

- Two major impacts of the human-AB experience have been humanity's alienation from its natural habitat and imagination of a supernatural realm.

- This dual diversion from a natural perspective fragmented human consciousness and caused an atrophy of our inner senses and self-learning ability.

- To restore fractured human consciousness to its wholeness requires use of all ways of knowing and recognition of humanity's place among all levels of beings.

A New Myth for the Twenty-First Century

Many people believe it is time to modify the conventional story we humans tell about ourselves and our history to take into account new scientific and historical discoveries. I believe this book demonstrates that an assessment of the implications of new insights from the fields of prehistory, archaeology, genetics, anthropology, linguistics, history of religions, consciousness studies, and many other areas inevitably leads to a new myth. Developing a synthesis of selected material relevant to the above hypotheses would provide a foundation for a "new myth for the twenty-first century" as called for by several writers.

Our conventional accounts of humanity's origins and development no longer square with all the facts known to us. The new twenty-first-century myth should give a reasonable historical account of all events required to encompass a universal worldview for the human species. Thus, it should posit explanations for all known areas of humanity's inner and outer experience. This book makes an attempt to be comprehensive enough to provide the initial framework.

A suitable myth for *Homo sapiens* must encompass an examination of the full range of our experiences in our exploration of the world. It should define the expansion of species consciousness as we have experimented with our mental and physical capacities, capturing human excitement at the discovery of new knowledge. It should account for the exhilaration we feel when surpassing our past standards. Our exuberance in unrestrained creative endeavor must be captured. The ecstasy that results from heightened senses and profound interactions with one another and nature demands inclusion in the new myth.

On the other hand, the myth should describe and posit explanations for human failures to achieve these natural states and levels of development. Learning from past defeats provides the foundation on which to build a new era. I hope that this book can serve as a catalyst for many creative minds who can help articulate such a new myth.

PART I

ABs in History

Introduction to Part I

Metaphysical, historical, and sacred sources contain voluminous evidence of beings that I have called ABs and describe various roles ABs have played in human history. Why this subject matter has not been treated as a legitimate discipline of research is one of the sub-themes of this book. It begs for serious scientific analysis, beyond simple anthropological speculations about myth.[1]

Some primal myths and sacred texts ascribe to ABs a role in the birth of Earth as an organism; a few assign specific ABs responsibility for creating the universe. However, all major cultural traditions report the involvement of Advanced Beings in their earliest beginnings, with several providing intriguing details about the ABs responsible for the genesis of the first humans. Some metaphysical sources and sacred texts point to general temporal milestones, but we must look to science for an historical time line.

Numerous metaphysical sources provide good starting points for addressing the AB-intervention hypothesis. Outside ordinary reality they may provide an independent measuring stick against which to compare tangible evidence. They provide information and insights that expand the physical boundaries in which science normally works.

This book is based on the assumption that our universe is multi-dimensional, but that all dimensions are aspects of one integral organism. This means that even though conscious beings may communicate with us from other dimensions, their knowledge, if valid, should ultimately be traceable in this dimension, the one we live in. If a nonphysical source suggests that ABs have influenced the development of *Homo sapiens*, we should be able to discover tangible evidence of that influence on Earth. In addition to physical artifacts, tangible evidence may be in the realm of ideas and useful knowledge (relevant to something humans can experience).

With these caveats in mind, chapter 1 gives samples of what some metaphysical sources say about AB contributions to human development on Earth. Chapter 2 reviews a selection of sacred or mythic accounts of early AB activity, and chapter 3 contains information from historical documents about AB involvement with humans. Together, these three chapters provide a basic introduction to what humans have believed over time and across cultures about AB intervention in human development.

A Note on My Format for Dating Events and People

In this book I present a cross-cultural perspective (assuming *a priori* that no particular belief system is more valid than another), which also means using a neutral dating system. Since the B.C./A.D. system reflects Christian assumptions about the timing of certain historical events not shared by other cultures, I have chosen alternatives now being used by some other writers.

For all dates in prehistory—prior to about 11,500 years ago, the start of the Neolithic Age—I write dates like this: 50,000 B.P. The B.P. stands for "before the present" and could be written 50,000 years ago. I most often use the shorter B.P. I accept the widely used starting point for the Common Era (written as C.E.) as being about 2,000 years ago. Therefore, after about 11,500 years ago you will see dates written two ways: 4500 B.C.E. to indicate 4,500 years "before the Common Era" and 675 C.E. to indicate 675 years into "the Common Era." For people who are accustomed to the B.C./A.D. system, B.C.E. may generally be taken as B.C., and C.E. as A.D. Dates written without letters after them can be assumed to be C.E., as in 1953 or the fifth century.

1 What Do Metaphysical Sources Say?

In the search for understanding of Advanced Beings, metaphysical material provides a good place to start. It includes information or knowledge about the universe or history that originates beyond ordinary human consciousness or that cannot be perceived by the so-called objective or physical senses. It comes in many forms, under many names and, because of its nature, must be handled with care.

In considering metaphysical materials, an experienced former editor (Sara Benjamin-Rhodes) had this to say: "No source of information is without distortion. Even the clearest channels are not, nor have they ever been, 100 percent accurate. Even within information that is 'mostly true,' there is some . . . that is not true. Even within . . . [the] 'mostly false,' there is some truth." Therefore, knowledge from any source ought to be checked for its correspondence with historical or other evidence before one accepts it as reliable.

In a book like this, one cannot begin to cover the range of contemporary and historical metaphysical material humans have received from and/or about ABs. Humankind has communicated with gods, angels, departed humans, ethereal beings, light bodies, and the collective consciousness throughout recorded history. People have taken advantage of a non-electromagnetic "Morse code" of energetic transmissions that somehow conveys information from one level of consciousness in the universe to another. Without understanding how the decipherment process works in their brain, humans have reacted to it. (See the website www.issc-taste.org for accounts of sane people experiencing inner voices.)

Such communications have resulted in dreams and prophecies that launched new religions, scientific inventions that shaped industrial society, inspirations that led to new heights in human creativity, and answers to problems mundane and cosmic. There can be no doubt about the awe-inspiring power of both the sources and material, even when a recipient feels the underlying intention may be questionable. After all, the source has a power the human does not: the capacity to access the human and initiate the communication.

William Blake (1757–1827, English artist, poet, and visionary seer) said many of his poems were dictated by the "Immortals," the gods and goddesses of other worlds he saw through his inner vision. The past-life memories of noted twentieth-century author Taylor Caldwell contained authenticated details of ancient and modern medicine, foreign languages, historical personalities, and (seemingly realistic) material on lost civilizations. They provided the basis for numerous best-selling novels. Many people believe prophecies of Nostradamus (sixteenth-century French physician and clairvoyant) have come true. They claim his one thousand published inner visions have already accurately predicted four centuries of major events and still extend almost two millennia into the future.[1]

Edgar Cayce, considered by many to be America's greatest psychic, lived from 1877 until 1945 and produced more than 14,000 documents of telepathic-clairvoyant "readings" given for more than 6,000 different people over 43 years. They covered everything from medical diagnoses to past lives, from prehistory to a cosmology of the universe. While in a trance, oracles at Delphi in ancient Greece received information and insights that guided the politics of a Golden Age. In 1921, noted artist and sculptor Walter Russell received a body of scientific knowledge ahead of its time through 39 days of "inner illumination."[2] One can cite numerous examples, but these show the range.

In writing this book, metaphysical information has provided important pieces of the puzzle. The following random selection of material does not attempt to demonstrate either the authenticity of the various sources or the reliability of the channels.[3] Like historical and scientific material, no single source alone can claim the label "ultimate truth" regarding ABs or human history.

The Pleiadians

With no particular attribution of relative importance, this survey starts with selected channeled material purporting to describe Pleiadian interest in humans and their perspective on Earth history. The Pleiades are a star system in the constellation Taurus estimated to be 500 light years from Earth. Many know it in the night sky as the "Seven Sisters" centered on Alcyone. Numerous books, websites, and individual psychic channels offer Pleiadian views on everything from the nature of the universe to desirable personal habits. Noted writers include, among others, Barbara Marciniak, Barbara Hand Clow, Lia Shapiro, Billy Meier, and Amorah Quan Yin.

The Pleiadians have been important to humans for at least 60,000 years. That's how long the Dogon of Mali in Africa claim Pleiadian connections in human history. Similar myths can be found among those of ancient Greece and China. Writers José Argüelles and Aluna Joy Yaxk'in link Mayan and Pleiadian cosmologies. According to Argüelles, the Mayans may have tracked and communicated with the Pleiades.[4] Other Central and South American peoples, particularly the Toltecs and the Incas, included the Pleiades in their rituals.[5] In more recent times, Swiss UFO researcher Billy Meier reported contacts with Pleiadians in the 1970s, and Barbara Marciniak began to channel them in 1988.

Marciniak's book *Bringers of the Dawn*[6] set the stage for an outpouring of Pleiadian material in the 1990s. The AB collective she channeled claims to have common ancestors with humans. Marciniak says they are concerned that we come to understand our true legacy and take responsibility for ourselves rather than remaining subject to ABs who have their own interests at heart.

These Pleiadians say some of their ancestors came to Earth in the distant past, seeded the planet with love and creativity, and gave some of their DNA to the human species. This shared DNA is why they consider us their distant cousins. They want to help us remember who we are, develop our telepathic skills, learn how we are connected to all facets of the universe, and understand our earlier incarnations on Earth. They tell us that another group of ABs

7

(creator gods) raided the Earth about 300,000 B.P. and rearranged human DNA. This point began a new phase in human history where we were disadvantaged by the DNA manipulation. They say the ABs spoken of in the Babylonia/Sumerian tablets were those who enslaved humans at that time. They also say these ABs engaged in nuclear warfare among themselves and left a legacy of radiation.

A favorite source for information on Pleiadians is the well-known writer and consciousness researcher Barbara Hand Clow. In her 1995 book, *The Pleiadian Agenda*,[7] the voice of a being who called itself Satya of Alcyone (the brightest of the "Seven Sisters" stars) described AB involvement in human history. Satya says Pleiadians have mingled with humans as our teachers for 26,000 years. Satya says Pleiadians tried to help humans avoid an atmospheric-based cataclysm, including a pole shift, around 11,000 B.P. (allegedly caused by Earth entering their star's photon belt). The Pleiadians allegedly tried to help the survivors afterwards by leading them to better locations. (Remember this later during my discussion of Noah.)

The channeled voices claim that in addition to Pleiadians there have been several interventions by other groups of ABs, including:

- The Anunnaki who ruled Earth for thousands of years, whom we learned to worship as gods, including Anu who said he was our Lord. Satya said the Anunnaki were from planet Nibiru, which long ago shifted from an orbit around star Sirius A to become the Planet X of our solar system.

- The Maya (Timekeepers) from a star near Alcyone in the Pleiades, from whose name came the Maya of Central America, and who visit Earth when their planet cycles nearby. They allegedly left the last time in the ninth century C.E., a date that coincides with archaeologists' estimated fall of the Mayan civilization.

- The Sirians who have long had our best interests at heart.

Amorah Quan Yin's Pleiadian voices[8] describe a planetary system (ours) embedded in a larger star system with the Pleiades at the center (also see Argüelles on this point). This celestial organism operates in several dimensions, where human souls have experienced many different stages of development. Before Earth, some of those stages involved incarnations on Venus, Mars, and Maldek—the name for the planet subsequently smashed into the asteroid belt between Mars and Jupiter. (Note Rudolf Steiner's perspective on this, following shortly.)

Theosophists

Theosophy, a philosophy grounded in metaphysical materials transmitted by ABs through H. P. Blavatsky in the late nineteenth century, holds that humans have gone through several physical forms on Earth.[9] According to Blavatsky, humanity in its second (Lemurian) and third (Atlantean) stages of civilization benefited from recurrent visits by the "gods." Theosophists believe that in the middle of the Lemurian era (14 to 16 million years ago) external forces (ABs) helped our evolving ancestors come into full physical form. (It is interesting to note that the earliest date attributed to fossils of proto-*Ramapithecus* by some paleoanthropologists is 14 million years ago.)[10] Regarding the Atlantean era, theosophy implies humans received outside help in "the use of fire, the building of cities, and the development of metallurgy."

Anthroposophy

Rudolf Steiner(1861–1925), the Austrian founder of anthroposophy, or what might be called modern spiritual science, wrote that "the spirit world was open to him from birth."[11] Akin to the theosophical movement in a number of ways, his work introduced a multidimensional perspective of reality to many fields of endeavor, from farming to science, education, and philosophy. He saw humans as incarnations of souls involved in a long process of evolution that had taken them to various planets for different stages. On each planet humans experienced several body types and stages, repeating epicycles within cycles.

On Earth, he said, there have been five "root races" (Polarean, Hyperborean, Lemurian, Atlantean, and Aryan), each containing subraces that progressively developed different aspects of the modern human. ABs, or "divine messengers," led by a being called Manu, assisted throughout this long process.[12] Humans descended to this world from an astral world and have remained connected to the advanced knowledge contained in the Akashic Records. (Pierre

Teilhard de Chardin's concept of *noosphere* and Carl Jung's collective unconscious reflect this notion of a memory pool [the Akashic Records] encircling the Earth.)

Remote Viewing

Of the many routes to metaphysical information, an interesting one came out of research done with support of the U.S. government's intelligence community. Called scientific remote viewing (SRV), the process involves sending a part of one's consciousness to "see" a remote location and "bring back" useful information about the site. This psychic method of reconnaissance has been used with success by military and civilian intelligence officers and by private individuals. Sometimes the SRVers reported encounters with noncorporeal beings[13] and experienced new aspects of ethereal reality, including unintended impacts of our own projections on the process.[14]

One college professor who was trained by a former U.S. government SRVer has reported on one form of ABs. Courtney Brown, in his book *Cosmic Voyage*,[15] identified a group of nonphysical beings who are based in the Earth's atmosphere who were labeled "Midwayers" by the military. According to SRVers, the Midwayers' purpose throughout history has been to help humans develop their potential by subconsciously providing useful information to us.

The famed psychic Edgar Cayce provided an interesting twist on the notion of information coming to humans through the subconscious from ABs. Believing in reincarnation, Cayce also believed that numerous souls (the super- and subconsciousness of physical beings) awaiting a rebirth can communicate their wisdom through the subconscious to living humans.[16] Since Cayce's time, literally thousands of individuals, including the SRVers mentioned, have reported communications with ABs in realms that appear similar to what he described.

A Sirian Channel

Devin, an AB of particular interest, given the extensive Sumerian documentation of the Anunnaki race from Nibiru, speaks through a human named Jelaila.[17] Devin claims to be a member of the "9-D Nibiruan Council" serving aboard the spaceship Pelegai from the Sirius star system. It describes Nibiru and its ruling families in terms consistent with Zecharia Sitchin's synthesis of the Anunnaki story (more details later on). Anu is named as the patriarch of Nibiru who has recently passed on his authority to his sons Enlil and Enki.

This ruling family is described as a hybrid of several races, including human and reptilian (remember the myths about the princess and the dragon), that reflects the tensions among the belief systems of various races. Devin says Nibiru's leadership (popularly known as Planet X and a member of the "Galactic Federation") has played a role in settling disputes among the Anunnaki warring factions.

In a vein compatible with Earth's cataclysmic history documented by widely respected authors D. S. Allan and J. B. Delair (see chapter 10), Devin describes Nibiru/Planet X's periodic passing near Earth in its elliptic around the Sun, and how its passages affect our Earth and current events on Nibiru. Devin says our collective unconscious (like the Akashic Records) carries memories of the great cataclysms that occurred with the passing of Nibiru through our solar system.

Devin claims the effects of the passage are dependent on the level of consciousness and social development of humans. (The explosion of AB-god cults discussed in chapter 20 may be associated with the last passage of Nibiru.) The next passage will be different, according to Devin, who says, "our world is experiencing unprecedented elevations in consciousness . . . evolving at a pace that is beyond any expectation." He further states, "Since free will is a major component . . . [humans] are the ones who determine the[ir] future."

What Regression Hypnosis Reveals

Use of hypnotic regression to explore past-life memories has uncovered information relevant to earlier AB lifetimes alleged by a great number of people. Hypnotherapist and prolific author Dolores Cannon has discovered many cases where humans have memories of being inhabitants of other planets. These memories support the hypothesis that humans are hybrid beings whose genetic memories combine extraterrestrial and Earth events.[18]

Cannon believes that humans have a soul or consciousness that transcends many lifetimes, and that none of us originated on the young planet Earth. One of her subjects reported a lifetime in an unnamed community near Qumran (home of the Essenes and the Dead Sea Scrolls). He described flying "watchers" who exuded a special energy or light and never set foot on the ground, but taught the human community and praised its members for holding on to the teachings handed down from Atlantis. The hypnotized subject suggested that the Star of Bethlehem was something like a spacecraft. Its crew ("messengers") described in advance the selection of Jesus' parents and birth date.

In another case, Cannon heard a woman's description of having lived in Africa in ancient times as a man who saw a "UFO." The man received telepathic messages about the place of the craft's origin and life there and why it was important to humans. He did everything he could do to make it return, but the craft never contacted him again. Another subject reported a lifetime when he was coerced to become the pilot of a craft engaged in extraterrestrial warfare. He believed himself to be an integral part of the craft, as if it responded to his thoughts. He reported involvement in a conflict that destroyed life on a planet.

Another subject reported a life to Cannon as a space traveler who arrived on Earth in a reconnaissance mission and became involved in teaching very primitive humans new construction and cultural skills. At the end of her hypnosis session, this woman had the sense she had somehow, back then, inappropriately interfered with the "locals." She apparently chose to be reborn several times on Earth to compensate for her interference.

Another subject reported having been part of a research/technology transfer team responsible for helping primitive humans solve a mystery behind their dying crops. She and her colleagues traveled in a bubble to protect themselves from toxins attacking local plants and animals. They took some of the humans away to ensure their survival, but she felt called to return and help the victims. In another case, the subject thought of himself as a hybrid from alien and Earth parents. He served as a teacher (with knowledge received aboard some sort of spacecraft) to help primitive humans improve their lives.

Further Hypnotic Regression

Taylor Caldwell, mentioned earlier, subjected herself to hypnosis from which came "remarkable passages that revealed a baffling knowledge of medicine, the Bible, Atlantis, and Lemuria."[19] Her detailed descriptions of Atlantis provide geographical data that has aided in later searches for this fabled land. She also described in this 1913 manuscript (as a 13-year-old girl) the process of nuclear fission before Einstein thought about it and the atom bomb that did not materialize until World War II.

In her 1967 novel, *Dialogue with the Devil*, a product of automatic writing, Caldwell reported conversations between the archangelic AB siblings Lucifer and Michael and described unknown planets and other ABs. The view that emerges in this novel is that beings from another planet would come and wreak havoc on Earth (as predicted in the Old Testament book of Joel) as they had done on an unknown planet called Melina. This would permit the intervention by more Advanced Beings to bring an end to an era of irresponsible behavior and establish a new age.

Channeled "Ascension" Material

Scores of books were written in the late twentieth-century's Ascension movement. This movement has the premise that humans are approaching a new phase in evolution that involves a transformation in human consciousness, one that will reconnect us with ABs and dimensions of existence higher than our 3-D world. Many of these books comprise messages from various "ascended masters," beings no longer incarnate who have in different ways already ascended to that next level.

This cosmology starts with the assumption of ABs as being "way showers" for humans; they provide humans with advice and moral support on their journey. The book *Crystal Star: A Guide to Ascension*[20] exemplifies this genre of metaphysical information. It purports to represent ABs such as Sananda (the etheric Jesus), Ashtar (who represents a group of human and angelic beings from several galaxies), the Archangel Michael, and St. Germain. These sources speak of the intervention of flesh-and-blood beings on Earth in times past and present, but they stress that nonmaterial beings now surround humans and seek to help us learn to be our true selves. St. Germain speaks of a hierarchy of ABs, including the Elohim referred to in the Bible, who have various creative powers.

Modern Prophets

Many individuals have gained a reputation as modern prophets, people who receive messages from one source or another about future events. Gordon-Michael Scallion, best known for his "future maps" of North America,[21] channels material he receives from what he calls "a group of intelligences . . . within." Scallion's sources say Earth-human contact with ABs has been going on for millions of years, from the first projection of souls (early human forms of consciousness) 18 million years ago, through Atlantean times (ending 11,600 years ago), into the historical period of Moses, Zoroaster, Buddha, and Jesus.

The "intelligences" say two forms of human-AB contacts continue today, Scallion reports. One is the "messengers" predominantly from the Pleiades and Sirius who communicate telepathically, offering humans assistance for the coming Earth changes. These messengers sometimes present themselves in physical form but generally appear as light or inner voices. They are not to be confused with another category of ABs, those beings involved with UFO sightings and human abductions. The messengers use the human inner senses to communicate directly with human minds when our "brain vibrations" are congruent with theirs.

Scallion's messengers confirm former civilizations on Mars and on a tenth planet involving beings not unlike life-forms on Earth. These beings no longer exist in our solar system, but other dimensions of conscious beings do, including some on our moon. A group of educators and scientists from Mars, at the termination of civilization there, moved to Earth and "melded" with some "mixed creatures" who were already evolving on Earth, Scallion reports. They began a "colonization" on a continent in the area of the Pacific known as "Lumania." The people of this civilization grew to a great stature and later moved into a part of Africa.

Jesus from the Other Side

Quite a number of books have been published purporting to be messages from Jesus, adding to or modifying the biblical material about him. Some purportedly represent his efforts to clear up any historical misunderstanding of who and what he was, to set the record straight. One has Jesus saying, "The purpose of this writing is to free up the many misconceptions which people have held about me through the ages . . . to clarify the entire human drama of the crucifixion and everything I stood for at that time."[22] Another, which has a profound ring of historical authenticity, has Jesus reviewing the book: "The foregoing is an astonishingly accurate account of my life and thoughts . . . consider this my second coming."[23] Such books portray a different Jesus from that of the New Testament and one more compatible with various first-century accounts later rejected by the Nicean Council in 325 C.E.

Some Implications

Some interesting aspects of the above sources become immediately evident. First, despite the wide variety of nonhuman sources and human channels, a remarkable amount of consistency exists among the substantive themes, if not the terminology or detail. In the social sciences an analyst would say, "The degree of internal congruency is significant." Second, the degree of similarity with other fields of knowledge (scientific and historical) also surprises me. I had not expected so much congruence between metaphysical materials and more conventional areas of knowledge.

The internally consistent information may be briefly summarized as follows. Human origins lie in the stars, whether from DNA from ABs being mixed with human or humans inhabiting other planets in earlier stages of development. Physical and nonphysical ABs have intervened in human development in both positive and negative ways. While some have sought to encourage human self-determination, others have pursued control of humans for their own purposes. Intervention has taken various forms: teaching, technical assistance, and advice. Humans have multidimensional natures and can access other levels of consciousness. The ABs have fought among themselves on Earth to the detriment of human progress. The presence of ABs was used to create the idea of God for control purposes. Most AB sources urge humans to control their own destiny.

ABs have been called many names in both metaphysical and historical documents. This has led to confusion that has hindered the development of a human consensus about the true nature of gods. According to the sources cited so far, from the beginning of human consciousness, individuals have had visions of nonphysical beings, heard voices, received channeled material, and come face-to-face with ethereal and flesh-and-blood ABs. Since the label applied to each experience depends on the perceiver's culture, strangers to that culture don't realize that they perceive the same reality.

Before we get too carried away with this material, we must do a reality check. Could humans just be making it up and then, through our subconsciousness, feeding our own fantasies back to ourselves? We can guard against this possibility by using a variety of materials, from different ways of knowing and periods of history. Using all epistemologies—the approach taken in this book—makes it less likely that we project phantasms into the *noosphere* and then merely tune in to them when in altered states.

2 Who Were the First Gods?

Remember the Greek tales of battles and loves among the gods of Mount Olympus, those beings who easily flew across the sky, launched thunderbolts at one another, dove into an underworld, and became enamored of mere humans? These and other universal myths take up the equivalent of several gigabytes on the hard drive of human consciousness. Some of them can have powerful psychological and behavioral implications for modern humans.[1] However, most scholars have treated such myths and legends as primarily fabrications of a primitive human imagination.

Some researchers, like Ignatius Donnelly in the nineteenth century, took them seriously as historical documentation of early human memories, but most have dismissed them as primitive, fanciful belief systems. Only in the mid-twentieth century did serious frontier historians like Immanuel Velikovsky begin to probe for possible confirmation of the facts underlying these so-called imaginary tales. Over the past few decades, archaeological and documentary research, like that of Zecharia Sitchin, Graham Hancock, D. S. Allan and J. B. Delair, Peter Thompson, and several others, has helped to demonstrate the 3-D reality of much of this so-called mythic material.

A Different Perspective

Traditional oral accounts (most captured in writing over only the last two centuries) and fragments of texts (a few thousand years old) deal with the basic issues that any conscious race would ponder. How did our world and life start? What is the origin of humankind? How did my particular race or tribe come into being? Who started our civilization?

Many legends and myths associate ABs with the answers to all these questions.

Seemingly implausible answers to such questions are treated in a surprisingly universal fashion by culture after culture. Practically every tradition in the world has gods (under local names) descending from the heavens in marvelous machines and with magic powers to intervene in the lives of humans. These traditions seem to point to a family of gods who settled on Earth from space but continued to flit about and fight one another in the skies. The startling specific details of these legends include: Advanced Beings from the sky creating humans; gods setting up dynasties of rulers, including demigods; gods having sexual intercourse with humans; humans receiving technologies from nonhuman inventors; and Advanced Beings serving as teachers of humans.

A leading scholar of ancient civilizations, Arthur Cotterell, perhaps unwittingly, supports the case made in this book for considering the basis of myths as actual experience with ABs. He believes the work of psychologist Carl Jung suggested that images in "the collective unconscious stem from the actual experiences of our remote ancestors."[2] Cotterell wrote, "The civilizations of the first planters— the cities of the Nile, the Euphrates-Tigris Valley, and the Indus— evolved mythologies connected with a priesthood. The Sumerians even looked upon themselves as the property of their gods; they were workers on the divine estate." He quoted anthropologist Bronislaw Malinowski: "The myth in a primitive society . . . is not a mere tale told but a reality lived."[3]

This chapter starts with the assumption that mythic and sacred material should be treated as at least a partial reflection of human experience and studied for its historicity. It contains accounts from various traditions that identify the earliest known AB encounters and the activities which humans have associated with them. We start with a review of texts respected by the major world religions and then include samples from various traditional and aboriginal cultures.

Judaism, Christianity, and Islam

One text provides a fundamental account of the prehistory shared by these three great world religions. Genesis, the initial book in the Pentateuch (first five books) of the Hebrew Torah, known to Christians as the Old Testament, provides much historical data that has been independently verified.

We now know from nineteenth- and twentieth-century research that large parts of the Pentateuch incorporate bits and pieces from much older documents.[4] Genesis states in its own text that chapter 5 restates the "Book of the Generations of Adam." The "Book of the Wars of *YHVH*" and the "Book of Jashar" are given as references respectively in Numbers 21:14 and II Samuel 1:18.[5] More extensive versions of biblical material have been found in millennia-old Sumerian clay tablets known as the Chaldean Genesis, the Seven Tablets of Creation, and other titles.

The Hebrew Genesis account of AB involvement in human origins and history seems to cover three stages. The oldest extant Hebrew (Masoretic Text) and Aramaic versions reveal nuances not found in English translations. Even there, ambiguities suggest older unknown texts may have been more explicit. For instance, the structure of the Hebrew Genesis 1:1 points to a single power in the original creation—"when God began" all things.[6] This is stage one. In the Aramaic version (written several centuries later), the various acts of creation—the heavens, the Earth, and various creatures—happen "in ancient times" but without precise order.

The Hebrew version of Genesis 1:26 implies a second stage when a group of ABs (identified by the word "Elohim," which means plural gods) said in effect, "Let's make an earthling in our own image, according to our likeness."[7] In verse 27, the same plural Elohim created "male and female" beings in their own image. The later Aramaic scribes substituted the four-letter *YHVH* (meaning not just any single god, but their own AB) for the original Hebrew word Elohim, indicating multiple gods created humankind.[8]

In the Hebrew Genesis 2:4 and 7, the theology changes with the introduction of *YHVH* Elohim (a phrase that suggests plural gods like or including *YHVH*) to identify the ABs involved in creation.[9] It may reflect a third stage: existing hominoids changed to *Homo sapiens* by *YHVH* and other gods. Or the above-mentioned second stage was revised to place *YHVH* among the ABs (combining *YHVH* with Elohim) responsible for the creation of mankind. In verses 5–9, the *YHVH* Elohim (inappropriately translated as the Lord God in the English Bible) is credited with having "formed the Adam (earthling)" to "serve the Adamah [ABs] . . . from the [matter] of the Adamah."

In chapter 4, Elohim is dropped altogether, and from then on *YHVH* is used alone to make it clear that the story is about one god, the tribal god of the Hebrews. Reading the English Bible one cannot see these distinctions. Such nuances become important in the next chapter because they suggest a specific group of ABs could have created Adam and Eve from earlier human types. This three-stage scenario makes Genesis compatible with Sumerian texts.

Chapter 3:8 of Genesis says multiple gods (*YHVH* Elohim) walked with our direct ancestors and talked to them, setting rules for their behavior. Later they gave humans clothing (3:21) and banished them from Eden for breaking one of the rules. Other ABs (Cherubim or Watchers) at that point were given specific roles vis-à-vis humans; they were assigned to guard Eden's gates with a "*whirling* and flashing sword" to keep the exiled humans from returning (author's emphasis). That appears to have ended Adam and Eve's intimate relationship with the *YHVH* Elohim who had created and nurtured them.

Some later parts of Genesis, depending on the context, leave the reader uncertain about the identity of the AB(s) to whom the text refers. It appears various ABs continued to walk and talk with Hebrews (Cain, Enoch, Noah, and Abraham, among many others). Humans continued to be able to call upon different ABs (4:26), and Enoch was apparently taken into the heavens by one of them (5:24). After their exodus from Egypt, the Bible makes it seem more certain the Hebrews' main AB contact was *YHVH*. His tetragrammation (the four letters *YHVH*) used alone identifies him as the AB exclusively worshiped by the Hebrews. (The terms God, King, and Lord replace *YHVH* in English Bibles.) After accepting him as the supreme AB, Moses and the children of Israel may have replaced other AB names with *YHVH* in succeeding Hebrew accounts. (Egyptian pharaohs did the same by erasing their predecessors' names from public places.)

At some point the ABs found the "daughters of men" beautiful and slept with them, producing hybrids that became "mighty men, men of renown" (Genesis 6:2–4). An AB walked with Noah, and one gave him advice on how to escape the impending flood. After it was over and the Earth had dried up, the ABs met him and his family and gave them help, for which the humans made them a great meal in appreciation. The ABs continued to interact with Noah's descendants over the generations to the time of Abraham. Then one AB ordered Abraham to leave Haran (his city of residence), saying he had plans to make a great nation around him (12:1–2). So goes the biblical story of the early days of men and ABs.

Hinduism

The earliest sacred texts of Hinduism (and Buddhism) are the Rig Vedas (hymns), whose transfer from oral tradition to written form is usually dated from about the time of Moses (1500 B.C.E.). The next Hindu material is the Upanishads (philosophical documents) followed by the Puranas (just over 2,000 years old) which include the famous epics Mahabharata and Ramayana. The Puranas cover creation myths and accounts of the lives of AB-gods on Earth.

The Ramayana relates the "history" of three gods: Rama (an incarnation of Vishnu), Sita, and Hanuman. The Mahabharata deals with many of the same issues as the Pentateuch: desirable culture, manners and morals, and, more specifically, the history of India in antiquity. This history covers the struggles between humans and the ABs, including the latter's knowledge of activities that would promote humanity's social development (not unlike *YHVH*'s admonitions to the Hebrews). The Mahabharata also includes the well-known Bhagavadgita, the philosophical sermon of Krishna (an AB-human hybrid speaking for Vishnu from whom he descended).[10]

These texts identify several gods who appear to be the first ABs in human awareness. Brahma was identified with creation of the natural world, analogous to the power in Genesis referred to in the first 25 verses as the creative source of the sky and Earth and everything between. Associated with Brahma were Shiva and Devi, involved in the creation of human beings. This trio resembles very closely the three Anunnaki gods (Enlil, Enki, and Ninsurhag) reported to be responsible for the creation of mankind in the Sumerian stories. Indra, referred to as one of the oldest gods, resembled Zeus/Jupiter in the West. Varuna, son of female god Aditi, was described as having broad creative powers equivalent to the Greco-Roman AB Ouranos/Uranus, and also compared to the sea-god Poseidon.

Japanese Traditions

The other major traditions of the East (shamanism, Shintoism, Taoism, and Confucianism) do not have such specific accounts of gods being involved in human origins. The Japanese indigenous Shinto philosophy saw life as the manifestation of "*Kunitokotachi,* the unseen, transcendent yet immanent, spirit of the universe."[11] However, the word "Shinto" means "the way of the gods," implying the existence of ABs and their relevance to human development.

The first people in Japan were reddish pygmy aboriginals. They were wiped out by the Ainu (now the most ancient people living in Japan) when they arrived from Asia. The name Ainu, found on the same stone that contained the Code of Hammurabi, implies "children of the bear" (associated with the star Arcturus which means "keeper of the bear" in Greek).[12] This suggests they were part of a more natural human tradition not familiar with the later AB involvement in human history.[13] However, the modern Japanese, immigrants themselves, who replaced the Ainu appear to have been exposed to some contacts with the AB leaders identified in the Sumerian texts.

This connection becomes apparent when one compares certain Japanese legends to those of Mesopotamia. One of the tales contained in the Sumerian texts (more fully described in chapter 3) states that AB Enki got out of control chasing after and sexually harassing his half-sister Ninti (aka Ninhursag). In addition to breaking the AB protocol on consensual sex, he caused so much physical damage to her kingdom that a council of the gods had to be convened to sort out the mess. The Japanese have a similar story of their primary goddess Amaterasu being sexually pursued by her half-brother Susanowo; as in the Anunnaki society, the child of a god by his half-sister becomes the next ruler. The royal family of Japan is believed to have descended from the progeny of this incestuous conception by the AB gods Amaterasu and Susanowo.

Traditional Societies of Africa, Europe, and the Americas

While traditional societies differ from "modern society" in many ways, they share a common heritage. They have memories of the first ABs known to humans in the mists of prehistory. Perhaps their images, less tainted by more recent AB interactions with humans, may provide insights not otherwise available to a species attempting to rediscover its roots.

Of all continents, the mythology of Africa contains the most diverse terminology in its reference to ABs. Part of this may be due to several thousand African languages, but it may result from a more ancient experience with ABs.

African myths frequently use peculiarly local folk tales to illustrate important principles. However, when one compares the cosmological assumptions implicit in such folk tales, fundamental belief structures appear to underpin the surface diversity. For instance, one common assumption, also shared by many early American myths, is that the universe arose from a singular spirit or force. This force or power is not the same as the concept of a supernatural, anthropomorphic deity that arose in the cradle of Western civilization.

The African concept is actually more evolved, in terms of our current scientific understanding of the universe, than the Middle Eastern theism that has generally influenced modern religions. The African notion of a primal source of creation was of one not external to humans and nature. It suggested an energy with a multidimensional or multifaceted nature (as in Asa, the creator, fashioner and distributor of the Akamba people of Kenya).[14] This energetic concept, also represented by Adroa of Zaire and Uganda, Mawu-Lisa of Dahomey, and Olorun of the Yoruba in Nigeria, recognizes the yin/yang or androgynous nature of the creative principle. It parallels the he-she nature of the Chinese T'ai Yuan and the (American) Zuni Awona-wilona primal sources of creation.

With regard to conscious beings more advanced than humans, the African perceptions of ABs were similar to those of the early Americas. The first ABs, in order of appearance, came from the heavens and traveled between Earth and the stars. The Dogon of Mali believed the AB gods who created humans came to Earth from the region of the star Sirius. The AB Nommo twins who arrived first on Earth were the sons of Amma who remained at home in the heavens. For the Ugandans, the AB working on Earth known as Kintu sent reports to his father Katonda who was also the parent of other gods living in the heavens. The Liberians called the senior AB who sent his sons to work on Earth Sno-Nysoa. He eventually ordered them home in the skies.

African accounts of the origin of humans at the hands of ABs bear many similarities to those in other regions of the world. In terms that remind us of Sumerian accounts of possible genetic manipulation discussed in chapter 3, an Ashanti myth says a male being and female being from the sky created human offspring with the help of a snake (think of the double helix). The Bantu of Kenya say the god Wele had two AB assistants who "on the fifth day" created the first man (Mwambu) and the first woman (Sela). Later a human female married an AB from the sky/sun.[15] Multiple male and female ABs were involved in the creation of humans according to several African accounts (remember the plural gods in Genesis who "made man in their own image").[16]

The coastal Celts (from the Iberian Peninsula to the shores of Northern Europe) may represent the best example of pre-supernatural beliefs in the Europe later dominated by the Roman Church.[17] Celtic myths (in Ireland) describe several ABs whose progeny (maybe involving one human parent) traveled to and from foreign lands (perhaps Atlantis) and served as early kings. The goddess Danann, with Elatha, gave birth to Bres who was given the kingship of Ireland by ABs.

Bran (the son of Febal—possibly an AB) was a hero and demigod who brought tales of a magical land to the West into Ireland. Cormac MacAirt, an historical figure, apparently possessed some advanced technology gained from a wandering AB. With one item he could discern when someone was lying, and with another he could anesthetize the ill and women at childbirth and help them recover. An early "good god" was Dagda, whose technology could result in instant death or instant healing. He and his daughter Brigit used technologies beyond the comprehension of the Celtic people.

Other contributors to the pre-supernaturalist tradition in Europe may be the Lapps of Finland, the Samoyeds of Russia, and the Uralians (including Voguls and Hungarians). As seen in chapter 16, these language groups fall outside the Indo-European family. Their beliefs correspond to traditional themes from Siberia and the East Asian mountains. The Buriat tribal people living near Lake Baikal in Russian Siberia speak of an AB named Morgon-Kara who revived the dead by bringing their souls back to Earth. The Samoyeds of Russia spoke of flesh-and-blood ABs from the heavens who influenced human culture. Their supreme god Num worked with nature in much the same way as did the first god reported in Genesis.

We also find that the early postcataclysm migration of Indo-Europeans from Central Asia to Europe, continuing until 4500 B.P., appears to have introduced AB-god personalities into the Germanic and Scandinavian cultures. For instance, the Anglo-Saxon god Thor was the Germanic equivalent to the Indo-European thunder god, possessing the same advanced aerial weapons as Jupiter/Zeus and Indra. He consorted with Odin and Frigg, two other gods from the skies.

During their confrontation with Roman culture before the Christian era, the Germanic peoples were still attached to the earliest system of Indo-European AB gods, reminiscent of the pre-Homeric period in Greece (1200 to 800 B.C.E.). Odin was supreme as well as the oldest of the gods; his wife was Frigg.[18] Their AB family included Njord, his son Frey (counterpart to Roman AB Priapus), and his daughter Freya; Frey and Freya mean lord and lady, respectively. The terms lord and lady were used by the Sumerians to refer to their local AB gods. (Lord was used in the early Bible in a similar fashion.)

In the Western Hemisphere, postcataclysm cultures seem to have retained the AB gods from a period that preceded the more detailed Sumerian and Hebrew documentation of post-Flood AB control in West Asia. Thus, the American pantheon of gods did not include the many AB personalities that one sees in Mesopotamia, Canaan, Egypt, and Greece from 3500 B.C.E. to the beginning of the Common Era.

In obviously older traditions, AB gods were described as beings who came from the skies. The AB credited with anointing the ruling class of first Incas was Inti, who came from the direction of the Sun. The Moche culture in Peru called its sky god "Ai Ayaec." The Carib and Arawak tribes (precolombian Caribbean peoples) worshiped a "sky god" who lived in the Sun.[19] A contemporary Brazilian shaman[20] uses present-day terminology to report "our legends say that a long time ago a flying saucer landed in the Amazon basin and men emerged from the spaceship."

A Common Theme

Combining the stories from all continents suggests the ABs were more than abstract concepts of gods or characters in science fiction tales. They point to robust flesh-and-blood characters who descended to Earth from the heavens, exhibiting awesome powers and fully engaging humans.

Numerous accounts indicate that humans walked and talked with the gods. In some cases they were able to negotiate some of the conditions of their relationship. Not only did humans walk with the gods on terra firma, several reports indicate humans occasionally rode in shuttle craft (called MU in Sumerian and Ben Ben in Egyptian) in the Earth's atmosphere. A few were even taken into deep space in the larger AB space ships (GIR in Sumerian).[21] The Bible reports the prophet Ezekiel was taken aloft in a "fiery Chariot" (Ezekiel, chapter 8, describes a classical abduction experience). Noah and Enoch were also reported to have been taken into space. Enmeduranki, a (demigod) prince of Sippa, was taken to an orbiting craft and taught science and math.

After the Cataclysm, Etana (Sumerian) and Thothmes III (Egyptian) apparently received a ride through the heavens. The *Epic of Gilgamesh* indicates Gilgamesh tried to get a space ride and failed. According to the Koran (18th Sura) and a nonbiblical Jewish legend, Moses was given a ride in space to convince him that to represent *YHVH* to the Hebrews was to serve a real god who descended from the sky. In this context, modern UFO/ET stories in which humans report being abducted and taught important information by alien beings are not new after all.

Where Does This Leave Us?

The odds that descriptions of the god-human interactions in this chapter could have arisen accidentally in local tribes across widely separated regions of the world are minuscule. Several alternative explanations (a pre-human world culture; a genetic basis for such visions; past-life memories from another planet; mass delusions induced by environmental stress; god-implanted memories) also appear incredible and lack supporting evidence.

Another explanation that at first glance appears equally incredible—that such things actually happened—is nonetheless supported by a cross-cultural content analysis of the myths. In the statistical logic used by most physical and social scientists, such a degree of congruence among apparently independent sources would indicate a high level of internal reliability. The corroborating evidence in the following chapters only strengthens the case for an AB-intervention hypothesis.

3 Were ABs Involved in Human Origins?

In recent decades, scientific and historical research has made it possible to validate much historical information in the Bible and other ancient texts or artifacts. For instance, we now know the Hebrew Pentateuch and the Hindu Rig Veda accurately describe geographical details (mountains, deserts, and rivers) of the Middle East and India respectively. They name kingdoms, rulers, and battles that can be corroborated by other sources. They describe cultures that can be verified through archaeology and anthropology. They contain authenticated facts about astronomy, agriculture, social practices, and institutions.[1] Therefore, that they speak of AB involvement in human origins should be taken seriously.

Creation myths around the world provide each culture with an interpretation of how the universe, Earth, and humans came to be. (Barbara Sproul's book *Primal Myths* provides an outstanding collection of primary sources of creation myths from around the world.) Some accounts begin with the creation of humans, usually as a result of the actions of more powerful beings from the skies, heavens, or another dimension. Other traditions also include ideas on the origin of Earth or the universe itself. In the latter category, several so-called primitive accounts unexpectedly speak of a powerful creative force from which the universe manifested itself. Many describe it as androgynous, with both genders combined to manifest (birth) matter/energy and all beings.

The Taoists called that force *Li,* comprised of yin and yang, respectively the female and male aspects. For the Aztecs, Ometecuhtli was the androgynous source of all existence. The Zuni's Awona-wilona resembles the Grand Couple concept I used in my earlier book, *Our Solarian Legacy.* This notion is consistent with the idea of a primal energy or consciousness, one integral source that creates through the rhythmic interchange of opposite polarities.[2]

As we'll see in chapters 8 and 9, science has offered preliminary hypotheses about sites and dates for the first appearance of humans. Scientists must base their findings on the physical data available at the time of their study. This means interpretations keep changing as new data appears. Given the evidence of cataclysmic changes that have reconfigured continents over the ages, destroying fossils and artifacts alike, we will never be able to piece together the full story from the physical evidence.

Human-created evidence, in written form and artifacts, is just as fragmented as the fossil record. Metaphysical sources, including the memories of humans and other beings, suffer from the influence of idiosyncratic interpretations. All this means that reconstructing a full and exact record of human history lies beyond human capabilities. Even using various inner senses along with physical senses, I believe the best we can hope for is an approximation.

ABs in Human Creation

While the universal creative power is only hinted at in most traditions, when it comes to the appearance of humans on Earth the stories contain more detail. And, almost without exception, human creation myths point to AB involvement in the act.

The preceding chapter described the Genesis creation myth most familiar to Western readers. That account is an abridged version of the Sumerian *Epic of Creation.* Together the two texts present the Earth as having come from a void, with its attributes of light, water, land, and nature's creatures made manifest by the voice commands of a godhead (the universal Elohim). This god force is credited with the creation of all life (including humans), but specific ABs (*YHVH* Elohim) from the heavens modify mankind by mixing earthly and heavenly ingredients. Varying from the Bible account slightly, Sumerian texts suggest the AB creation of "Eve" provided fertile humans to replace the neuter Adamu.[3]

In the Western Hemisphere, in a parallel scenario, the Quiche legend from the Andean region of South America also describes the creator gods traveling between the heavens and the sea and making humans upon the Earth. As in the Genesis account, the Arawak tradition of the Caribbean says the AB creators Kurumany and Kulimina created man and woman after a different and remote Aluberi had created the world.[4]

Like the biblical story from the Middle East, an Andean account also attributes the creation of humans to plural gods. The Quiche list them as the Dominator, the Designer, and the Feathered Serpent— interestingly enough, analogous to the Sumerian ABs Enlil (commander), Enki (life scientist), and Ninhursag (medical specialist). Genesis states the gods (Elohim) formed man of the dust of Earth, and the Quiche translation says they made man of clay. Around the globe in India, a Vedic myth says the gods used the power of light and water in creation of the Earth and its creatures. Does all this mean there was a pre-human creature before *Homo sapiens*, as the fossil record indicates?

We have some hints of what the ancestors of aborigines in Australia and the Dogon in West Africa may have thought prior to the Cro-Magnons in Europe. They both claim their oral traditions go back 60,000 years. Both groups believe their first ancestors were the products of magical acts by male and female beings who came to Earth from the skies. This suggests these two widely separate cultures date from the beginnings of the Anunnaki (Sumerian) intervention but were left out of the subsequent experience of the Anunnaki colonial culture described later in this book.

Atlantis As Evidence

The unsinkable tale of Atlantis pops up in every category of evidence used by modern science to study our past. This evidence includes historical accounts from early Greece and Egypt, the folk tales of countless peoples, comparisons of rituals and languages, animal behaviors, monumental ruins and physical artifacts, metaphysical sources, DNA profiles of isolated groups, and cultural dispersion.

Enough evidence now fits such a coherent pattern that no reasonable analyst can deny the broad outlines of the story. It points to an Atlantean civilization, under the rule of AB gods, that persisted down to the last major Earth cataclysm only 11,500 years ago. However, the relationship of the Atlantean "gods" to the Indo-European (in the better documented Anunnaki story) and other "gods" remains unclear and demands further research.

Just after 600 B.C.E., the Athenian political leader Solon heard accounts of the history of Atlantis from the Egyptian priest Sonchis. The Egyptian, reading from inscriptions on stone pillars, told Solon that Atlantis sank beneath the seas more than 9,000 years earlier (at the time of the above-mentioned 11,500 B.P. cataclysm). Solon said he was also told that before that time, Atlanteans had attacked and defeated Egypt, but that the earlier Greeks had beaten the invaders back.

About 200 years later Plato began a trilogy that included the work *Critias,* containing details passed on from Solon to Plato's friend Critias through his great-grandfather and grandfather. Plato referred to Atlantis as being "larger than Libya and Asia put together." He described it as a sub-tropical place with a glittering capital, with a magnificent science and a society of harmony and proportion. Other early Greeks (Crantor, Proclus, Plutarch, and Clement of Alexandria) independently corroborated the sources of Plato's material.

Atlantis was associated by Lewis Spence (1874–1955) and others with occult arts or linked to the esoteric schools of natural and perennial science and philosophy (reviewed here in chapter 23). The immortal Calypso in Homer's epic poem *Odyssey* was portrayed as the daughter of Atlas, one of the gods considered to be from Atlantis. In the same epic, Circe, identified as one of the Titan offspring of AB Helius/Apollo and a demigod mother, used knowledge of magic (Atlantean science) to cause Odysseus' men to act like animals.

In some other Greek accounts the Titans were associated with Atlantis. The Atlanteans were considered descendants of three thousand daughters by AB Oceanus and demigod Tethys or progeny of the granddaughters of Uranus and his Earth wife, Gaea, depending on your interpretation of the various Greco-Roman versions of the gods' family trees. Atlantis researchers, including Plato, tend to see the Titans or demigods as progeny of the AB Poseidon and his human wife Cleito in Atlantis.[5] They allegedly produced five sets of male twins, with Atlas the oldest.

Shirley Andrews, one of the preeminent modern researchers on Atlantis,[6] postulates that the Titans may have been the Cro-Magnon peoples who originated in Atlantis instead of Africa or the Middle East. Even if they had the same mixed AB-human parentage as other *Homo sapiens*, thousands of years of microevolution in a hospitable climate (as Atlantis is almost universally described in history) could have produced a more robust race. Andrews believes the presence of Cro-Magnon fossils only in Europe, North Africa, and South America suggests they were immigrants from Atlantis around 55,000 B.P.

The dating of Cro-Magnons, with their highly developed art and stones with numerical notations, "suddenly" appearing in Europe around 40,000 B.P. adds credence to Andrews' view. Their art and artifacts reveal cognitive skills and a well defined cultural perspective.[7] This culture produced houses, graves, shelters, fires, and thousands of tools. It excelled in every form of art: painting, sculpture, decoration, drawing, and engraving. Its people (standing as tall as 6'4") engaged in ceremony, ritual, music (their whistles and flutes have been discovered), and dance (suggested by cave art figures).

Andrews has developed a timeline of major events in Atlantis that helps us compare its history with Indo-European history up to the Cataclysm. She reports that ABs arrived on Earth around 450,000 B.P., that *Homo sapiens sapiens* appeared circa 100,000 B.P., and that Cro-Magnons arose by 55,000 B.P. (These dates correspond with fossil and DNA evidence presented in chapters 8 and 9.)

As a result of a planetary pole shift around 50,000 B.P., Andrews says Atlantis was left with only five islands. With another pole shift around 30,000 B.P. and the beginning of a new Ice Age, more land was lost, and only one island and an archipelago remained of the once mighty Atlantis. About 14,000 B.P. a bird-serpent war occurs, and about 12,000 B.P. the final destruction of Atlantis takes place, with the death of most inhabitants. Andrews believes a few remnants of that culture survived on various islands and shorelines. Around 4000 B.C.E., she believes another cataclysm destroyed a final outpost on Bimini Island off the coast of Florida, mostly underwater at the time. (Geological research findings support the pole shifts and cataclysms she describes.)

Other Mysterious Vanished Landmasses

Atlantis is not the only alleged prehistoric center of human civilization. Rudolf Steiner and other sources of metaphysical material refer to Mu and Lemuria as predecessors to, or co-existent with Atlantis. While one can identify some anecdotal evidence of these mythical places, we do not have enough facts to construct as much of a history of them as we can with Atlantis.

Briefly, the legendary Lemuria has been viewed as a continent that linked many of the then Southern Hemisphere lands, including the present India, Madagascar, the Malay Archipelago, and the south coast of Asia. (Scientists have given the name Gondwanaland to an ancient mega-continent that had something of this configuration before it fragmented into the current continents.) Esoteric sources claim this area was the birthplace of an earlier form of humanity, with some saying ABs intervened in human development during the Lemurian era. Oral traditions say Lemuria broke up due to extreme geophysical stresses and sank into the sea. Mu has been described as another mythical continent in the Pacific Ocean just south of the equator. It was allegedly destroyed by the effects of the Cataclysm of 11,500 B.P., with survivors escaping to other sites.

The "How" of Human Creation

Traditional myths contain specific details that make their claims of AB involvement in human origins seem credible, implying the involvement of "prehuman" species already existing on Earth. They include details that make sense to modern science in the current context of biological engineering. This possibility receives support from ancient Sumerian documents. The manipulation of proto-human ova, semen, and blood by the ABs obliquely described in the Sumerian cuneiform texts and elsewhere is now feasible in genetic laboratories.

Quetzalcoatl (from the Toltec and Aztec traditions) reportedly sprinkled his blood with the bones of earlier creatures to create humans. In the American West, the Selish tribes' creator AB Amotken used hair from his head to create the first five women. The Quinaults of the Pacific Northwest believe their "changer god Kwatee" created humans from his own sweat. All these methods could imply a contribution of the gods' DNA. And these gods, as did the Anunnaki, came from the sky. The Chaco tribe from the Pampas in South America said a female named Kasogonaga hanging from the sky created humans. The Algonguins and the Blackfeet of North America say their gods (Kici Manitu and Napi respectively) made man from the Earth with a breath of spirit.[8]

Gods, Genes, and Consciousness

Similarly, the old Norse traditions recorded in the *Eddas* report humans were created from two trees (ash for male and alder for female) that could also symbolize the Tree of Life (or genetic knowledge). The Norse tradition—like the Hebrew, Quiche, and Sumerian—had multiple gods. (Was it a team of medical scientists?) The first beings created by the three Norse/Germanic gods Odin, Vili, and Ve were refined in several steps before being placed in Middle Earth where they became the progenitors of the human race (remember Eve being made fertile in Eden). As in other legends, each god had different skills to contribute to the genetic engineering. They came through the sky from the home of the gods "across the rainbow" in Asgard.

A Greek tale of Prometheus has ABs making man in the image of the gods by combining earth and water, i.e., combining existing mundane elements. The Toltecs portrayed the first woman in a garden (as in the Bible) with a serpent (two snake figures form a double helix, the chemical structure of DNA). The Quiche story includes four men from the sky being put to sleep to help make women creatures (the Bible implies that Adam might have been caused to sleep while bone marrow was taken to create Eve). These accounts may imply the use of technology like anesthesia and gene splicing to create hybrids,[9] as suggested by nonscientific Sumerian texts describing what the Anunnaki did.

In his metaphysical "readings" regarding Atlantis, Edgar Cayce portrayed Atlantean humans as beings seeded by the gods. A lower form of humans with more of an animal nature (which we might define as genetic castoffs today) remained after the AB "seeding." Cayce said they served as beasts of burden and even slaves for the more refined beings. He suggested the Indian caste of Untouchables could perhaps be traced to this group of deformed and somewhat frightening hybrids.

Later chapters in this book provide further details that reinforce the thesis in this chapter that some stage of humans (*Homo sapiens,* or at least *Homo sapiens sapiens*) did not just arise naturally, but were products of deliberate intervention by ABs. These ABs worked with Earth materials and/or animals and somehow combined them with something of their own essence.

As we have seen so far, the meaning of this "essence" varies from account to account. Some Sumerian and metaphysical materials track better than others with dated gaps in the fossil record and match several DNA phylogenetic trees prepared by genetic researchers to date "Adam and Eve" and human subspecies. So let's explore the details of human origins as seen through Sumerian eyes.

Who Were the Anunnaki?

In the 1850s, European amateur archaeologists began to dig into mounds in the Tigris-Euphrates Valley (present-day Iraq), seeking to uncover the ruins of fabled cities of Mesopotamia. In the process of excavating the ruins of Nineveh, Nimrud, and other mythical centers of early civilization, thousands of cuneiform and engraved clay tablets were discovered. Many thousands of them have been translated over the last century and a half, with literally more than 100,000 to go. In addition to revealing details of human life 6,000 to 8,000 years ago, they re-introduced humans to the gods of old, along with accounts of their heavenly and Earthly exploits.[10] (One can check them out at these websites: www.eee.bham.ac.uk/cuneiform/ and www.jhu.edu/ice.)

The foremost contemporary interpreter of this material is Zecharia Sitchin, mentioned earlier. He is best known for refining earlier translations in light of present knowledge. Although I do not agree with his cosmology (basically the Judeo-Christian supernaturalism analyzed later in this book) for reasons that become clear in my later chapters, his elucidation of historical details and connection of them to other fields of knowledge stand up under comparative review with the work of other scholars. His summary of information relating to the "olden gods" known in Sumeria as the Anunnaki presents a cohesive and defensible mixture of textual material and judicious interpretation. The following overview draws upon several of his books.

Our solar system has a mystery planet named Nibiru in Sumeria and Marduk in Babylonia (astronomers refer to it as Planet X), Sitchin writes. Its elongated orbit takes it far beyond Pluto, but approximately every 3,600 years it passes near the Sun and inner planets. It is inhabited by humanoid beings known in Sumeria as Anunnaki (in the Bible as Anakim). Nibiru originally appeared from outer space and was captured by the Sun's gravitational field, doing considerable damage to the original solar system. (As we'll see in chapter 10, it may continue to pose threats to our planet in its periodic near passage.) During one of its transits near the Sun somewhat less than half a million years ago, Niburians were reportedly dispatched to Earth for explorations. Earth's gold deposits were desired on Nibiru to solve an environmental problem (involving a loss of atmosphere).

A mining colony was established upon a continent in the Earth's southern hemisphere (the Anunnaki called it Abzu), and facilities for space landings and takeoffs were set up in an area that included the Giza Plateau in Egypt, the Sinai Peninsula, and the Tigris-Euphrates Valley. The Earth expedition was supervised from Nibiru by Anu, who assigned his two sons Enlil and Enki to manage separate parts of the operation. Enlil was in charge of the headquarters in E.DIN and most of the space facilities. Enki was responsible for Abzu. It included mines that might have been in southern Africa (ruins as old as 100,000 years-plus have been found) and the Nile Valley.

At its peak, the Anunnaki expedition had only about 600 individuals, divided among the Mesopotamian facilities, the mines, and orbiting spacecraft. It contained only a few female officers (members of the royal family represented by Enlil and Enki), who assumed command of various areas and activities. The Anunnaki technology was probably only somewhat more advanced than that of humanity's twenty-first century, but for early humans it must have seemed like magic.

AB Genetic Engineering

Various Sumerian, Babylonian, and Chaldean texts, some thousands of years older than the Bible, when considered as a composite, give significant detail on aspects of the Anunnaki intervention in human evolution. With the advantage of current knowledge, Sitchin helps translate ancient medical terms into twenty-first-century science. The following paragraphs liberally draw on his findings. (Readers seeking more depth can delve into Sitchin's eight volumes of compelling research.)

In the Abzu gold mines mentioned earlier, junior Anunnaki, tiring of the back-breaking labor, asked if the team's chief scientist Enki could create workers from some of the local beasts. Enki and Ninhursag (his half-sister, medical colleague, and sometimes lover) agreed to experiment. They concluded they could take a primitive Earthling and through DNA manipulations create a hybrid being suitable for heavy work in the mines.

After some trial and error with ugly results, Enki (his double helix symbol, like that of modern medicine, consisted of intertwined serpents) and Ninhursag found a way (in genetic engineering terms) to splice hominid DNA with their own. There appeared to be no ethical concerns about using our ancestors in this fashion, not unlike human genetic experimentation with other species.

Sitchin's interpretation of the Sumerian account suggests a process of in vitro fertilization (with human sperm) and in vivo gestation (by AB females). (For the Bible student, this appears to be simplistically alluded to by the Genesis 2:7 reference to the creator god breathing "the breath of life" into the newly formed creature.) After the in vitro fertilization technique proved successful, a small group of Anunnaki females in the outpost were assigned to carry equal numbers of hybrid male and female embryos to term.[11]

The limited number of AB females in the astronaut crew soon became tired of being surrogate mothers for the Adamu. In response, Enki and Ninhursag used a few hominid mothers from Abzu (perhaps what is now part of Africa) to provide ova for and to gestate the hybrids. As we'll see in chapter 9, this account corresponds with geneticists' hypotheses that all current humans came from one female or a small group of genetically homogenous females sometime around 250,000 B.P. in Africa. Sitchin believes the first hybrids were neuter. (See earlier similar biblical suggestions.)

Self-replication was not deemed necessary for slaves working in the mines, but their success set in motion a chain of events to change that. The Anunnaki crews based in E.DIN (their space launch control center in Mesopotamia) saw how useful the hybrid slaves were to their colleagues in the mines. They wanted to take some of them from Abzu to work in E.DIN (the apparent Sumerian analog to the Garden of Eden). There, Adam and Eve (the latter a new kind of being created as a mate to Adam in E.DIN) broke an AB rule, learned more than they should, and were told they had to start taking care of themselves, including having children.

This Sumerian scenario is also reflected in the Bible. Genesis 1:26 reports on the creation of the worker (Adam). Verse 1:27 refers to the neuter male and female workers. Verse 2:8 marks their journey to E.DIN. Verse 2:7 suggests a genetic upgrade for the worker Adam, and verses 2:21–22 describe the creation of the new version of woman to partner with the new Adam.[12] Verse 3:16 finishes the tale with the charge to bear children. From the Sumerian tablets we learn the DNA changes to permit fertility also made humans sexually compatible with the Anunnaki.[13] Thus, junior Anunnaki began intercourse with humans.

Not only does the Sumerian scenario track with the Bible account, it corresponds on significant points with recent scientific findings. These will be more fully discussed in chapter 9, but they warrant mention in this context. Phylogenetic dating of the appearance of "Adam and Eve" places Adam before Eve in sequence. That is compatible with the above scenario from the millennia-old clay tablets. DNA studies suggest the appearance of Caucasoids (assumed by conventional scientists to have migrated from Africa to the Middle East) dates from around 100,000 B.P. The Sumerian accounts suggest that around this time the Anunnaki began to intermarry with *Homo sapiens*, resulting in a new, rapidly multiplying hybrid. This sexual mixing of AB-human genes may account for the sudden appearance of Caucasoids in the Middle East.

Much later, selected and apparently deliberate impregnation of human females by ABs (sexually or artificially) would play a great role in the procreation of special individuals who would make significant contributions to the course of human history. Jesus (Mother Mary, born 7 B.C.E.) came in a long line of such *virgin births* (a term used to imply an AB-god was somehow involved in conception). Thus, Mary, the mother of Jesus, reportedly said something to the effect that "the Lord came unto me and told me I would have a child." Other such virgin births allegedly included Zoroaster (1500 B.C.E.), Krishna (Mother Devaki—1200 B.C.E.), Indra (in Tibet—700 B.C.E.), Gautama Buddha (Mother Maya—600 B.C.E.), and Attis (Mother Nama—200 B.C.E.).

In review, these first three chapters have provided an incredibly consistent story, from many different time periods and locations, of the worldwide human experience of AB involvement at crucial points in human development. To simply dismiss it as figments of a primitive imagination would suggest that the basis of our own intelligence and modern consciousness may not be as reliable as we think.

PART II

Different Types of ABs

Introduction to Part II

One person wakes in the middle of the night sensing another being in the room. A man sitting in a forest receives a message from a voice outside himself. A woman having a difficult delivery sees a luminous being hovering over her while giving birth. Someone else feels himself taken into a vehicle suspended above the Earth. What determines the individual's reaction to such an experience? How will she describe and label it to others, if she decides to do so?

The feelings we have about such encounters and the words we use to describe them depend on several factors. Our core personalities (whether we are basically calm or prone to panic attacks) govern our initial emotional response to the AB's presence. However, our personal religion or philosophy can shape the way we subsequently interpret and label the experience. As we seek to communicate what happened to others, our maternal language and its vocabulary set the parameters of the actual description we relate to them.

Part 2 explores similarities among experiences like the above and why we give them disparate names. It seeks to identify generic terms that cut across the cultural labels that greatly confuse current discussions of AB experiences. The following three chapters demonstrate that no single worldview has the exclusive truth regarding nomenclature, much less reality.

Gods, Genes, and Consciousness

Due to its key role in defining Western culture over the past two millennia, the perspective of the three large supernatural religions (Judaism, Christianity, and Islam) has been the lens through which most reports of ABs have been interpreted. Chapter 4 deals with this worldview. Chapter 5 reviews the secular or scientific perspective, paramount only within the last century, that uses terms such as "alien" and "ET." Chapter 6 covers a metapsychological orientation that deals with nonhuman beings as part of a transcendent consciousness, using terms such as "higher beings," "spirit guides," or "higher frequencies and dimensions."

When botanists dig up a 100 million-year-old plant fossil or recover fragments of an unknown plant, they compare bits of the evidence to see if they point to the existence of carpels (hollow chambers to protect and nourish seeds that grow into fruit). If it has carpels, the botanists know they have a flowering plant. Similarly, regardless of the cultural interpretation, if we find evidence of advanced consciousness interacting with humans, we know we have an AB.

4 What Makes Angels and Demons Different?

Modern Egyptian society almost totally consists of an Islamic culture largely unrelated to that of ancient Egypt. The roots of this culture can be traced to a metaphysical encounter in the year 610 C.E. between a human from the poor Kuraish tribe and an AB. From Mecca, in Arabia, the town associated with a black stone from the heavens, Mohammed reported that the Archangel Gabriel appeared to him in several visions and instructed him to propagate a new religion. By 630 C.E., enough people believed in this allegedly "divine" message to organize themselves into a social and military force that took over the sacred city of Mecca. They established Islam (meaning "absolute surrender to Allah").

Roughly 1,370 years later this Muslim religion, encompassing more than a billion believers worldwide and acting through the Egyptian courts, locked up an Egyptian who said he received messages about some secrets of the universe from one of Allah's angels. In September 2002, Sayed Tolba was sentenced to three years in prison for "insulting religion and supporting extreme ideas." Such actions (and more extreme punishments, including torture and death) have been part of all religious cultures that claim an exclusive message from an AB.

41

Why does a religion based on the channeled messages of one AB (Archangel Gabriel through Mohammed) punish an individual who claims to have had messages channeled to him from a similar AB (Allah's angel)? In the 3,500 years between the time another unseen AB named *YHVH* spoke to Moses in the same land of Egypt and poor Sayed Tolba's case, innumerable people in Jewish, Christian, and Muslim societies who said "angels" had spoken to them have been punished for contact with "demons." Is there a difference between angels and demons? Or, is the difference between the two in the eye of the beholder?

Who Were the First Angels?

While many traditional cultures had names for subordinates of major gods, they had no "good/evil" or "godly/satanic" dualism. Such theological or moralistic polarities as "angels" versus "demons" arose only recently in human traditions, and only in the history of the Indo-European culture. Other references to a lower level of ABs (including early Indo-European ones) generally described them as subordinates who carried out orders as messengers, aids, watchers, etc. Some of them were described as flesh-and-blood beings, while others were considered ethereal. The Ganda in East Africa recognized nonmaterial beings in the natural world, calling them *balubaale,* while the Mende tribe in Sierra Leone called such genii *dyinyinga.* A term used by other tribes for the same phenomenon was *mingehe.*

Discarnate beings (sometimes called "spirit guides" in New Age terminology) were considered to be messengers among African groups who received advice or warnings from them. Ugandans called them *emandwa* or guardian spirits. The Ashanti had names for several levels of ABs: *abosom* for lesser gods who were messengers from the AB Onyankopom, *asuman* for spirits, and *nsamanfo* for disincarnate humans.[1] The Dan tribe of the Ivory Coast has a more descriptive memory of the angels who walked with their ancestors: attractive human-like birds who knew all the sciences given to mankind.

In the Germanic tradition these personal assistants of the gods were called Valkyries. Like the "angels" sent by *YHVH* against the Egyptians, the Valkryies went forth from Odin over the battlefields to choose who would die. They equally served the gods at home or on dangerous missions, just as any good soldiers would do for their leaders. The roles assigned to these assistants of the AB-gods had no divine connotation.

In the Celtic culture, the names for entities who were nonhuman, but less than gods, number at least 12: elves, sprites, fairies, leprechauns, gnomes, dwarves, sylphs, and undines. The Celts also incorporated names such as devas, elementals, and spirits from other cultures to capture this in-between group of beings.

A Sumerian View

The oldest references to angel-like beings are found in Sumerian texts using the term *sukkal,* which scholars consider equivalent to our word "emissary." For instance, Anu, the ruling Anunnaki who remained in the heavens, reportedly had an "emissary" on Earth named Papsukkal. When Anu was absent, his grandson Ninurta (possibly aka *YHVH*) could use him to carry out assigned tasks. Ninurta's personal emissary was Sharur. Enki, second in charge among the Anunnaki and Ninurta's uncle, called his emissary Nusku.[2]

The Sumerian scribes did not see theological implications in these beings and their activities. For instance, they described the GI.GI (junior Anunnaki), pilots of shuttle craft between orbiting spaceships and guards of the facilities of the gods, who engaged in combat and carried out other duties.

The GI.GI were known as "bird-men" and were portrayed on Sumerian artifacts with wings to indicate their ability to fly. (Such images led to the modern depictions of angels sporting wings protruding from their shoulders.) Their various duties led them to be called "messengers" or "watchers." They hovered over the daily affairs of humans. They allegedly shouted to Alexander to go back when he tried to approach the abode of the gods on Mount Sinai after his conquest of Egypt. They had challenged Gilgamesh at the same spot, millennia before, when he sought the "fountain of youth." In between these widely separated dates, they had guarded *YHVH*, standing between him and Moses.

The Egyptians referred to these lower-level ABs as *neter,* which has been interpreted to mean "watchers." They also had a term *Ta Neter* ("Place of the Gods") to refer to a specific base for the ABs on Earth overseeing human affairs. The Sumerian use of the term DIN.GIR for this category of ABs corresponds to the Hebrew use of the word *Nefilim* in the Old Testament.

Books of the Old Testament add to this portrayal of such beings.

Two angels accompanied Abraham to Sodom and Gomorrah to search for righteous people to keep them from destruction, but an AB god came along and revealed himself as the one in charge. Angels flew the King of Tyre to Eden for meetings (Ezekiel 28); they transported Enoch into space in a "fiery chariot."

The so-called esoteric tradition always portrayed angels as tangible beings, materially involved with human affairs. The Essenes referred to them as guardians of the places where the gods lived (in their earthly abodes and in space). The Gnostics saw angels as a broad category of beings between humans and the ultimate power source of the universe. They thought a low class of angels (archons) led by *YHVH* had created mankind. For them, *YHVH* was the son of senior AB Sophia who had contributed some of her essence—possibly genes—to the creation of humans. Some believed the most senior god sent Jesus to save mankind from the regime of *YHVH*.[3]

Early Kabbalists shared something of the Essene and Gnostic perspective. In their view, the Shekhinah (the female god aspect analogous to Sophia) mothered humanity. In a hierarchy of archangels (divided into groups of ten) and angels (with similar subdivisions) she played the role of human liberator. The Hermetics believed the angels were responsible for protecting humans. The Magi recognized angels as ABs who taught humans advanced truths.[4]

Early Indo-European terms for angels connoted a neutral role for a class of actual beings. They were a normal part of reality, a world that contained ABs in various guises. In early Persia (Zend), the term *yazd* meant angels or beings from the skies. Another Persian label was *dev* or *div* which simply means an AB, a personage of higher class than humans. The Hebrew term *mal'ak* simply meant "messenger of the gods" (*irin* meant "those who watch"). Sometimes they were called *Bene Elohim* or "Sons of the Gods."[5] In Greek the word *angelos* (from which the Latin *angelus* derived) meant messenger as well. The Greek word for "watcher" was *grigori*. Even the Greek word *daimon* originally indicated an ordinary AB before it came to mean an evil being or devil.

Why Polarization?

The origination of this division of Advanced Beings into God's good angels and the Devil's evil demons must have an historical explanation. The supernatural Christian view attributes it to an ethereal conflict between God and Satan (Lucifer) that resulted in this "devil" and his followers being kicked out of Heaven into Hell. If this metaphorical explanation points to a real-world event, we may be able to identify it and the basic issue causing the conflict.

Could the conflict among the gods have had any relevance to human affairs? If so, how did it play out in the human society affected by the particular ABs involved? Whose interest was served by making a religious tenet out of a policy difference between AB factions? Did it enable psychological manipulation of humans? Does it exacerbate societal divisions, fanning the flames of war, and serve covert agendas in today's world?

Simply put, the answers to these questions seem to be fivefold: One, the policy conflict waged by two or more of the ABs dealt with their opposing attitudes toward humans. Two, the human followers of the two AB factions adopted the hostile attitudes of their AB lords. Three, the name-calling helped incense humans, motivating them to help the ABs fight their internecine battles. Four, these AB-instigated divisions incited humans to hate other humans for superficial reasons. Five, internalizing this AB conflict on Earth and dismissing it as supernatural made human nature subject to psychological manipulation for covert agendas.

These bluntly asserted answers become more clear as we review various religious texts. Books like those of Enoch were accepted by Jews and the early followers of Jesus. Thus, I assume the following materials represent at least partially valid descriptions of actual events, or fragments of culturally-transmitted memories of them. The named ABs refer to the Sumerian/Hebrew documented Anunnaki.

The first Book of Enoch [6] describes a moment that possibly solidified the division of ABs into opposing camps. It tells us that two hundred angels had made a compact to marry human wives and to teach them arts and sciences. Led by Azazel, they had provided secrets of metallurgy, jewelry, medicine, "enchantments," astrology, and astronomy to their human consorts. When Archangels Michael, Uriel, Raphael, and Gabriel learned of this, they reported it to a senior AB-god. He decided that angels educating humans (women in this case, maybe symbolized by Eve in the Garden of Eden) would be labeled "sinners" (perhaps after Enlil's "unofficial" son named Sin whom he favored—with a throne—over his legitimate heir Ninurta [7]).

The "sinners" were sentenced (note the alliteration) to various punishments, exile on Earth, and assignment to mortal combat. They and their offspring were declared evil for all time. If the senior AB behind this sentence was Sin's offended half-brother Ninurta, such epithets and curses can be understood. Sin had deprived him of his father's blessing but then later took his Uncle Enki's side against their father Enlil in supporting policies that favored humanity. (Chapters 20 and 22 suggest Ninurta as *YHVH* favored authoritarian, AB-god supervision instead of human self-determination after the Anunnaki withdrawal from Earth bases.)

If this account has any validity, it explains why people who did not worship *YHVH*, or agree with his priesthood and believers, were later on labeled sinners. They were seen in the same category as demons (fallen angels) and in league with the devil (a likely reference to the Anunnaki leader Enki described in chapter 3 who always favored helping humans to become independent and self-sufficient). This means the original AB "sinners" were the good guys, interested in improving human welfare.

Origins of Satan and Good versus Evil

The separation of ABs into the "angel/demon" dichotomy based on this policy dispute has been linked to the origin and evolution of the Judeo-Christian-Islamic image of Satan. Two authors, one an established academic and the other an independent scholar, have researched and added depth to our understanding of this issue.

Elaine Pagels, a noted professor of religion, in her analysis of Hebrew sacred texts, does an excellent job of demonstrating the evolution of the concept of Satan from the era of neutral names for the "messengers and watchers" described earlier. She progressively identifies steps from the first occasion in the Bible when an angel (Satan) seems to challenge its god (rather than simply carrying out orders) to the stage when early Christians divided all humanity and any other beings into "God's people and Satan's [people]."[8]

Beginning with *YHVH*'s instructions to Moses on what to tell the Pharaoh and the way he described their future enemies, the Israelites saw themselves as above other nations, referring to them in pejorative terms. (Pagels points out that the Hebrew root of the word Satan means "one who opposes or obstructs.") This name-calling characterized Hebrew international relations from the beginning of Israel, but as internal Jewish conflicts developed, particularly after the exile in Babylon, use of hate-baiting terms was brought home. The adversarial connotation of Satan began to be used by one Jewish faction against any other faction that disagreed with its views. By the time the Essenes ("the sons of light") rebelled against the Jerusalem temple hierarchy, use of the "sons of darkness" (people who depart from the way) clearly referred to their Jewish opponents.[9]

This history makes it clear that the Hebrews had simply followed the example of their patron god. They labeled their opponents, foreign or domestic, Satanic, worshipers of Beelzebub, Belial, and the Princes of Darkness. In return, their opponents likely shouted their own epithets of "infidel" (meaning "unfaithful to the 'true' god"). One of the Dead Sea Scrolls has a title that accurately describes its contents: "The Scroll of the War of the Sons of Light Against the Sons of Darkness." While some theologians consider this scroll to be the prophecy of an apocalyptic struggle between heavenly forces in some future scenario, the historicity of language suggests otherwise.

"*Its purpose was to supply an urgent and immediate need* [emphasis in original], a guide for the problems of the long-predicted war, which according to the sect would take place in the near future."[10] The Essene writer used pejorative terms in the manner of modern propaganda to arouse the emotions of the faithful against their enemies to gain a psychological advantage in an imminent war. Two thousand years ago, there is no question that calling one's opponents "evildoers" served the purpose of psychologically rallying the Hebrew troops for war.

Independent scholar Andrew Collins researched the origin of three cryptic verses in Genesis (6:1, 2, and 4) that describe the "sons of the gods" (Bene Elohim) taking wives among the daughters of men and bearing children by them, children known as the "giants of old."[11] (This appears to refer to the same incident as the Enoch story identifying the etymology of "sin.") His study led him to deeper historical roots than the Hebrew material recapitulated by Pagels. He found links between the Jewish "angel/demon" duality and earlier Zoroastrian beliefs (possibly developed while some Israelites were in Babylonian exile from 586 to 538 B.C.E.). By this time, Zoroastrianism was clearly dualistic (good versus evil) and tending toward supernaturalism.

The Zoroastrian sacred text, the Zend-Avesta, was rooted in the earlier Magi tradition of Persia/Iran and the Vedanta tradition of India. The Magi accepted the Hindu Rig Veda's idea that creation in our universe involves a continual and reciprocal process of construction and destruction. In the early Vedic texts, the labels Sura and Asura distinguished these two equal and necessary forces of creation. Sharing the

Vedic view, the Magi believed that humans should respect and honor both Ahura Mazda and Angra Mainyu, their terms, respectively, for the Vedic-named Sura and Asura aspects of creation. The early Magi, rooted in the "natural perspective" (see chapter 7), appreciated this positive/negative, constructive/destructive polarity as necessary for progress in all levels of life.

Asura originally meant just an energetic aspect of the creator. But as the AB-gods fought among themselves, the terms began to take on theological implications. With one faction victorious one day and toppled the next, humans had to decide what to do about them. The Hindu word Asura (and the Persian Angra) became associated with the loser, seen as a dark being[12] (*daeva* means dark god in Persian) or group of dark beings (the Asura, or antigods). When that happened the word Sura was reserved for the winner, a light AB.

The Hindu Ramayana and Mahabharata tales of these wars of the gods make it possible to see the links among Hindu, Aryan, and Sumerian names. Angra/Asura paralleled the AB Enki in Sumeria (the Serpent in Eden who shared knowledge with humans). In Persia the *daevas* taught living by natural laws (as taught by Enki, Thoth, Hermes, etc.) known as *daevo-data*, against which Zoroaster so fervently preached.[13] This suggests the Zoroastrians, Hebrews, and others who bought into the angel/demon dualism took the side of ABs who wanted to keep humans subservient to the Anunnaki regime.

Adopting the Zoroastrian light/dark polarity, the Hebrews called their Prince of Light Michael and their Prince of Darkness Belial. The Essenes described themselves as the Sons of Zadok (truth) arrayed against the Sons of Lying (Belial). "A son of Belial will plot to oppress my people, but I will not allow him to and his dominion will not exist . . ."[14] As the phenomenon of AB-god cults spread throughout the region (see chapter 20) humans used "good and evil" to imply ideological opponents. Thus began the AB-based religious justification for smiting your alleged enemies because of the god they choose to follow.

The use of the "light/darkness" metaphor to divide the angel and human followers of different gods into "good and evil" categories seems to go deeper than just name-calling. Although Collins does not reach a conclusion identical to mine from the same material, his tracing of the evolution in India and Persia from neutral angels to good and evil ones helps answer our questions. Yes, the story of Sin and Satan's origins (along with the demonization of certain angels) did start with conflicts between two AB camps. Yes, the labels did relate to different AB policies towards humans. But, given today's hindsight, it turns out the apparent good guys were really the bad guys.[15] The AB and human winners in the policy debate described by Enoch took positive labels for themselves and tagged their opponents (those favoring full access to knowledge for human independence and self-development) with words like devils, sinners, and demons.

Satan and the Serpent

The association of Satan and his demons with serpent terminology and symbols supports the hypothesis that this icon was based on Enki, the Anunnaki god who supported human independence. In the Sumerian account, Enki the scientist not only helped genetically improve humans, he warned Noah of the impending flood and provided knowledge and technology to humans on many documented occasions.

Remember, in the Bible, a serpent urged Eve to eat of the "tree of knowledge." Enki's symbol as a healer was the entwined serpents of a double helix (DNA today). According to several sources,[16] Enlil and the "gods of Eden" have thereafter tried to stamp out the influence of Enki of Abzu (sometimes known as the Serpent or Lucifer). Enlil's followers, disingenuously referring to themselves as the "good brotherhood," reportedly taught humans to fear snakes in all forms. But their covert objective appears to have been keeping humans dependent by discrediting the Enki/Thoth/Hermes support of human freedom.

Jesus and Angels

To the extent that we know of Jesus' actual teachings, he took the Magian view (natural law) and attempted to enlighten his followers. (Recall that the Magi sought him out by the light of the Star of Bethlehem at the time of his birth.) By credible accounts, Jesus of Nazareth did not seek to found any cult or religious institution.[17] Mary Magdalene's account is particularly relevant. Described in the earliest versions of the Gospels of Philip and Mary Magdalene, she, as Jesus' intimate companion, was the first to see him in his ethereal (ghostly) body before his final transition after death.

Mary Magdalene reported to the other disciples that Jesus told her in this encounter that the essence of his teachings dealt with seeking union with the divine through direct inner knowing (*gnosis* or self-knowledge). This requires inner preparation, introspection, and inner transformation. Jesus, as "teacher," told her: "All that is born, all that is created, all elements of nature are interwoven and united with each other. . . . There is no sin. . . . It is you who make sin exist, when you act according to the habits of your corrupted nature: This is where sin lies. . . . If you are out of balance, take inspiration from manifestations of your true nature." She concluded, "He is calling upon us to become fully human *[anthropos]*."[18]

Peter and Andrew and other male disciples were disturbed by this view. They asked, "Must we change our customs and listen to this woman?" In the end their contributions to Pauline Christianity reinforced the patriarchal, external god concepts. Jesus' teachings were lost as Nicean Christianity went back to the Zoroastrian view of good and evil (sin) instead of the earlier Magian view.

The third-century Manicheans, like some Gnostics, believed the history of "flesh-and-blood" angels. But, Greco-Roman Christianity decided in the fourth century that angels were ethereal beings and that early references to angels were metaphorical. The Church wanted to clearly blame man's "sinful nature" on Eve's falling for the serpent-god's cunning. This would serve as the linchpin in its arguments for the use of Jesus' death and alleged physical resurrection as the only way to salvation from that "original sin." So, even though the Manicheans agreed with them that humans were sinful by nature and needed to find God, the Christian power structure persecuted them. This became the Church's official reaction to suggestions that squabbling ABs on Earth could have been involved in shaping human religions.

A New Religion Chooses Sides

Using Jesus' name for purposes his teachings did not suggest, the first-century cult of Christos (see chapter 20) became the human implementer of the policy of restraint on human development (the objective of the Enlil/Ninurta/*YHVH* group). Its leaders, including Saul/Paul, took the traditional Old Testament notion of *YHVH* as the most powerful among AB-gods and redefined him as the one supernatural God.

The late fourth-century Roman consolidation of the Christian Church, largely adopted from the Greek-instigated federation of churches, during and after the Council of Nicea, strengthened the policy of strict controls on human freedom. Strong conversion campaigns, often accompanied by military force and the threat of death, sought to destroy groups that continued to worship the various AB-gods or live by natural principles. The purpose was to erase the memory of the time when *many* AB-gods, including *YHVH*, were active on Earth. Those who reminded society of when *multiple gods* walked the Earth were labeled pagans/sinners and deprived of livelihood and even life itself.

By the end of the fourth century, Christianity had refined the notion of Satan as the embodiment of Zoroaster's evil Ahriman (the Prince of Darkness). The "evil" Satan represented for the Church the recognition of a body of AB knowledge given to help humans and the reality of AB influence in human history. As the Israelite had embodied *YHVH*'s enmity toward his competitors (the AB-god Baal or Belial and others), the Christian Church condemned as Satanists or devil-worshippers the Jews and others who would not forget that *YHVH* was only one AB among many. Collins pointed out that St. Augustine helped to expunge the record of ABs by declaring the Book of Enoch too antiquated to be included in the official Bible.[19]

The time is now overdue to assemble in public view *all* AB-originated and AB-related material hidden in the Vatican, royal palaces, museums, and covert government repositories and subject them to a review of people representing all cultures. The natural rights of humans demand no less. Only then can we distinguish the real "demons" from the "angels," by observing which groups are open to all aspects of AB history.

5 Are ETs Angels by Another Name?

Since World War II hundreds of thousands, if not millions, of people have reported seeing UFOs, and untold thousands have reported (and documented) encounters with ETs. Thousands of these reports have been thoroughly investigated by government agencies, scientists, private researchers, and healthcare professionals. They provide convincing evidence that humans now living have experienced various forms of contact with various types of Advanced Beings. The ultimate truth about what has been experienced still eludes us, but the truth of the reality of the experience is beyond question. Are today's ET contacts different from human contacts with angels described in sacred texts?

Traditional legends and sacred texts, including the Old Testament, described heavenly (meaning "from the stars") angels in both material and energetic terms, just as humans describe ETs today. While some ET contacts over the last half century have seemed illusive to humans, many have been described by data perceived through the physical senses, just as they were reported in Old Testament times. So, does evidence support an assertion that ETs and angels are not the same?

We cannot answer that question with direct evidence. However, the preceding chapter made a well-documented case that the current supernatural-being interpretations of the ABs we now call angels differ from the way ancient people actually perceived these "angels." The Bible and other texts describe them as real, physical beings. This chapter makes the argument that the difference between the Old Testament, angel-as-physical-being idea and the modern belief in angel-as-supernatural-being reflects a redefinition of history. The objective reality of ABs has not changed, but human interpretations of it have.

Instead of seeing the ABs as natural aspects of ordinary reality (even if not understood) as the ancients did, during the medieval period of Western history most people adopted a supernatural way of thinking that assumed all nonhuman beings were ethereal entities. Our transitional culture now lives with a mix of ancient, medieval, and modern perspectives regarding the ABs discussed in this chapter. The ancient human saw angels as natural beings, whether material or energetic, with a culture superior to that of humans. The medieval human believed they must be supernatural—from a divine realm. The modern person says if they are not humans but exhibit intelligence and fly they must be ETs.

Different cosmologies, with different assumptions, generate these different terms for a common reality. The terms "ET" and "alien" came into popular use only in the latter half of the twentieth century. People wishing to avoid religious terminology started to use "extraterrestrial" to replace "angels" when referring to beings "from the skies." The problem with this practice is that in discussions about ABs people talk past one another, letting the larger truth fall between the cracks. This chapter looks at some implications of this Tower of Babel of terms for ABs.

To achieve mutual understanding we must begin to speak the same language. That requires us to transcend cultural labels and refer to comparable events in comparable terms.[1] Let's assume I meet a luminous being in my yard on a dark night, one who warns me of a danger to come, and a luminous being appears in your bedroom and warns you to beware of meeting a certain person. Why does it matter if I call mine an angel and you call yours an ET?

With regard to the warning and the fact of the messenger, it doesn't make any difference. But when it comes to our respective reactions, it could make a significant difference. You might be frightened if you called it an ET encounter, but if you were a Christian you would be reassured by calling it an angelic visit. In one society you might be venerated by telling people you had seen a messenger of god but ostracized if you reported having seen an ET.

Even though the event does not change, your perception, your reactions, and those of your neighbors would depend on the term you use. Understanding this connection between labels and beliefs and behaviors is essential to developing a global consensus about the effects of ABs on human history. I have described in the preface my reason for offering the term AB or Advanced Being (and its equivalent in other languages) in an attempt to find a term as neutral as possible. You can be the judge of how well the AB concept works by the end of the book. The French equivalent of AB would be EA for *Être Avancé,* and Spanish would be SA for *Ser Avanzado.* The nearest possible equivalent would need to be identified for each language.

ETs Are Among Us

The credible reports of UFO encounters since World War II are too numerous to summarize in one book, much less a chapter. Thousands of serious people, people who neither sought nor desired to profit from their stories, have convinced professionals of the veracity of them. Many have presented physical evidence to back up their memories. What does the evidence say?

There is no question that contactee experiences of personal anxiety, pain, joy, happiness, rage, and terror are very real. There is no question that body scars and other marks or wounds are real. There is no question that the psychological and psychic changes in the experiencers are real. There is no question that much knowledge received by them is real. Such real effects have real causes.

Some Case Studies

In 1990 a well-established psychologist with considerable experience using hypnosis to access abduction memories published 13 case studies that exemplify ET encounters in the second half of the twentieth century. The experiences of contactees described in Edith Fiore's *Encounters*[2] seemed to fall into three categories. The most numerous seemed to involve physical examinations (some quite painful) in settings and with equipment that indicated a medical research program. Many people felt they were also recipients of educational efforts by the ETs. A number of the participants believed they were treated for and healed of various ailments. Some saw their encounters as positive experiences revealing insights beneficial to humankind.

The examinations involved physical manipulations, probing with various devices (including nasal, oral, vaginal, rectal, and urinary tract insertions), use of X-ray and sonograph machines, and collection of blood, nail, and hair samples. Sperm and ova were sometimes extracted. Laser-like surgery was performed on some. A few contactees reported they were taught self-healing techniques. Reported treatments included growth of new cells, rebuilding a damaged liver, elimination of worms and yeast, dissolving a blood clot, shrinking tumors, and healing cancer. Generally the contactees felt that the ETs did not intend to hurt humans.

Some were told that the purpose of the monitoring program was to check up on humans because the ETs had been physically involved in human development thousands of years ago. Most abductees reported, under hypnosis, that their abductors had used some sort of suggestive techniques that suppressed memory of the events. However, a small percentage of abductees had retained direct conscious recall of the events.

ETs Take Advantage of Humans

Widely read ET abduction researcher Budd Hopkins has a less benign perspective on the phenomenon. In his second book, *Intruders*,[3] Hopkins investigated the childhood-to-adulthood case of a woman abductee whose experiences also included friends and members of her family. The subject was hypnotized by Hopkins after she had partial recall of certain aspects of her experience. The investigation revealed her abductions started when she was seven years old, if not before, and continued to the point when her two small sons were also abducted and given implants of some kind of sensors. When she was 18 she experienced an abduction with a gynecological operation that appears to have resulted in a pregnancy. A second abduction three to four months later ended in the removal of her fetus. She felt a part of her had been stolen.

This case is quite compelling, since after the gynecological operation mentioned above, the woman was medically considered pregnant after an examination that included blood and urine tests. After the second "operation" she was no longer pregnant. Her abductors promised her she would see her child again. A few years later, during another abduction, she was shown a strange looking "little bitty" female who was very fragile and was introduced as her daughter. She felt the abductors' claim was true, as she had always "known" that she had a daughter somewhere.

Hopkins collected data on a large number of cases that led him to believe that despite the psychological trauma for the abductees, the aliens did not intend to harm them. They seemed to have done their examinations efficiently, trying to keep the abductees calm and inducing a partial amnesia that would facilitate their return to normal routine. But the results were usually psychologically scarring as well as physically scarring. The aliens seemed to be surprised by the psychological effects of their actions in what Hopkins calls a "highly complex, morally ambiguous, and self-contained external reality."[4]

ETs Offer Help to Humanity

The publicity for Harvard psychiatrist John Mack's excellent book *Passport to the Cosmos*[5] mistakenly called "encounters with alien life-forms" a new phenomenon in human consciousness. Mack does not hold that view in regard to his abduction research, but it reflects the general public's lack of historical awareness. In fact, his case studies (over 200 in nine years) reveal so many similarities with historical accounts that Mack (raised in a secular German Jewish heritage) cannot escape comparing experiences of his interviewees to biblical accounts.

The events described by Mack's human reporters include personal encounters with lights, sound, energy fields, odd craft, and human-like beings. Many associate the same phrases with the appearance of the ETs that one finds in biblical accounts: "loud noise and flashing lights," "vibrating," and "rushing winds." Their ETs sometimes appear as "beings of light," glowing or luminous.[6] People often report feeling like the subjects of a research effort, and that they are being periodically checked on. Often the individuals receive information about the challenges facing the Earth (most of them human-caused) and suggestions (even warnings of catastrophe or apocalypse) on how to avoid its demise. Some of these reports sound like the messages of olden prophets of Israel.

A common theme reported by the subjects of his research involves being taken by humanoid beings, voluntarily or not, for various medical procedures. Many of these reportedly result in the taking of ova or semen to be used either for strengthening the alien species' own stock or the conception of ET/human hybrids. Some contactees report having seen their alleged progeny in subsequent visits to space craft. (Recall the Sumerian accounts of what we've interpreted to be in vitro and in vivo procedures and the biblical accounts of ABs mating with humans.)

Some contactees described profound sexual relationships with ETs that continued for long periods. The reports resemble the Sumerian tales of the AB Ishtar with human lovers or the Greek stories of Zeus with the mortal Niobe (who bore the demigod Argos). Given biblical descriptions of human-AB sexual relationships, these modern stories do not appear so new and strange after all.

Communications from the ETs come in different ways: telepathically, eye-to-eye, on screens with projections of images of things to come (like the images shown John in the Book of Revelation), and access to libraries in the sky (like that of the Egyptian god Thoth). Sometimes spheres or balls of light transmit the information. Training in psychokinesis, a sixth sense, and telepathy often occur in what one contactee called an "alien boot camp."

Cases of knowledge and technology transfers like the ancient ones described in chapters 13 and 14 reportedly occur with some frequency. One South African medicine man reports being taught geography and art, and how to build telescopes, jet engines and ships, a crossbow, and a new kind of gun.

Another Perspective

Researcher Jacques Vallee takes an iconoclastic perspective on aspects of the modern UFO phenomenon. An astrophysicist, computer scientist, and former U.S. defense contractor, Vallee finds the physical evidence of alien activity disturbing. The title of one of his books, *Confrontations*,[7] sets him apart from writers like Whitley Strieber, with books entitled *Communion* and *Transformation*. Based on personal investigations of 100 cases in the United States, Brazil, France, and Argentina, Vallee questions the pervading extraterrestrial hypothesis, speculating that "we are dealing with a yet unrecognized level of consciousness independent of man, but closely linked to the earth. . . . UFOs represent a technology capable of harmful action."[8]

Of the 100 cases Vallee interviewed, 47 involved secondary (beyond the abduction itself) physical and medical effects, with 12 cases of fatal injuries. The physical effects included material fragments left by UFOs, energetically caused damage, demonstrations of power or force whose magnitude could be realistically estimated from physics calculations, and electromagnetic (electronic failures in machines) and gravitational disturbances. Vallee concludes that although the UFOs may operate in a dimension beyond 4-D space-time, they certainly make an impact in 3-D reality. Landing sites are marked; nearby living plants are affected; areas are covered with fog or burned; strange substances are left behind; humans have wounds, fevers, and organ failures; and some people die.

Vallee questions why such physical effects and medical consequences do not get the attention of eminent researchers. He believes study of them may lead to an explanation of the reasons for the apparently hostile intentions of the alien perpetrators. It appears he shares the U.S. government's alleged view that the phenomenon poses a threat to human society.[9] He believes governments possess proof of the UFO reality but do not understand it. One concern of Vallee's is that ill-founded UFO beliefs (like religious ones) make people subject to psychological manipulation. (On this point he and I are in full agreement.)

That the modern UFO phenomenon closely parallels historical accounts of AB interactions with humans (including sex) is self-evident to Vallee. His earlier book *Passport to Magonia* establishes that the phenomenon is not new, but is history repeating itself. Vallee says this evidence "teaches us a new measure of humility before the universe and its bewildering potential to reveal alien forms of consciousness and, more importantly, perhaps new insights into our own."[10]

Hierarchies of Beings

Several different types of beings have been reported, from the small "Greys" of sci-fi poster fame, to those with reptilian features, to those who cannot be distinguished from humans. Brazilian shaman Bernardo Peixoto, Ph.D., an employee of the Smithsonian Institution (one of Mack's subjects) separates the Greys from a group of spirit-beings they call the *ikuyas*. He believes the former are sexually involved with the creation of hybrids and make trouble, while the latter are helpful to humans. While many contactees see their ET experience in terms of their religions, the ETs do not seem to portray themselves as divine.

ETs Serve As an Ark for Humanity

One of the best-documented life stories of an abductee in the literature involves the Andreasson affair, reported by noted UFO/ET researcher Raymond Fowler. In three books he portrayed the involvement of Betty Andreasson Luca and members of her family with various UFO and ET events that covered a period of more than 40 years. According to material recovered from hypnotic regression sessions and the corroborating statements of family members, Betty had been exposed to contacts with ETs from age seven. The contacts included seeing lights, hearing voices, UFO sightings, meetings with aliens in the woods and in her bedroom, missing time, anomalous scars, and abductions aboard spacecraft. Luca believes she was chosen as a messenger to make public the reality of the current ET program on Earth.

Fowler believes Luca's abductors have been involved with humans from our beginnings, and that both the ETs (Greys and humanoid types) and modern humans are the creatures of one earlier race, probably the tall, blond Nordic types reported by many people who claim contact with ETs. These watchers or messengers have as their sole purpose helping humans (from a distance) and maintaining the life-forms resulting from the earlier AB intervention on Earth. Luca (as the contactee) and Fowler (as the analyst) agreed that one purpose of the ET "examinations" was the harvesting of human ova and sperm (and perhaps "seed" from all Earth species) as a hedge against the extinction of all life on Earth. They also speculate that the ETs use the genetic material to reproduce themselves, as they always were or have become sexless.

In the third book of the Andreasson series, titled *The Watchers*,[11] Fowler explores the ramifications of Betty's reports in a manner somewhat compatible with the larger story represented in this book. Betty was raised in the Judeo-Christian tradition and naively called her first visitors (the small Greys) "angels." Once, when being taken to meet an ET commander, she assumed she was going to meet the One, the ultimate creator of the universe. Years later she pressed Fowler on the connection between biblical accounts of angelic activities and her own experiences. Although speaking from a general Christian perspective, he attempted to deal objectively with the similarities. He provided Betty a list of examples from the Bible (including many I and others use in illustrating the same point) that describe events that very nearly parallel modern UFO/ET accounts.

Of these parallels he said, "Again, I would stress that the [listed] events, if reported by modern witnesses, would be called UFO experiences. One must also assume that if ancient witnesses did indeed observe UFOs that they would describe them in nontechnical terms . . . All these references presuppose that *aliens are angels* [his italics]."[12] Fowler goes on to recognize that evidence of such activities[13] challenges any religions that do not include ABs in their theology.

Account of an Intimate Journey

Scientist Angela Thompson-Smith describes almost 40 years of encounters with ABs that exposed her to weird experiments, high-tech implants, visits to spaceships, and nursing an alien-human hybrid.[14] She represents one of two categories of so-called abduction experiences, the ongoing childhood-to-adult type, instead of a seemingly spontaneous event. As a neuropsychologist and cognitive scientist, Smith approached her contacts in as objective and systematic a manner as the strange circumstances would permit. She used the neutral term "Visitors" and described her encounters with them as "Interfaces." For 13 years she kept a detailed journal of her AB contacts and relevant parts of her daily life.

Using primarily a self-guided process of memory and dream recall, she pieced together an account that corresponds to many less detailed records. The most intrusive aspect of the series of medical examinations involved strange technologies, the embarrassment of being undressed, paralyzed, swabbed, probed with needles, and subjected to various procedures. She documented physical evidence from her encounters, including scars and wounds, scratches, dried blood, and leaks from her navel (from laparoscopy insertions into the abdomen). She also endured tests of her psychological reactions and attitudes.

Over the years, her state of mind went from fear of the aliens to excitement about studying and learning about the phenomenon, only to return to fear as the U.S. government subjected her to its own form of abduction. In the end, with nothing more to hide, her fears had disappeared. She concluded that her experiences were real, that similar occurrences were widespread throughout the population, and that even though many events involved altered states of consciousness, the body suffered physical effects. Her perception was that the Visitors were interested in studying us, were interbreeding with humans, but had no desire to intervene in any way to save us from our own mistakes.

Smith's experience with and perception of the U.S. government's program of monitoring and intimidating humans who experience AB contact offer insights relevant to the theme of consciousness manipulation in this book. She believes a largely one-sided *de facto* war is being waged against the ABs by official groups who fear the obvious power of the Visitors. She counts as evidence the continued build-up of the unilateral Star Wars program and efforts to intimidate and marginalize abductees. This is part of a historical campaign to reinforce the dualistic, secular, and religious consensual reality that declares ABs are not real.

From Examination to Cooperation

One highly publicized case of what the ABs involved called "unsolicited visitations" had the purpose of laying groundwork for an eventual AB-human diplomatic meeting. Prepared as a brief or treatise by veteran journalist Phillip Krapf (retired from the Los Angeles *Times*), his book titled *The Contact Has Begun*[15] declares that one AB race called "the Verdants" (named after their home planet) will offer help to humans to make the transition from a planetary to an interstellar society. According to Krapf, professionals like himself have been exposed to "orientation and education" meetings aboard a spacecraft about the peaceful objectives of an intergalactic organization. High-level "ambassadors" have been chosen and are preparing to officially announce the presence of ABs.

Based on several detailed briefings by the Verdants, Krapf believes the end of the 1,000-year-long program of AB medical examinations and psychological analyses of humans is near. He says several hundred people have by now been engaged by ABs to prepare for a period of cooperation. This preparation involves *Homo sapiens* changing from a warlike culture to one that meets the behavioral standards of more advanced worlds.

Krapf has written that the Verdants confirmed that other AB species have been involved with humans, some to positive and some to negative effects. The Verdants allegedly verified the reports of the Roswell crash in 1947, indicating it was an accident. They said the bodies were recovered by the U.S. military, which fortunately restricted access to them and avoided the mass hysteria that would have occurred just after the end of World War II. The details published by Krapf do not contradict the historical material presented so far in my book. They do suggest an *evolution* of the nature of AB *interest* in humans and the possibility of a public resolution of religions' misunderstanding of their true nature.

ETs by Many Names

This and the preceding chapter are important steps in removing the curse of the Tower of Babel from human society. The confusion sown by distortions in terminology among various texts and through multiple languages over the centuries has had serious consequences, consequences that have hobbled human development, limited human vision, and, in turning humans against humans, have diminished the realization of our natural potential.

Translators and educators dealing with AB material, unintentionally and/or with malicious intent, have imposed their own religious or cultural assumptions on the consciousness of others. Now we must make a joint effort, collaborating in public forums, to recover as much as possible of the original experiences. With very few original records, to close the historical gap will require a judicial cross-cultural comparison of terms by modern linguists and historians.

A synthesis of old and new terminologies should help us build a consensus that permits society as a whole to discern the truth of human experience with ABs, if not the truth about them. This new look at the AB story will shift the focal point of human consciousness from a homocentric one to a cosmic perspective. Such a change in focus will have ramifications greater than the earlier Copernican shift from a geocentric to a heliocentric view of Earth's place in the universe. The divisions between sacred and profane, religious and secular, scientific and magical, natural and supernatural, will disappear.

6 Are Allies, Guides, and Higher Selves ABs?

The last two chapters dealt with conscious entities experienced as being external to humans. Contactees still maintained a sense of separateness from the ET even when it communicated telepathically. Similarly, when they sensed the AB speaking inside their heads or merging its mind with their own, most still perceived the AB as a distinct being. This chapter moves to the other end of the spectrum, where distinctions between the source of an apparent AB communication and the person receiving it remain elusive.

Readers of Carlos Castaneda's books[1] learned from the sorcerer don Juan, with whom he apprenticed, the concept of an "ally," a noncorporeal being imbued with consciousness and energy. This ally behaved in many respects like an AB, with the power to teach and protect, to be a helper to humans willing to experience states of nonordinary reality. However, whether the ally was an independent being or a manifestation of Castaneda's own consciousness remained unclear.

Castaneda's experience was reportedly accessed through the use of natural psychedelics (*Datura inoxia* and *Psilocybe mexicana*) and a regime of shamanistic training. In such altered states the boundaries between self and other become imperceptible. This practice of using psychedelics to connect with other dimensions of consciousness predates Judaism and Zoroastrianism.[2] Archaeologists and anthropologists believe the use of such substances may go back to early humans and has been a continuous feature of aboriginal and traditional cultures. In its desire to prevent people from directly accessing a "divine" realm, supernatural religion stamped it out wherever possible.[3] However, in the course of Castaneda's training, he learned that power (i.e., psychotropic) plants are only an aid to perceiving the larger world.

Castaneda learned to "stop the world" and "see" things differently. By his willpower he became a "warrior" and a participant in encounters with his opponent, a coyote, or his ally. (Yogis have always maintained that the focusing of one's intention is sufficient to access these other dimensions.) He learned he could engage the ally by "tackling" it.[4] A person of knowledge could count on the specialized power of this ally in the form of a "helper."[5] Not human, these entities were "luminous beings" who were not constrained by the rules of ordinary reality; they could assume human form and act in the physical plane. The net effect was not unlike encounters with an AB.

Encounters with Other Beings

The 50,000 year-old shamanic tradition, including that described by Castaneda, involves the use of specific substances and techniques that enable the practitioner's separation of his/her mind from the body to commune with the spirits of animals and other beings. However, many routes exist to such ethereal excursions, termed "out-of-body experiences" (OBE for short) by psychologist Charles Tart in the 1960s. Some methods are deliberate and appeal to the modern mind, while others are involuntary. In fact, many people have had to nearly die to experience it (near-death experiences, or NDEs). Most of these encounters with ABs are different from those described earlier because, with the exception of the near-death experience, the human can take the initiative.

Out-of-Body Experiences

Charles Tart's friend and early OBE enthusiast Robert Monroe developed the first electronic technology to assist one to consciously leave the body and travel to nonphysical realms inhabited by other beings. Monroe founded an institute now known by his name and developed the Hemi-Sync method (used in The Monroe Institute's programs) to help people achieve different states of consciousness. It "uses patterns of sound to help create simultaneously an identical wave form in both brain hemispheres."[6]

Through the Gateway Program at The Monroe Institute in Faber, Virginia, many individuals have been trained in a unique process of self-exploration and discovery. This includes the ability to consciously take leave of one's physical body and communicate (using various forms of energetic exchanges) with a variety of other entities in different levels of conscious development. (Readers interested in more details of this outstanding program can contact the Institute through the means given in this chapter's endnote 7.) Monroe's information gathered from the realm of ABs concerns us here.

After several validations of the information received from these beings, Monroe (now deceased) no longer questioned its validity. Some of these helpers had been in human form, even thousands of years ago. Others had never been in human form, but could choose to be. Ones with different forms inhabited other regions of the universe. Monroe reported the most highly developed "had knowledge and technology far beyond that drawn from human experience."[8]

The ABs with whom he communed (in a nonverbal form of communication that involved direct, immediate experience or an instant knowing) said they did not create us. Further, they said that we and they were created by the ultimate creator, but that they and we were creators in our own right, and that though there are hundreds of billions of beings similar to us, humans have their own unique experience. Monroe recognized that he had been "consulting with a being or beings whose penetration into human life had been interpreted to be God, gods, angels, [and] the devil." They said unilateral intervention in human affairs was "not [their] intent . . . [but that] adjustments had to be made."[9] Monroe said the beings with whom he had contact indicated UFOs and flying saucers were manifestations of other types of beings, and they had different agendas.

In her book, *Cosmic Journeys*, one of Monroe's longtime fellow explorers, Rosalind McKnight, provides her perspective on the beings she called "Invisible Helpers." She, Monroe, and all their colleagues who traveled to levels outside the physical realm were met with some kind of "guiding force." This force appeared as a presence, voice, light, or energy, depending on what the explorer expected. The humans used their own terms to label them: "an angel, Jesus, a guardian, an inner-self-helper, a guide, a higher self, a control, a universal consciousness, an invisible helper, a super-ego, or a guiding voice."[10]

McKnight came to believe that her "Invisible Helpers," whom she met through the Institute, had always been with her from childhood, guiding and directing her, especially when she was in trouble. The Hemi-Sync technology made it possible for her to make those preexisting connections overt and conscious.

McKnight's Invisible Helpers assisted her in making contact with extraterrestrials, who visited Earth as part of their space exploration program. She was taken aboard some of their crafts and learned that they could function at different "frequency levels," including the one inhabited by humans. Most of the so-called "abductions" of individual humans take place at this level. Monroe was interested in learning about the AB's technology, and he and McKnight gained many useful insights into their activities involving Earth. One of the important lessons for her was the realization of her own various dimensions, all operating simultaneously in different facets of the universe. Other beings, too, have these.

Near-Death Experiences

Most readers probably already know about the phenomenon of near-death experiences (NDEs). People who had ceased all physical functions have been revived to describe being conscious during various encounters with other beings in luminal or energetic form. Foremost NDE researcher P. M. H. Atwater has collected several thousand stories of people, young and old, who, in the course of being between worlds, met various conscious entities. They are described as angels or religious figures (depending on the orientation of the individual). Between 9 and 14 percent of her subjects report they have had encounters with aliens in a UFO.[11]

Atwater reports in *The Complete Idiot's Guide to Near-Death Experiences* that about 70 percent of children NDEers encountered "angels" or ABs by other names.[12] Children seem more likely to use the term "angel" for any such entity than adults, who have a larger vocabulary from which to choose.

Best-selling author Dannion Brinkley, a two-time NDEer himself, reports in his book *Saved by the Light* that a spirit guide took him to a "crystal city" where 13 "Beings of Light" gave him 117 predictions about future events. They included items dealing with changes in governments, the rise and fall of nations, economic collapses, health-care problems, and social problems.[13]

Reports of such encounters were first popularized in the now classic *Life After Life* by Raymond Moody in 1975. He said his subjects invariably encountered a being that could only be described as "a being of light" who had a personality (in my view, an anthropomorphic term) with love and warmth. This being gently guided the person through a series of questions to determine if he or she should return to the physical body. The communication was nonverbal, but the individual understood clearly what transpired.[14] This method of knowledge acquisition resembles the "instant knowing" through telepathic communications described by Robert Monroe in his OBE experiences.

Conversations with the Gentlemen Upstairs, God, and One's Higher Self

Communications with nonphysical AB entities do not always involve such dramatic encounters as out-of-body or near-death circumstances. For most people, they occur in more "ordinary" situations. Sitting in meditation, daydreaming, prayerful intellectual searching, and many different approaches have resulted in encounters with other intelligences. The subject areas and validity of the information seem to be no less significant than that received in moments of greater drama. Scientists and philosophers are still trying to figure out *how* this works, but in the lives of individuals it *does* work.

Some psychologists and physicists today hypothesize that life in this universe consists of multiple dimensions and that consciousness is one of those dimensions, itself consisting of different levels. This could account for human perceptions of the self experiencing various aspects of matter, energy, and consciousness as integral parts of their universe. ". . . Although we see ourselves as 'individuals' separate from each other, in fact—and not at all metaphorically—we are all connected one to another [and with all parts of ourselves], by way of our intimate connections with a larger being."[15]

"The Gentlemen Upstairs" is a label given by Frank DeMarco, author of *Muddy Tracks: Exploring an Unexpected Reality*, to such a part of himself, or something larger of which he was a part, that provided him wise counsel and perhaps soul-saving insights. In DeMarco's experience, this aspect of consciousness operates in a realm he called Upstairs, a level that often knows what is better for us than what we think we know while living Downstairs in ordinary reality. Upstairs seems to him to be good at orchestrating events so one is in the right place at the right time, to meet the right people, and so on.

Of the Gentlemen Upstairs (also called inner guides, "the Boss," and simply "TGU"), DeMarco says, "They and I function as close friends, joking with each other, but serious at the same time; trusting in each other's good intent and basic ability. . . . For a long time I wondered if 'they were real'—meaning were they truly independent intelligences offering assistance, or were they part of my own subconscious or semiconscious mind, helping me to fool myself."[16] He reports receiving mounds of material from TGU in response to his continual questioning, "advice that turned out to be invaluable." One time he asked for a novel plot. He was promptly given ten pages of plot, characters, motivation, etc. He then asked how he should tell the story and got three paragraphs of instructions.

DeMarco concluded: "The world contains real forces and abilities that haven't yet been explained, and cannot be explained away, but can be experienced." One of the unexplained is that the larger being sees things differently from how we do; it contacts us and we can contact it.[17] (He strengthened his ability to interact with such beings at The Monroe Institute, mentioned earlier.) This remains consistent with philosophical concepts of a larger being of which humans are only aspects, like local concentrations of consciousness (including ABs) within the whole.

Best-selling author Neale Donald Walsch's first book, *Conversations with God,* introduced millions of readers to the idea that they could have two-way conversations with the AB they called God. Over the course of more than five years he posed questions that he thought the "Source of all things" should be able to answer. The answers that came to him, he wrote down in three books.[18] Where did the answers come from? In Book 2, God said to Walsch, "You must stop seeing God as separate from you. . . ." The answer obviously implied that both our questions and answers come from the same field of consciousness, the same realm that comprises gods and humans.

Through this process, Walsch recorded "God's views" on almost every subject of interest to humans wishing to live a more consciously aware life. Topics included the nature of God and consciousness itself, the church, death and the devil, free will, health, judgment, karma, laws and love, mind and matter, pleasure and relationships, sex and sin, the soul, truth, and war and wisdom. Relevant to the themes in this book, God told Walsch that "extraterrestrial beings" have visited the Earth many times and "gently assisted" human development with "a boost now and then."[19] Walsch's writing suggests anyone can access this wisdom.

Many groups refer to experiences like those just described as conversations with one's "higher self." These include transpersonal psychologists, Theosophists, and Religious Science practitioners who think of all beings as aspects of one multidimensional, universal soul, spirit, or consciousness (not unlike the concept of Atman in Hinduism). To some, this interpretation may seem another version of Freud's "superego" or Jung's "collective unconscious," or correspond to what most Catholics and some Protestants call "guardian angels."

Even if they are connected at some level with the consciousness these terms refer to, most individuals perceive such a realm as being composed of separate entities. Other people may wonder if these are some aspect of their own consciousness. Whether the experiencer thinks she is talking to herself or to another being, the reality of the outcome remains clear. Individuals receive information regarding events, people, and topics about which they have no conscious foreknowledge.

This discussion of process applies equally to the two categories of metaphysical experiences introduced in chapter 1. The production of information by psychics and religious prophets involves a similar *modus vivendi* with the source of such material being unknown. Such prophets purport to access all sorts of information, from the most personal details of individual lives to scenarios of a future Apocalypse.

One of the most famous of twentieth-century prophecies was that associated with the small town of Fatima, Portugal. Believers accept that the Virgin Mary revealed three important prophecies to three peasant children in the period from 1915 to 1917. They allegedly dealt with the onset of World War II, the spread of communism, and the Cold War, and some subjects that have not yet been revealed by the Vatican.

An interesting aspect about the reliability of predictive information received through this process is that some researchers claim the general success rate for even the best psychics and prophets of any category is no more than about 66 percent. Does this mean the information itself is not perfect or that the human interpreter is at fault? Or, does the operation of free will and the human capacity to intervene in the cause and effect relationship account for the other 33 percent?

Channeling

A final category of AB communications with humans falls under the rubric of channeling. In this situation, individuals go into altered states of varying depths, and what appears to be a different being (in terms of voice and language) speaks with its own message or responds to questions posed by a third party. The quality of information is quite similar to that produced in the "conversations" described earlier.

One such channel is the well-known Ron Scolastico, who transmits personal and general information from what he and others call "the guides." The guides, in terms of substance and relevance, in many instances appear similar to allies and higher selves. Some purport to be individuals from other dimensions, while others claim to be humans who have lived before and wish to share their accumulated wisdom. Buddhism, too, has its own name for enlightened beings who give spiritual guidance to humans. Bodhisattvas, earthly or transcendent, dedicate themselves to compassion and service. Those free of rebirth are believed to assist humans on their path, much as do Scolastico's guides.

An example of this phenomenon is a person named Allison who goes into a trance state and channels a group consciousness called Sextus. Allison receives general words of advice from these beings, who claim to inhabit other dimensions but have a particular interest in human progress. One quote from Sextus illustrates this phenomenon:

> There are so many civilizations, so many groupings of consciousness, of intelligence, of frequency within and without your immediate universe, that were you to still the mind from the everyday movement of your activities you would witness an overwhelming realization how vast, multifaceted, and multidimensional existence truly is. . . . What is so difficult for the peoples of Planet Earth to comprehend is that they do not create their reality independently from others.

Although all creation is renewed in every moment of existence, no creation is truly birthed by one individual consciousness.[20]

Many Christians have reported their own channeling experiences,
but in terms compatible with the Church's nomenclature. For
instance, Hildegard von Bingen, the twelfth-century mystic of
Rhineland, saw multiple categories of ABs in her now famous visions
from another realm. She interpreted them as largely symmetrical with
the accepted Christian hierarchy of supernatural beings. In the context of the previous chapter on the labeling of angels and demons, von
Bingen clearly "heard" her AB voices to be angelic.[21] The Church
regarded them that way, too, while she was alive. Pope Eugenius
authorized her to write whatever the Holy Spirit inspired her to write,
but after her death her writings were suppressed (considered to be
demonic) for 800 years.

Mark Russell Bell, a former Hollywood publicity specialist who
channels material related to Christian themes, has stated: "I found parallels between the account of the Angelic Force called 'Michael' by the
family in Oklahoma with what has been recorded about the angel who
spoke to Moses on the mount . . . [it] was mentioned as an 'angelical
spirit' in a Nostradamus 1555 letter to his son, used Edgar Cayce as a
channel, was referred to as 'The Mahatmas' by *The Secret Doctrine*
author Madame Blavatsky, communicated via the ouija board to inspire
the *Messages from Michael* books, and was glimpsed in a near death
experience by George Ritchie as described by Raymond Moody in *Life
After Life.*" Bell believes there is a common source for the various AB
communications that have appeared in apparently different guises for
over three millennia.

All Pieces of the Same Puzzle

As Mark Bell suggests, I believe we can reasonably conclude that
all human encounters with Advanced Beings described in the first six
chapters of this book point to a universal phenomenon. While we may
not yet be able to fully characterize that reality, some individuals seem
to have grasped its multidimensionality in ways that suggest that all its
participants—including humans—comprise one integral organism, a
universe much more complex and filled with more nuance than we
have thus far imagined. One such individual, a talented artist,

respected teacher, and profound scholar named Edward Carlos, has spoken publicly and written on a life of encounters.[22]

As a small child he saw an "angel" outside his window who took him for a flight over the farm country where his family lived. Thus began a progressively more insightful exposure that involved unsolicited journeys to sophisticated craft he prefers to call *vimanas* (a term used in the Vedic tradition). In what he considered shamanic-like experiences of a healing nature, he received teachings about important areas of concern to humans and the Earth. His face-to-face mystical encounters with other beings involve a range of sensations and exposures to lights and energies that progressively transformed his awareness to higher dimensional levels, perhaps approaching that of his "hosts." Exposure to vistas of Earth and the cosmos from space have informed his artworks while introducing him to other lives and situations analogous to near-death experiences.

His life has included many of the types of AB encounters described so far in this book with the exception of any concept of direct rule of humans on Earth, which Carlos believes "is contrary to their nature and capability." His experiences apparently progress in terms of consciousness but are completely outside of any notion of direct manipulation. The manner of connection is always metaphoric and in the mode of a teaching experience.

What makes this case so important is Carlos's intellectual ability to comprehend and describe (as a gifted artist and photographer) both the spiritual and physical aspects of his relationships to the beings, and his emotional maturity to grasp the nuances of the interactions. He understands that even though some aspects of the examinations cause "pain," they also contribute to improving something in the body. He described the techniques of transporting the human through physical barriers as a sort of transmutation from the ordinary body to an energetic body. He recognized the transformative impact of moving between worlds, learning to appreciate the "alien" perspective and thereby expanding the horizon of his own consciousness.

In short, Carlos's experiences recapitulate much of the collective history of humanity's perceptions and interpretations of ABs and their ongoing empathic relationship with humanity. Trying to understand the experience from the inside out, Carlos and people like him bring all of humanity closer to the time of realistic relationships with Advanced Beings who up to now have been seen as phantasmal, magical, or supernatural.

Rooted in Fantasy?

Perhaps this six-chapter introduction to the complexity of AB history and the variety of conscious human experience has left you with many questions. If so, you are not alone. One cannot be faulted for wondering if human consciousness has fooled itself by creating fictional stories whose repetitions over generations project "false memories" into the dreams or other altered states of future humans. Could we have been fooling ourselves from the beginning of human consciousness? If that is the case, what sort of "hard-wiring" in the human brain could account for it? And how would that hard-wiring have come about in our species?

Some observers have noted that during the period between 1880 and 1940 (the beginning of the current UFO/ET era), science fiction became a very popular genre. Books described abduction of humans by strange creatures, flying vehicles chasing after trains and automobiles, cars stalling, and people being hit by light beams. One could speculate that these same images have since been fed back into public consciousness as the alleged reports of actual experiences with ETs. Would that mean every generation of reports described in these first six chapters had a preceding generation of science fiction authors? Who then were the creators of the first science fiction? I believe it more likely that the science fiction writers of a century ago disguised and built upon human *memories* of actual events and beings from earlier times.

When so many sources describe this variety of human encounters with ABs, it becomes rationally difficult to dismiss them. To do so would force us to conclude that at some level humans have conspired to be hallucinatory and delusional throughout history, and that sounds illogical. The evidence suggests that ABs come in both physical and nonmaterial forms. They tell us we and they are intertwined in the same multileveled reality, all connected to the One Source of the universe. Should we not at least take that possibility seriously enough to study it?

That neither the mass of UFO/ET evidence nor the proliferation of materials from higher levels of consciousness has been examined by established institutions is a staggering indication of the self-imposed limitations of modern consciousness. Scientists and the media spend many million times more resources on the images of objects and energies light years away than they do on these daily, and nightly, aspects of human life on Earth. More time and energy is spent by scientists in research on the sex life of bees and ants than on the AB experience that one in ten humans claim to have had.

This indifference is actually more difficult to defend *scientifically* than to hypothesize a consciousness-filled universe. Science's top priority for today should not be the search for evidence of ABs, but to understand why humans fear the possibility that they might exist.

PART III

Science Corroborates AB Intervention

Introduction to Part III

The scientific method cannot definitively prove any particular hypothesis true or false unless it can control *all* the variables and forces relevant to the assumed cause and the observed effect. Given the complexity of our multidimensional universe, the most we can ask of the scientific method is to define the probability of a given hypothesis being correct. The probability is a statistical calculation (itself based on assumptions about the nature of nature) of how many chances out of 100 or 1,000 the finding did not occur by chance (accident). However, given that humans (even with multidimensional senses) remain local incarnations of consciousness, we cannot aspire to better odds.

Remember that even hypotheses based on intuition or psychic knowing still require testing of their reliability or validity in ordinary reality to be called truth.

Therefore, we cannot expect to be able to prove with 100 percent certainty that at x date, ABs y intervened or did not intervene in human history and had a positive or negative effect. The most we can hope for is corroboration, more evidence to support the hypothesis than evidence to counter it. If the preponderance of evidence were to prove AB intervention was impossible, then we could give up the quest in this book. However, I believe you will agree that the existing evidence must compel any serious scientist to test the AB-intervention theory.

Gods, Genes, and Consciousness

In this third part we examine physical evidence related to the appearance and evolution of the genus *Homo* and its species *Homo erectus*, *Homo sapiens* (including Neanderthals and Cro-Magnons), and *Homo sapiens sapiens* (modern humans). Most of humanity's physical remains have been destroyed by biological, climatic, or geophysical processes, including the rotting caused by almost invisible microbiological organisms. These conditions mean the assumptions that currently shape the conclusions of archaeologists, anthropologists, and geneticists rest on a limited database. You may find it very surprising that, even with these shortcomings, the tentative findings of these disciplines serve to corroborate the AB intervention hypothesis.

7 Were Humans on a Natural Path?

What niche did the first humans fill in the web of life and the hierarchy of consciousness in the universe? This question raises broader issues than has the twentieth-century simplistic debate between Darwinism and Creationism with its Earth-focused and Man-centered themes. It assumes consciousness and organic life are universal phenomena, and that Earth-based humans are only pieces of a much larger puzzle. It suggests forms of life elsewhere preceded those in our relatively new solar system. It implies a sort of purposefulness in the cosmos. At this point, we should not assert an answer not based in our own direct knowledge.

However, just posing the question without a final answer gives us a different starting point from that usually presumed by science or religion. Unable to begin with some *a priori* answer concocted by one group or the other, only the evidence before us can provide a reasonable basis for our answers. This and the following two chapters are an attempt to review the physical evidence of human origins and early development outside the paradigms of "accidentalism" and "supernaturalism." In other words, we begin by letting nature's record show us its direction. Then we refrain from accepting as truth any interpretations that fall beyond our ability to judge their validity based on our collective experience.

Retroactively uncovering the natural human path of development requires us to jettison our childlike notions of how a god created two people in the Garden of Eden or how a flash of lightning caused a few genes in a cell (that had appeared accidentally) to mutate and mandate sexual reproduction. Let's see if any reasonable inferences can be drawn from looking at many fields of study that would suggest a purposeful, natural path of human development.[1]

Historical evidence points to such a natural era for early humans. Many legends speak of a "golden age" or a "peaceable kingdom" in prehistory. These stories seem to point to a natural time before the ABs. They suggest that early humans were part of the natural setting, and that an AB intervention resulted in the creation of modern humans, with everything that means with regard to "progress." Interestingly enough, such a scenario seems to be confirmed by the Sumerian accounts of AB manipulations of early humans. As we'll see in the next two chapters, it may be corroborated by studies in paleoanthropology and genetics.

This present chapter then attempts to illustrate how humans fit into the overall schema of life, assuming we have a natural place in a universal order. It presents some ideas on the human role in the ongoing evolution of life and consciousness in an evolving universe, governed by inherent natural principles.[2] The chapter describes perennial human efforts to maintain a natural perspective on our development and to understand the fundamental realities of our universe, including other conscious beings. These efforts may be seen as a metaphysical thread woven throughout prehistory and history.

Humans in Their Place

Early humans seemed to have fit easily into the descriptive taxonomy established in 1758 by Swedish botanist Carolus Linnaeus. The primate order of mammalians included about 180 species of prosimians (lemurs and tarsiers, for example), monkeys, apes, and humans. Relative to other mammals, primates had binocular vision (with enclosed eye sockets), mobile fingers and toes (with nails instead of claws), a reduced sense of smell, and large brains. The hominid family of the primate order seemed to naturally encompass upright-walking primates (early humans) with relatively large brains. But, as we'll see in the next chapter, the question remains whether this taxonomy naturally provided for *Homo sapiens* and *Homo sapiens sapiens*.

Were Humans on a Natural Path?

According to the fossil record, about five million years ago genus *Homo*, like all animals preceding it, began its own path of natural development, engaged in a self-learning process necessary to adapt successfully to its environment. The process of microevolution permitted several subspecies of these evolving humans to differentiate themselves in separate locations depending on diet, climate, and other physical conditions. Their remains, found around the world where conditions supported fossilization, are considered to be those of our human ancestors. We will use the term "human" to include all the commonly labeled *Homo* groups down to ourselves (although the recent record indicates we are quite different from our putative ancestors).

Conventional Retrospective

The first archaeo-anthropological interpretations of primitive peoples' lives were made by scholars schooled in the Christian tradition of the late eighteenth and nineteenth centuries. Interest in archaeology only began in the late 1700s with the excavation of Pompeii and Napoleon's later expedition to Egypt. Physical anthropology only developed after the 1850s; cultural anthropology did not develop until the twentieth century. These researchers carried to the field the basically medieval assumptions about a supernatural god and used them to determine the way they imagined primitive people thought of gods, arbitrarily applying their findings to art objects and other artifacts in Mesopotamia, Egypt, Europe, and the Americas.

The modern anthropological perspective, shaped before recent discoveries about prehistory, assumed a gradual evolution from the first humans roaming about by instinct, picking up random fruits and nuts and eating lesser animals for survival. According to this view, female "gatherers" would harvest ripe foods, and the male "hunters" would wander afar in search of game. It assumed that external factors slowly made establishing farms and domesticating animals expedient. Increasing populations in turn led to towns and cities, and then great civilizations. However, the artifactual, genetic, and fossil-record evidence summarized in this book does not support this scenario.

Alexander Marshack, a revolutionary researcher in archaeology and anthropology, concluded in the 1970s that scholars had assigned labels to "primitive man" which were derogatory, based on unproven assumptions and not the evidence (art, stone, and bone artifacts). He pointed out the cranial capacity of *Homo sapiens* has not changed from the size found in the oldest fossils.³ He also reminded us that the archaeological records of tools and artifacts do not necessarily represent the evolution of human cognition and intelligence.⁴ His analysis confirmed that time-factored thought (involving seasons and other natural cycles) and knowledge of other species and geography are revealed in notations (quantitative information) and art as far back as 35,000 B.P.

Since Marshack's shattering of some of academe's shibboleths regarding prehistory, many have come to agree that reality appears to have been much more complex. Paleolithic and Neolithic humans demonstrably had a natural path of complex conscious development. Thus, to know who we are, we must attempt to discern something of the indigenous human path before we try to hypothesize the influence of more advanced beings.

According to traditional societies the early humans were able to tune in to the consciousness of plants, discerning their particular properties and beneficial uses.⁵ Sensitive to the vibrations of all life-forms, these early humans learned to read their "messages." Some myths report that animal friends assisted early humans in the identification of edible plants, but don't say how. The Cherokee tell another aspect of this history: The plant kingdom's council of spirits (group consciousness) decided to inform the primal Cherokees which plants were antidotes for human diseases.⁶

Early humans, capable of conscious interaction with their environment, would have exercised a high degree of self-consciousness. While progressing slowly (by our modern standards) with tools, fire, foods, and habitats, they could have developed more complex communication and social systems. They would have likely learned how to wisely relate to their environment, taking what they needed, storing seeds and roots for the winter, but leaving the plants and animals capable of replenishing themselves.

Something extraordinary happened. After hundreds of thousands of years, the gradual process of unfolding exploded in what is known as the "big bang" of human culture. Less than 50,000 years ago, social inventions began happening with increasing rapidity, and in the last 10,000 years full-blown civilizations burst upon the scene.⁷ Conventional theories simply cannot explain such a phenomenon. Other chapters deal with the problem by offering the AB-intervention hypothesis. The following paragraphs illustrate an increased appreciation of the inherent self-learning capacity of natural humans.

Nature's Own Program

Scholars are beginning to understand the inherent drives under-lying nature's self-learning process, based on the need to survive and adapt to changing environments. Theories fabricated to explain obvi-ously different inventions and social traditions among animal and human groups are giving way to inferences drawn from direct obser-vation of nature (science's own method of learning). The academic sociobiological theory assumes gradual genetic mutations influencing behavior occur by chance and get reproduced because they enhance the survival capacity of a species. However, observations of humans and other species by researchers reveal very rapid rates of change. Thousands of generations would be required to account for the appearance of even relatively simple cultural variations if they depended only on genetic change through natural selection. Thus, natural selection cannot satisfactorily account for the cultural "big bang."

Due to this problem, some sociobiologists have turned to envi-ronmental factors for an explanation. However, observations of nature show that different groups of a species subjected to the same environmental conditions can still develop vastly different cultures. This invalidates the notion of ecological determinism. Neither acci-dental genetic mutation nor environmental determinism can account for the observed variety of choices made by conscious beings, includ-ing our genetically closest relative, the chimpanzee.

Traditionally, science has considered "culture" to be those behav-iors that set humans apart from other animals, according to the logic that humans have culture and animals have instincts. That simplistic assumption has now been called into question by primatologists and cultural anthropologists.[8] Some have observed that the gap between the tool-using practices in wild chimps and some aboriginal humans is not so definitive. They have also documented a significant number of primate behaviors that cannot be readily explained by biological and environmental determinism. For instance, chimps have been observed learning to use sticks to "punish" other chimps.[9] It has become clear that different cultures exist within many species. (Culture for all animals includes the species' relationship to food, its sexual practices, individual-group relationships, ways of relating to environmental challenges, communications, and social norms.)

Some basic aspects of culture can be linked to the requirements for species survival, but the specific practices become quite varied within a species. While each species has inherent needs that must be satisfied within the conditions of its physical environment, they can be met in different ways. For instance, an animal that requires meat for survival will develop the minimum practices necessary to secure food in its particular habitat. However, the specific modes chosen for distribution of that meat to other species members vary among groups within the same environment. They have "chosen" different patterns.

Such examples of animal learning and choice require a new explanation for cultural development. Individuals of all animal species, through an inherent level of consciousness, discover new insights and learn new skills in the process of experimentation. This learning is then communicated to and accepted by other members of the species. The new patterns then become embedded in traditions, taught to succeeding generations. The result is culture, a system of beliefs and practices that remain stable until new learning occurs.

This new direction in research supports the idea of self-learning and a capacity for choice in all species. Early humans would have been engaged in that natural process of self-learning. If the evidence in this book is valid, we can never know what the outcome might have been had they been left to their own devices.

Sensing Nature Inside and Out

Early humans would also have been able to access the multidimensional aspect of nature. Research with animals and humans has revealed an innate capacity for inner-dimensional communications that enhances their learning process.[10] Having learned of the inner realities through their own experimentation, early humans would have had no reason to conceive of an inaccessible realm. What supernaturalists today call a "divine realm," our ancestors would have seen as just another aspect or dimension of "ordinary reality." They would have felt just as natural as a modern intuitive or psychic person does tuning in to physical and nonphysical channels of information.

These nonphysical channels appear to include all species, including Advanced Beings able to communicate telepathically with humans. Jacques Vallee and Ingo Swann[11] have reminded us that the mutual telepathic channel reportedly still working between humans and ABs shows such faculties are apparently universal. In an extraordinary example of anthropological insight, Hungarian-born Felicitas Goodman found a key that permits modern humans to perceive altered states of consciousness as early humans apparently did.[12]

With years of field work and experimentation, Goodman and her colleague, Belinda Gore, have discerned that particular body postures depicted by artifacts from early cultures around the globe can induce trance states. The trance states, duplicated by modern practitioners, can lead to healing, divination, and out-of-body journeys. This indicates prehistoric cultures could use posture, dance, and sound (some of their artifacts are whistles) to access subtle energies and other dimensions of consciousness.

Some of the integrity of these natural beliefs still lives in the myths of Early Americans and others who appear to have lived largely outside the sphere of AB influence. Belief in the reality of consciousness beyond humans and the power of still poorly understood energies did not arise from fantasy, but from an experienced reality. They are concepts now finding support among frontier scientists. One of these is the concept of *mana*, a mysterious form of energy described by Melanesians of Papua New Guinea, known as *prana* in the ancient Vedic science. Modern science has now experimentally developed an understanding of that subtle energy known by at least 52 names around the globe.[13]

Natural Science and Spirituality

Given what we now know about human capacities, we can reasonably speculate on how our ancestors would have experienced the universe. Early humans would have seen the Earth and sky that we see and felt the forces and rhythms of nature that we encounter. Although they would not have had the same terminology and concepts we use today, with a good translator we could have succeeded in communicating effectively with them about the following aspects of nature.

They would have sensed the connections and communication between and among natural organisms (intra- and interspecies). They would have observed that specific behaviors were related to certain later events, particularly where their own activities were concerned. Some sense of cause and effect likely evolved very quickly. They would have been aware of different levels of communication with other species. They would have sensed the presence of nonmaterial, but conscious entities. They may have easily learned that their own thoughts and intentions influenced plants and animals, and even parts of their own bodies.

Early humans would have discovered that certain rituals, some probably including the ingestion of consciousness-altering drugs, enhanced their perception of subtle energies and influenced external realities. Evidence would suggest they engaged in such rituals because of the results: the healing of a member of the family, or a rain dance that brought rain.

Probably very early on, early humans realized that they shared a field of consciousness with one another and other dimensions. (Australian aborigines still report the tradition of sharing dreams.) They would have routinely accepted the value of dreams and out-of-body states (in shamanic practices) as a source of sometimes useable information. Thus, early humans would have integrated their inner-channel and five-sense experiences in a natural manner, seeing all sources of knowledge as integral aspects of their own reality. But, the sudden appearance of beings dropping from the skies, exhibiting awesome technologies and living seemingly immortal life spans, may have been too much to grasp. It was magical.

Although we have been taught that early humans were naïve and that their spiritual lives were based on mistaken beliefs about the universe, the preceding argument suggest that we may have been wrong. When we look at historic artifacts and traditions, and think logically about human nature without interposing our supernatural ideas on them, a very different picture emerges. Early humans may have been closer to many current scientific insights about the universe than our supernatural traditions of the past two millennia.

ABs Share the Natural Perspective

Early humans were not alone in their natural perspective on life in the universe. More Advanced Beings would have had their own view of reality, based on their self-learning experience. It would have been considerably different from the human one, due to a longer period of development and their species' unique history. ABs apparently have shared some of their learning (knowledge and insights about the multidimensional universe) with humans.

From the earliest days of civilization's 10,000 B.P. "big bang," some humans have reported they were made privy to the secrets of AB wisdom. These AB initiatives are treated more fully in later chapters, but several independent traditions date their introduction to the early phases of civilization in Egypt, Mesopotamia, and the Indus Valley. This natural scientific and philosophical school of thought probably resulted from a combination of human introspection about their own experiences and what they had been taught by AB gods.

As we'll see in chapter 19, the Anunnaki leaders had different policies about helping humans. Some wanted only slaves, and others desired to help their human progeny realize their own potential. Because of the conflict among the ABs, groups of independent human thinkers apparently had to draw together in Mystery schools, dedicated to maintaining the secret teaching of the past. They, apparently helped by some Egyptian priests and other patrons, maintained a body of natural science from fields including cosmology, medicine, mathematics, and astronomy.

This advanced AB-human synthesis of naturalism appeared publicly from time to time, but since the purported era of the Anunnaki gods in Mesopotamia it has never comprised the mainstream of human thinking. Hellenic culture (Greece and Ionia) 2,600 years ago saw a blossoming of this independent naturalism. Philosopher-scientists espoused the notions that "the more we know the less we believe" and that man had the capacity and responsibility to determine his own destiny. Three centuries later, Alexander the Great may have operated on the assumption that the natural wisdom of all cultures (Greek, Assyrian, Babylonian, Anatolian, Persian, and Judaic) could be synthesized for humanity's benefit. This theme, kept alive by groups like the two discussed below, re-emerged in the sixteenth- and seventeenth-century Renaissance in Europe.

The Hermetics

A body of knowledge now known as the *Corpus Hermeticus* came to the modern era from Egypt through the early Hebrews and Greeks, through Neoplatonism and Gnosticism. The Hermetics recognized the unity of all things and beings in an interdependent universe. They saw the individual as part of a universal mind, only separated from it by one's sense of self. The closest we have to the original Egyptian texts are materials preserved in Greek documents produced at the Library of Alexandria around 2,000 years ago.

These texts make it clear that the Hermetics did not speak of a supernatural, anthropomorphic god.[14] The Greek word for the creative force of the universe was *nous*, implying an endless, pure form of knowing. The concept is not unlike the universal field of consciousness that early humans would have experienced and that many modern physicists now see as the source of all form.

The Kabbalists

Parallel with orthodox Judaism, a group of scholars known as the Kabbalists tried to maintain a naturalist perspective. The Kabbalist

Yagel, a sixteen/seventeenth century Jewish physician, believed a natural thread of perennial human wisdom ran through several individuals in Western civilization. Starting with one of the Zoroasters,[15] Yagel added Plato, Asclepius, Hermes, Homer, Prometheus, and Pythagoras. He saw them as representing the same approach to knowledge that the Kabbalists stood for, one that "explore[d] nature in all its multifarious dimensions . . . [where] the truth follows its own course . . ."[16] Although Yagel believed that humans received advanced knowledge from other dimensions and angelic ABs, he believed it had to be tested by humans with their own senses. Knowledge from the inner dimensions, in his view, should be tested in practice.

Inner Conflicts of Self-Learning

This chapter has set forth some arguments for the existence of an innate, self-correcting natural perspective motivating human consciousness since the advent of early humans. It may be something like the hardware of a modern computer, built into the neural pathways and animated by a species-specific focus of consciousness. It likely includes an inherent need to experiment with one's environment (physical and nonmaterial) to achieve a fuller sense of one's personal and environmental reality. This suggests humans have an intrinsic need to figure things out, or at least to believe they have done so. Only when an experience with objective reality demonstrates they have been wrong can new learning occur.

The thesis of this chapter has been that humans, absent contact with ABs, would have followed their own path of discovery and development. They would have taken as a natural part of their reality any experience that might befall them. Most humans would likely have been content to learn a few things and rest on their laurels until confronted with situations that forced new learning. As in the animal kingdom generally, other humans could have been more inclined to try new behaviors or ideas just for the satisfaction of learning. Could the latter group account for the previously mentioned cultural "big bang"? Or did beings more advanced than early humans inject technology and knowledge into human culture that stimulated leaps in consciousness, and thus civilization? The following chapters strongly point in the direction of external intervention.

8 Can We Explain the "Missing Link"?

When I first began to consider the possibility of AB physical or genetic intervention in the development of modern humans, I wondered how presently available fossil evidence might be relevant to that hypothesis. Current evolutionary theory holds that our earliest human-like ancestors descended from even earlier primates and that various species branched off that trunk of the family tree, with the most successful evolving into modern humans. The absence of "transition fossils" that clearly show intermediate stages between very different alleged successor generations calls this assumption into question. The 150-year-old search for these "missing links" is described in this chapter.

Could such missing links that have undermined evolutionary theory with regard to humans be related to AB intervention? Given that the current fossil record contains only fragments of previous life-forms on Earth—climatic and geological changes have destroyed much of the evidence—I did not expect to find incontrovertible proof one way or the other. But, with new discoveries from paleoanthropologists appearing almost monthly, always revising the previous month's picture of the *Homo sapiens* family tree, I was encouraged to look.

I found that the fossil evidence unearthed to date certainly does not disprove the AB-intervention hypothesis, and, in some important ways, it appears to corroborate it. Recent use of the most advanced dating techniques suggests dates for the appearance of genus *Homo* and *Homo sapiens* species that appear to be compatible with the AB-intervention time frame described in part 1. The Sumerian (historical) and Pleiadian (metaphysical) reports of Anunnaki colonization and genetic engineering correspond in significant ways with the fossil evidence.

The Art and Science of Paleoanthropology

The first modern discovery of fossils that appeared to belong to some of our human ancestors occurred in 1856. For almost 150 years the discipline of paleoanthropology has sought to reconstruct the five-million-year history of human evolution. That first discovery involved a skeleton found in the Neander Valley in Germany. We now know it as one of a subspecies of *Homo sapiens* and call it Neanderthal in honor of its burial place. Similar fossils discovered since point to a global history for Neanderthal humans from over 300,000 years ago to as recently as 28,000 years ago.

In 1866 the bones of what we now call Australopithecines were discovered in southern Africa. The first skeletons that appeared to be early *Homo sapiens*, labeled Cro-Magnons from their location in a French cave of that name, were discovered in 1868. Remains of an older species now known as *Homo erectus* were not found until 1894 on the island of Java in what is now Indonesia. The late 1920s saw the discovery of fragments in China of what has become known as the 420,000-year-old Peking Man (a subspecies of *Homo erectus*). Many nonhuman fossils were also uncovered in various sites, providing a record of animal diversity. Since the 1920s, many new fossil finds have been given labels as other genera, species, and subspecies, but the fossil record of human development remains fragmented and partial.

When the first hominid bones were discovered, most Christians denied they were human ancestors or even related to humans, due to their belief that mankind had been directly created by their Judeo-Christian anthropomorphic god just over 4,000 years ago. By the late nineteenth century the battle for public opinion pitted the idea of divine creation against Darwin's notion of natural evolution by a process of random mutation and selection of the fittest. Religious believers vociferously rejected the possibility that mankind and apes might have had a common ancestor. But the concept of natural evolution as the only reasonable explanation of human origins had captured the imagination of those seeking to dethrone the supernaturalism espoused by Western religions.

Most scientists became proponents of Darwin's biological adaptation model, including those in the relatively new academic disciplines of archaeology and anthropology. They, without considering other options, attempted to piece the fossil fragments together in a manner that would confirm the gradual development of new species from earlier ones. Their art of dating fossils, in order to make them fit Darwin's schema, was dependent on several interlocking assumptions. They assumed the bones were deposited along with other items found within a stratum of rock formation. Not until the late twentieth century did science develop precise fossil and DNA dating techniques that would undermine these findings.

To understand reports of fossil evidence, we need a few definitions to help us with the specialists' labels. "Hominid" means the family of bipedal, primate mammals that includes humans. "Hominoid" implies a resemblance or physical relationship to humans. "Humanoid" connotes having a human form or characteristic, but not necessarily any direct relationship. These labels and those used for various genera and species are descriptive, not explanatory. They do not give the reader a self-evident historical scenario.

To give a sense of their chronological progression and to relate them to the AB hypothesis, I divided all the scientific labels referring to various fossil groups into three categories. They suggest a progression from the first seemingly indigenous humans, through various hypothesized AB interventions, to the appearance of species *Homo sapiens* with its several subspecies.

Recognizing the continuing uncertainty that results from the ongoing discovery of contradictory fossil remains, I tentatively use the term *prehuman* for the various hominid fossils that may have been mislabeled as human ancestors. They include everything from the seven-million-year-old Toumai skull found in Chad in 2002 to the long-identified *Ardipithecus, Australopithecus,* and *Kenyanthropus*. These fossils range in age from three million to seven million years old.

After these prehuman fossils, I label as *early humans* only the species considered to be in genus *Homo*. Using this approach, the most ancient currently known early human fossils date to four-plus million years ago.[1] Such an early appearance suggests the genus *Homo* coexisted with the prehumans and did not genetically descend from them. This lack of intermediate fossils between those considered to be prehuman and early human can be described as the first missing link.

Two species of genus *Homo*, *heidelbergensis* and *erectus*, lived from two or more million years ago until well after 250,000 B.P. Genus *Homo* also includes the currently recognized older, but more short-lived, species of *habilis*, *ergaster*, and others. Some believe all of these may be only subspecies of one generic *erectus* type that arose independently of other hominids. Such diversity within the single *erectus* species has recently become more plausible, given what we understand of the potential for intraspecies genetic adaptations through microevolution.

The fossils of early humans have been found in Africa, Europe, and Asia (including China and Java), demonstrating they were not limited to one habitat. This array of fossils includes an interesting 1.7 to 1.8-million-year-old site in the republic of Georgia, between the Black and Caspian seas. The bones of six individuals have *habilis* characteristics, proving a type formerly assumed to have been limited to Africa was actually more widespread.[2] Members of this general *erectus* group overlapped with *Homo sapiens* for what could have been several hundred thousand years.[3] Such overlaps suggest that one did not directly evolve *into* the other by a process of natural selection.

I have defined as *transition humans* the groups that fall on this side of the second missing link in the fossil record. (We have not found fossils to fill the gap between the *erectus* types and *Homo sapiens*.) Under transition humans, I include all *Homo sapiens*, including Neanderthals and Cro-Magnons. The Neanderthals were shorter and broader with larger bones and muscles than their contemporary humans. The Cro-Magnons were in general taller and more robust than other *Homo sapiens* with whom they co-existed. However, it appears likely that genetically they all fell within one integral species.

As last in this three-stage taxonomy, I include under the label *modern humans* only those who survived into the Common Era known as *Homo sapiens sapiens*. They include aboriginals, Negroids, Caucasoids, and Mongoloids, and every conceivable twenty-first-century combination of them. As we'll see later, the fossil record has a *third missing link* between *Homo sapiens* and *Homo sapiens sapiens*. It makes the appearance of modern humans seem spontaneous.

The three-stage *(early, transition,* and *modern human)* model outlined above reflects recently estimated time periods for the important specimens among fossils discovered to date. It recognizes the gaps in the fossil record that have led some evolutionists to postulate the notion of "punctuated equilibrium." This concept does not *explain* the almost spontaneous (in evolutionary terms) leap from one hominoid type to another. It simply *describes* an unexplained exception to the very slow process of evolution. Since no physical evidence indicates how such leaps could have occurred through any known natural process, terms like punctuated equilibrium remain *labels* instead of testable theories. However, interestingly enough, the three-stage model tracks very closely with the AB-intervention hypothesis and timeline introduced in part 1 and referred to throughout this book. This hypothesis, with the evidence in these chapters, provides a more plausible explanation than speculative labels.

As you read the following assumptions made by myself and by scientists studying the fossil record, remember that we have discovered only a small percentage of the total original fossils from an unknown percentage of the areas inhabited by our ancestors. Also keep in mind that dating techniques are still imperfect. Our assumptions remain just that.

Fossil Record and Dates

Techniques for dating fossils and artifacts have evolved with the advances of science. In the early twentieth century, science could provide only hypothetical relative dates for organic materials by estimating their antiquity in relation to an assumed age for the rock or sediment stratum in which they were found. This biostratigraphic approach involved an assumption based on an assumption. The lack of a technology to date the rock around the fossil made the estimates meaningless. Scientists then demonstrated in the 1940s that potassium/argon ratios could be used to date volcanic rock deposits. Potassium-40 turns into argon-40, so the more argon-40 one finds in the rock the older it is. Given the 4.1-billion-year half-life of argon, the process can date rock from 500,000 to several million years ago.

While helpful in dating the rock strata, this process still left problematic the assumption that the fossil's age was the same as the rock stratum in which it was found. So, more precise dating techniques were invented for organic materials. The first was the carbon-14 method that was effective for deposits no older than 50,000 years. Later developments included accelerator mass spectrometry, electron counting, and other electromagnetic spectrum analyses.[4]

To cover the gap (between 50,000 and 500,000 B.P.) left by radiocarbon and potassium-argon technologies, several newer dating methods have been developed.[5] Two of these techniques work well with flint tools, ceramics, and sediments by counting the time since the object was last heated by fire or sunlight before being buried. The third works with materials like tooth enamel, coral, or mollusk shells. All these techniques have shortcomings and are best used with other techniques for corroboration. The review of dates below uses data collected from all of these techniques as appropriate.

Predecessor Species

Prior to the appearance of humans in the fossil record, the remains of several assumed predecessor species have been dated. Many scientists assume they are our direct ancestors but have no demonstrable proof of that connection. As you will learn in the next chapter, current genetic theory would hold that the timelines found in the fossil record are too short for random, adaptive genetic mutations to produce the obvious dramatic changes. Nevertheless, the record does show a category of bipedal creatures arising on Earth who could have included our protohuman ancestors.

Prehumans

These hominids fall in the category that included the Miocene Apes. They ranged from the size of cats to others eight to nine feet tall and weighing 700 pounds. We call the latter *Giantopithecus* and date them from 20 million to 8.5 million years ago. The earliest hominid remains that most paleoanthropologists place in the human family tree were labeled *Ardipithecus ramidus* and have been first dated at 4.4 million B.P.[6] However, the 2002 discovery of a skull in

Chad, in central Africa, accepted by some scientists as the oldest pre-human hominid, pushes the date back to 7 million years.[7]

After *Ramidus* came *Australopithecus* (with a cranium one quarter the size of *Homo sapiens*) at 4.0 million B.P. Hominids known as Laetoli (in Tanzania, where Mary Leakey discovered their footprints) were dated at 3.5 million B.P. The famous "Lucy" and "First Family" fossils (different types) were dated to 3.2 million B.P.

However, these hominid creatures cannot reasonably be thought of as humans. Although bipedal, they had small skulls, very different feet, sloping foreheads, and significantly different bone structures. Several of these basic types existed in parallel for millions of years, remaining in stable species with only intraspecies changes. Several types survived until about 1 million years ago, when all of them drop from the fossil record (as we now read it). But long before they disappeared, beings we label genus *Homo* (from the Latin for "man") came on the scene as early as 3 million years ago. This lengthy co-existence of different species with no known transition fossil undermines Darwin's natural selection theory, giving us the first so-called "missing link" between humans and other hominids.

Early Humans

The first beings we can reasonably call hominoid were *Homo habilis* (a tool user with long arms and short legs and a brain one-half the size of modern humans) and *H. ergaster* who appeared well before 2.5 million B.P. and lasted until perhaps a million years ago. They overlapped more than a million years with *H. erectus,* the most humanoid of this era, who may have survived until after 250,000 years ago. The *erectus* cranium size was larger than that of the other *Homos,* but their physical proportions resembled the seemingly older types. Their global diaspora indicates skills at adaptation and potential for development. They left artifacts of a surprisingly sophisticated stone tool technology, plus wood and seeds.

The currently available fossil record shows *erectus* lived beyond Africa, reaching at least from Western Europe to Eastern China and the Pacific Islands to Australia. Some of them, or their cousins, lived along the Jordan River approximately 800,000 years ago. That archaeological find was dated through evidence of a magnetic pole reversal about 780,000 B.P.[8] They inhabited one site in what is now Israel for at least 100,000 years. Similar *erectus* sites in Europe date from 500,000 B.P. All this suggests *erectus* had a very early and widespread habitat.

Other possible early human groups overlapped with *erectus*: *Homo antecessor* arrived at 800,000 B.P. and *Homo heidelbergensis* appeared at 500,000 B.P., with brain sizes apparently three-fourths that of modern humans. *Erectus* largely disappeared from the record about 300,000 years ago (a very important date as we will see), but some may have survived well into the modern era. Given the wide-ranging evidence of dates and geographical locations for these various types, there is a strong probability that a number of genus *Homo* species, or more likely subspecies, were scattered around the globe a half million years ago.

Now we come to the second infamous "missing link," another hypothesized stage of development for which no fossils have been identified. If found, it is believed this missing species would show the evolution of early humans (the above hominoids who perhaps were the last natural humans) to transition humans. The continued existence of that missing link, after 150 years of unsuccessful searching around the world, only adds credence to the AB genetic intervention hypothesis. But that gets ahead of the fossil story.

Transition Humans

The being that appears to be physically in between the early genus *Homo* category and Common Era humans was named *Homo sapiens*, indicating not only anatomical differences, but also evidence of greater intelligence. Fossilized remains available to us so far show *Homo sapiens* appeared without direct antecedents much less than half a million years ago. Their fossils have been found in Asia (China 200,000 B.P.), Africa (Ethiopia 160,000 B.P.), the Middle East (Israel 100,000 B.P.), and Australia as late as 10,000 B.P.

This new category of hominids could have been any one of three possibilities. A totally new category of primates (not considered likely by most scientists), direct successors to one of the early humans in the *erectus* species, or they could have been some sort of hybrid. The possibility that one or more of these significantly different and overlapping groups descended from one another becomes less tenable with the more blanks we fill in in the fossil and genetic record. The last possibility would have required some sort of genetic mixture between the early humans and an as-yet-unknown species. This "unidentified-species alternative" provides an opportunity for input of AB genes, as implied in oral traditions and described in Sumerian and Akkadian and sacred texts (including the Bible).

What I have called the transition human category of *Homo sapiens* included Neanderthals and Cro-Magnons. Debate continues on whether they should all be considered the same species. Some believe Neanderthals—who appeared over 300,000 years ago and survived until 25,000 years ago, with a smaller brain capacity—should be considered an independent species. They do not appear to have reached Asia or the Western Hemisphere. The most recent transition human fossils (Cro-Magnon subspecies) have been discovered in Europe (40,000 B.P.), in Lebanon (37,000 B.P.), and in France (27,000 B.P.).

Modern Humans

Once again we have considerable overlap between different stages of human development. *Homo sapiens sapiens* (modern humans) appear in the fossil record alongside transition humans for more than 100,000 years. The earliest dates for modern humans range from 100,000 to 150,000 years ago. In southern Africa, their fossils date from 75,000 to 120,000 B.P. The oldest modern human fossil samples discovered outside of Africa to date have been in Israel, dated between 90,000 and 100,000 years ago.

In evolutionary terms, 100,000 years is a very short time. The number of dramatic "improvements" one finds between *Homo sapiens* and *Homo sapiens sapiens* in such a brief period is not compatible with the concept of random genetic mutations. During this period we find not only skeletal and muscular changes, but differentiation of races and other secondary characteristics. Such a plethora of "mutations" unrelated to obvious environmental causes again raises the possibility of outside influence.

Reported Intervention

The 6,000-year-old Sumerian clay tablets, which provide the most coherent story of an AB intervention, interestingly, were discovered about the same time Darwin and Wallace were developing their concept of evolution. It has taken 150 years for interpretations developed in the two areas to be compared.[9] How does the Sumerian material relate to the fossil record?

The Anunnaki allegedly took a brutish Earth being and mixed some of its genes with some of their own to produce a worker suitable for labor in their gold mines in Africa. This point of initial AB genetic intervention identified in the Sumerian tablets appears to have come approximately 300,000 years ago. As mentioned above, current state-of-the-art dating of early *Homo sapiens* fossils (transition humans) places them between 200,000 and 300,000 B.P.

As we'll see in the next chapter, a third perspective places the appearance of *Homo sapiens* in the same 200,000 to 300,000 B.P. range. Its corroboration comes from the mitochondrial DNA study attempting to identify "Eve" (the female African gene pool from which all modern humanity is assumed to be descended). The resulting phylogenetic tree (see next chapter) dates her between 250,000 and 300,000 years ago. An intervention in the evolutionary process (like that described in Sumerian texts and worldwide legends) would explain the "missing link" and obviate the need for unconfirmable concepts like "punctuated equilibrium" (described earlier).

The Sumerian texts suggest that a second major Anunnaki intervention occurred in human development around 100,000 years ago in the Middle East. Is it only coincidental that the earliest known *Homo sapiens sapiens* remains (modern humans) have been found in Africa (the area of Anunnaki mines) and in a cave in Israel (part of the Anunnaki culture)? The site lies near "Eden" where the Anunnaki-oriented human civilization allegedly flourished, involving the sexual intercourse between gods and humans described in the Bible and other texts. Could such an astonishing situation be what led to another level of human physical and social development? This correspondence of three sources (fossils, DNA studies, Sumerian texts) for the same general period cannot prove the AB-intervention hypothesis, but the coincidence is compelling.

Before this development, Zecharia Sitchin believes there were human workers in West Asia, but they do not appear to have been *Homo sapiens sapiens*. The Sumerian tablets suggest the first artificially-bred workers, the Adamu, may have been taken by the Anunnaki from Abzu to E.DIN 200,000 years ago. The date is not incompatible with the currently accepted period for appearance of the stronger and more flexible Neanderthals. Their presence in Europe after this era suggests they could have been the first version of transition humans to be transported from the AB mines to their central location. This "rougher" version of humanity (discovered in Germany's Neander Valley) overlapped with other *Homo sapiens* for more than 100,000 years, surviving almost unchanged until less than 30,000 B.P.

The ABs could have then "improved" these "brutes" through further genetic manipulations less than 100,000 years ago, thereby creating the Cro-Magnon subspecies. The Cro-Magnon fossil dates uncannily coincide with the Sumerian description of a more civilized Adamu who was useful for agricultural and construction work for the "well-bred" Anunnaki in Mesopotamia.

(Some authors cited in this book believe the disjointed references to the creation of humans in Genesis 1 and 2 refer to such a two-stage process. See the discussion in chapter 2.)

Combining the fossil record and clay-tablet story[10] surprisingly accounts for paleoanthropological thinking about three stages in the origins and diaspora of human development. Early humans were scattered over the globe more than a million years ago. Perhaps a quarter million years ago, transition humans arose in Africa (Abzu in Sumerian lore) and migrated to other continents. They included variations (Neanderthal and Cro-Magnon) with a limited migratory range. Then modern humans appear in the Middle East about 100,000 years ago and further divided into modern groupings.

The transition humans would have been likely to cross paths with versions of their *Homo erectus*-type ancestors still living outside Africa but would probably have had little interest in interbreeding. Some transition groups may have stayed near the mines, becoming the Khoisa and other so-called Bushmen in southern Africa. Their migrations from the early African sites would help explain the dispersion of the same human creation myth among the more primitive aboriginals as well the more advanced Hebrews and Hindus.

These transition humans would not have been involved in the genetic developments in the Middle East, so they carried only memories of aspects of the early days in Abzu (the land of mines and genetic labs) to other continents. Having left the Anunnaki hegemony early, their myths would not have details of later AB-human developments. The traditional legends about the gods referred to in chapter 2 and elsewhere support this notion.

While by no means final, the above associations between fragmented historical accounts and an equally fragmented fossil record clearly do connect some of the same dots in our search for the full picture of human development. The unexpected degree of correspondence can only reinforce our confidence in the path we have been slowly reconstructing. In the next chapter we look at the new field of genetic mapping of group differences in search of the human family tree. Will it reinforce the lines between these dots and provide new ones?

9 Can DNA Studies Provide Answers?

Millennia-old religious texts and indigenous traditions claim that our human ancestors descended from essentially one mother and one father, who had been created by the gods. Modern science now offers corroborating evidence for such claims. In the 1990s, several spectacular "Adam and Eve" stories based in DNA research hit the headlines. Teams of geneticists, using mitochondrial and nuclear DNA regression techniques, claimed to have identified a common father (around 270,000 B.P.) and a common mother (around 250,000 B.P.) for all current humans. In a slight variation of having discovered Adam and Eve, some scientists claimed to have traced all humans back to a very few females.

DNA studies and fossils suggested Caucasoids appeared outside of Africa around 100,000 years ago. Both fossil dates and genetic estimates suggest a new genetic type settled southeast Asia and Australia around 60,000 B.P. (Oral traditions among the aboriginals in Australia also allegedly date them to this period.) Other parts of Asia and Europe were reportedly peopled by a different genetic type around 40,000 B.P. Later DNA studies alleged current Europeans descended from a few hundred ancestors as late as 25,000 B.P.

These dates roughly coincide with significant developments

described in the Sumerian texts and metaphysical sources covered in part 1. All this suggests we should take more seriously the worldwide reports of ABs from the heavens creating humans. It raises the question: Can DNA research help trace the origin and dispersion of human populations in ways that test the AB-intervention hypothesis? While this debate cannot be resolved on the basis of the still-rudimentary science of phylogenetic theory,[1] several DNA studies seem relevant to the AB-intervention hypothesis. A brief review of recent DNA research[2] may help us understand its promise and limitations in reconstructing human history.

For instance, the above-mentioned studies place "Adam and Eve" and the "primal mothers" in Africa at various times between 200,000 and 300,000 B.P. Unexpectedly, these dates coincide with the period inferred (prior to the DNA studies) from the Sumerian texts for the creation of Adamu (the workers). The fossil record (see chapter 8) of that period shows *Homo* remains with the body and brain sizes of modern humans. Underscoring the importance of this point, leading evolutionists agree that the basic gene pool and the human brain have not changed since the first appearance of *Homo sapiens*. Can mere coincidence explain how three DNA techniques and the fossil record all point to the same time, place, and process as Sumerian and metaphysical texts?

In another instance of corresponding information, Genesis and Sumerian texts described in chapter 3 appear to speak of two stages in human creation. First, they describe the forming of one creature at a time before several were created simultaneously. Then, the Sumerians specifically reported the use of 14 AB females to carry to term additional hybrid zygotes comprised of human ova fertilized by Anunnaki sperm.[3] These stages are corroborated by the calculation of dates for "Adam and Eve" and the DNA family tree suggesting a "spontaneous" emergence from a few females of a new species in genus *Homo*. Let's review the basis of such "findings."

Phylogenetic Family Trees

In the absence of measurable DNA from the early period of human origins, we must use surrogate techniques in attempts to tease out the hidden story. The development of phylogenetic trees (somewhat like a family tree of succeeding generations) assumes the greater the diversity within a group's DNA the more ancient its origins. This makes it possible to construct a diagram of various groups' DNA profiles that places each group in chronological order. Using this process, native inhabitants of Sub-Saharan Africa appear to represent the earliest group.

In addition to the degree of diversity, the presence of particular genes in certain groups and the latter's estimated ages can help us chart each group's history. Two gene characteristics help identify the genetic links of current groups to earlier generations: One is the fact that mtDNA (mitochondrial DNA) can only be transmitted by the mother[4] and the other is that nuclear DNA is transmitted only through the male Y chromosome.

Use of these two kinds of data led to the highly publicized discovery of the existence of "Adam" about 270,000 B.P. (average date from several estimates) and "Eve" about 250,000 B.P. (average of dates given). Such studies reach a hypothesized cutoff in DNA branching where no more ancient generations are considered necessary to account for current humans.[5] This research may point to the second "missing link" described in the preceding chapter. The possibility of genetically engineered beings could explain the acknowledged gap between early humans (indigenous genus *Homo*) and transition humans (*Homo sapiens,* Neanderthal, and Cro-Magnon) discussed in chapter 8.

Let's see what DNA studies say on the question of gaps and dates. In a seminal study, Jonathan Marks reported he had discovered a "founder effect" which indicates that only a small group of *Homo sapiens* gave birth to *Homo sapiens sapiens* around 200,000 B.P.[6] (The fossil record indicates they did not replace other *Homo sapiens* subspecies, which continued to exist in parallel.) Hugh Ross[7] has written, based on his mtDNA data, that *Homo sapiens sapiens* date from 150,000 B.P.

These and other regression studies (using mtDNA)[8] show all modern humans appear to be genetically related possibly as far back as 230,000 years. Africans (the oldest) are considered to have been clearly well established between 130,000 and 80,000 B.P. The next oldest seems to be Caucasoid, Middle-Eastern types, dating from about 100,000 years ago. The next oldest are believed to have been Central Asians dating between 73,000 and 56,000 B.P. Next, such estimates suggest, came the Europeans between 50,000 and 40,000 B.P.

One study[9] suggests that maybe there were two dispersals from Africa, an Asian one 50,000 years ago and a later European one.

Another mtDNA study by Bryan Sykes of Oxford University[10] suggests most people in Europe descended from seven women ("daughters of Eve") as far back as 45,000 years ago. Sykes says their location of origin seems to be Northern Greece and the Caucasus Mountains near the Black Sea.

Before we jump to conclusions, we must remember that such studies are still almost as much art as science. The date-range of their conclusions illustrates the great variety in what can be inferred from these techniques. For instance, they place the advent of *Homo sapiens sapiens* anywhere from 300,000 B.P. to as recently as 50,000 B.P. Similarly, Europeans, depending on which study, could have arisen as recently as 25,000 B.P. However, their median estimates place the events in the same time frame as metaphysical and historical material presented in part 1 of this book.

Despite such obvious variations in dates, the rate of all these estimated genetic splits marks a dramatic departure from the 2 to 4 percent-per-million-year mutation rate geneticists have calculated for microevolution. All these changes were too significant and happened too quickly to have been the result of random mutations in the nuclei of human cells, followed by selective interbreeding.

Such *rapid* diversification is more compatible with *deliberate* genetic *intervention* than the *laissez faire* route assumed for natural evolution.

Subspecies, Races, and Genotypes

In addition to the so-called DNA family tree, other genetic studies relating to more recent stages of human development may also support the AB-intervention scenario. One area of interesting research has to do with the dating and geographical placement of various subspecies, races, blood types, and ethnic distributions. While this data cannot prove the theory of human hybridization with ABs, it provides independent commentary on a timeline for AB-human events drawn from historical, legendary, and metaphysical sources.

What Is Race?

The word "race" has come to have many connotations: a species (as the human race), a genetically distinct group within a species (as the Ainu in Japan), a different skin color (as black, white, red, and yellow), or a cultural Homogeneity (as in European). Whatever the origin of racial differences, current distributions of DNA show that variations other than race more logically divide humans into distinctive groups and no known "purebred" human races remain.

Distributions of DNA variations sampled by researchers across racial lines generally show wider ranges within a particular group than the average variations between different races. While skin color has been shown to relate to the interaction of ultraviolet light and the body's need for vitamin D[11] (light skin helps people produce more vitamin D in areas with weaker ultraviolet light), evolutionary biologist Jared Diamond writes, "Evidence of natural selection of color dissolves under scrutiny."[12]

Diamond writes that anthropologists trying to support the theory of climatic influence stress the dark skins of African blacks, southern Indians, and New Guineans but make no mention of the pale skins of Amazonian Indians and Southeast Asians living under similar conditions. He points out that people's length of time in a climatic zone seems not to account for the differences either. He illustrates the principle by noting that the ancestors of fair-skinned Swedes arrived recently in Scandinavia, while the ancestors of Tasmanians were black-skinned despite living for at least 10,000 years in Siberia. Diamond concludes his argument by noting the many obvious internal contradictions among theories on the evolutionary survival value of skin color.

Some DNA studies suggest that genetic patterns commonly accepted as distinguishing race (color, facial features, and body types) appeared quickly and quite recently. Gradual adaptation to changing lifestyle or environmental circumstances can happen through natural microevolution within a species. But changes in several traits, like those related to race, would involve a slow, incremental process of random selection over many generations. The genetic timeline developed by the phylogenetic-tree approach shows that different races appeared much too quickly, almost bursting upon the scene, for that process to work.[13]

Subspecies or Genotypes

Given such leaps in human changes, AB intervention may offer as reasonable a basis for some of the unexplained and recent appearances of subspecies, races, or genotypes as other theories. We have already mentioned the coincidence of the Caucasoids' appearance with the reported widespread intermarriages between Anunnaki and humans about 100,000 years ago.

As we'll see in chapter 11, Noah was reportedly warned of the impending flood by the AB god Enki.[14] The ark he built to Enki's specifications is believed to have beached on Mount Ararat, not far from the prehistoric site of Catal Huyuk associated with early postcataclysmic agriculture. Following the Flood, the Semitic (Near East), Hamitic (Africa), and Aryan or Indo-European (Anatolia and Caucasus) genotypes (pure families of skin and eye color, hair, and body types) are believed to have appeared almost overnight in historical terms.

These genotypes have long been associated with Noah's sons (Shem, Ham, and Jephath). Their genetic legacies produced the three centers of postcataclysmic Western civilization along the Nile, Tigris/Euphrates, and Indus river valleys. Each was part of the reputed Anunnaki-based civilization. Could they have resulted from gene-mixing by AB lords to mark their respective protégés? No simpler explanation exists for the quick appearance of these three genotypes.

If distinctive genotypes correlate with areas of hegemony by different ABs, then human genetic history could be a reflection of the history of AB colonization. Did the establishment of a different AB kingdom in Central or East Asia before 50,000 B.P. result in genes that led to a separate Mongol genotype? Or did the Mongols represent migration to Asia out of one of the reportedly lost AB colonies? The culture reflects an Asian perspective on ABs unlike the Sumerian.

Within what people consider to be the Negroid race today, we find genotypes so different that we need an extraordinary explanation for such an obviously complex history. Two-thirds of black Africans belong to one group that further subdivides into four groups: Kung, Western Pygmy, Senegalese, and Eastern Pygmy, with the two Pygmy groups quite different from each other. The remaining third is more similar to certain European and Asian groups in all respects except skin color (which we have seen is not a racial characteristic). Current DNA studies can only describe the variations, not explain them.

Another intriguing example of a genotype that cuts across modern geographical divides includes some Amerinds, including the Navajo, and certain Europeans. Some geneticists estimate this gene pool to have developed into an independent one between 12,000 and 36,000 years ago.[15] Could they have been products of Atlantis or some other region genetically isolated for a long time from the area we now call the Cradle of Civilization? Other such independent genotype groupings (like the Lapps in northern Norway, Finland, and Arctic Russia, unrelated to other Europeans) raise the same issue.

AB manipulation of human characteristics could have served one or more objectives: to help humans cope with changing environmental conditions, to mark the followers of one AB ruler or inhabitants of his/her kingdom for identification purposes, or to make humans more desirable as servants or sexual partners. (These last two interbreeding goals have been observed in recent behaviors by European colonials vis-à-vis their subjects and by human masters toward their slaves.) Another objective could have been to enhance the level of human intelligence or increase conscious awareness of other dimensions (see comments later in chapter).

Blood Types

Blood groups may be another phenomenon potentially related to the history of AB interactions with humans. Blood types cut across all racial lines. In fact, all current racial divisions are assumed to have preceded the divergence of Type A from Type O (the original blood type). The appearance of Type A seems to have resulted from a gene mutation rate four times faster than the common fruit fly. Thus, we need to seek explanations beyond random mutations, geography, diet, environment, and race to account for this.

One hypothetical history from the medical field provides a time-line for our four major blood types.[16] The dominant and oldest, Type O is associated with meat eaters. Type A is assumed to have appeared 15,000 to 25,000 years ago somewhere in Asia or the Middle East. Associated with cultivated grains and other agricultural crops, its highest percentages are among Western Europeans and their descendants.

Type B is believed to have developed between 10,000 and 15,000 years ago in the Himalayan highlands (currently Pakistan and India). Its highest numbers are in India, Japan, China, and Mongolia, and in Russia up to the Ural Mountains. (See earlier mention on the Mongol genotype and a different AB perspective.) Type AB blood is rare, found in less than five percent of the population, and apparently only came into existence 1,000 to 1,200 years ago.

In the context of our AB intervention hypothesis, the appearance of Type A appears to coincide with the migration to Europe of humans from AB colonies in the Fertile Crescent during the period from 30,000 to 15,000 B.P. Plant dispersion patterns suggest these migrants also took agricultural samples from the AB colonies in the Fertile Crescent.[17]

Type B seems most likely to have occurred just after the cataclysm of 11,500 years ago, as ABs rescued humans and created AB-human city-states. Historically, Jews and other non-Arab peoples in the Middle East have a higher-than-average Type-B percentage than the generally Type-O Arabic population around them. Perhaps blood type, like other physical features, was a marker of identification for human groups related to particular AB regimes. Blood samples played a role in distinguishing Israelites from Egyptians when an angel was sent to kill the oldest sons of Egyptian families (see biblical story in Exodus).

The concept of "blood brothers" permeates several traditional societies. The idea of "blue blood" associated with royal families, allegedly with "divine" rights, suggests a connection to an Anunnaki blood type (see chapter 15). The book *Holy Blood, Holy Grail*[18] develops this theme with regard to Christianity, but much more research is needed to illuminate the linkages only hinted at here.

Some metaphysical or esoteric schools of thought accept the possibility of AB genetic intervention in human development but have different interpretations of its purpose. Sources in chapters 1, 2, and 3 and references elsewhere in this book portray AB contributions to humanity as advanced knowledge, physical refinements, technology and social innovations, and enhanced consciousness. Genetic changes of the type covered in this chapter and perhaps others not so evident may have been intended to increase the human capacity to understand and communicate with other levels of consciousness (including that of the AB donors). For instance, Carlo Suares, a Spanish Kabbalist, believes the creation of Adam may have involved genetic inserts that enlarged humanity's range of consciousness about more advanced realms.[19] These ideas are not incompatible with the intimations of Sumerian and biblical texts.

Other Genes

The presence of specific genes may also provide clues to AB contributions to our genetic heritage. For instance, the HLA gene (histocompatibility) appears to predate the period when early humans and apes lived in parallel, suggesting HLA is a part of the early human's gene pool. On the other hand, scientists estimate the gene that "writes" hemoglobin appeared somewhat less than 100,000 B.P. That date coincides with the period of reputed widespread sexual inter-course between "the gods and the daughters of man."

AB and Human Gene Compatibility

The Sumerian account in chapter 3 suggests ABs could snip DNA from their own chromosomes and mix it with human ova to be carried by AB females. If true, it indicates an initial, high degree of genetic compatibility between the two species. The later accounts of AB-human sexual intercourse resulting in offspring further supports this idea, raising the interesting possibility of a proto-gene pool common to both the Anunnaki and early *Homo sapiens.* Given the already documented high degree of DNA overlap between humans and other primates and an apparent overlap between humans and the Anunnaki, beings in our genetic range may be more widespread *in the universe* than we have imagined.

One obstacle to proving the AB-human hybrid hypothesis is the apparent absence of pure Anunnaki and pure *Homo erectus* DNA. Without such separate genomes we cannot deduce their respective contributions to the *Homo sapiens* gene pool. DNA is not easily pre-served; the oldest we have is a sample of the genus *Homo* from Neanderthal remains dated to 50,000 B.P. Since the first hypothesized hybridization would have occurred hundreds of thousands of years ago, we have to assume that the more recent transition humans (Neanderthal and Cro-Magnon) and modern humans *(Homo sapiens sapiens)* would all contain some combination of AB and early human genes.

Currently a DNA difference smaller than two percent exists between humans and our nearest primate cousins (chimps). It seems logical that early humans (a distinct species) would have had an even smaller percentage of DNA variations from other hominids. Therefore, only a very small percentage of our current DNA could be uniquely from the Anunnaki genome.

This line of speculation, placing *Homo sapiens sapiens* on a spectrum somewhere between *Homo erectus* and the Anunnaki, may provide some insight into the Anunnaki physiology. Historical accounts of the "giants who walked the Earth" may suggest the ABs were taller than early humans. The AB bodies could have been phys-ically weaker with smaller bones and muscles, but with more finely developed motor skills. They may have had a proportionally larger brain capacity, less body hair, thinner and lighter skin, and more prominent sexual features. The ABs could have represented potential, but undeveloped characteristics of future humans. Seen in these terms, AB genes shared with us may have only speeded up an intrinsic process of *Homo sapiens* microevolution.

Various Judaic sources provide details describing the progeny of intercourse between angels and humans which may offer further insight into some of the AB characteristics added to the human DNA pool. A fragment of the Book of Noah discovered with the oldest known version of the Book of Enoch[20] (an Ethiopian text) tells about a son (Noah) born to the wife of Lamech (son of Methuselah) who was thought to be fathered by an AB. In this version of the story, Enoch, who was Methuselah's father, was asked his opinion about whether Noah had an AB parent. Lamech had suspicions that his wife had been impregnated by one of the "watchers" and wanted his father to check with Enoch, who was now living among the ABs.

The exchange between the two gives *prima facie* evidence that Noah was a hybrid. Methuselah told Enoch that Lamech had said his son was "unlike man, and resembling the sons of the God of heaven." Enoch responded by saying that in the time of his father Jared "some of the angels of heaven . . . united themselves with women . . . [and] have begotten children by them." The implication was that this family line carried with it the DNA of those angels. So, even if Lamech was the immediate biological father, he would have passed on the genes of the angels.

What are some of those genes, or what features did they express? Lamech described his wife's son as having skin "white as snow," yet "red as the blooming of a rose." His hair was long, woolly, and white. His eyes were beautiful and bright; they "lighted up the whole house." Enoch predicted Lamech's son Noah would be one of the "giants on earth." Other texts underscore the AB lineage Enoch described for Noah (known as Zuisudra in Sumerian, Atrahasis in Babylonian, and Utnapishtim in the *Epic of Gilgamesh*). All these sources agree he was a demigod.

Subspecies Interbreeding

The prevailing theory of species definition holds that successful interbreeding can occur usually only among members of the same species (in terms of producing fertile offspring). It is unclear whether early human and other hominoid groups could mate with one another. It also remains unclear whether Neanderthal and Cro-Magnon peoples were interbreeding subspecies of the Anunnaki-human hybrids (if one accepts that hypothesis) or parallel species descended from early humans.

A 1997 DNA study of Neanderthal remains (using a small amount of mtDNA) concluded modern humans are not direct descendants from Neanderthals.[21] However, other researchers, examining 25,000-year-old fossil remains from Spain, believe Neanderthals were able to interbreed with Cro-Magnons and produce hybrids. Current scientific opinion, reflected in the June 2003 *Smithsonian,* suggests Neanderthals and modern humans may have mated or tried to. Interbreeding among modern *Homo sapiens,* Neanderthals, and Cro-Magnons could explain why they were all able to peacefully co-exist for tens of thousands of years. If they did, the present *Homo sapiens sapiens* gene pool would include the results from such mixing.

Current AB-Human Interbreeding

Modern UFO/ET contact and abductee reports are replete with accounts of nonhumans mating with humans, sometimes producing hybrid children. The idea of wide-ranging reproductive compatibility is supported by twentieth-century descriptions of Siberian village children born from sexual matings between humans and savage humanoids. Apparently credible reports of a few pregnancies from such intercourse portray these wild beings in a manner that suggests they could be survivors from the Neanderthal/Cro-Magnon era. An interesting potential source of indigenous DNA might be available if we could isolate genetic material from an apparent prehuman line like the variously called and elusive Bigfoot, Abominable Snowman, or Yeti.[22]

Added credence to the notion of an interstellar species, of which modern humans would be only a subgroup, comes from reports of AB-human sexual procreation (like those mentioned in chapter 5). Science fiction tales of interplanetary sex may not be as fictional as we have imagined.[23]

Convergence of Evidence

How does this chapter on DNA research mesh with the previous chapter on fossils and the material presented so far on the AB-intervention hypothesis? The DNA research agrees with paleoanthropologists and the Sumerian account that modern humans originated in a location somewhere in Africa. The presence of ancient gold mines in southeastern Africa seems to coincide with the Sumerian accounts of the location of the first human hybrid workers. Geneticists also place the earliest ancestors of modern humans somewhere in sub-Saharan Africa. Both the genetic studies and the dates for the AB genetic engineering with humans calculated by Zecharia Sitchin (from dated king lists) fall in the same general time period: 200,000 to 300,000 years ago.

We cannot conclude at this point that scientific DNA research proves or disproves the AB intervention hypothesis, but the above coincidences are intriguing. Of several relevant research avenues, DNA research has an edge over the fossil record. A truism among geneticists goes, "Genes always have ancestors while fossils may not have descendants." Further research along the lines suggested by the chapter could be useful in resolving the AB question.

Comparing DNA patterns with language distributions, locations of specific fields of knowledge (as mathematics) or cultural institutions (as kingship), and religious practices could shed light on the AB intervention hypothesis. A population diaspora study like that done by Cavalli-Sforza and referenced earlier should be conducted with the AB intervention perspective as one of the screens through which the data are interpreted. I believe it would strengthen the findings in this chapter and, when combined with the chapters to come, reveal significant circumstantial support for the AB-intervention hypothesis.

PART IV

Rescuing Flood Survivors

Introduction to Part IV

World myths share common reports of great natural cataclysms, including the Flood associated with Noah, that have uprooted human societies and changed the course of history. Science now reveals that such accounts contain more reality than myth. Our planet has had a tumultuous past.

The Earth that seems so solid under our feet is in reality a fragile sphere of interconnected parts that can "shake, rattle, and roll" when confronted with an equally powerful energy field, like that of another celestial body. When this happens, its human passengers experience a wild ride of earthquakes, thunder and lightning, flooding rains, erupting volcanoes, and much more. When the floods and dust settle, the humans still alive find an altered landscape. Amid the ruins of their past they face the task of starting over.

Chapter 10 describes Earth's most recent cataclysm of this type and its effects on humanity.[1] Hundreds of dates assigned by scientists to anomalous physical and biological effects converge around the date of 11,500 B.P. Considerable geophysical evidence points to this cataclysm as the one that legends describe as largely destroying human society. (In this book that event is written with a capital C [as in Cataclysm], in the same manner that we capitalize Flood in referring to the biblical event, which appears to be part of the overall Cataclysm.)

Chapter 11 addresses evidence that several groups of human survivors received technical assistance from ABs after the Cataclysm. This aid appears to have jump-started the revitalization of several centers of human civilization. Whether intended or not, the echoes of this AB help reverberate through history to the present.

Chapter 12 reviews evidence that suggests that at least one group of survivors received special attention. The gods' selective technical assistance and knowledge transfer may have helped some human societies leap dramatically ahead of others. The Anunnaki involvement in the Middle East appears to have redirected the course of history. Their input may account for aspects of the Indo-European culture that gave it several advantages over other cultures.

10 Did a Cataclysm Convulse Earth?

During the last two centuries, researchers around the world have accumulated evidence regarding an 11,500 B.P. cataclysmic event that caused the Earth to tremble and nearly wipe out *Homo sapiens sapiens*. The most familiar story is the biblical Flood and the survival of Noah's family, but numerous other traditions have their own versions. A Vedic myth tells of destruction by a great flood, when only a few humans survived. These were led by Manu who took refuge in a ship that ended up in the Himalayas. ABs came to the aid of these survivors, who later repopulated India. Other such stories are summarized later in this chapter, but let's first examine their human and planetary context.

Ending a Golden Age

One gauge of the Cataclysm's impact comes from a comparison of reports of how it affected humans with their memories of a prior era. While few records or artifacts have been found to illuminate what life was like before the last worldwide catastrophe, many societies have guarded precious memories over the millennia.

Greek poets eloquently spoke of a golden age before the gods when humans enjoyed an idyllic life in harmony with nature. For people of the Judeo-Christian tradition, the Garden of Eden described in Genesis constitutes a powerful symbol for an era when humans went without shame, enjoyed the fruits of nature, and knew few or no hardships. Buddhist texts describe the Shambhala of antiquity as a place of wisdom and peace. The Mandeans of Iraq and Iran speak of an earlier "ideal world" called Mshunia Kushta.

Taoism and the Vedic tradition share a common tale of a Golden Age before the fall of humanity (the "fall" being a possible reference to the effects of the Cataclysm). That age was characterized by an organic outlook on nature, with social tolerance and respect for the gods.[1] The Hindu sagas describe a time related to human origins and their gaining of knowledge when "Seven Rishis" (sages) ruled during a period of enlightenment. With telling symmetry, the Babylonian story of "Seven Sages" describes an era when great cities were ruled by these seven immortal beings.

What was the precataclysm global culture like? Reconstructing prehistory, a difficult task under any circumstances, has been rendered almost impossible by the effects of the Cataclysm. Before the discovery of lost cities in the Americas, pyramids in the Canary Islands, monumental architecture under the sea, and evidence of a worldwide seafaring culture that predates modern history, scholars felt safe declaring that civilization first arose in the Fertile Crescent and spread from there. Thor Heyerdahl in 1947 shattered that myth with his 101-day, 4,300-mile voyage by a balsa-log and reed raft from Lima, Peru, to the Tuamoto Archipelago in the South Pacific. Over the next half-century he demonstrated that a common "pyramid culture" had stretched from Egypt across the Atlantic and on to West Samoa.

Heyerdahl did not question the prevailing view that the history he uncovered only started 5,000 or 6,000 years ago. His schema did not take into account recently discovered undersea evidence that shows a more extensive "pyramid culture" in a much more distant past. We now have corroborating evidence that much of this architectural detritus predates 11,500 B.P., but putting the broken pieces together will take several decades.

Various legends refer to an age before the Cataclysm with tribal homelands on great plains. Sources include the Lushai of Assam, the Bunun of Formosa, and the Tsimshian of Columbia. Other legends associate great civilizations with as-yet unidentified mountains or mountain ranges. They include the great mountain Meru, the Riphaean range, and

Atlas.[2] Interdisciplinary research like that attempted in this book will be necessary to sort out the relationships of these and other legends to geophysical, archaeological, fossil, DNA, linguistic, and cultural data dated to before and after the Cataclysm.

Apparent antediluvian maps (including one known as the Zeno map) show Greenland, Iceland, Norway, and Western Europe as an area without snow. Tree trunks in Greenland date from the period when an earlier theory would have the area covered in 100,000-year-old glaciers. This apparent discrepancy between the emerging human story and "conventional wisdom" can be partially explained by magnetic records of polar shifts that interrupted long-established patterns.

The evidence that follows suggests that prior to the Cataclysm the Earth's axis was more perpendicular to its orbit (with less differentiated seasons), and the planet had more extensive flora and fauna, smaller polar ice caps, lower mountains, fewer deserts, and shallower seas. The atmosphere had more carbon dioxide and oxygen. With fewer clouds, the humidity was high with light precipitation.

The geological record indicates the Earth has been subjected to various global cataclysms over the last five billion years, a number of which occurred during the life span of the *Homo sapiens* species (from five million years ago to the present). Accounts of both local disasters and universal cataclysms are contained in many cultural traditions. Given modern scientific dating techniques, it is possible to determine the internal reliability of some of these accounts. This chapter will now give a brief overview of Earth's uneasy history and describe the physical effects of its most recent global cataclysm.

Local Views of Cataclysm

Of course, no single Weather Channel report of events around the world for the year 11,500 B.P. has been discovered. With no global overview of what happened on Earth at that time, we must depend on limited local reports to piece together a comprehensive picture. Some descriptions of local conditions that give us a human perspective have survived throughout the millennia. The accounts from simple and frightened people describing local experiences of what was obviously a global disaster seem credible. There is no reason to believe such congruent tales could have been created from thin air in widely separated locations without some actual experience. Later in the chapter we review pieces of physical evidence and inferences that may be made from them.

We can start with the familiar tale of Noah and his family in Genesis chapters 6 through 8 (also described in the *Epic of Gilgamesh* where the Lord Enki warned Zuisudra). The immediate cataclysm lasted for 40 days and nights, and it consisted of rain that fell unceasingly for that period. The waters swelled, covering all the mountains, and lifted the Ark up to ride the surface 15 cubits above the mountaintops. This account of the Flood (the most prominent local effect of a global event) places it in a time after the period "when the sons of the gods had intercourse with the daughters of men and got children by them."

The Hebrews saw it as punishment by the Lord (a likely reference to Sumer's Enlil) for man's evil thoughts and inclinations, but the physical effects seem real: ". . . all the springs of the great abyss broke through, the windows of the sky were opened, and rain fell on the earth for 40 days and 40 nights. . . . More and more the waters increased over the earth until they covered all the high mountains everywhere under heaven. . . . Every living creature that moves on the earth perished. . . . The water gradually receded . . . and by the end of the 150th day it had disappeared."[3]

Suggesting an early cultural link between the Middle East and the Andean region, an Incan account sounds this same theme: Viracocha (creator of the primal people) used the Flood to destroy mankind. (He later repented, like Noah's god, and helped the survivors.)[4] Mayan records point to three deluges in a time before the Common Era.[5] The Babylonian *Epic of Gilgamesh* (from which the obviously partial Genesis account may have been taken) includes descriptions of hail and wind like a cyclone accompanying the flood. It provides more detail of the event than the Genesis story. Norse accounts in the "Elder Edda" and "Prose Edda" mention smoke, dust, ashes, and stone. The effects include a shaking of the earth, with trees being torn out by their roots. The Mayan Troana Codex tells of the breaking-up and sinking of the land of Mu, with 64 million inhabitants lost.

A summary of available traditional stories would describe the trauma along the following lines: horrendous thunder and lightning; 40 days of rain, ice, and hail pelting the Earth; hurricane-force winds; and boiling temperatures. Then the water in the Earth's seas, lakes, and rivers was pulled northward, followed by an overwhelming wave of water cascading back over the globe, moving debris and great rocks before it. The Earth wobbled on its axis, pausing in its rotation. There was widespread volcanic activity, magma flowing to the crust of the Earth and igniting raging fires, and the subsidence of land and the lifting of mountains, with continents being cracked by great chasms.

With passage of the early stages, the Earth entered a period of darkness, with sunlight blocked out and glacial conditions. Rains of fire and dust, including metal and stones, made it appear as if the sky had collapsed. Flora and fauna had been destroyed. Mud and gravel were everywhere, and the atmosphere appears to have been poisoned. People reported the moon had moved to a new orbit; the lengths of the days and the seasons had changed; the polar axis had shifted (evidenced by changes in the constellations located at the galactic pole, from Earth's perspective).

The overall effect of the variously described physical events was a world with new climatic zones and a new biological regime. These changes marked what geologists call the end of the "late Pleistocene Era." That point in time marked a new period in human and Earth history.

A Fragile Earth

Why do memories of a single cataclysmic event vary so much from region to region?

Think of the Earth's layers like the skin, soft fruit, and solid core of a peach. In the Earth, these layers, while interconnected, operate somewhat differently. The Earth's diameter is almost 8,000 miles, but the crust (or skin) is at most only 22 miles thick (under the land) and just 4 miles thick under the oceans. The mantle (or fruit) represents 80 percent of the volume of Earth. At the center the core (or seed) is mainly iron with some nickel, with a 137-mile layer of liquid separating the mantle from its solid core (1,600 miles in diameter). In addition, the atmosphere and Earth's electromagnetic sheath interact with both the surface and the inner core to cause changes in temperature and pressure.

By studying the flow of seismic waves like those caused by earthquakes, scientists have developed a model that helps them understand how the Earth would react to stresses caused by the gravitational and electromagnetic forces of a passing celestial body.

Action on one side of the globe would result in a different, but corollary action on another part of the Earth's surface. This accounts for the variety of effects described in the following section.

The Phaeton/Nibiru Event

A masterfully researched book, *Cataclysm*, by D. S. Allan and J. B. Delair, has established better than any other the period during which the above-reported event must have happened. Based on carefully tabulated geologic and archaeological evidence from around the world, dated by many different and independent scientists, Allan and Delair arrived at the date of 11,577 years ago. Since the publication of their book, other research (including some referenced in this book) has corroborated this "new beginning of human civilization."

The horrific, devastating effects, permanent and temporary, described in the preceding summary of historical accounts would have required a causal agent of gargantuan proportions. The most likely candidate appears to be a near-miss by some celestial body: A comet, asteroid, or even a wandering planet could have had similar effects. Allan and Delair deduce that it was a large fragment of a star (perhaps from the explosion of the Vela supernova, 45 light years away, about 14,000 years ago) pulled into our solar system's gravity field. They called it Phaeton, the Greek name found in several myths about the Cataclysm. The Sumerian account of what appears to be the same event attributes it to the planet Nibiru (described earlier). In this chapter I have chosen to label the destructive body Phaeton/Nibiru.

Such a body careening through our Sun's satellites could account for several anomalies that astronomy, which assumes a single birth experience for all the Sun's satellites, has thus far been unable to explain. These out-of-phase or out-of-orbit peculiarities include the fact that Mercury's orbit is irregularly shaped, Venus's rotation is slow for its size, and Venus and Pluto rotate in the opposite direction from other planets. Mars's orbit is eccentric and too slow for its size, with two irregularly shaped satellites. Jupiter, Saturn, and Uranus rotate too rapidly for their mass. In addition, Jupiter has a moon at each pole, going in opposite directions. Saturn has a ring of debris, and Uranus has an irregularly shaped orbit and an inclined equator. Pluto's slow and eccentric orbit appears unnatural. An asteroid belt exists between Mars and Jupiter where a planet might be expected.

Allan and Delair illustrate how Phaeton's entry into the solar system in the time frame suggested by Earth evidence could have caused this list of perturbations. It is also possible that some of these anomalies could have been caused by earlier intrusions into our solar system. Observations that survive in historical accounts describe a rogue heavenly body's impact on various planets before it crashed into the Sun. Zecharia Sitchin, introduced earlier, holds the view that there have been several such passes of the planet Phaeton/Nibiru in what Sumerian texts call the "war in the heavens."[6]

Depictions of the wandering body that caused so much damage appear in stone carvings and cave drawings, in pictoglyphs on rocks, and on Sumerian seals.

Different cultures have various names for the rogue star responsible for their perceptions of cataclysmic damages to Earth: Phaeton (Greek), Typhon (Roman), Tistrya (Persian), Ta-vi (Early American), and others. Babylonians labeled the body Marduk, after their chief god.

Marduk in Babylonian texts was described as spewing jets of fire toward the outer planets. After wreaking havoc with planets in its path, it was charged with destroying a large planet known as Tiamat. Tiamat's fragments could explain the now improbable asteroid belt between Mars and Jupiter. Greek descriptions of the intruder growing in brightness, to almost rival the Sun, could have referred to its collision with a large planet far beyond Pluto. Its explosion could have provided the pieces of rock now known as the Kuiper Belt beyond the planets of our solar system.[7]

Remnants of Phaeton/Nibiru's explosive encounters with the Sun's planets still roam the solar system more than 10,000 years later. Persian tales describe it as a fiery dragon or monster coursing across the heavens toward the Sun, with its tails scattering fire along its path. Evidence of remnants seen in the sky, crossing the face of the moon and other planets, include oddly shaped dark objects, clouds that obscure light, and brilliant spots of light. The Earth has experienced unexplained falls of ice, stones, mud, and dust from space. Objects like these would long ago have been pulled into planets or the Sun by gravity if they had been leftovers from the Sun's original planet-formation process five billion years ago.

As Phaeton/Nibiru approached the Earth, its magnetic forces, gravitational pull, and accompanying field of ice and debris would have resulted in the cataclysmic conditions described in this chapter. They could have included the reported axial shift and a speeding up of Earth's rotation from 30 to 24 hours.[8] It could have displaced the Earth's oceans and submerged large areas of land (perhaps including those known as Atlantis and Mu in the Pacific Ocean, and Lemuria in the Indian Ocean). The aftereffects could have been what scientists now call a "nuclear winter," which destroys life left untouched by an earlier conflagration.

Damages to Earth

Most scholars still think all these changes happened 11,000 to 12,000 years ago as a result of the gradual ending of an Ice Age on Earth, leaving humans somewhat smarter in a New Stone (Neolithic) Age. But the physical evidence shows something very dramatic happened two or three millennia before the appearance of Nineveh, Sippar, and Nippur as flourishing metropolitan areas in Sumeria.

According to Allan and Delair, the following impacts came from the interactions between the Earth and Phaeton/Nibiru as the latter passed nearby, perhaps between the moon and Earth (leaving them more separated than before). The Earth's and Phaeton/Nibiru's magnetospheres would have served as mutually protective sheaths to prevent an actual collision, but the geomagnetic impact would have been considerable. In fact the passage seems to have caused a temporary weakening of the Earth's dynamo (reversal of polarity) and a disruption of the precession of the equinoxes.

This means a shift in the tilt of Earth's rotational axis (from 30° to 23.5°), with a rearrangement of the equatorial bulge, and a commensurate shift in the positioning of continents and oceans. This torque would have disrupted the normal flow of magma beneath the surface and resulted in the volcanic and seismic activity described in many locations. Subsidence of continents would be offset by upheavals in mountain ranges (like the geologically documented recent lifting of the Andes, Rockies, Alps, and Himalayas). The combined impact of such shifts would result in climatic changes and widespread biological extinctions (like mammoths and other species that disappeared 11,500 B.P.).

The close passage of Phaeton/Nibiru ignited parts of the Earth; seriously damaged the atmosphere; whipped up hurricanes; rained fire and brimstone on Earth; and sent every being that could move pell-mell in search of safety. The effects lasted more than the biblical 40 days, with the subsequent equivalent of a nuclear winter lasting for generations.

Did a Cataclysm Convulse Earth?

That global disaster turned sea sediments to stone, rearranged climates, and created new shorelines and mountain ranges. It sank and covered a luxuriant continent; ended an ice age; caused the extinction of the saber-toothed tiger, giant bison, humped-back camel, and the famous woolly mammoths frozen with undigested food in their stomachs. But most important of all it destroyed everything but vestiges of an advanced civilization.

Some Had Advance Warnings

Noah was not the only human warned of the impending cataclysm. Most of the individual and small group survivor reports identified by Allan and Delair indicate that many humans had some advance warning. Famed psychic Edgar Cayce (innumerable details of his many readings have been authenticated) reported (reading number 1681) that the Atlanteans had been warned by the ABs who flew in vehicles over Earth.

Not all those warned of the impending flood were lucky enough to get technical assistance from the ABs circling the Earth in their spacecraft. The Haida people who live on the Queen Charlotte Islands off the northwest coast of Canada have a story similar to the Sumerians, but the ending is not the same. Whereas the Sumerian Zuisudra received specific instructions to build a seaworthy submersible and was later rescued by the gods, the Haida were left to escape to the hills. And only those who reached the still-dry mountain peaks in canoes survived. Suggesting they referred to the same event, archaeologists estimate the Haida arrived on their present island home 11,000 to 12,000 years ago.[9]

According to the Sumerian texts, the Anunnaki first agreed among themselves to not warn humans of the impending disaster. But Enki, always more favorably disposed toward his creatures, decided to break the oath and warn Zuisudra. Apparently other ABs around the globe also took pity on favored humans and warned them or, as in the case of Zuisudra or Noah, gave technical advice on how to cope with its effects. A few humans seem to have by chance been in more secure areas, likely caves in elevations untouched by the giant waves circling the globe, and survived.

Survivors

Mostly small, scattered groups of humans survived the Cataclysm and its aftermath. As mentioned earlier, many of those who lived did so because of advance warnings. If the Sumerian account of events leading up to the Cataclysm is correct, any ABs on Earth would have been aware of the implications of the impending interplanetary encounter. They would have had sufficient time to retreat to their spacecraft and sit out the disaster taking place on Earth.

The humans most likely to escape on their own lived in the mountains or high plains and knew how to farm and hunt. Some had other survival skills and were lucky to be able to find shelter in caves, along with plants and animals to support themselves until things returned to a new level of normal. Some people with high skill and knowledge from the AB colonies escaped, but without their support systems. They could only offer ideas and memories. They were known as great teachers among the aborigines and other traditional societies. This assistance may have helped some centers of survivors to regain at least a shadow of their past glory. The major exception was the planned survival of "Noah's family," who were able to take advantage of extensive AB technical assistance in Asia Minor after landing on Mount Ararat.

Intangible effects elude the geologists and biologists, but they may be as real as the physical. For instance, historians puzzle over the conundrum of memory loss. Why have all humans not retained in their oral traditions memories of some of the physical cataclysms evident on the Earth's surface? Could one of the effects have been an erasure or suppression of memory? We do not yet understand the role of electromagnetic fields in human consciousness, but it stands to reason that there is an interaction. A scrambling of the Earth's magnetic field or a polarity shift could have caused some humans to lose parts of their stored memories, especially those associated with painful events.

Cataclysmic Dislocations

Among all the accounts of the geophysical effects of the Cataclysm, the most significant story is the almost complete disappearance of solid Atlantean territory. But some other changes to existing continents are more easily envisaged. One was the separation of aboriginals living on the Tasmanian Peninsula of Australia from the mainland. They had arrived from the mainland only two or three thousand years before, although their ancestors had already been on the continent for fifty thousand years. When the sea level rose as a result of the melting of glaciers and other ice packs, it made Tasmania an island.

A similar thing happened with the continental shelf of the Americas. Coastal plains were submerged, burying—among many others—settlements dating from 12,000 B.P. and older in the Gulf of Mexico and along the coastlines of Florida, Cuba, Bimini, Belize, and other areas.

Such local changes happened all around the world, and some of them would have significant impacts on the future of humanity. For example, the land routes to North America from Siberia and via the Bering Sea area (it only became a sea again after the Cataclysm) and from Scandinavia via Iceland and Greenland disappeared under the sea as well. That slowed the reintegration of peoples from the upper part of North America with Europe and Asia.

The cataclysmic end to the Ice Age did not totally wipe out the highland civilizations in Central and South America. Survivors in those regions, whose lowland relatives perished from rising sea levels and land falling into the ocean, still encountered difficult living conditions, struggling for many generations. Due to the uplifting of their mountains, they suffered from new climatic extremes and the effects of higher elevations on crops and living conditions. (Airplane passengers above the Andes can still see scattered villages that remain in the cold, arid conditions that faced the pre-Incan survivors.)

Readers may have seen maps that show how Antarctica 80 to 100 million years ago connected what is now Africa, Madagascar, India, and Australia. Prior to the Cataclysm, a similar land mass played the same function at the North Pole. North America, Greenland, Siberia, Scandinavia, and Western Europe were all linked together above sea level. When the new sea level settled into place, the part of the Arctic land mass, named Appalachia by geologists, that had connected North America to Europe lay beneath the sea. An area known as Fennoscandia that extended the Scandinavian coastline almost to Greenland was also below sea level. The terrain labeled Beringia that connected Alaska to Siberia and the Asian coast almost to Japan had been drowned too.

These areas now below the waves had provided land routes among North America and the other two continents during the inter-glacial period between 50,000 and 11,500 B.P. They could have provided access to North America for the Asians and Europeans whose 20,000- to 30,000-year-old remains have caused anthropologists to abandon the late twentieth-century idea that the first North Americans came from Asia by a coastal route after the last Ice Age.

In Noah's part of the world, all living creatures left on dry land perished, and the waters did not recede enough to reveal the mountaintops for ten months. It took another two months for the ground to become dry, and four weeks more for the survivors to venture out of the ark. Noah, his wife, and his sons and their wives, and all the livestock in the ark were the lucky ones.

Traumatized humans could not have aspired to achieve a level of civilization that matched their memories without the assistance of the ABs. With the loss of the precataclysmic knowledge and skills base, they had to start almost from the beginning. For instance, a Yoruba (Nigerian) tale relates that Orunmila, leader of the "*ara orun*" (visitors from the skies), sent an SOS to the heavens requesting help. Assistance came in the form of ABs with special equipment to help rid the Earth of excess water, but no other assistance was provided.

The lack of AB assistance was not universal. The following chapter discusses the evidence of assistance allegedly provided by ABs to some humans.

11 Did ABs Help Revive Civilization?

Popular science writers start with the assumption that Neolithic humans all began on about the same footing everywhere in the world at the end of the most recent Ice Age. For instance, Jared Diamond rhetorically asks why some societies developed much more rapidly after 11,000 B.P. In his book *Guns, Germs, and Steel*,[1] he developed the thesis of environmental influences that favored some groups over others (all groups assumed to be biologically equal). This approach completely begged the questions of how such complex civilizations appeared in Sumeria without any visible historical antecedents, and how to account for the sophisticated physical and biological texts and other evidence of advanced knowledge found in the ruins.

The range of artifacts we now have access to for the period between 6,000 and 10,000 years ago challenges historians in two ways. First, the lack of evidence for proto-societies (the gap problem) from which the great city-states evolved. Second, the apparent rapidity with which Neolithic man moved (the great leap problem) from hunting and gathering to creating the star tables, medical texts, and philosophical and legal treatises found on 6,000-year-old clay tablets (see part 5).

A Rebirth of Civilization?

The "gap" and "great leap" problems become obvious in the Fertile Crescent, where highly developed civilizations can be dated shortly after Neolithic or survival-level settlements have been dated. In the environs of Asia Minor near the suspected landing site of Noah's Ark, domesticated crops and animals can be dated to the period shortly after the drying-up of flood waters. Further, within a blink of evolutionary time, humans left records of very advanced knowledge in life and physical sciences, constructed buildings marveled at by today's engineers, and created complex social systems.

Even a rate of change like that seen in twentieth-century technologies could not account for such accelerated institutional developments among Neolithic peoples. Habits of thought, complex social patterns, and deep psychological shifts require much more time to emerge than new material inventions. Abstract terms like "punctuated leap" cannot explain how hunters and gatherers, who reputedly had only recently left their caves, could evolve to having modern city-states like Kish, Uruk, Akkad, and Babylon in just a few centuries. Scenarios like "rebirth of a pre-existing civilization" or "external assistance" can better explain the development of such complexity in the short period of time available.

This chapter provides an answer to Diamond's question with reports from the people involved. Survivors from practically every region of the globe reported their people had been aided by ABs. Whether these were surviving elders or visiting AB teachers is not always clear. A few samples from scores of historical accounts describe how Advanced Beings provided assistance to selected Neolithic survivors of the Cataclysm.

Reports of Aid

Indian survivors reportedly led from the Himalayas by Manu were taught by three great ABs: Vasishta, Vishwamitra, and Agastra. They helped reestablish Vedic culture along the Sarawati River.[2] In the Andes, legend has it that Inti (the AB from the sky mentioned in chapter 2) took pity on the backward humans in their misery and sent the first Incas (meaning rulers) to help them redevelop civilization. The Mayans reported that life was renewed by Hunab Ku (their supreme god) after the Cataclysm.[3] The Chibcha people in Peru reportedly appealed to their AB cultural founder Bochica to mitigate effects of the Flood, and he helped drain the land.[4]

A Plausible Scenario

Stories like these suggest that as the earthquakes, fires, and flood waters of the Cataclysm began to settle, some survivors received the equivalent of modern-day disaster aid from powerful benefactors. The story of Noah's Ark stands out in Western history, but Noah and his family were not the only survivors to receive technical assistance. In the Germanic tradition, the Noah figure was named Bergelmir, who was saved from drowning along with his wife by "going up in his boat" (designed by ABs). The Zoroastrians, Aztecs, Indians, Celts, Scandinavians, and others have stories similar to Noah's, with ABs who came to the rescue of their own ancestors before or just after the disaster. Whence came these ABs?

Legends already referred to (and others to come in later chapters) suggest that prior to the Cataclysm, ABs reigned over or cohabited with humans on several continents. In addition to the Fertile Crescent, they may have been established in east Asia, southern India, and South America. If the multiple reports on them have any validity, the gods also ruled on the to-be-lost lands of Atlantis, Lemuria, and Mu. Given their capability for space travel, most of them should have been able to escape the planet's terrifying disasters and then return.

According to the Sumerians,[5] the Anunnaki possessed spacecraft that enabled them to escape the turbulence on Earth. Before the situation became untenable, their launch rockets (GIR in Sumerian) had lifted them off Earth to reconnect with mother ships orbiting the Earth beyond the stormy atmosphere. After the air cleared, command modules (MU in Sumerian) or shuttle craft detached from their landing vehicles and flew around the Earth to locate human survivors.

It is also possible that if non-Anunnaki were involved on a physical plane, they would have done the same, and that ABs functioning in a nonmaterial dimension could have resumed inner contact with survivors. The metaphysical sources referred to in chapter 1 indicate the AB assistance was both material and involved inner communications.

Technical assistance from ABs could have been motivated by any of several reasons. One may have been purely scientific interest.

Perhaps some ABs, safe in craft high above the maelstrom, had been emotionally touched by the devastation taking place on Earth and had taken pity on the destitute and forlorn humans who lived through it. As Phaeton/Nibiru approached Earth on its deadly trajectory, some gods had apparently been forced to abandon human lovers and hybrid progeny. Even though humans were second class, compared to their own AB families, such a tie would likely have evoked compassion for the suffering humans. Whatever the motivation, most of the support described in worldwide legends seemed short-term, like Red Cross emergency relief.

The Lucky Few

Not all humans were left to their own devices or limited to short-term aid. The area widely known as the cradle of civilization was more likely merely a relative safe haven for the lucky. The Anunnaki apparently decided to reestablish their Earth colonies with the biblical Ark's passengers and their descendants. They needed human help to fulfill their own requirements for food production and other support. For 5,000 to 6,000 years, the AB assistance allowed humans to recover earlier levels of civilization faster and more completely than survivors in other parts of the globe. No wonder they thought the gods had blessed them as a chosen people!

These lucky few received the ancient equivalent of the postwar Marshall Plan (the economic and technical aid program the United States provided to European countries destroyed by war). Aid of that order of magnitude to survivors in the Middle East could account for the otherwise unexplained appearance of full-blown civilizations there 8,000 to 10,000 years ago.

The technical and economic ramifications for the proto-Indo-Europeans' "luck of the draw" are still visible today. Their position of dominance in the modern world cannot be blithely attributed to greater intelligence or harder work. Their ancestors simply benefited from their proximity to the AB gods and the favoritism given them. Chapter 12 covers the story of this special attention.

The Anunnaki

When the aftereffects of the Cataclysm had subsided, the Anunnaki apparently decided to try to recover their operations on Earth. Here, let's review some of what the Sumerian texts tell us of the resettlement effort. One text relating to these decisions, the *Epic of Etana*, reports the reorganization of AB authority after the Flood. Enki assigned his son Gibil to supervise the gold mining area, another son Nergal to manage the south of Abzu (probably sub-Saharan Africa), and Egypt was placed under Marduk's authority.

The spaceport was rebuilt in the Sinai highlands (after flood waters had destroyed the earlier facility in the plains of Sippar and Mippu) and placed under the authority of Enlil's grandson Utu. He was known as Shamash in Akkadian and was the twin brother of Irnini (Ishtar). Ishtar was given control over the Indus Valley area. Utu and Ishtar's father, Sin, had commanded the spaceport before the Cataclysm. Sin was Enlil's firstborn son by his wife Ninlil. Since Ninlil was not Enlil's half sister, according to Anunnaki rules of succession which defined the legitimate heir as the firstborn son of the king by his half sister, Sin could not be considered his legal heir. Nevertheless, the Sinai peninsula still carries his name.

Ninurta, Enlil's son by his half sister Ninhursag/Sud and thus his legal heir, got control over Mesopotamia, which included AB mission headquarters. Another son, Ishkur/Adad became the leader of Asia Minor and the Eastern Mediterranean islands. The plains area which had included the old spaceport, from the land of Sumer to the Mediterranean, remained in the hands of Sin/Nannar.

This particular organization chart would later cause conflicts that affected humans (already mentioned in chapter 4 in the discussion of the origin of the words "sin" and "sinners"). In the postcataclysm period, as prior to it, the AB exercise of power over humans was direct (resembling slave owning in the southern United States before the Civil War), and the relationship was clearly understood.

The Anunnaki demonstrated their miracles of technology, taught their superior understanding of nature, and shared their concepts of agriculture, construction, and the handling of social issues. Humans could learn from the ABs by observation and imitation. In return for being good citizens, humans received the patronage of ABs. The result was, in evolutionary terms, the almost spontaneous rebuilding of human civilization in the "cradle of civilization."

For several thousand years, these AB-gods ruled their revitalized areas, generally through local demigod kings (of partial AB lineage) who had responsibility for a city or particular geographical area. Around 5,700 years ago, according to the calculations of Sitchin, these demigods began to be replaced by humans, as the role of kingship was lowered to their level. King lists in Sumerian, Akkadian, and

Egyptian name the successive rulers that we now associate with the rise of civilization. For instance, Egyptian lists make it clear when humans took charge for a transition period and when the role of pharaoh was established, about 3,100 B.C.E. In later chapters, I go into detail on the implications of the gods' input into human history.

The archaeological and DNA record indicates that the lucky Middle Eastern survivors quickly started to share their bounty of seed and stock with their linguistic and racial cousins in Europe. From about 8,000 B.C.E. to 6,000 B.C.E. they passed on the food production innovations gained from AB assistance. This was most likely done through extended family networks (still visible in modern genetic patterns) that had been laid down over tens of thousands of years prior to the Cataclysm.[6]

Other Possible Civilizations

Readers familiar with the view that a high civilization arose quickly in the Fertile Crescent after the Flood may not be aware that other traditions suggest relatively advanced civilizations restarted in several places. Archaeological findings and oral traditions point to the existence of sophisticated human settlements on other continents contemporary to those in West Asia around 8,000 years ago. These well-developed cultures far removed from Mesopotamia reflected what might be considered AB influence but did not adopt the Anunnaki extended family or develop a proclivity for the supernatural. This suggests that if they had AB help, it was before the Cataclysm or did not involve the Anunnaki regime that shaped Indo-European culture.

People of the Vedanta (a Hindu system of history and philosophy as expansive in scope as the Judeo-Christian system) believed that a new civilization arose in the Himalayas and on the Indian subcontinent. The Vedanta was apparently refined enough to have a singular cosmology and a comprehensive history (in the oldest, most perfectly preserved Vedas) by 6000 B.C.E. The Indian subcontinent apparently did not feel the effects of the Anunnaki until Ishtar's move into the Indus Valley, well after the Cataclysm.

Another center appears to have been in China, where tradition has it that by 8000 B.C.E. survivors were moving from the Tien Shan Mountains down to the great Yellow and Yantze Rivers and on toward the sea. (Many ancient cultural sites have been identified along these two rivers.) The Andean Plateau appears to have been another center revitalized to some degree along the lines of precataclysmic cultures. Ruins in Bolivia (including the Lake Titicaca area) and Peru point to highly developed architecture and astronomy that survived the Cataclysm. They suggest these areas had some sort of "expert help" not available to most societies in the Americas. Both these cultures lack the documentation to enable a profound historical study as can be done in Sumeria.

Scholars have no explanatory theory for how such high civilizations could have arisen spontaneously and independently in indigenous cultures in different parts of the world. The descriptive theory, calling them "sister" or "equal partner" cultures, simply asserts they somehow arrived at the same level from disparate experiences. Simply too many common features—notions of kingship, writing, calendars, and other attributes of civilization—existed for them to have occurred by chance so widely apart. A precataclysmic, widely disseminated culture offers a plausible basis for such similarities.

A cultural legacy without a postcataclysm Anunnaki orientation would be necessary to explain the significant differences between Eastern (particularly the Chinese and the Indian) and Western consciousness. These Asian survivors developed languages and philosophies quite at variance with the Indo-European culture, harking back to a more naturalist orientation (summarized by Lao Tzu in the sixth century B.C.E.).

Chinese society did not have access to or benefit from the Indo-European alphabet. Their complex and unwieldy pictograph system of writing persists until today. Their scientifically advanced tradition could have derived from Atlantis or Lemuria, both of which reportedly had nature-based rituals, including a focus on the Sun. Shamanistic and yogic practices incorporated into Chinese culture fit nicely into the more natural orientation reportedly shared by the Atlanteans and the Lemurians. Perhaps the Chinese today represent a legacy independent of the Anunnaki colonial regime, one able to avoid the AB-god cult era and the development of supernatural religion as described in part 7.

India seems to have been the repository of advanced knowledge about the multiple dimensions of the universe and an enlightened view of the human place in the natural order. Before the recording of the Vedas in the Indus Valley, the sages there knew of the practice of kundalini yoga (the infusion of subtle energy throughout the body that heightens awareness). There is some evidence suggesting the priests of postcataclysmic Egypt may have also practiced releasing this internal, subtle energy.

Current theories and research on the role of subtle energies and conscious intent can be traced to the same ancient Egypto-Hindu roots as advanced mathematics. This leaves unclear just how closely the Egyptians followed the dictates of the Anunnaki leadership based in Mesopotamia. It may have been that Egypt and India enjoyed help from more naturalistic, "progressive" AB gods.

The early Greeks also appear to have benefited from a natural perspective taught by Mystery schools in Egypt and India. It is possible some Anunnaki willingly shared much advanced knowledge with these independent societies without attempting to subjugate them. Or, these more independent-thinking cultures could have had the benefit of teachings from Atlantean survivors.[7]

Atlantean Connections

As mentioned elsewhere, metaphysical and traditional accounts suggest that several categories of ABs have been involved in human history. They could account for some of the obviously non-Anunnaki influences on more advanced cultures prior to and after the Cataclysm. I simply am not aware of enough evidence to hypothesize at this point about such independent influences. I refer to such interactions as the Atlantean connection, understanding that the reality is likely more complex.

The fact that the early Hindus, as reflected in the oral Brahmin tradition, attributed a solar origin to their multiple ABs suggests an Atlantean origin. Allusions to such a Brahmin Atlantean origin does not necessarily mean they were the last survivors of the continent. (Recall its demise has been ascribed to the 11,500 B.P. passage of Phaeton.) The first Brahmins could have emigrated from Atlantis in one of the earlier groups fleeing its breakup, or fled the sinking islands of Lemuria or Mu.

The only certainty at this time is that the Indian culture that confronted the Anunnaki hegemony in the Indus Valley (Mohenjo-Daro on the Indus River and Harappa on the Ravi) over 6,000 years ago already had a highly advanced, non-theistic Vedic tradition. When corrupted by the Anunnaki-sponsored invasion, local Hindu philosophy began to closely resemble essential features of the Sumerian and

Egyptian cultures. It was after this experience that Indians adopted allegiance to AB-gods. Only then did Hindu myths come to reflect the lives, battles, and loves of the Anunnaki.

In addition to the previously mentioned differences between non-Indo-European cultures and the Anunnaki colonies in West Asia, the non-Anunnaki-AB assumption seems to be supported by two other factors. First, the Vedic people (the mingling of groups from south India and survivors from the Himalayas—not Tibetans) were a maritime culture, comfortably living along great rivers and seaports. Some of their AB teachers were referred to as skilled sailors. Atlantis, commonly referred to as the island kingdom, seems to have been a great seagoing ancient culture—unlike the Anunnaki society.

Second, the Hindus used Sanskrit, thought of by some scholars as a maritime language due to its similarities to Polynesian languages and Hawaiian.[8] (Some speculate these languages came from one of the lost continents of Lemuria and Mu.) The fact that arguably the most significant AB technology transfer to humans (the alphabet) appears not to be an Anunnaki contribution suggests other AB races also worked with humans before and after the Cataclysm.

The settlements in the core of Asia (the Tibetan Plateau and the Tien Shan mountains) were cut off from the oceans. Whatever its AB connections had been prior to the Cataclysm, this region also appears to have been ignored by the post-Flood AB "angels of mercy." Advanced agricultural practices were quickly revived and social institutions are believed to have flourished as early as those in Mesopotamia. The racially similar Tibetan and Chinese peoples appear to have been left with an AB heritage independent of Mesopotamian Anunnaki.

Other independent centers of advanced knowledge may have survived the Cataclysm. In the Himalayas, Tibetans claim to have been the guardians of ancient knowledge and technologies which they credited to either Atlantis or Lemuria. (The Bon of Tibet speak of the ABs who started their culture as the Og-Min.) The fabled, but still elusive Aryans may have survived somewhere in the Caucasian and Caspian Sea region. None of these areas experienced anything like the extensive involvement of ABs in human affairs that we see in West Asia.

Precataclysm Atlantean traditions seemed to have fragmented, along with the Atlantean land mass, and been widely dispersed in parts of the Americas, Europe, and North Africa. Even if they carried some Atlantean knowledge and skills with them, they would have been at a disadvantage to the descendants of Noah, who had direct AB help to restart their civilization.

Greek historians claim that Atlantean invaders after the Cataclysm were defeated by the proto-Greeks around 9,000 years ago. Atlantean survivors in the Western Mediterranean (then an inland sea) could have evolved into the Etruscans. The early Roman elite may have had roots in this culture. Until they became caught up in AB-cult movements of West Asia less than 2,500 years ago, the Romans had a strong independent tradition, intellectually and psychologically free of the Anunnaki.

Some Were Left Out

Survivors who were not met by descending AB craft or reached by traveling, benevolent AB teachers were left to their own resources. Most of these survivors probably had only a rudimentary understanding of the institutions and technology that had just been destroyed (like most humans would have following such a cataclysm today). Vague memories of complex areas of knowledge probably led to practices that were mere shadows of the glories of the earlier civilizations.

In some instances, a few people may have retained key knowledge. This knowledgeable group might have included a few surviving priest-scientists or specialists with technical skills. Various legends refer to them as "the old ones" or "the wise ones." These scientists, philosophers, or engineers may have had expertise to share with their fellow survivors. However, the lack of back-up from precataclysm infrastructures or advanced equipment likely handicapped their efforts to demonstrate what they remembered.

Survivors in several areas reported to their children that they had received only limited AB recovery assistance. Often, this only amounted to directions or guidance to more habitable areas. An example of the less lucky, or maybe less prepared for advanced knowledge, who received only minimal assistance can be found in the American Northwest. The Quinaults report that AB Kwatee only showed their ancestors how to use stones as mallets or cutting tools.

The African story of minimal AB assistance was similar to that of the lesser-developed tribes of the Americas. It seems as if the ABs who came back to Earth after the Cataclysm did not include Africa, with the exception of Egypt, in their redevelopment programs. (Does this sound familiar?) For instance, the Dogon of Mali report that the "sons of gods" became involved in worldly affairs, including the development of agriculture and taking part in wars on Earth, but do not describe any kind of aid programs for survivors.[9] (This probably refers to precataclysmic AB activities.) Some African groups report having received some basic AB aid. The Zulu god Unkulunkulu reportedly made doctors available to treat disease and advise humans in food preparation (sounds like the Peace Corps). The god Mawu-Lisa is credited with providing humans with some technology, but this seems to have been in the course of early human history instead of just a few thousand years ago.

The survivors who did not benefit from programs of technology transfer and development assistance were left to struggle. They had only rudimentary implements and memories of simple ideas about nature and earlier human history, including the earliest activities of the gods. Some of these left-out groups have survived until the present day in a subsistence mode. Others who were more broadly experienced or better educated before the Cataclysm managed to achieve more than a subsistence level. These intermediate cultures can still be identified by their levels of development (primarily in Africa and Asia) between those of aboriginals (who always remained outside the AB culture) and those "blessed" with access to AB knowledge and technology.

Self-Restarting Cultures

Clearly many humans who did not receive advanced assistance after the Cataclysm still were able to get on their feet again. While we cannot discern whether specific information was brought forward or learned after the recovery, we do know that knowledge more advanced than one would expect from Stone Age people can be found around the world. For instance, the artifact known as the Ishango bone found near Lake Edward in Central Africa and dated at 8,500 B.P. demonstrates humans lived a time-factored life. Its notations relate to moon phases; they are "intellectual" material and not art.[10]

Intercontinental trade routes appear to be the most reasonable explanation for how quickly the 11,500 B.P.-Cataclysm survivors achieved the capacity to conduct commerce with humans in distant lands. Evidence of Sumerian mining colonies has been found in early postcataclysm Peru and Bolivia, as have ancient Hindu cotton and jute plantations in early Mexico. The Vedic people of India apparently navigated around Africa, across the Atlantic, and up the Amazon River to take copper and tin from mines in Peru and Bolivia. Several coins used in this ancient trade, found thousands of miles from each other and from their points of origin, had exactly the same weights.[11] More recently, Roman coins have been dated to sites in pre-Columbian Venezuela.

"Early Americans along the present-day Mexican Gulf Coast were raising maize, sunflowers, and a variety of other crops" 7,000 years ago.[12] Maize was cultivated near Panama about the same time. Although some scientists consider these areas to be the first in the Western Hemisphere to domesticate plants, radio-carbon dating of such plants tells us only that they were there at that time. It does not speak to their earlier existence in the region or elsewhere.

Two or three millennia after the Cataclysm, ships were sailing the oceans again, carrying goods from areas with special resources or skills to consumers with comparable things to trade. Tokens and other symbols of value facilitated transcontinental trade. Ores of copper and tin were transported across the Atlantic from the Americas to Europe and the Middle East. Ships plied the Mediterranean-area seas and rivers. Egypt had copper ore to contribute to the rise of bronze industries. They mined iron and began to use it for household purposes. People with free time used metal mirrors to focus on personal appearance.

Sturdy stone and kiln-fired brick houses were built by people all over the world where climate and population density warranted it, including out-of-the-way places like the Guernsey Isles in the English Channel. Pottery, candle making, the smelting of gold and silver, writing paper, cloth production, and other industries added to a comfortable lifestyle.

The Psychological Legacy

Human psyches coming into the modern era would have been shaped by both the memories of their ancestors' traumatic experience of the Cataclysm and their reactions to AB assistance. The psychological trauma caused by the disappearance of a world with a stable physical environment and established lifestyles would have resulted in what we now call a post traumatic stress disorder. The human mental landscape would have been turned upside down. Humans' earlier beliefs had not protected them from the Cataclysm, and they would have been looking for new explanations of how the universe works. Anyone offering authoritative answers provided much-needed solace; any previous dependency on the ABs would have only deepened.

The fact that ABs had easily survived would have made humans even more credulous. Anything connected to the ABs may have been seen as magic or divine, from the unknown and unknowable realm in the skies. Traumatized humans would be predisposed to believe anything they were told about the hidden powers of the Anunnaki or other groups of ABs. Since ABs had flown into space to escape the devastation wrought by the Cataclysm, humans readily believed they could also save humans if they chose to, or if humans convinced them of their value. The continuing AB warfare kept humans impressed with their powers and their control over matters of life and death on Earth.

The chaos that Anunnaki internecine conflicts precipitated among the various human families left them predisposed to seek a sense of stability. A covenant that promised AB protection and support as long as the humans remained faithful to their particular god or gods would have found many ready to sign on.

When the Anunnaki finally pulled out, humans who had never conceived of life without their rule would become desperate for their return. Anyone prophesying a return of a respected god immediately got the public's attention. Anyone suggesting a certain form of behavior as a way to gain favor with the now-invisible god received a hearing and collected many troubled followers. These psychological conditions would have helped set the stage for the changes in human consciousness described in the rest of this book. Today they manifest in various forms of the Second Coming movement.

Members of some groups today look for signs of the return of Christ.[13] Such signs may be political events like the rebirth of Israel, increasing earthquakes, the appearance of a personality who can be labeled the Antichrist, psychic phenomena, natural spirituality, and growing violence. Some members of these groups may take action to precipitate events they can call "signs." Later chapters give further details of the events and the likely resulting psychological stress that led to such delusions in the past.

12 Which Survivors Got Special Attention?

After the Cataclysm, according to Sumerian and biblical texts,[1] ABs returned as the floodwaters receded back into the marshes of the Tigris/Euphrates river basin. For their own purposes, the Anunnaki decided to set up three administrative regions. Publicly expressing regret for having abandoned humans (Enlil/Lord God promised never to do so again[2]), they organized relief and reconstruction efforts to make Mesopotamia habitable again. These efforts also included reclamation of the Nile River valley and the reestablishment of space port and flight-control facilities on the Sinai peninsula. Noah (Zuisudra in Sumerian), his sons, and the other human survivors were brought into these operations. Provided additional tools and seeds, humans resumed agriculture and animal husbandry (with Enki's genetic expertise being used to domesticate animals and wild grains) for themselves and the gods.

According to the *Myth of Cattle and Grain*, the Anunnaki genetically modified Earth plants when they first set up E.DIN and had stored the improved seeds back on Nibiru. They were available for the resuscitation of agriculture in the highlands before the lower plains dried out. (This explains why scientists have been puzzled as to why the so-called first fruits and vegetables were grown on the mountainsides instead of in the valleys.) While hillside food production was given priority, to avoid further famine, the gods set about clearing river channels, draining off excess water, and preparing the previously fertile valleys for easier cultivation. When that was accomplished, former population centers were revived on or near the old sites. (If the sites survive modern wars in the Middle East, priority should be given to excavation of deeper layers under the known ancient cities of Mesopotamia to confirm and explore this history.)[3]

One can only speculate on the factors beyond their own interests that motivated Anunnaki selection of recipients for technical assistance. The reportedly extraordinary level of AB support in the Middle East appears to have been based on precataclysm AB involvement with humans, including even family ties with Noah and others. Evidence of such AB/human connections comes from the king lists and other genealogies that have survived in Egypt, Mesopotamia, and the Hebrew Bible. *Atrahasis* texts record that the gods, led by the female ABs Sud and Ishtar, wept for humans as they observed the Cataclysm from the sky.[4]

Intermarriages with humans prior to the Cataclysm (Genesis 6:4) likely added to the motivation of the junior Anunnaki to work with survivors. Another possible, more mundane, factor was the gods' desire for the foods humans had produced for them before the cataclysm. This is implied in Genesis 8:20; favorably disposed toward the human offerings, the ABs considered their sacrificial meats to be "sweet."

Sitchin's *The Wars of Gods and Men* provides insight into some of the likely technology transfers and reconstruction that followed Noah's reconnection with the ABs. Within a short time, Enlil's son Ninurta had dammed rivers to make Mesopotamia habitable again. The Nile Valley was reclaimed for human habitation by Enki. The Sinai Peninsula was prepared for the Anunnaki postdiluvian spaceport, which included a control center on Mount Moriah (the future Jerusalem). From these geographical areas of AB focus would spring the three seminal civilizations whose combined influence would someday shape what is known today as Western civilization. First came Sumeria and then Egypt, followed by Israel. The next four parts of this book present an overview, based on the best currently available evidence, of how that might have happened.

Can we trust the validity of the Bible and other texts used in this portrayal to represent something of the historical truth about the role of the gods in the aftermath of the Flood? The record itself appears to establish the credibility of those texts. With AB help in Mesopotamia and Egypt, agricultural and urban sites could have sprouted there almost overnight, as the archaeological record suggests they did. Technology could have quickly blossomed and spread from this region, as the record indicates it did. Humans in these favored areas would have gotten a head start in knowledge and technology, as they did.[5]

Birth of the Indo-European Culture

The documentation of the efforts of Middle-Eastern human survivors, with support from their gods, gives us better access to this region's history than any other. This fact alone stands as testament to the assistance given by the gods to that group of humans. This assistance is well described in part 5, including the gifts of language and writing. Evident in the historical documents, but ignored by modern institutions, is the degree to which ABs gave the West Asians an advantage over the rest of the world.

Although the AB legacy is now known as Indo-European culture, it involved three distinct groups which apparently predated the Cataclysm. First, and on the east, were the Caucasian people who may have originally been from the Caspian Sea region. In Egypt were the Hamitic people who had evolved in northeast Africa. In the middle were the Semites of the Arabian peninsula. (The Caucasians were also known as Indo-Europeans, who earlier had spread eastward into Persia and westward into central Europe.) The loyalty of these and other groups to the gods associated with their homelands would result in conflicts that persist into the present era.

The first area to leave its mark on post-Neolithic history was Mesopotamia (now called Iraq). Along the Tigris and Euphrates arose (or re-arose) the cities of Eridu, Shuruppak, Kish, Erech, Nineveh, Uruk, and Babylon, among others. These cities were surrounded by large agricultural areas to support urban populations up to a hundred thousand or more. As society progressed, more examples of monumental architecture could be found. Walls encircled some of these cities, and all were governed by a resident AB who required a ziggurat for his use. Local priesthoods developed to serve as channels of communication between humans and the reigning gods. People captured in battle and conquest became slaves.

Which Survivors Got Special Attention?

Within a few thousand years of the Flood, Sumerians created artifacts that demonstrate writing and mathematical systems with evidence of professions like medicine, astronomy, architecture, and law, among others. However, the records of their views showed that the Sumerians clearly believed they were "created to serve, to labor for the gods."[6] Art produced by them left us images of the people, their gods, and their activities (including waging war for the gods). The gods helped set the tone for human institutions. By 8,000 years ago, human society in this part of the world was back on its feet, if not rivaling the legendary Age of Atlantis.

While the culture appeared authoritarian and hierarchical in structure, the early years were not totally patriarchal. A few female ABs apparently held their own among the gods.

Within the region, AB centers of power shifted around. Babylon rose above all other cities and ruled from the Persian Gulf to Syria in the north. Babylon's civilization remains a legend. Great palaces and courtyards and underground structures rivaled any of the modern world. Science and learning rapidly exceeded any expectations that might have been based on the gradual pedestrian and mundane progress of almost still-Neolithic tribes. The Code of Hammurabi (really a compendium of common law already in existence) epitomizes Babylon's level of civil society.

Egypt was not far behind. After helping get reconstruction going in Mesopotamia, the Anunnaki Enki turned his attention to the Nile Valley, which was reconfirmed (according to Sumerian texts and validated by Egyptian king lists) as part of his hegemony in Africa.[7] The fertile river valley supplied a comfortable lifestyle for most people (slave laborers would be an exception). A series of gods, demigods, kings, and pharaohs ruled over a complex social structure. Public buildings (and palaces, tombs, and memorials) surpassed anything known at the time. We know so much about early Egyptian life because a system of writing existed almost from the beginning. Its history and culture influenced later Eastern Mediterranean societies in ways that lived into the modern era in science and religion.

Their art was highly developed and even now provides a pictorial tradition of more than two millennia. It and other records indicate that women in Egypt were much more independent and enjoyed power and attention far beyond the other Indo-European societies. Egyptian life seems to have had a style of informality, relaxation, and even erotic tenderness. The emotions of relationships and families appear to have been public and respected. In sum, a complex and socially sophisticated society appeared in less than 5,000 years after the Flood.

Rise and Fall of Civilization

Conventional historians have documented much of the apparent warfare and cultural conflicts among the post-Flood city-states in Mesopotamia and beyond. Such bloody struggles involving the same cultures that left records of advanced laws and philosophy leave the historian with a single question: Why?

Sitchin has helped uncover the roots of this violence in the Sumerian stories of humans drawn into conflicts by ABs fighting among themselves. As other scholars corroborate important aspects of his work,[8] researchers can no longer avoid seeing so-called "sacred texts" with new eyes. As illustrated in this book, the reader can discern for herself the references to ABs and their human contacts in documents previously read as only metaphorical.

According to Sumerian texts, AB-assisted human centers peacefully reestablished themselves after the Cataclysm. For almost a thousand years they existed with no great upheavals. But shortly after 9000 B.C.E., a new round of squabbling broke out among the Anunnaki. They resumed fighting over the control of space facilities, and, according to Sitchin, a peace conference was convened, Anunnaki were reassigned, and new facilities built. With a few thousand years of peace, humans made great advances, and by 3800 B.C.E. the urban civilizations of Eridu and Nippur were flourishing. Uruk came into its own as the city to host the chief AB Anu on an inspection trip to Earth.

Continuing with Sitchin's interpretation, a few years later mankind was granted kingship, starting with Kish, the capital under the aegis of AB Ninurta. Humans began to think they could emulate the gods, but they were punished for it in the biblical incident of the Tower of Babel. (Chapter 16 explains how humans attempted to construct a means to reach the heavens—the domain of the gods—but were scattered and given different languages to prevent it.) The gods continued to fight among themselves and change the leadership of various city-states several times. Around 2900 B.C.E., Innana (one of the Anunnaki female leaders) received authority from her peers to move into the Indus Valley, and history saw the mixing of Sumerian/

Aryan culture with that of the Vedic/Dravidian peoples. By 2200 B.C.E., Sumerian civilization had risen to its greatest heights, as had Egyptian culture. But serious trouble was on the horizon.

In Egypt the gods resumed direct rule after the Flood, but around 7000 B.C.E. demigods assumed the throne. By 3350 B.C.E., in a very chaotic period when the country was divided into Upper and Lower Kingdoms, rule had passed to human kings. This lasted until about 3100 B.C.E. when the first pharaoh was installed in Memphis (the site of the "watchers" described in chapter 4). Known as the Old Kingdom, this period lasted for about a thousand years.

Around 2000 B.C.E., Egypt entered the period of the Middle Kingdom. As the ABs withdrew from the picture, the pharaohs changed the definition of the basis of their authority. They continued to claim the powers of gods but also stressed they personally were descended from the gods and, as if to further shore up their authority, promised that the gods would return.[9] By 3,500 years ago, Egypt was in decline. The peak of pharaonic power, the end of the New Kingdom, was fading in Thebes under the leadership of Amenhotep III.

The role of the Semites (unless one also considers the Sumerians and Babylonians to be Semites) in shaping Indo-European culture was different. Part of the Mesopotamian culture almost from the very beginning, they did not coalesce into a single empire of significance. They are not known for large cities or vast armies. Their triumphs and defeats were on a regional scale. Yet, as we will see, a special role in history for one group (Hebrews) was to provide the route for the survival of the oppressive legacy of the gods into modern times.

A New Level of Conflict

Indian, Roman, Sumerian, and other accounts describe wars among gods that could be compared to journalists' coverage of modern missile battles. Descriptions like those in Genesis 18–19 could just as well be referring to the effects of nuclear weapons. Sumerian accounts of the destruction of Sodom and Gomorrah seem even more to the point. Several sites (near Rajasthan in India, and parts of the Sinai Peninsula and Libya) provide possible evidence of nuclear explosions. Radiation, glass-like substances (similar to those produced at the Trinity atomic blast site in New Mexico), and blackened rock unexplained by any other hypothesis give credence to the following interpretation of Sumerian warfare.[10]

Six thousand years after reestablishing their presence on Earth, the Anunnaki had not resolved the internal divisions that reportedly rent the precataclysmic settlements in Egypt and Mesopotamia. In a great fit of frustration, Anunnaki leadership made the mistake of authorizing the use of nuclear weapons to settle the struggle for control of their Sinai space facilities between two pairs: Nergal and Ninurta versus Marduk and Nabu. The apparent nuclear conflagration in 2020 B.C.E. between the warring gods decimated the populations and natural habitat of the whole region. The flourishing civilization dissolved into scattered and ill survivors; there was no infrastructure, and the communities were surrounded by barren soils and poisoned waters. A period of stagnation befell all the city-states in the Near East. But from that desolated region came a line of Abraham's descendants who would later team up with an AB-god with a long-range strategy for the AB legacy in the Middle East.

After several hundred years of such conflicts, the Anunnaki apparently decided to pull out of their Earth bases. If they had reasons other than their own internal breakdown for the departure, translators have not yet found them in ancient texts. As we saw earlier, traditions in other parts of the world also have only simple explanations for the apparently precipitous departure of the gods.

When the Anunnaki made their decision to abandon their overt ties to human communities, we do not know what they foresaw for the future of the humans who had become dependent on them. However, it appears that they (like most modern colonial powers) gave little priority to the long-term developmental needs of the humans left behind. On the basis of what followed in the human societies, we can surmise there was no AB commitment to any sort of transition policy. (Remember how the U. S. government deserted its supporters in Vietnam in 1975 and in Afghanistan in the late 1980s.)

Regardless of the lack of an overall policy, at least one AB decided about 3,500 years ago to prepare a group of humans for a special role. He may have hoped they might become a model for a successful human society. Unfortunately, the last-minute effort at institution-building and social engineering (terms we might use today) was implemented in the middle of this chaos. The brainchild of an AB who identified himself as *YHVH*, the intervention called for creating a new nation-state from Hebrews then living in Egypt.

The disappearance of AB control over city-states and the loss of focus they and their activities provided to humans resulted in a deep social breakdown. It unleashed a well-documented reign of political and social chaos that lasted for almost two millennia. As long as the Anunnaki gods remained visibly active in the Near East, the twin pillars of their hegemony (Sumeria and Egypt) remained "superpowers" and remained relatively immune from attacks by independents from the Arabian peninsula, the Aegean seacoasts, and Asia Minor.

But, as soon as the dust had settled from the final Anunnaki political implosion and likely nuclear explosion, things began to change. The Hittites (from what is now Turkey) extended their empire eastward into Mesopotamia. Sumeria fragmented, with Babylon the cohesive center still loyal to the god Marduk. Egypt, in its already weakened Middle Kingdom, was soon conquered by the Hyksos (shepherd kings from West Asia).

Around 1600 B.C.E., the Kassites conquered the Babylonians. Egypt entered the period of Empire, engaging in struggles with different powers. A few centuries later the Hebrews completed their conquest of Canaan. Israel itself went from monarchy to tribal fragmentation as it broke into the kingdoms of Israel and Judah. Around 722 B.C.E. the Assryian Empire dominated West Asia and 50 years later conquered Egypt. During a 200-year period, the Assyrians rose to be taken down by the Chaldeans, who, along with Egypt, fell under the Persians.

By Alexander the Great's campaigns around 300 B.C.E., the Anunnaki heritage was weakened to the point that a Greek society representing an independent perspective was able to topple most of the remnants of "divine kingship." The Hellenistic culture of Alexander's empire spread a new perspective to the former AB-ruled societies. It was replaced by the widespread imposition of the new institutions of the Roman Empire (which had been developing for 1,000 years independently of Anunnaki rule).

A Chosen People

Historians have documented that for twenty centuries, armies surged back and forth across the plains of modern day Kuwait, Iraq, Syria, and Jordan; the mountains of Lebanon and the Sinai Peninsula; and the Egyptian river valley. Kings vying for power kept the region in turmoil,[11] but one human's legacy with roots in the earlier days of the gods wove a religious thread through the area that would reshape not only Middle Eastern history, but the history of the world. The transmitter of that legacy was a Sumerian-born aristocrat named Abraham who joined the Semite people who would eventually overshadow the Caucasian and Hamitic people of the region.

According to Genesis 11, Abraham was the son of Tehar, a Sumerian descendant of Noah's son Shem. First called Abram (meaning "father's beloved" in Hebrew), he and his wife Sarai (meaning princess) may very well have been descendants of demigods. (Recall the discussion earlier about the Book of Enoch that, like Genesis, traces this lineage back to Noah whose forebears included ABs.) Abraham's career appears to have been guided by both Enlil and his son Ninurta, and supported at times by other AB gods.[12] During one period of internecine conflict among the AB-sponsored kings and their followers, Abram was ordered by an AB to move to Canaan.[13] There his negotiations with other groups implied he had high status and AB-based authority.

Around 4,025 years ago, the time some believe the AB nuclear destruction (see chapter 19) of Sumer and Akkad (including Babylon) occurred, Abram became Abraham. He submitted to the circumcision ritual of the Semites to be accepted under the command of a different AB. Abraham's entanglement in the regional conflicts reflected the AB struggle for control of the spaceport in Sinai. Serving an unidentified AB, Abraham's body of troops and supporters headed for the Negev area to serve a defensive role. Afterwards he went into Egypt (where infighting pitted the sons of Enlil and Enki against one another) in an apparent diplomatic role (see Book of Jubilees). After perhaps five years there, he and his wife Sarai returned to Beth-el (a key AB stronghold) in Palestine.

With his death around 2000 B.C.E., Abraham passed the torch to his son Isaac. Isaac begot a son, Jacob, who begot a son Joseph (of the multicolored coat), who, in a likely apocryphal story, was sold into slavery in Egypt. After the nuclear holocaust had decimated their homeland, the Israelites had apparently gone voluntarily to Egypt (about 1830 B.C.E.). Some spent almost 400 years there, much of it apparently in service to the same Marduk/Ra dynasty against whom Abraham had served in Canaan, Egypt, and elsewhere. One of Joseph's descendants, Moses (born almost 300 years after the death of Jacob), was reared with access to the elite of both the Egyptian and Hebrew worlds. He was chosen, with his brother Aaron, by *YHVH*—one of the now invisible gods—to serve as instruments for reestablishing an AB-oriented hegemony in the midst of the desolation wrought by the gods' wars.

Under *YHVH*'s direction, Moses (born circa 1510 B.C.E.) led the Hebrew exodus from Egypt around 1430 B.C.E. when he was 80 years old. He marched the state-less people (not unlike modern Palestinians) around in the Sinai desert for 40 years.

From the books of Moses (Exodus, Leviticus, Numbers, and Deuteronomy) and the Book of Joshua, a picture emerges of an AB who wished to institutionalize a new kind of society among the heretofore squabbling mini-states that had occupied the Middle East until about 1500 B.C.E. His vision, spelled out to Joshua, who assumed tribal leadership upon the death of Moses, was to establish a model nation from the Sinai Desert and the shores of Lebanon to the Euphrates and across to the Great Sea (probably the Caspian).

For centuries, Israel did not make much progress in establishing the utopia *YHVH* seemed to have had in mind. The Israelites fought and mingled with the Canaanites, adopting some of their ways. In the process, the clarity of thought that *YHVH* had hoped for dissipated, and the Jews became mired in the minutiae of ritual and petty competition for status. For more than 1,500 years, *YHVH*'s notion of a well-ordered, utopian future for humans became lost in factional squabbling among the Israelites, and it attracted few followers from other AB-cults.

It was easy for the Roman Empire, a little over 2,000 years ago, to divide the Jewish nation and render it a provincial backwater. In one of the great ironies of history, leaders of the very same empire that suppressed *YHVH*'s people would turn to the use of his name and history (incorporated into the new religion of Christianity) in attempts to shore up their crumbling support among Roman citizens.

The Hebrews

For a people who became so important, and as the seed for a supernatural culture that would eventually dominate the world, the origin of the Hebrews remains an enigma. They did not represent a distinct race nor have especially distinguishing characteristics vis-à-vis the other Semites around them. Long before their migration into Egypt (escaping the devastation of the Dead Sea region), the Hebrews lived in an area of northwestern Mesopotamia in Harran at the foothills of the Taurus mountains before moving to Canaan (Genesis 11:31–2).

At the time of the above-mentioned AB-caused holocaust, they were under the leadership of Abraham. He had apparently been a

Babylonian military officer whose AB genes may have seeded the Israelites and Ishmaelites.[14] The original name "Habiru" (for Hebrews) may have been applied initially to any groups of nomads or immigrants, but later was associated only with people living in Israel. The name Israel came from the term Isra-el, the title Jacob used when the Hebrews reoccupied Canaan around 1400 B.C.E., 40 years after their exodus from Egypt.

The Role of *YHVH*

YHVH introduced himself to Moses in Exodus (chapters 3 and 4).[15] In 3:14 he told Moses, "I am who I am." He claimed he was the same god who ruled over Abraham, Isaac, and Jacob, but he clearly acted in a different manner. He hid himself from Moses and used miracles now known as materialization or teleportation, like changing a wooden staff into a snake, to prove his divine powers. His stated purpose was to liberate the Hebrews from their "servitude" in Egypt and make them into a powerful kingdom in the land of Canaan (part of the larger Palestine). He said he was prepared to protect them from the other gods and enemies along the way and to instruct them on developing their own society if they would remain loyal to him.

From the beginning, *YHVH* remained invisible, wanted no image made of him, and did not want his Hebrew followers to worship other gods. Through various channels—a voice in the Ark of the Covenant,[16] a telepathic channel, and a messenger—he offered advice to improve the Hebrews' social behavior. In exchange for their becoming his people and accepting him as their only god, he promised their liberation. He ordered his male subjects circumcised (as Abraham had been) as a special sign of allegiance.

To secure the Egyptians' acquiescence to the departure of the Israelites, *YHVH* apparently used biological weapons to create havoc among the Egyptians by inducing a series of plagues.[17] Though common Egyptians quickly agreed to let them go, the pharaoh (Amenhotep II or Ramses II) held out against *YHVH*'s demands. The final coup, communicated to the pharaoh through Moses and Aaron, was *YHVH*'s decision to send his soldiers (angels of death) to slay all the firstborn sons of the Egyptians. (The Hebrew sons were passed over because *YHVH* had warned them to mark their door posts with lamb's blood before the fateful night. Such young male genocide has since been used in many religious or ethnic conflicts.)

Which Survivors Got Special Attention?

After this bloody demonstration of *YHVH*'s wrath the Hebrews were permitted to cross the Red Sea. They then spent 40 years of indoctrination in the wilderness of the Sinai Peninsula before *YHVH* led them into the land of Canaan. During those years they learned how *YHVH* wanted them to live and how to ensure his continued protection. *YHVH* distanced himself from the earlier practices of the AB-gods, avoiding social or sexual contact with humans.

YHVH's 40-year training program reveals his attitude toward his human subjects. It was reflected in three books that later became part of the Hebrew Bible. Leviticus established *YHVH*'s priesthood for the community, set forth his ordained laws of behavior, and explained rituals required of his followers. The Book of Numbers explained the basic covenant required by *YHVH:* People must accept his authority on faith and trust his promises. Doubt would not be acceptable. Devotion to other gods would be punished. In exchange for this loyalty he promised to protect his people.

Deuteronomy, after a preamble, set forth a constitution for the theocracy of Israel, gave ten commandments regarding forbidden behaviors, ordered the Israelites to destroy the Canaanites, and prescribed how they were to treat the sanctuary (*YHVH*'s center for communicating with his priesthood). This book also ordained dietary rules, titles, and festivals in *YHVH*'s honor and described the nature of expected leadership practices and interpersonal relations. It set forth a "carrot and stick" contract between *YHVH* and his followers (depending on their behavior they would either be blessed or cursed). The Israelites, according to their own accounts, accepted his definitions of right living, learned to hate what he hated, and felt eternally indebted to him.

YHVH seemed to have wanted the Israelites to follow a strict moral code, but he did not appear any more mature than the other Anunnaki in terms of peaceful resolution of conflict, concepts of justice, ideas of the family, and rules of social intercourse. He ordered terrorist acts against the followers of other gods. Even with the Israelites, he resorted to coercion and punishment to control behavior (not unlike parents using corporeal punishment in child-rearing practices). If he was not actively hostile toward women, he exhibited no plan to make them equal partners in his ideal society.

YHVH demanded that his people so identify themselves. As mentioned earlier, males were required to do so through circumcision, and everyone had to wear the correct clothes and perform strict rituals. He ordered, "Have no other gods before me." He appeared to be without female companionship; his teachings and institutions underrepresented the feminine aspect of life. By all accounts he reflected the orientation of a patriarchal, authoritarian, rule-oriented Anunnaki space command.

A Mixed Legacy

The situation described in this and the two preceding chapters must be described as a mixed legacy in two senses of the phrase. In one sense it means that not all humans benefited equally. In another it means even those who received special attention from more Advanced Beings suffered some negative consequences.

According to stories in traditional societies, many groups of Cataclysm survivors were left to their own devices. Some destitute humans reportedly received immediate succor and perhaps a little training. Only a few benefited from longer-term aid, enabling them not only to recover from the trauma of extended material deprivations and psychological terror, but to prosper. These civilizations revived much more quickly with AB input than they would have been able to on their own. AB technologies and organizational support, including advanced science and other fields of knowledge, facilitated rapid development in a few societies. Part 5 and chapter 17 amply survey the positive benefits of this AB knowledge and technology transfer.

However, where Cataclysm survivors found themselves subjects of AB colonies, they developed a dependency syndrome based in an unnatural reliance on external power. Chapters 19 and 21 explore the psychological and social implications of having been colonized.

PART V

Evidence of Advanced Knowledge

Introduction to Part V

The scientifically dated evidence in this section leaves us with a forced choice between two fascinating conclusions. Either a very high level of human civilization has existed much longer than currently accepted theories permit, or beings more advanced than humans left evidence of their presence on Earth hundreds of thousands of years ago. The myths and legends of early humans do not claim human credit for this technology; they support the AB option.

In addition to dateable physical evidence, we can discern from the records of various intellectual disciplines that some beings had access to knowledge far in advance of that which primitive humans could have managed a few millennia ago. Much of it was equal to or even beyond that of current science. The next three chapters deal with evidence from various fields of knowledge for which the only logical explanation seems to be the presence of ABs during early human civilization.

Long before the rising seas flooded Mesopotamia, Sumerians were predicting the future positions of celestial bodies, enjoying the benefits of electric batteries, using advanced medicine, and carrying on sophisticated social intercourse. They had developed astronomical calendars good for 25,920 years, and their astrologers worked with a finely tuned sense of the mental and psychological impact of the stellar zodiac. Other precataclysm evidence points to professions, including architecture, agriculture, astronomy (derived from an off-planet perspective), mathematics, and various sciences that can be dated to at least 65,000 years ago. The evidence places human knowledge of or involvement in these professions. These three chapters then call for a rethinking of our traditional theories of human development.

Chapter 13 provides an explanation for the mystery of why so many genetically manipulated crops appeared in the general region of Mount Ararat so soon after the biblical Flood. It accounts for the still unexplained architectural wonders of the ancient world and shows why modern astronomers are just catching up with ancient knowledge. Chapter 14 pushes the origins of science back beyond current estimates of the origins of Western civilization. Chapter 15 deals with the question of how such complex social institutions appeared in the Fertile Crescent on the heels of Neolithic villages.

13 How Did Civilization Arise?

Conventional history reflects the belief that Neolithic humans first domesticated plants and animals and established small villages less than 8,000 years ago. Without hesitation, such books also state that 6,000 years ago humans almost spontaneously developed civilization with arts and sciences supported by complex political, social, and economic institutions. Mesopotamia and Egypt are described as having miraculously developed mathematics, architecture, astronomy, law, philosophy, and medicine in the period of a few centuries, with no visible antecedents.

Such an incredible "great leap forward" begs elucidation. However, to explain how a quantum jump in human consciousness and development could have happened without a long trail of gradual innovations requires thinking "outside the box." The evidence in this book offers two possible explanations. One is that parallel to the hunter/gatherer societies inferred from the archaeological record during the Paleolithic period, a higher level of civilization also existed. The second, not antithetical to the first, is that Advanced Beings provided humans with scientific and other superior knowledge after the 11,500 B.P. Cataclysm. This chapter reviews selected evidence supporting that thesis.

Transfer of technology from ABs to modern humans would have been a long and complex process, involving several modes of interaction.

One would have clearly been direct instructions from AB teachers, as worldwide myths describe. Another could have involved human observation of AB activities while working in their mines and on their installations. For example, if humans worked for the Anunnaki, they could have learned something of the gold smelting process. Some of what other laborers observed could be taken home and adapted to their own communities. In special cases direct demonstrations or gifts of technology could have been involved. (Many of the twentieth-century accounts of ET contact—sampled in chapter 5—describe situations similar to these processes.)

Nonhuman Teachers

Many apparently independent cultural stories about the origins of civilizations (including the early Sumerians, Egyptians, and Hindus) report that basic scientific principles and whole fields of knowledge came from nonhuman sources. These stories of technical assistance often attribute the basic concepts for civil institutions and social standards to ABs. In the latter category, the previously mentioned Book of Jubilees reports that a class of beings called Watchers "instruct(ed) the children (of the gods so) that they should do judgment and uprightness on Earth."

Humans today have a strong tendency to identify new ideas and inventions with the individuals or groups responsible for their introduction. When somebody does something important and unique, they want to get credit for it. It is likely that our human ancestors were similar, and if they had been responsible for the discoveries and inventions described in these myths, would not humans have claimed the credit? Instead they gave Advanced Beings the credit. The following accounts, selected from varied traditions, consistently corroborate the theory of widespread AB contributions of advanced knowledge to human civilizations.

Often, when researchers attempt to identify the oldest memories in a current culture, they find that its traditions point to earlier peoples and their receipt of knowledge from ABs. For instance, an Inca shaman/teacher in Peru once told me the megalithic ruins in the Andes attributed to the Incas were traditionally known to be constructed by ancients who preceded them. Further, he said those ancients were reportedly taught the construction techniques by the Apus (light beings). Similarly, in the Amazon, the AB Abe Mango reportedly taught the Tukano tribe building technologies, pottery making, weaving, and cookery.

At the end of the last ice age, the Chippewa's Manaboshu (a Noah-like personage) received instructions from an AB on how to make a good bow and arrow and how to work with copper. These technologies defined their early culture. In Old Mexico, Zanna, who is believed to have led the ancestors of the Aztecs to the Yucatan, was considered the "author of civilization" and the source of their alphabet. The Algonquins consider a being named Gluskap, who did feats too amazing for a man to have done, to be their cultural founder.

The Mayans' ancestors reportedly received advanced ideas from Kukulcan who arrived from the West and helped found a new culture.[1] Quetzalcoatl, credited with having taught the Toltecs many important areas of knowledge, was deemed to have made the greatest contribution to the founding of their culture, including setting ceremonial calendars and religious practices. Kukulcan and Quetzacoatl, different cultures' names for what is obviously the same being, remind one of *YHVH*'s activities with Moses and the Hebrews.

On other continents, only space limitations here preclude me from presenting scores of legends like that of the ancient Frisians of Northern Europe. An AB seer and philosopher named Minno helped start their civilization. Their Earth-mother Frya also gave them—as *YHVH* gave the Israelites—laws that would result in a good society.

Written Accounts

Turning to written documents, we find the same themes. The Bible's Old Testament is replete with stories of ABs communicating higher knowledge to early leaders: Enoch reportedly walked with the gods and was instructed by them. In another reference, he was taken into the heavens and taught "wisdom." Noah learned of the impending flood from one of the gods sympathetic to the human plight. Ezekiel received plans from the gods for the Temple at Jerusalem, walked with them, and even left the Earth with them in a "fiery chariot." The god *YHVH* handed Moses engraved tablets and dictated civic and religious instructions for the creation of a unique Hebrew society.

From other traditions we also find written accounts with a very similar perspective on early history. An Azerbaijani legend credits an antediluvian personality, a wise Enoch known as a demigod in other texts, with being the first teacher of the Kiyumars and the first ruler of Iran.[2] In Indian antiquity (see the Hindu Ramayana) the Nagas, known as the "educators of the world," taught navigation, military principles, and architecture. The people from whom the Mayans say they descended, according to their history collected in the *Popol Vuh*, received "fabulous knowledge" from an AB.

The Serpent God (probably the AB Enki mentioned earlier) gave knowledge from the Tree of Life to Eve and Adam. Prometheus gave "fire" (wisdom?) to prehistoric Greeks after stealing it from the heaven inaccessible to humans. A "water spider" who swam to the burning island no human could reach presented the "gift of fire" to the ancestors of Cherokees and other Southeast U.S. tribes.

The Sumerians admitted that the ABs they knew as the Anunnaki gave them all the sophisticated knowledge (described in their clay-tablet libraries) that current historians call "human firsts": mathematics, astronomy, medicine, agriculture, business, engineering, law, and music, among others. Gods common to Mesopotamia/Egypt and India have been identified with teaching humans advanced information: Sarasvati, the teacher of science and writing (like Ninki and Venus); and Ganesa, the giver of learning (like Thoth). Other gods are described who fit the Anunnaki pantheon: Kali of thunder and destruction, Vishnu the preserver (like Enki), and Shiva the destroyer and regenerator (like Enlil, who wanted the Cataclysm to destroy humans but was then convinced to give the survivors seeds and tools to revive civilization).

Familiar Greek "advanced teacher" stories are accepted by scholars as replays of fictional accounts passed on from the Egyptians, but the Egyptians claimed they received the advanced knowledge from nonhuman, tangible beings. For instance, Solon spoke of a goddess who gave proto-Greeks cosmology, divination, medicine, and law in the antediluvian era. However, his Egyptian mentors said the AB Thoth gave this knowledge to their ancestors. Thoth was credited with the invention of writing, arithmetic, architecture, surveying, geometry, astronomy, medicine, and surgery. According to the Egyptian Book of the Dead, he possessed all secret knowledge on 36,535 scrolls (maybe computer disks) in a vault (maybe a space-ship) in the sky.

In an extensive review of documented world myths, I have not discovered a single story that portrays the founding of its civilization as resulting from the *unaided* efforts of humans. They never say "this or that human did that," or even discovered it. ABs get the credit for the seminal turning points of all these societies. Such a universal practice, given the tendency of human egos to claim credit wherever possible, gives credibility to a surprising theme: Human societies benefited from advanced teachers at various times and places within our collective memory. A careful rereading of myths and legends and classical literature reveals this history of knowledge transfer has been in plain sight.

Technology Transfer

A frequent corollary to teaching or training by Advanced Beings is what modern development specialists call "technology transfer." In this process, advanced humans demonstrate devices or provide new equipment. For instance, pictures of papyrus being presented by the ABs who established Egyptian civilization exist among the oldest Egyptian engravings and paintings. Greek legends place the use of iron in the era when the gods reigned over the "great race" that was submerged in the great deluge.

The following pages give examples of teaching or "information transfer" and technology transfer. This theme is so important in human history that it requires two chapters (13 and 14). One particular area of technical assistance that deserves special treatment has to do with AB influence on language and writing (chapter 16), including the introduction of the alphabet (chapter 17).

Agriculture

Before the intervention of the AB-gods, humans found the food they needed in nature. Genesis 1:29 describes the situation. Speaking to humans, the original creator says, "I give you all the plants that bear seed everywhere on Earth, and every tree bearing fruit which yields seed: they shall be yours for food." But after the AB intervention and the transfer of humans to E.DIN, the gods "planted a garden. . . . and made trees spring from the ground, all the trees pleasant to look at and good for food" (Genesis 2:9), and then said in 2:17, "You may eat from every tree in the garden, but not the tree of knowledge. . . ." After being banished from E.DIN, humans were told (3:17), "With labor you shall win your food from [fields] all the days of your life."

Notwithstanding the biblical account of prehistory (including references to Adam being a husbandman and his sons Cain and Abel respectively tilling the land and shepherding), most historians start the history of agriculture after the Flood and as follows. Wild grains date to just over 11,000 years ago in the highlands of the Fertile Crescent. Then within less than a thousand years, genetically uniform strains of plants (requiring human cultivation for their propagation) became widely evident. Wheat and barley and domesticated sheep, goats, and cattle appeared in Persia, Mesopotamia, and Canaan around 8000 B.C.E.

Within a thousand or so years, the Sumerians were growing flax, apples, plums, and grapes. About the same time, Egyptians were using flax in textiles. They also used spelt, a grain that was a mixture of botanic genes, not a new generation of an earlier grain or a mutation. The question remains: Where did knowledge of the genes and their manipulation to domesticate plants come from?[3] The Sumerians and the Hebrews said it came from the gods.

Chinese survivors apparently *recovered* crop production by 7000 B.C.E. near Xian in the North and close to Shanghai and Taiwan. (The reason I use the term "recovered" will be explained shortly.) Millet appeared in China soon after the Cataclysm, and evidence points to the existence of the Chinese silk industry after 3000 B.C.E. Mesoamerica and the Northern Andes were producing crops by 6000 B.C.E.[4] They included potatoes and beans in Peru, pumpkins in the Americas, wheat and lentils in Mexico, and rice in Indochina. Flax appeared in Asia.

Survivors who found themselves in the equatorial and tropical regions should have been able to depend on copious local food plants without the need for AB development assistance. But, as in other areas of human knowledge, ABs are given credit for giving agricultural knowledge and skills to humans. Quetzalcoatl reportedly taught the primal Toltecs how to grow maize.[5] In Africa, the AB Juok gave the Shilluk tribe cattle, millet, and fish for their sustenance.[6]

The agricultural techniques made available to "Noah's descendants" after the Cataclysm were quickly spread by travelers diffusing seeds and ideas through family networks from previous migrations to Europe. Radiocarbon dating tells us that the "new agriculture" covered the Middle East and Turkey within several hundred years of the Cataclysm. Then it spread to Greece and the Caucasus Mountains by 6000 B.C.E., to Southern Europe by 5000 B.C.E., and five hundred years later to Italy and Central Europe. By 4000 B.C.E. it had spread to Spain, Southern France, and Germany, and on to the coasts and islands surrounding Europe, including the Scandinavian Peninsula, by 3000 B.C.E.[7]

The reason humans attributed agriculture to their AB benefactors goes farther back than the Cataclysm. The Genesis account and the Sumerian *Myth of Cattle and Grain* explain why. The ABs developed the first domesticated crops and livestock, i.e., domesticated them and made them available to humans. The myth states, "Vegetation that luxuriates they multiplied in the land. Four-legged animals they artfully brought into existence." The Anunnaki then taught humans the tilling of land and the keeping of sheep for the ABs.

Sitchin has speculated that when most food plants and animals were destroyed in the Cataclysm, humans had to depend on the Anunnaki to restock Earth from their genetic records on Nibiru. This would explain the (re)appearance of these food items within a few centuries after humans were consuming wild grains in the highlands of Asia Minor. As incredible as this story may sound, mitochondrial DNA research (technique described in chapter 9) on domesticated cattle and dogs[8] place their origins, respectively, at about 200,000 years ago and over 100,000 years ago. Based on the same DNA analysis, African and European cattle split into two strains over 20,000 years ago.[9] Such technical assistance from the ABs indebted humans to them as long as the ABs remained on Earth.

Thus, the story of agriculture is one of a more primitive species receiving help from Advanced Beings and, for many generations, paying the price of servitude. (This scenario had been repeated in any number of modern colonies and slave-holding states.) It is no wonder that humans reported in Sumerian texts that they were dependent on the AB colonists and considered their livelihood to be at the mercy of the AB leadership. Obliged to the Anunnaki for agricultural knowledge and skills, humans tended their fields, orchards, and cattle. They also served as cooks, clothiers, and artisans. They worked as musicians, entertainers, and "sacred prostitutes" for the gods. They were even willing to take on the battles of their respective gods when the gods fought among themselves.

Architecture

How do we explain huge prehistoric complexes of which the ruins are still visible in various regions of the world? They include the Great Pyramids of Egypt, the complex of Baalbek in Lebanon, the magnificent Tiahuanaco near Lake Titicaca in Bolivia, Machu Picchu and

Sacsahuaman in Peru, the temple at Angkor Wat in Cambodia, great temples in Mexico and Central America, and others still under the sea and Earth. Seven are now known only in legend: the hanging gardens of Babylon, the statue of Zeus at Olympia, the Colossus of Rhodes, the temple of Artemis at Ephesus, the Mausoleum at Halicarnassus, the Alexandria lighthouse, and a huge, fabled building in Egypt described by Herodotus. Researchers suspect many of these extant sites sit atop the ruins of earlier structures that precede the Cataclysm.[10]

The first unanswered question regarding all these structures is the date of their construction. The second is how could primitive people accomplish such perfection in huge pieces of stone, some of which cannot be so precisely cut and placed (without mortar) even with twentieth-century technology.

The engineering of the Giza plateau pyramid structures, using the same materials as the builders, could not be replicated today with the degree of perfection they exhibit. These three great Egyptian pyramids contain from one million to three million stones with average weights of three to four tons each. The structures would have to have been started at the bottom where a deviation of less than an inch on one stone at the bottom would produce a 20-foot error by the time the masons reached the apex. This discussion does not even include the exact astronomical measurements built into the structure. The pyramids' master builders reportedly taught humans their architectural and engineering skills (see Freemasonry discussion later).

The scale of the platforms at Baalbek are still out of the range of today's technology; they cannot be duplicated with current crane lifts and other equipment. This huge complex of so-called temples and royal structures in modern Lebanon contains a platform comprised of five million square feet of stone blocks. Most weigh hundreds of tons, and three (the trilithons) quarried at several miles distance weigh more than 1,000 tons each. We have no obvious clue to the technology involved. Clearly a civilization beyond primitive humans just graduated from the New Stone Age was required.

The ruins in Tiahuanaco (Bolivia) and Cuzco (Peru) involved similar huge blocks that were reportedly put in place by beings more powerful than humans. The astronomical layout of the "temple" in Tiahuanaco suggests it was built 27,000 years ago. Some speculate that an anti-gravity technology was used in these projects, and there is some evidence that at least a few humans understood its principles.

A published report of observations by a Swedish doctor alleges Tibetan monks had mastered the levitation of heavy stones using sounds generated by musical instruments and chanting.[11] Similar techniques were allegedly used in wall construction for Thebes and Troy in Greece, the latter attributed to ABs Apollo and Poseidon. Given what we can now accomplish with various sonic devices, this concept is not farfetched.

The entire Andean Region, and Peru in particular, is filled with little-known ruins of unknown civilizations (beyond the better-known Machu Picchu and at Lake Titicaca). New discoveries occur every few months. Gene Savoy discovered 40 ancient sites in a little more than 40 years—all in the Peruvian rain forest east of the Andes. They are believed to have been built by the Chachapoyas (meaning the "cloud people" in Incan language), people, the Incans say, who were an ancient people before history.[12]

Astronomy

Artifacts with astronomical data from prehistory have two important characteristics. First, some of the information can be dated by computer regressions to the time when a configuration found on an artifact would have been visible in the sky. The correlation of the date with the ancient star data probably indicates the time it was observed. Second, some of the information appears to be knowable only from an off-planet perspective, thereby suggesting that the beings who created it (human or AB) did their analysis from a point not on Earth. For instance, analyzing prehistoric stone sculptures in the Egyptian desert, astrophysicist and archaeoastronomer Thomas Brophy has demonstrated that humans more than 20,000 years ago had precise knowledge of major star coordinates, the location of our Sun, and the dimensions of our galaxy.[13]

Once again, humans often credit ABs as the source of that early knowledge. For instance, Quetzalcoatl, the source of seminal knowledge for the Toltecs, reportedly taught their earliest ancestors how to measure time and study the progression of the stars. He allegedly invented the calendar that tracked their movements. The quantity and quality of evidence indicating humans had complex knowledge of the planets and stars is so persuasive it cannot be ignored by credible historians. Selected samples of information illustrate the thesis of this book, but an interested reader should check the references in the chapter notes.

Seasons and Calendars. Organized horticultural activities handled by human workers depended on knowledge of the seasons and moon cycles, i.e., accurate calendars. This was particularly true in Egypt where agriculture was based on the periodic flooding of the Nile. The calendar used by postcataclysmic Egyptians (per Diogenes Laertius, an early Greek historian) started counting about 51,214 years ago. Its year was based on 365 days, with two adjustments (like our leap year) made periodically for the actual time it takes for the Earth to revolve around the Sun. One slightly longer year occurred every 1,460 years and another occurred every 2,336 years. These two cycles coincide with the movements of the star Sirius and the planet Venus, something that could have been known only by advanced astronomers.

The Egyptian calendar's starting date, according to Maurice Chatelain, is within 400 years of perhaps the oldest Mayan date, recorded as 51,611 years ago on the Chincultic ceramic disk. These calendar starting dates preceded the Cataclysm. Others, like the Zoroastrian *Bundahishn* (beginning in 9630 B.C.E. and written in the late Persian Pahlavi language) appear to have restarted their calendars after the Flood.[14]

Evidence that such advanced information possessed by prehistoric humans survived the Cataclysm can be found in artifacts. In 1901 Greek divers recovered a bronze astronomical calculator from a Grecian ship wrecked in 83 B.C.E. This finely tooled instrument with zodiac signs and differential, gears, pinions, and dials was set to sky charts of 86 B.C.E., three years before the ship apparently sank. But even more importantly, its calculations came from the Egyptians' Sirius-based (Sothic) calendar which had been developed thousands of years earlier by someone with a non-Earth perspective.

One Sumerian tablet and a Persian account of the Cataclysm indicate the dating of eras by the constellations (specifically Leo and Cancer) existed prior to 9500 B.C.E. Another clay tablet documents the exact positions of the constellations in the sky as early as 7700 B.C.E. These artifacts indicate the continuity of knowledge on both sides of the Cataclysm

Movement of Stellar Bodies. Sumerian clay tablets discovered by George Smith in the buried ruins of the ancient city of Nineveh in 1873 contain tables of advanced astronomical data. One table contained a numerical constant (195,955,200,000,000, since called the Nineveh constant)[15] recognized in 1955 by Maurice Chatelain

(French mathematician and space communications manager for the Apollo moon landing program). With it he discerned that Sumerians knew how to calculate the revolution periods of all the planets and their moons in our solar system (counted in seconds not days). The table was accurate to several decimal points, with each calculation corresponding to modern tables of U.S. astronomers, and encompassed a time span of more than six million years.

The time it takes for the Earth to complete one rotation on its axis, as contained in the tables, makes it possible to date the calculation. The Sumerian figure for the Earth's rotation varied slightly from the current cycle. We now know the Earth's rotation has been decreasing by 0.000016 seconds per year (established by the cesium clock used in modern astronomy). Taking the difference between the prehistoric rate of rotation and the current one and dividing it by the annual rate of decrease indicates when the tables were calculated: The tables engraved in clay established the Earth's precise rotation 64,800 years ago.

When Chatelain then analyzed ancient Hindu, Maya, and Greek astronomical tables, he discovered they had one thing in common with the Sumerian tables. The rotations of solar bodies contained in the tables from four different cultures came from the same time: 64,800 years ago.[16]

While the Mayans calculated astronomical measurements based on the same constant as the Sumerians, their table was based on days instead of seconds as used by the Sumerians. Counting back 13 Mayan cycles, of 5,163 years each, from the projected end of the current cycle in 2020 takes us to 67,119 B.P.—very close to the Sumerian date. The same information known to both cultures suggests either connections between the prehistoric Sumerians and the Mayans or access to the same teacher. That the number 360 used by Sumerians in their calculations (360 degrees in a circle, etc.) played a central role in Mayan calculations also suggests a common source.

From the beginning of recorded history, the Brahmans of India had knowledge of the precessional cycle of 25,920 years (the number of years it takes the Sun to move through all 360 degrees of 12 constellations) and used it for measuring periods spanning millions of years. Greeks and Babylonians, respectively Hesiod about 700 B.C.E. and Berossus about 260 B.C.E., wrote of similar time periods, as did the Yezedis of Kurdistan. This information found its way into the Manichaean gospels of the third century C.E. (See chapter 20 for discussion of why the Christian church in Rome persecuted these people. Apparently they promoted knowledge from AB sources helpful to humans.)

Astrology. Not only did the AB-trained humans have detailed working knowledge of heavenly bodies and their influence on planets, they seem to have had some understanding of the minute but significant influences of the energetic impulses of various configurations of celestial bodies on human behavior.[17] By the time humans assumed kingship from the ABs, they considered astrology to be a reliable science. It had apparently been seen as useful in understanding the affairs of any conscious beings by human priests working with AB astronomers.

The antediluvian Sumerians used a well-developed system of astrology based on 12 signs of the zodiac—meaning "circle of animals" in Greek. (Some evidence suggests the Chaldeans added Libra to the other eleven only after 3500 B.C.E.) Sargon I calculated astrological predictions in Babylon 4,350 years ago. The Aryan invasion of India around 1500 B.C.E. introduced Mesopotamian astrology to the Hindus.[18] The Essenes just before the time of Jesus used horoscopes to predict the adult physical characteristics of newborns and forecast their social destinies.[19] Later the Mayans used a zodiac based on 13 signs, now recognized by some modern astrologers as more accurate than the Chaldean 12.

Most of today's astrologers use star/constellation positions that are more than 2,500 years old (from the time of the Chaldeans when the Hebrews were captive in Babylon). Although modern astrology describes the effects of various conjunctions, no one understands how the energetic interactions between planetary and star positions and human behavioral predispositions actually work. Apparently the human priesthood that learned it only understood how to manipulate the system, not why it works.

14 Who Invented Mathematics and the Sciences?

Conventional history books[1] say science began about 600 B.C.E. with the Ionian school of Greek philosophers (located in Asia Minor, now part of Turkey), but the reader is aware by now that is not the whole story. Historians of science recognize that various well-developed techniques for dealing with the physical world (metallurgy, medicine, construction, mathematics, and astronomy) played roles in human society before the Ionian Greeks articulated a rational perspective on nature. Nevertheless, their rational and systematic inquiry into natural phenomena is seen as the birth of Western science. The material in this book makes the case that such an approach to knowledge originated long before the naturalist Greeks and even before the advent of *Homo sapiens sapiens*.

Several samples of technology dated to at least 100,000 B.P. or earlier highlight that possibility. Michael Cremo and Richard Thompson in their book, *The Hidden History of the Human Race,* describe a coin-like object (circular with obviously symbolic markings) found while digging for a well in Illinois that has been dated to over 200,000 B.P.[2] Carbon dating of the prehistoric and abandoned mines in South Africa places their most recent period of activity at least as far back as 100,000 B.P. In another example, a Russian scientific institute reported finding in 1996 microartifacts of tungsten, molybdenum, and copper in 100,000-year-old deposits of gravel and sand on the Balbamyu River.[3]

With regard to the preceding chapter and this one, we cannot be certain how or which knowledge or technology was made available to humans before the Cataclysm. What appears more certain is that humans had access to a widespread, universal knowledge base. Whether AB experts lived in different locations or human migrants took the information with them after they dispersed from AB areas of operation remains unclear. Worldwide legends of traveling teachers or wise men boosting local cultures give credence to the traveling expert theory.

Supporting the traveling expert view, widely spread counting systems had interchangeable base numbers: Sumerians (60), Egyptians (10), Mayans (20), and Gauls and Babylonians (12). Note that 60 is a multiple of all the last three. The flexible Egyptian decimal system became the most widespread in the world. Why the British and Americans ended up with feet and yards based on units of twelve inches can apparently be blamed on the Gauls for dividing the Anunnaki 60 by five rather than three or six.

Starting at 600 B.C.E. as the beginning of science implies that developments like those to be described later in this chapter were based on accidental experience, intuition, or magical thinking that hit on solutions to everyday problems. From that point of view, and very illogically, domestication of plants and animals happened more than 10,000 years ago (remember the preceding chapter), metallurgy 8,000 years ago, medicine and mathematics 6,000 years ago, complex constructions 5,000 years ago, etc., and they all came before the birth of Western science. Conventional history does recognize that some forms of higher mathematics were used by humans over 4,000 years ago.

Mathematics

Six thousand years ago, Sumerians, Egyptians, and perhaps Minoans left evidence of a number system that could deal with large quantities. A particularly troubling point for the science historian is the Sumerian 60-base system of numbers that led to the mathematical solving of quadratic equations (requiring two levels of solutions). Both the Mesopotamians and Egyptians had precise systems of measuring area and volume (using the sexagesimal system). They used multiplication tables and calculated basic geometry. They used the transcendental number π (3.1415....) to define the ratio of the circumference of a circle to its diameter and the Pythagorean theorem, the relationship of the hypotenuse to the lengths of the other two sides of a right triangle. Note that Pythagoras only rediscovered it later.

Some evidence suggests that at least four postcataclysm civilizations used place values (to break whole numbers into fractions): Mesopotamians, Chinese, Indians, and Mayans. The Chinese and Indians appear to have learned fractions from the Mesopotamians, although the Indians may have gotten them indirectly through the Chinese. Decimal numbers (used for calculations in the abacus) have been dated to 1350 B.C.E. in China. The symbol for zero was believed to have been invented around 900 B.C.E. in India or Indochina. The early Greek mathematicians Thales and Pythagoras built upon this knowledge base.

These concepts were obviously in use before the Greek development of rational experimentation with the physical world. Dates in this discussion are based on the ages of artifacts containing the information. So, it is likely the concepts and skills would have been known much earlier. Where did these skills come from? With access to information six millennia old, we now know the Sumerians had access to advanced mathematics, whether they understood it or not.

Pythagoras, around 500 B.C.E., held the view that all reality exists in a state of harmony. He believed harmony (proportions and order) could best be represented by numerical relationships. (He is the first recorded to have represented musical harmonies in terms of ratios of the pitches of notes.) The legend that he traveled throughout Asia Minor, especially Egypt and Babylonia, before settling down in Sicily in 529 B.C.E. makes sense. He possibly learned the famous "Pythagorean theorem" in Mesopotamia (heart of the AB colony).

We have the same ambiguity about origins in this area of human knowledge as in many others. The humans identified with mathematics point to earlier and earlier sources. For instance, the Greek mathematician Eudoxus, around 350 B.C.E., worked on complicated models of planetary rotations.[4] The likely origin of his concepts which led to modern trigonometry lies in Egypt, where he traveled with Plato.

In 300 B.C.E. Euclid compiled all known principles of plane and solid geometry,[5] undoubtedly using Egyptian papyri that show knowledge of geometry and simple equations before 1700 B.C.E. A little later, Aristarchus, credited with first proposing the heliocentric theory of the universe, was only restating ideas long lost in Mesopotamia. In another example of the scientist standing on the shoulders of the past, Copernicus, more than 1,800 years later, used Aristarchus's work to put forth a heliocentric theory that helped fuel the European Renaissance.

Other Greeks, like Apollonius, Archimedes, Eratosthenes, and Hipparchus, who received training at the great library in Alexandria, elaborated on this body of universal knowledge. Essentially researching the documentation left over from the AB regime, they achieved an understanding of the principles taught by the Anunnaki. Only after having access to the Sumerian tablets did historians realize this had happened. (A few researchers believe some of the information in the library came from Atlantis, different from that offered by the Anunnaki.)[6]

Ptolemy, who lived in Alexandria between 200 and 100 B.C.E., also reviewed the work of earlier eras and compiled the *Almagest*, a textbook on astronomy that used mathematics to demonstrate how all the heavenly bodies revolved around the Earth. Persuasively, using only the math Eudoxos used 450 years earlier, apparently without access to Sumerian astronomical tables, he convinced philosophers that his inaccurate Earth-centered model was fact (demonstrating that numbers by themselves can be used to prove just about anything).

Using the Sumerian and Egyptian artifacts, we infer precataclysmic knowledge from the content or dates related to astronomical events that can be dated by computer. However, cave art in Europe, which can be dated to between 20,000 and 30,000 years ago, appears to provide direct evidence of precataclysmic mathematical knowledge. This means Cro-Magnon people appear to have had knowledge of a decimal system that we mistakenly believe was invented only a few thousand years ago.[7]

Given these examples and much more, the history of mathematics in the West seems to be one of working with fragments of leftover advanced knowledge. Were these fragments developed by earlier humans or simply material left by departed ABs and then rediscovered? The teachings of Freemasonry, Hermeticism, Rosicrucianism, Kabbalism, Sufism, and other occult traditions for more than two millennia imply that the information was taught by ABs. Supporting this contention is the fact that most of the historically identified figures seem to have had earlier, unidentified assistance from advanced teachers in the region of Mesopotamia or Egypt. A glaring exception to this record of human access to advanced knowledge exists in Africa. No evidence of complex mathematics has been dated in sub-Saharan Africa prior to its colonization by Indo-Europeans in the second millennium.

Science

In one of the earliest civilizations recognized by conventional archaeologists,[8] 8,000-year-old Catal Huyuk in Turkey, they have no explanation for artifacts that could have been produced only by an advanced technology, including the existence of a perfectly polished mirror of obsidian (hard volcanic glass), stone beads with bored holes so small that only modern technology could duplicate the feat, and the smelting of copper and lead.[9] What would the Catal inhabitants tell us if we could ask them where the objects came from?

Would they, like traditional societies, attribute them to nonhuman origins? Like the Egyptians, Greeks, and Romans attributed their ability to control and use fire to the Atlantean gods Phos, Phur, and Phlox (giving rise to the Greek-based word phosphorous, meaning light-bearing)? Earlier mention has been made of ABs providing fire to primitive humans. More examples in the Americas are Abe Mango, as noted earlier, teaching the Tukano how to use fire, and Kanassa bringing fire from the sky to the Kuikuru peoples in Brazil. The Aztecs also had a fire god: Xiuhtecuhtli.

The interesting point here is that the more primitive traditions speak only of the gift of fire from ABs; they did not proceed from basic uses of fire to the more advanced technologies described in the next paragraph. In contrast, a higher level of technology, the use of fire and its explosive potential, is part of the history of the societies associated with the presence of Anunnaki colonies.

For instance—the manufacture and use of gunpowder: early Greeks talked of the god Zeus in the War of the Titans making use of weapons that caused the Earth to tremble as in earthquakes, and whose continual flashes set fires on Earth. The Bible describes YHVH, on behalf of Moses, destroying the unfaithful with explosives (Numbers 16:31–41) and Gideon intimidating the Medianites with small jar-like bombs (Judges 7:17–22). India reportedly used exploding rockets to repel Alexander the Great (and sold them to China in the century after Jesus' birth). In some accounts, the Carthaginian commander Hannibal also used fiery rockets against the Roman armies. Were these human uses of explosives made possible because an AB, Zeus, gave his technology to humans?

Human societies outside the Indo-European/AB culture report only observations of AB use of such technology and do not indicate they had access to it. The Fon people of Africa state the Gu or magical weapons were available to ABs, but not to humans, who were only taught metalworking.[10] The Navajo report that their sun god Tsohanoai gave his AB sons weapons that were not available to humans. They had "chain lightning arrows, sheet lightning arrows, sunbeam arrows, and rainbow arrows."[11] Navajo descriptions of these weapons remind one of the weapons used by the Hebrews, Indians, and Romans mentioned above. But, it appears that the Navajo were only eyewitnesses to scenes of night bombing, strafing, and anti-aircraft fire (like our wars on international television).

The Vedas speak of gods in human form who had special types of powerful weapons, not just bows and arrows. In the Vedic descriptions, their activities suggest these gods also used advanced equipment, ranging from diving suits to flight suits, with all sorts of technical capabilities for communication and flight.

The accounts described above that some see as only myths can be read as human descriptions of AB technology transfer not limited to fire and explosives. The foundations of practically all fields of science, in one culture or the other, have been attributed by ancient peoples to contributions from resident or visiting ABs. This wealth of knowledge includes specific inventions still in use. For instance, the invention of the magnetic compass was attributed either to the well-known Atlantean god called Hercules by the Romans or Typhon, the son of the Greek goddess Rhea.

The Egyptians credited the invention of the compass to Harveri (son of the god Osiris). Reports from antiquity suggest a compass was used by ancient navigators well before the Christian Era. It was reportedly widely used even in China 5,000 years ago. Such a compass would have made it possible for the Etruscans, Egyptians, pre-Incas, and Olmecs to site temples and other monumental buildings on the cardinal compass points.

Yoga: A Natural Science

An AB known to Hindus as Ishwara has been credited with teaching humans yoga (a system for the development of consciousness through various categories of physical and mental practices). According to David Frawley, yoga may have originated in a pre-Vedic, Dravidian Shaivite culture. If true, that could place these stories in a precataclysmic time frame.

Such an early date for the development of yoga suggests it could have been part of a benevolent and supportive transfer of knowledge or training by ABs outside the West Asian colonies. It includes the central principles of natural science and philosophy. Classic yoga teaches self-mastery and self-discipline, with each individual taking responsibility for his/her contribution to society. It promotes social change through evolution, not revolution. It values unity in diversity. This ancient philosophy contrasts favorably with the much more recent Indo-European, AB-oriented culture.

Using Technology versus Mastering It

A perennial dilemma for developed nations today that wish to provide technical assistance programs to lesser-developed peoples is how to ensure that the beneficiaries not only learn how to use a device, but master its internal principles. Given the previously assumed Anunnaki space travel and genetic engineering skills, humans would have been exposed to technology considerably beyond their understanding at the time.

Humans could have observed advanced technology or even learned to use some of it without understanding how to produce it. For instance, some researchers believe ancient humans probably cast the scale models of flying machines found in Egypt, Colombia, and Mexico but apparently did not learn to build or pilot them. Aids to flight still exist on Mount Fuerte in Bolivia and near Nazca, Peru, but they do not prove humans mastered the technology at that time.

Humans may have only observed but not mastered how to manufacture items like the following: A six-ton, wrought iron shaft located in New Delhi with a surface like polished brass that has weathered Indian monsoons for perhaps thousands of years. A crystal skull from Belize, with near perfect detail of a human cranium, created by an unknown technology. Spheroids (one to four inches in diameter) found in South Africa with exteriors made of a nickel-steel alloy, filled with a strange material that disintegrates when exposed to air.[12] Perhaps humans are only finally catching up with Anunnaki technology of 300,000 B.P.

Even if humans did not master AB science in ancient times, it is quite possible that exposure to it planted intellectual seeds in those cultures that bore fruit in later generations. This possibility can help explain why more AB-oriented cultures made greater technological strides than societies not so exposed.

An Ignored Science

For centuries, techniques of divination (accessing energetic and noumenal information through use of the subtle senses) have not been considered to be part of science. However, some may have been integral to the AB portfolio of scientific tools and part of the technical assistance package I have hypothesized was made available to humans. They may have included several techniques for understanding the inner workings of the universe, including dowsing and other modes of sensing energetic and mental force fields. The ABs' use of astrology and numerology was based on a scientific combination of physics (particularly quantum wave functions and sonic vibrations), astronomy, mathematics, and the effects of subtle energies on consciousness and behavior.

These so-called "esoteric sciences" led to greater understanding of the multidimensional, energetic interactions among individuals and between individuals and natural events. For instance, the science of astrology helped people discern the electromagnetic, gravitational, and perhaps subtle energy impacts of heavenly bodies on their biology and emotions.

Numerology as we now attempt to use it appears to have been based on an advanced understanding of the energetic nature of the universe and the role of vibrational frequencies in shaping the physical, behavioral, and emotional manifestations of natural phenomena, including humans. The ancients, whether human or AB or both, appear to have grasped that numbers and letters represent subtle-force vectors that interact to shape all life in the universe. Considerable effort must have been dedicated to understanding the inner meanings of numerical combinations and the influence of letters and words (through subtle and sonic vibrations) on nature. The science provided insights into the role of energetic relationships and timing in the course of human events.

While astrology and numerology are based on competence with advanced physical sciences and mathematics, other forms of divination could have been derived from systematic observation of apparent cause-and-effect relationships in natural events. For that reason

I suspect that approaches to synthesizing the complex of factors converging on a given situation, such as the Chinese I Ching and the Nordic runes, may have sprung from independent human experience. The I Ching offers an intuitive process for ascertaining the influence of, or options for choice within, energetic forces at work in individual and group activities. The runes work in similar ways to access energy fields relevant to specific human choices in decision-making.

Regardless of the specific contributions of ABs or wise ancient humans to these areas, each system or specific technique reflects an advanced understanding of the multi- and interdimensional nature of the universe. They are clearly the products of a sophisticated science or extremely long-term and detailed studies of natural processes incompatible with modern notions of the intelligence and level of development we attribute to our ancestors.

Over the last few millennia we have lost much of the detailed understanding of both the science and techniques of divination and now use partial and distorted versions of them. I believe the primary reason they have been excluded in the development of Western science is the fear that their use would undermine Christian cosmology. A religion that depends on keeping communications with other beings under its control must discredit nonphysical human powers as evil. Thus, anyone who used such techniques (shamans, medicine women, psychics, esoteric scientists) were labeled pagan or heretical and subjected to sanctions.

Rediscoveries of Earlier Science

The evidence for advanced knowledge in prehistory, whether human or AB-originated, undermines the claim made by various developed nations that they deserve credit for this knowledge and the right to be "king of the mountain." Their ancestors were lucky enough to gain access unavailable to others. In this context, the dominance of Indo-Europeans in modern knowledge and technology is not the product of superior intelligence and harder work or the divine grace of their religion's god. The arrogance that now motivates so many citizens of the industrialized world has no basis on which they can claim exclusive rights.

Many important discoveries claimed during the last few centuries are only rediscoveries of forgotten knowledge from the times when ABs provided technical assistance to humans. Although finely specialized and elaborately developed in many areas, current societies are not necessarily the most socially and intellectually mature examples of civilization that humans have created or are potentially able to create. Most areas of the world we call "highly developed" result from the special attention (material and other-dimensional) given to selected survivors of the last global Cataclysm on Earth. For that reason, many explanations for the different levels of development among nations today have nothing to do with who we are, but whether our ancestors lived close to Advanced Beings.

For example, an eminent cosmologist extrapolating future human development bases it on the belief that "for maybe a hundred thousand years, humans held the Earth was in the center of the universe." He considers, along with most academics, that people living before 500 years ago were not even evolved enough to know the Sun was the center of the solar system. When he assumes that earlier humans were too primitive, he concludes the last five centuries of Western science and technology are the inevitable triumph of Judeo-Christian culture. This ignores the ancient existence of such knowledge, and its availability to the Indo-Europeans.

In another example, Copernicus postulated the Sun was the center of our solar system in 1543, but we now know the Anunnaki had named all the planets, placing the Sun at their center, thousands of years before that. Sumerian tablets, 6,000 years old, only repeated that information. The Mayans knew of the planets Neptune and Uranus by at least 3144 B.C.E. and, with the Sumerians, knew their periods of revolution around the Sun. Yet, we claim the planets were discovered in modern times by William Herschel (Uranus in 1781) and Johann Galle (Neptune in 1846). They were simply rediscovered. Should we not give credit where credit is due?

Newton articulated his Law of Motion in the same century that Copernicus set forth his heliocentric view of the solar system, but just as Copernicus was only rediscovering earlier knowledge, Newton, too, was rediscovering the principle recorded in 500 B.C.E. by a Chinese philosopher. In October 1957, a Soviet satellite obtained the first modern precise measures of distances between points of latitude and longitude. But as Maurice Chatelain pointed out in *Our Cosmic Ancestors,* the Sumerians, Semites, Olmecs, and Mayans all had this information and based their ordinary units of measurement on those distances at their respective locations on the planet.

Using the Soviet satellite telemetry, we settled on the circumference of the Earth as 40,075 kilometers. How did the ancient ancestors of modern-day Arabs determine it was 40,083 kilometers? From their AB patrons?

Three nineteenth-century scientists (Proust, Dalton, and Pront) are credited with the atomic theory, but the Greek Atomists (Democritus and Leucippus) described the same basic concepts in 400 B.C.E. Scientists became excited in the past decade about the useful role chaos theory could play in understanding the complexity of large systems. Interestingly enough, the Egyptians more than 5,000 years ago had an even more comprehensive systems theory in what is now known as the Hermetic (Thoth) Principles. Intellectual and moral integrity demand that we recognize our legacy from the past and share it freely with all our contemporaries.

The Benefits Continue

This chapter has suggested that the evidence for selective AB technology transfer to certain human societies disadvantaged the rest of the world. That process may still be going on. Many scientists report that their discoveries or inventions result from inner communications or inspirations from an unknown source. Popular metaphysical sources assert that ABs channel higher knowledge through their chosen human spokespeople.

Some UFO/ET researchers claim recent transfers of technical information have benefited the U.S. military and a few private businesses. One of the most compelling contemporary accounts on this subject is the late retired Lieutenant Colonel Phillip Corso's *The Day After Roswell*. He reports on his alleged participation in U.S. Department of Defense transfers of transistor, microchip, laser, and other technologies derived from crashed UFOs to private U.S. corporations. The resulting financial gain benefited a select few private companies and helped perpetuate their economic and political dominance.

If the science and technologies described in this chapter derive from nonhuman sources, who owns them? Do they comprise the birthright for all humanity? Have some humans taken advantage of knowledge to which they have no exclusive right?

15 Who Were the First Kings and Priests?

One can understand how naïve humans, if faced by an overpowering invading culture, might acquiesce to an already established regime led by an alleged royal or religious ruler, particularly if it is backed up by physical power and perhaps some tangible benefits. One cannot so easily understand how the first instance of such authority, based on an unseen and assumed supernatural figure, could occur in a natural human community. No currently known psychological or learning principles explain why humans earlier in our history would have voluntarily decided they were of such a lower nature that they needed to invent such a system. Could it be that such institutions were imposed on *Homo sapiens* the way the British crown was imposed in colonies in half the world?

The AB-intervention hypothesis offers a plausible explanation for the introduction of divine or royal rulers, without having to resort to convoluted and unprovable sociobiological hypotheses. Encounters with ABs as hypothesized in this book could account for the birth of key Western political and religious institutions and their development over the last 6,000 years. This explanation would account for the early spread of Middle Eastern forms of authoritarian government to southern Europe, western Asia, and northern Africa.

Cultures in Africa, Latin America, Asia and other so-called under-developed areas did not have such deity-based models of governance until exposed to the Indo-European, AB-based model. For instance, in the Swahili tradition, before Arabic invaders set up the divine ruler system on the East Coast of Africa, community leaders did not have to have the notion of divine rights of rulers to carry out functions of governance. Rulers were accepted in such roles because they were perceived to have a high form of inner purity.

In Mayan villages in Guatemala, the position of leader was deemed to be a common obligation for which volunteers served a year and returned to normal life. In areas outside the AB-influenced cultures of West Asia, such as early Greece and the Iroquois Nation of North America, other forms of government evolved where humans were free to work out their own processes of self-governance.

A Modern Analogy

U.S. foreign aid programs designed to help lesser-developed countries include more than just gifts of money and technology. The term "institution building" comes to mind when one thinks of U.S. foreign assistance in Russia, Afghanistan, Iraq, and elsewhere during the last few decades. "American ABs" have attempted to help locals build new political and economic institutions based on the free market and democratic principles the U.S. values.

One can reasonably assume that other-dimensional or extra-terrestrial ABs would use similar approaches if they decided to offer assistance to human survivors of the Cataclysm. They would naturally favor their own models of how a society should be governed, whether as colonists or in an assistance mode. What evidence do we have that such a scenario actually unfolded? We have Sumerian, Egyptian, and Hebrew descriptions of AB systems of governance. A simple review of modern human governments reveals a surprising similarity to AB organizational practices.

The most detailed accounts of AB contributions to human institutions come from the land of Babylon, what we can consider the "command center" of the Anunnaki regime. Examples range from Tell Hamoukar (discovered in Syria in 2000),[1] an agricultural center established or reestablished after the Flood, to later settlements in the Indus Valley. Widely separated geographically, all contain evidence of the same foods, art, simple writing systems, and cultural practices. This chapter focuses on institutions of kingship and priesthood in the Fertile Crescent.

AB Governing Practices

According to a Hittite text (*Kingship in Heaven*), the Anunnaki model for governance of the Earth colony was imported from their home planet Nibiru. On Nibiru, according to the text, a king (Alalush and later Anush) ruled from a throne surrounded by appointed officials, including his trusted cup-bearer. As the king was only one of a circle of offspring of older gods, competition among siblings and half-siblings caused turnover from time to time as a usurper bested the incumbent. According to the *Atras Epic*, conflicts were resolved by means ranging from physical struggles to casting of lots.

The sovereign, on Nibiru or Earth, had the authority to establish cities and appoint the rulers of those cities, and divide resources among groups. Thus, the AB equivalents of "princes" were given thrones in the first Sumerian cities: Eridu, Bad-Tibira, Larak, Sippar, and Shuruppak. They ruled by divine decrees enforced by junior ABs who swore allegiance to their lords. Punishment for disobedience could range from banishment to execution (as explained in the Sumerian text, *The Myth of Zu*).

The Anunnaki dynastic order of succession was so precisely designed that positions in the Great Circle of Twelve (the most senior members of the ruling family) were known by their numerical values. Several Sumerian texts show them ranging from 60 for the supreme ruler (Anu) to 10 and 5 for the most junior male (Ishkur) and female (Ninhursag) respectively. Numbers in between included 55 for Anu's wife (Antu) to 50 and 40 for the male heirs (Enlil and Enki) in order of precedence.[2] (Remember that the legitimate heir was always the first son born of the king by his half-sister.)

This succession system appears to have been widely copied, with minor variations, by some human cultures, even before the Cataclysm. Among the Hawaiians, the throne went first to the child of a king born from intercourse with his sister. If this union did not produce an heir, the next in order was the progeny of the king's mating with his niece, and then with a daughter.[3] The Inca ruler was someone who was born of a brother-sister marriage.[4] The Japanese believed their line of emperors started from a brother-sister mating. Orders of precedence much like those of the Anunnaki caused

European royals, up to the twentieth century, to practice something close to what we would now call incest.

A ruler with special status and mysterious powers would be expected to receive deference from his subjects. Sumerian and biblical accounts provide numerous examples of ABs taking advantage of their mastery of the skies to condition humans to worship them. If we read Exodus 13:20–22 with the AB hypothesis (as set forth in the preface of this book) in mind, that an aircraft exhaust would account for the described "pillar of cloud . . . by day" and "pillar of fire by night," then *YHVH*'s movements in front of the Hebrews exiting Egypt makes sense. The scenes portrayed on Mesopotamian cylinder seals and other artifacts show ABs wearing wings (symbols of flight) and displaying "magical" weapons and apparent communications equipment that would have dazzled primitive humans.

The Mesopotamian texts make it clear that layers of authority—from the gods to demigods, then to anointed humans and appointed officials—were created by the Anunnaki to keep themselves separate from the growing number of humans in the new civilizations.[5] Humans were required to keep their distance, bow their heads when in the presence of the ABs, and kneel as they approached the throne. Like modern dictators, ABs used intermediaries to carry out their orders and demonstrate their authority.[6] Others required humans to speak to them through a screen (as in the Catholic confessional booth). These and other practices exalted the ABs to a super special status among naïve humans.

Acts like bowing, curtsying, kissing the AB's hand or foot, averting their eyes, and using honorific titles (while the individual is simultaneously addressed as a lesser being by the ruler) condition humans to think of themselves as less worthy. A sense of self-deprecation results in the institutionalization of hierarchical castes or classes. Learning to be obsequious also has the undesirable effect of relieving one of a sense of responsibility for what happens in the society. Royalty in human monarchies have utilized all these AB practices to keep their subjects in place. To the extent that democratic nations elevate elected officials to a status of "near royalty," the same psychological conditioning occurs. (Many—including some U.S. presidents—now treat the role of the presidency as having divinely endowed powers.)

How did such a psychological gap between the ruler and his subjects develop? For people to accept such a supernormal status (beyond that of ordinary mortals) for the first kings would have required extraordinary circumstances. Under natural conditions only a society-wide delusion or forced acquiescence could account for this dramatic development in human history. However, observation of the Anunnaki's reportedly awesome technology would have provided convincing evidence that to disobey the AB-king's commands would be foolhardy. Generations of the experience described in the following discussion would reinforce the archetypal energy associated with royalty only now dissipating from the human psyche.

Initially only the direct AB descendants of the ruling Nibiruan family reportedly occupied the thrones of city-states. However, according to Sumerian and Egyptian king lists, about 50,000 years ago, the ABs Enki and his half-sister Ninhursag gave demigods the right to rule in Shuruppak—the medical center they controlled.[7] Apparently Enlil was enraged and tried to limit subsequent AB involvement with humans. However, it started the tradition of kingship by divine right (discussed below), reserved for AB-human hybrids with "blue blood," meaning AB blood. (See Baigent, Leigh, and Lincoln's *Holy Blood, Holy Grail* for further evidence of this hypothesis.)[8]

The Idea of Divine Kingship

No human culture appears to claim the invention of kingship. The Bible and Sumerian king lists record that ten demigods, from Adam to Noah, reigned until the Cataclysm.[9] Then after the Flood (as the Cataclysm of 11,500 B.P. was known in West Asia), kingship by demigods resumed in the city of Kish.[10] According to Sumerian texts, the demigods ruled until 3760 B.C.E., when a meeting of the senior gods took the decision to grant kingship to mankind.[11] At that time, according to both Sumerian and biblical sources, Nimrod was anointed to the throne of Kish by the AB Ninurta.

In Egypt, king lists and the historian Manetho (in an interview with Greek historian Herodotus) indicated the first human king was ceded authority in the Nile Kingdom about 300 years after Nimrod was crowned in Mesopotamia. Ten human kings ruled (during a reportedly chaotic period) until about 3100 B.C.E., when the first pharaoh, Men or Menes, established the capital of Memphis.[12] The position assumed by human rulers had previously been filled by two dynasties of gods and one of demigods for a period of 17,520 years.

The power of a human king to rule derived from a widely held belief in his divine right to do so. This means that his coronation, or the anointment of the first in his line, originated in the act of a god.

The notion that an AB had somehow designated him (seldom her) became the divine right of kings (and queens). European and Japanese royalty successfully defended this right until the middle of the 1900s.[13] Certain African chiefs made similar claims.

In Africa, the Shilluk people of the Upper Nile believe that the first kings were the AB sons of the supreme ruler who flew away from Earth ("went up" and "became like the wind") and occupied the "divine throne."[14] Bushman mythology makes the same point, that the first kings (chiefs) were the sons (Cogaz and Gewi) of Kaang who left Earth to go to their abode at "the top of the sky." Such beliefs appear to be linked to early experiences with the Anunnaki, before the "lowering of kingship to humans" described in Sumerian postcataclysm texts. Most Africans seem to have learned of the idea of "AB-anointed humans kings" through the European and Arab empire-building expeditions made to Africa during the second millennium.

On the other side of the Atlantic, the Incan tradition also mirrors the early Anunnaki demigod model of kingship. Only children of an AB (a light being—a sky or Sun god) could be rulers; their divine origin gave them the divine right. To ensure the preservation of the bloodline, a new ruler, as in the Anunnaki world on planet Nibiru, had to be the son of his father's sister whose marriage had been for the purpose of producing an heir. The new heir would in turn marry his eldest sister to carry on the line. Other children could be produced by the Inca (ruler) in polygamous relationships (like the Anunnaki). Eligible for government, religious, or military roles, these second-class progeny were not deemed eligible for kingship.

In most parts of the world, the human king's claim to a divine, AB basis for authority was generally reinforced by the local priesthood. Claiming to speak for the absent AB, they assured people that the king had indeed been chosen by their god. Some priests asserted that only they could serve as the channel for such a divine anointing. Successive popes maintained the power to anoint new kings in Europe as long as they could (see further discussions which follow).

While ancient humans gained increasing authority, the gods were still obviously in charge. Although humans exercised the rights of kingship in most cities, the Anunnaki apparently kept locations vital to their space facilities in their own hands. For instance, in 3450 B.C.E., Marduk (the son of Enki, one of the original AB colonists) officially designated Babylon the "Gateway to the Gods," and it remained under direct AB control until the ultimate war of the Anunnaki gods in 2024 B.C.E.

Outside the Anunnaki System

If the concept of kingship came from the gods, how did natural humans govern themselves? We can only surmise what might have happened in human societies where we don't have the benefit of thousands of written records. Nineteenth and twentieth century studies of traditional societies by scholars suggest that important decisions were made by consensus or a collective authority. In larger clans, different individuals may have assumed leadership responsibility in certain functions—e.g., hunting, rituals, healing, etc.—but fundamental decisions were made in council. Roles and work assignments apparently evolved without a few assuming a special power over the majority.

Early American peoples reportedly made decisions by a council process. Some used a system of checks and balances, perhaps requiring agreement by various elders before significant decisions could be implemented. For instance, in one Cherokee tribe, warriors could not undertake military action unless both a male and a female elder agreed. The concept of a paramount chief apparently did not develop in most African and American tribes until they had to designate one to meet a representative of the Indo-European king of an invading nation. (An exception is the Ganda people's kingship model, which is similar to the Anunnaki one.)

Even with our limited knowledge of natural human traditions, voluntary tribal or clan acceptance of an absolute, top-down ruler based in an imaginary/divine source of authority seems unlikely. Without physical evidence or a logical extrapolation from primal memories, the kingship institution requires an extraordinary explanation. The AB-instigated scenario described above presents a plausible explanation of such an unnatural development.

Who Were the First Priests?

It is likely that most people observing the elaborate papal costumes and rituals observed at St. Peter's in Rome and similar practices in churches, temples, and synagogues around the world have never wondered about the origins of these rituals. The few who do probably assume they gradually developed over thousands of years from simple beginnings like the ceremonial wearing of animal skins by traditional shamans. Actually, the historical record does not show such an evolution. Most of the priestly accoutrements now used by supernatural religions appear full-blown in the historical AB-civilizations.

The earliest Sumerian and Egyptian representational sculptures and drawings include individuals holding scepters, staves with ankhs, varied crosses or helicoids, cups, and incense burners. Officious-looking figures wear elaborate robes, girded with decorative belts or aprons, conical hats with various flaps and distinctive symbols, and special necklaces. These personages frequently surround an enthroned individual or someone with other symbols of power. In other scenes they appear to be performing ceremonies around a table or altar. Current church officials performing devotions or sacraments would feel at home in those ancient scenes.

If the AB-intervention scenario proposed in this book in any way resembles actual events, the birth of our modern priesthood can most likely be found in the interactions between ABs and the first humans to serve them. As soon as large groups of humans became involved in carrying out various tasks for an AB, some individuals were likely given the role of translating the AB's requests or demands. In all probability the professional priesthood grew from the routine role of transmitting orders from superior beings to naïve workers.

The best documentation of this priestly function comes from west Asian cylinder seals, figurines, and fragments of sculpture, and from paintings of the early Egyptian Pharaonic period four to five millennia ago. These depictions show ruling figures separated from the ordinary workers by a corps of retainers. If the 600 Anunnaki alleged to have descended to Earth spread themselves over a large area, they, like the chiefs of modern bureaucracies, needed such staffs. Whatever their first titles might have been (and we have no definitive record), these intermediaries between the ABs and other humans were the forerunners of the later priesthood. They would have controlled access by ordinary humans to the ABs, interpreted AB policies, and reported how well the human followers behaved. This group of "go-betweens" would have then ultimately become the priesthood (humans exercising power over other humans in the name of a ruler not accessible to ordinary persons).

Priestly Role

One major difference distinguishes the role of priests in a supernatural religion from the spiritual leaders of other traditions. Among a priest's various functions, the most important is to serve as the official interpreter of the views of his god. Although ordinary members may believe they can pray to their god directly, they still depend on the priest (by whatever title) to ratify their interpretations of what they believe to be divine experience. In most religions the priests claim to be divinely chosen for the role, either by family tradition or self-selection (a self-defined "inner calling").

Shamans, medicine men, and spiritual teachers play more of a facilitating role in the natural traditions, not as intermediaries for a divine presence. They share their experience and knowledge received through ecstatic states but stress the need for individuals to gain self-knowledge. While the priest stresses dogma, the natural teacher emphasizes experiential knowledge.[15] "Shamanic knowledge can only be acquired through individual experience. . . . 'learning from the trees' is considered superior to learning from a . . . shaman."[16] This principle remains consistent in the natural perspective across cultures separated by oceans.

The Evolution of Priests

While the role of shamans in natural traditions appears to have remained constant over many millennia, the religious priesthood has probably seen at least three different phases. In the initial phase, speculatively described in preceding passages, the priests would have served at the will of their AB patron. While they carried out duties assigned to them (as the Egyptian priests did) they would have enjoyed the protection and authority given them by the AB-gods.

The second phase, inferred from historical comments on the activities of the AB-god cults (see chapter 20), involved the roles of salesman, recruiter, and cheerleader. These roles were in addition to those of leading rituals and activities designed to motivate cult members and keep them faithful to the memories of the departed gods. They had to promote the idea that the gods were still interested in the affairs of humans and deserved allegiance (at least to their name).

This meant creative marketing of the absentee AB by ascribing linkages between the activities of the cult and either joyful or painful events in the lives of individuals or the cult community. To the extent they could make seemingly plausible claims that what the worshipers did actually had an impact on mundane events, the priests were able to recruit new members. Once members were enrolled in the group, the priests had to keep praising them (or shaming them) and urging further religious practices, including material support of the cult and the priests.

An Example of the Aztec Priesthood

The Aztec priests appear to have been a good example of the second phase of priesthood. They contributed to maintenance of an AB cult in two ways: 1) serving as the channel for appeals to the gods and interpreting natural events as if they were caused by the gods, and 2) educating the people in a manner that perpetuated the religious control systems and kept citizens subservient to the ruling class. The priesthood had a hierarchy of different classes of priests to carry out the different duties.[17] Nominally under the king, but pretending to represent the departed ABs, they were largely free to manipulate the consciousness and behaviors of citizens as they saw fit.

One group took care of the ceremonial and sacrificial duties, using their exclusive access to the altar to claim direct access to the gods. Next to them in power was the group keeping contact with the believers, overseeing penance, vigils, ablutions, fasting, and prayer. Individuals in these roles were required to maintain a high sense of asceticism and self-sacrifice. Others maintained the religious facilities, taking care of the physical needs of all priests. A special group was responsible for education and the formation of new priests as well as training of devotees. In addition to temple beliefs and practices, they taught astronomy, principles of government, history, and writing.

The priests of the third, or supernatural, phase had a much more difficult job. They had to convince potential followers of the merits of believing in and supporting an institution built around a social delusion (see chapter 22). They could use stories, some possibly true and some apocryphal, of ways in which their supernatural but anthropomorphic god might have been involved in extraordinary past events. Because such claims had to be taken on faith, potential followers had to be conditioned to believe that they were lacking some status or right that only the religion could give them. Thus the first job of the priests was to convince people that they were unworthy—fallen from some higher state or unknowingly guilty of a great sin—and could expect eternal punishment if they did not believe in the religion's god.

The supernatural-phase priest's second task was to convince people that in order to avoid the bad consequences (either in this life or the hereafter), conversion to the religion was essential. They used many subterfuges to attract new followers. They incorporated into their programs popular celebrations enjoyed by the people and gave them a religious label to entice participation by nonbelievers. Their recruiting activities and level of public support were greatly enhanced when political and military power began to support conversion campaigns with force. People coerced into entering the religion were subjected to intensive reeducation by priests. Once indoctrinated, they passed the religion to the next generation, which accepted it unquestioningly.

Priests as Guardians of Knowledge

Because of their close relationship with particular ABs, many first-phase priests would have been exposed to AB knowledge unavailable to other humans. This seems to have been particularly true of some Hindu, Magian, and Egyptian priests (see chapter 23). For this reason, many later priests played dual, and frequently incompatible, roles. They knew the truth of the ABs and their level of science but had to suppress it in deference to the supernatural perspective on which their church had evolved. In some instances, this inner conflict led to overt conflicts with the hierarchy (see discussion of "renaissances" and inquisitions). In others, first-phase priests (like the Brahmins) attempted to maintain the early knowledge through exacting oral traditions.

According to Vedic history, the Brahmins (now the priest class) appeared to have been among the few survivors of the Cataclysm in the high Himalayas. Learned beings, they reportedly had advanced knowledge and skills, much reminiscent of the Atlantean culture. They practiced teleportation, sending objects from one place to another at will. Tradition has it that they could control some of the forces of nature, causing rain and parting bodies of water. These feats were accomplished without mechanical technology, through focusing of the mind with meditation and special mantras. The Vedic culture suggests this particular priesthood existed prior to 11,500 B.P. and used rituals similar to those of shamans in Greece, Rome, Egypt, China, and among American Indians.[18]

Conflict between Priests and Kings

History is replete with stories of religious leaders conspiring to overthrow political leaders and vice versa. This conflict involved more than personal competition and jealousy. Their tradition of exclusive access to the ABs gave the priesthood a psychological advantage over humans in administrative or political roles. When humans, whether direct descendants of ABs or not, assumed leadership roles, a natural conflict developed between the priestly and the political assertions of power.

The result was intrigue, including covert assassinations, between leaders of the church and inhabitants of the palace. Prophets, popes, rabbis, and imams asserted they had the right, by divine authority, to anoint or crown political rulers. This finally led a king of England— Henry VIII—to declare in 1534 that Pope Clement VII had no authority over him and that he alone possessed the power to appoint the head of the Anglican Church. The Czars of Russia engaged in the same battle with the Eastern Orthodox priesthood, and Ivan III asserted Czarist authority (saying he was "autocrat by the grace of God") over the Patriarch of the church. By the time Aztecs became the dominant culture in what is now Mexico, the role of king had achieved superiority over that of two equal high priests.

Some Africans believed they had to communicate with deities through a special group of people. For instance, the Masai in East Africa turn to one clan to serve as their equivalent of priests. These medicine men (*iloibonok*) claim hereditary powers back to the beings who descended from the sky. (Note the parallel here to the claim of apostolic succession maintained by most Christian clergy.) Another East African people, the Ganda, maintained a priesthood, including some women, very similar to the priestly family concept in Middle Eastern religions.[19] (Note the similarity to the priestly Hebrew tribe of Levi.) More research on these African and modern religious connections with Sumerian traditions is needed.

Legacy Passed to Humans

The preceding paragraphs summarize the characteristics of Anunnaki top-down, authoritarian governance and suggest how it could have provided the foundation for human royalty and religious leadership. I believe the large degree of similarity between those reported AB systems and later Indo-European institutions suggest a direct linkage and long-term Anunnaki influence on human development. The spiritual and political approaches of such institutions differ greatly from those only recently touched by Indo-European culture.

One may reasonably conclude on the basis of the Sumerian, Egyptian, and biblical texts that kings and priests today follow in the footsteps of the gods. The king lists and accounts of early human rulers suggest that in Sumeria and Egypt humans did more than just imitate the gods. They apparently assumed the mantle of AB kingship, stepping into previously established roles and taking control of existing structures. Directly assuming the AB powers—crowning themselves, living in AB buildings and using royal devices—they obtained the same obedience and loyalty from citizens.

How was it possible to maintain the charade of "divine rule" after the apparent departure of the Anunnaki described in chapters 19 and 20? Linking their political power to the practice of AB worship allowed the new human rulers to psychologically manipulate the naïve humans who did not understand that the real situation had changed. Perpetuation of the AB-colonial model made it possible to satisfy the desire of the elite to control the masses for their own purposes. They used the priesthood and AB-worshiping foot soldiers to carry out their wishes. Because these two groups benefited from the prerogatives of the former AB regime, they served the new pseudo-AB rulers without question.

Independent Societies

Does the absence of correlation between principles of government in traditional cultures and the Anunnaki practices tend to support the notion that the Indo-European model is not a natural product of human development? It is impossible to answer this question on the basis of current evidence, but it remains an intriguing probability. Early cultures that remained independent of the Indo-European mind-set shaped by its self-reported AB colonial rule did not develop an extensive priesthood.

For instance, according to their legends, the Teutonic and Norse peoples believed consciousness pervaded all aspects of nature. They had no need for a specialized class to serve as intermediaries between common folks and the natural powers of the universe. They treated all forms of life, including human souls whose bodies had died, with respect and believed anyone could directly communicate with unseen dimensions. All events could be explained through human interactions with the forces of power in all aspects of nature. Their "temples" were meeting places, treasuries, and storehouses. Likewise, Shintoism in Japan did not develop a priesthood to serve as AB interpreters to humans or as human representatives to the ABs.

In its early stages, Indian society lived by the Vedas (in which all beings and other parts of the universe were seen simply as manifestations of the one creative force, without the necessity of a formal priesthood). After the Aryan invaders imported the Indo-European system of AB worship, the informal groups of different professionals became an official caste system. The priests of Aryan culture appear to have changed the Brahmin role in Hinduism from "learned one" to "arbiter of dogma." Subsequently, they claimed direct lineage from or access to the gods.

Buddha, as would Jesus 500 years after him and Martin Luther many years later, rejected the established priesthood, discarding the Brahmanic caste, theology, and rituals. Pure Buddhism had no room for ABs as stand-ins between humans and the ultimate creative force of the universe. It had no room for gods, priests, prayers, rituals, or temples. Buddha, like Jesus, sought to liberate people from the go-betweens, setting individuals free from the formal dogma fostered by the AB cults and religions. With no sense of dependence on supernatural ABs, one did not need to appease them or pray for their help.

PART VI

Development of Language

Introduction to Part VI

Attempting to make sense of a language map of the world is more challenging than deciphering a galaxy's star map; the languages are more diverse and more confused geographically. The well-known Genesis tale of the Tower of Babel—the gods became angry with humans for trying to ascend to the skies and confused their language and scattered them on the face of the Earth—seems germane to current reality. As with other major developments in human history, many cultures echo this story of AB intervention in the development of human language.

To understand why *Homo sapiens sapiens* languages and cultures have their current variety, we must answer key developmental questions about various points in history. All animals communicate with one or more methods. Why did humans choose speech over hand signals, body language, or telepathy as their favored means of early communication? Was there one natural language? When and why did humans perceive the need to develop visual symbols like pictures and writing to communicate abstract thought? Who invented the alphabet? Why are such divergent language systems in use today?

Chapter 16 provides an overview of human languages, their development, and the record we have of writing systems used in various parts of the world before the introduction of an alphabet. It reviews what cultures say about the role of ABs in the origination of such systems. It also addresses why humans have speech in contrast to the sounds of other primates. Chapter 17 traces the currently available historical record of the introduction and development of the modern alphabet, including the reported contributions of ABs in that process. Some explanations for why a generic alphabet was not universally accepted are offered. It describes the relationship of the alphabet's structure to the possible range of human sounds. Chapter 18 explores the implications of the spread of the alphabetic writing system, with particular emphasis on its impact on human consciousness. It explores the importance of archetypes associated with significant words.

16 Why Do We Have Different Languages?

Each species, from bacteria to humans, has multiple modes of communication among its members and with other species (including not-yet-understood telepathic and energetic senses). Many animals communicate with one another and with other species through vocal sounds. However, humans seem to have more flexible and highly developed skills in this area than other primates. The human capacity to design and speak abstract sounds appears to set them apart from other animals perhaps more than any other attribute.[1] Surprisingly to modern humans, several animal species have shown the ability to adapt and use communications involving human words and other abstract symbols.

If we can teach lesser species our forms of communication, an advanced species should have had no problem teaching humans its language. By now it should be no surprise to the reader that most mythical traditions around the globe point to ABs as the "giver of language." Whether this refers to a DNA code inserted which allows us the capacity to speak or to the introduction of a specific language is not made clear in the various legends.

We have no definitive understanding of how such widely different languages evolved within our single species. The differences not only involve words and grammar, but fundamentally different techniques for making sounds. For instance, Sino-Tibetans use more of a tonal system, while some aboriginals use mechanical-sounding clicks and pops, and Indo-Europeans depend on guttural inflections. Some Asian languages use different pitch levels to give a word different meanings.

Some linguists believe all these variations came from one ancient root language. But so far the search for persuasive evidence of a single language tree with one taproot has eluded us. Other linguists try to make the case for independently arising regional protolanguages that connect several families together, like a proto-Indo-European or a Nostradic that would unite all Indo-European and Sino-Tibetan families. Even proof of this hypothesis remains elusive.

Physical Basis of Speech

Many species have vocal chords in the larynx, but the fossil record does not reveal when and how humans differentiated from other animals and developed the capacity for complex sounds. Only humans have the hyoid bone at the base of the tongue and the muscles necessary for the range of sounds used in spoken languages. Recent discoveries indicate transition humans, including the Neanderthals, possessed the hyoid bone, but it has not yet been found in older fossils.[2] Since the soft hyoid deteriorates easily after death, we can't say for sure our *erectus* ancestors lacked it.

Did the Anunnaki genetic experiments described in chapter 3 involve manipulation of the physical traits required for speech? In August 2002, researchers from the Max Planck Institute for Evolutionary Anthropology in Leipzig, Germany, identified the gene (FOXP2) that gives humans control over muscles of the mouth and throat. They reported that this gene's mutation may have occurred about 200,000 B.P., and that it differs from that of chimpanzees by just two molecules. To cause a two-molecule shift would not have been very difficult for AB genetic engineers.

Even though speculative, the 200,000 B.P. date attributed to the FOXP2 gene's appearance puts it in line with other evidence supporting the thesis of language as a "gift from the gods." This date falls in the range of times associated in earlier chapters with AB interventions, including: 1) the Anunnaki "creation" of *Homo sapiens* from earlier humans, 2) metaphysical reports of the arrival of mankind from other planets, and 3) phylogenetic tree dates attributed to "Adam and Eve."

Language Families

The world has thousands of living languages, and many dead ones. Philologists divide them into scores of "families," believed to share a common ancestor language.[3] Languages in the same family share many common features and many key words, especially older ones that show a common origin. Families logically break into "branches" (like the Latin branch of the Indo-European family). Languages in the same branch are "sister" languages, believed to have diverged within a period of 1,000 to 2,000 years. Languages in different branches of the same family are known as "cousin" languages estimated to have diverged more than 2,000 years ago.[4]

These family, branch, sister, and cousin relationships help us to infer whether cultures with different languages share the same history (substituting local words for the same events) or have had a different history. For instance, although the Egyptian pharaonic civilization preceded the Hellenic by at least two millennia, the gods described by the two societies appear to be the same beings with different names, suggesting a common prehistory. As Indo-European languages, both derive from the same cultural source, in this case, Sumeria. The Egyptian and Hellenic gods (when one does comparative text analyses) largely parallel those described in Sumerian texts, indicating that all three cultures harken back to the same set of historical events. Examples include: Ptah/Hades/Enki, Ammon/Zeus/Enlil, and Isis/Hera/Ishtar.

Proto-Language and Divergences

Without answering the question of whether ABs modified human capacities for speech, language history can be divided into at least three stages: first, the inception of a natural, primal language; second, the possible development of regional languages before 11,500 B.P. (with or without AB input); third, the postcataclysmic language dispersal patterns, which suggest some influence from the AB colonization described in Sumerian and Akkadian texts.

Some traditions say the ancients believed that at one point (perhaps more than 100,000 years ago) all humans spoke one language and were divided linguistically only relatively recently. Etymologists also speculate a "world language" existed about 100,000 B.P. This date, from both ancient traditions and modern scholarship, coincides with that associated with the following significant human developments.

Paleoanthropologists have postulated the appearance of *Homo sapiens sapiens* about 100,000 years ago (in Africa or the Middle East). DNA research points to the appearance of Caucasoids in the Middle East about the same time—Sitchin discovered the same point in history for a new era in AB-human relations (intermarriage and expanded interactions) in the Middle East. The common date suggests the four factors may be connected.

Although we have no direct evidence of the hypothesized world-language's content or structure, some scholars believe that single language first divided 10 to 15 thousand years ago. Linguists arrive at such dates from their calculations of the time it would have taken for languages to evolve to their current level of diversity. Selection by the experts of the 10 to 15 thousand-year time span for the initial language division straddles the well-documented, worldwide Cataclysm of 11,500 B.P. That leaves us with the question of whether divergences in a basic language occurred before the Cataclysm or after.

The Snohomish people in the northwestern United States claim mankind was created by an AB named "Dohkwibuhch" who also gave humans different languages.[5] But these traditional peoples did not share memories of the West Asian AB-colonial era, and we can assume they referred to a precataclysm intervention. This fact could strengthen the possibility that different ABs contributed to fundamentally different approaches to language.

Modern Babble

The following discussion addresses the global diversity of language. Given conventional assumptions of the time needed for languages to evolve and the few thousand years allocated to post-Neolithic civilization, no one has yet developed a persuasive explanation for such complexity. The AB-intervention scenario may offer the most plausible alternative explanation.

Twenty of the most-spoken languages today fall into six distinct families: Indo-European (about three billion speakers), Sino-Tibetan (more than one and a half billion), Altaic (200 million), Afro-Asiatic (almost 200 million), Malayo-Polynesian (150 million), and Dravidian (130 million). Many other languages also fit into these families, and there are thousands of languages in more than a hundred other families. The language spoken by the largest number of people is Mandarin Chinese, but English (with the largest vocabulary) is the most widely spoken on the planet.

The Indo-European language family includes ten branches that, until a few centuries ago, primarily functioned in the Middle East and Central and South Asia—the general domain of the Anunnaki. Currently, this family includes most of the European languages, plus Persian (Farsi) and Sanskrit. One other family seems to have grown from postcataclysmic Anunnaki influence: The Afro-Asiatic family includes, among others, Arabic, Hebrew, Berber, Cushite, Hausa in present-day Nigeria, and extinct Egyptian.

Primal Language

Speculations about the possible language of early humans can't be much more than fanciful musings. Early *Homo* fossils (*erectus, habilis,* and *ergaster*) have been found on several continents (described in chapter 8), but we have no way to link them to any known language. I believe we are on much firmer ground to make plausible inferences about the possible languages of transition humans. Using the 300,000 B.P. threshold as the most likely date for *Homo sapiens* gives us a place to start the "language origins" search.

Three different factors point in the same direction: to someplace in Africa.[6] First, fossil and genetic research supports the idea of Africa as the birthplace of *Homo sapiens.* Second, the Sumerian texts point toward Africa as the site of the first AB genetic intervention in human development. Third, DNA samples show the oldest genotype groups are found among current African populations.

In Africa, my candidate for the most likely current language to have derived from the one spoken by the first *Homo sapiens* is Khoisan. From the mists of time, aboriginals, with their unique Khoisan language involving clicks and pops, have been largely outside the other cultures of Africa. While they are currently focused around the Kalahari Desert in Southwest Africa, there is evidence of their wide ranging habitations over much of the continent in earlier times.[7]

The clicking sound central to the Khoisan language is one of the earliest means of vocal communication available to babies. Within a few weeks of birth, infants master the communication techniques of eye contact and the smile. Within months they can use the tongue to click against the roof of the mouth to make responses to similar adult overtures. That suggests the Khoisan language may be a more natural human creation than ones influenced by ABs.

This language could have developed even among "AB-originals" who started out as Anunnaki workers. In the Sumerian scenario, the first Adamu worked in the mines of Abzu/Africa. Except to understand basic orders, such duties would not have required humans to use AB languages. Outside AB control, workers could have developed an indigenous language. Used by migrating aboriginals, its vocabulary would contain terminology for the early AB interventions in human life. (Aboriginal genetic compatibility with other humans suggests the common gene pool known as "Eve.") That could account for worldwide myths about the AB involvement in human creation.

Precataclysm Languages

Chapter 2 made a case for multiple sources of AB influence in human history, beyond the Sumerian-described Anunnaki role. If Atlantis and other stories of AB rule are correct, we should be able to see some residual effect in the area of human languages as well as culture.

Let's start with the Sumerian story (the best documented). It posits that *Homo sapiens* (transition humans) under AB control remained in or near the Abzu/Africa mining facilities until around 100,000 B.P. Anunnaki at headquarters in E.DIN had decided they, too, wanted workers to do agricultural, administrative, and technical work. The Sumerians recount that the Anunnaki then took some Adamu (possibly second- or third-generation Negroids) to the area of Eden in Mesopotamia.

These humans would have evolved closer to the Anunnaki physically and linguistically. Remember earlier references to widespread AB-human sexual intercourse beginning at this time. Chapter 9 told us geneticists estimate that the Caucasoid race appeared in this period. (This story eerily parallels the creation of mixed breeds from African slaves brought to antebellum America and sexually used by some plantation masters.) Does this suggest the proto-Indo-European language (based in guttural sounds) of 100,000 B.P. posited by linguists was based in the mixing of AB and human communication systems?

Other AB Language Centers

The differences in language structure and use of sound in other regions of the world could indicate either indigenous human development or different AB influences. Several language families differ from the Indo-European family in both respects. The evidence of links to ABs in the Tien Shan area of present-day China (described earlier) suggests the Sino-Tibetan family (with its complex tonal character) could result from another group of ABs.

The other obvious candidate for separate AB origins may be the Indo-Iranian branch of the Indo-European family. It has the oldest living language, Sanskrit, and the *devanagari* script (the name means "from the gods"). Discussions elsewhere in this book suggest a different AB cultural influence affected the development of pre-Aryan philosophy and religion in that region. It is suggested in the next chapter that the origin of the universal alphabet was part of an AB technical assistance program in this part of the world. Subsequent use of the alphabet by modern Indo-European and Afro-Asiatic languages may account for the current language links used by linguists to cobble together the idea of a proto-Indo-European prehistoric language.

Many small language families may be the result of primarily indigenous human developments. They include the Malayo-Polynesian languages (based on very simple grammar) that cover a part of Southeast Asia and the Pacific.[8] North and South America may have had as many as 1,600 languages according to the estimates of some linguists. A controversial theory has divided them into only three families.[9]

A few fundamentally unique languages have been identified: Ainu (in northern Japan), Basque, Vietnamese, and Burushaski (spoken in only one valley in Kashmir). No apparent basis exists to label these as having been involved in any particular period of exposure to an AB colonial culture. Interestingly enough, DNA research[10] suggests these disparate peoples may have shared the same location at some point in time. Were any of them elements of a diaspora from Atlantis, Lemuria, or Mu? DNA studies suggest the Basques arrived in Europe earlier than their Indo-European neighbors—15,000 B.P. (a date associated by author Shirley Andrews with Atlantean migration).[11]

Postcataclysm

Although having experienced a very traumatic period, most survivors of the 11,500 B.P. Cataclysm should have retained their language skills. The reviving population centers of Central Asia, China, South India, the Andean region, and Central America seemed to have retained and evolved their respective languages. Isolated tribes on islands and insular shorelines and in parts of North America, Africa, and Asia would have kept their respective languages alive. In both cases, the languages would have naturally evolved depending on the ratio of isolation to migration and intermingling with different cultures.

Protected by mountains from roaming bands of survivors and by a favorable climate, the proto-Chinese culture was apparently left on its own to resuscitate agriculture and animal husbandry shortly after the Cataclysm's effects waned. It maintained what was probably the precataclysm Mandarin-language homogeneity without outside interference for millennia. Its single language eventually split eight ways as it speakers moved into adjacent areas in southeast Asia.

Africa in Stages

With one quarter of the world's languages spoken in Africa, the continent provides an interesting context for the study of stages of AB influence on languages before and after 11,500 B.P. Apart from the aboriginal language discussed earlier, Africans claim primal AB contributions to their languages. If these legends are true, one should be able to reasonably infer early-AB input in African languages in contrast to the postcataclysm period when no evidence for direct AB influence has surfaced.

Brothers and sisters of the Adamu who were not shipped off to E.DIN and were living outside the Nibiruan mines would have continued independent development of human society and languages. They would have evolved physically and linguistically over the millennia. The existence of the Niger-Congo language family (including Bantu, Yoruba, Zulu, Ewe, and Wolof) may be evidence of this scenario. The roots of the word Bantu itself are interesting: "ntu" means man and "Ba" means plural. It may be more than coincidence that "ntu" seems related to Ninti, a name for the Anunnaki female who allegedly helped create Adamu in Africa. These people retained some of the basic cultural aspects of the Anunnaki culture (including the concept of ruling family lines of succession described in chapter 15) but were apparently free from direct rule by postcataclysm ABs.

However, this freedom meant loss of the benefits of AB technology transfer and the gifts of advanced knowledge made available to humans clustered between the Eastern Mediterranean and the Persian Gulf. Even today these African societies have not been able to catch up with the AB legacy enjoyed by the Caucasoid and Mongoloid races.

Why Do We Have Different Languages?

The postcataclysm stage of AB input into their languages probably came indirectly via Arabian colonists. These Arabs, with their Indo-European culture, appear to have reintroduced the Anunnaki legacy to East Africa long after the ABs had departed Earth. For instance, the Swahili language could be the result of mixing the pre-11,500 B.P. Bantu language with tongues of the Arabian peninsula's Afro-Asiatic-speaking people as they invaded Africa in the post-Flood era. Thus, in Africa we may be seeing three stages of language development: the indigenous primal languages, followed by languages shaped at least to some extent by early AB contributions, which in turn incorporated the late postcataclysm AB linguistic and cultural influences from West Asia.

The West Asian Case

This book postulates that the only area of postcataclysm, direct AB involvement in human development was in West Asia, the cradle of the Indo-European culture and languages. That region produced only two of the current 100-plus language families: Indo-European and Afro-Asiatic. That these two families have their roots within the region of Anunnaki hegemony supports the notion of a singular proto-language associated with the AB colony from Nibiru. History reveals that these two language families undergirded the dispersion of Sumerian/Anunnaki culture around the world.

The Afro-Asiatic family, considered to have derived from the proto-Indo-European group of languages, is now dominant in the northern half of Africa. It includes, among others, Amharic, Cushite, Berber, and Hausa. I suspect that the presence of the Afro-Asiatic family in Africa signals AB cultural influence moving back into Africa from the Middle East, not originating there. This would be consistent with the 100,000 B.P. transfer of Africans to E.DIN and the return of subjects from the AB colonies within recent millennia.[12]

Tower of Babel

Why would the Indo-European and Afro-Asiatic families split into so many branches in a small area with a concentrated population in such a short period of time? The circumstances surrounding the Tower of Babel story suggests an AB-based explanation. The word "Babel" has at least two possible origins. The Hebrew root "*balal*" means "to confound or mix." In Akkadian, "*bab-ilu*" means "gate of the gods." Both usages point to the same event.

Genesis 11 describes the tale familiar to Jews, Christians, and Muslims alike. In it, humans decided to build a tower to reach the heavens. The gods reacted, saying in effect that if they let humans do this they would expect to do anything they set their minds to. To prevent that sense of empowerment and independence, the gods descended on the project, confused the local language, and scattered the group responsible for such uppity behavior. Many people consider this story a biblical metaphor designed to teach humans that they should not be at cross purposes with their god's religion. However, it appears to be more historical than metaphorical.

An older version of the tale apparently about the same event has one AB involved, with human supporters, in a power play that offended the other gods. An Akkadian version of an earlier Sumerian text and a Babylonian source describe AB Marduk's desire to exercise Sumerian kingship in Babylon. His palace was to be a towering ziggurat (a huge structure of seven levels) that gave him ascendance over other gods. Its name was E.SAG.ILA, meaning something like "the house whose head reaches highest."[13]

But other gods had different plans. They wanted to transfer kingship to Erech and Ur from Kish and let Babylon fall in disfavor. They axed Marduk's plans and broke up his community of supporters. Thus, the humans who had been recruited by Marduk to build his tower were pawns caught up in the power struggles of squabbling ABs.

Sumerian texts suggest that on two occasions ABs may have undermined human unity by forcing the adoption of different languages. But each Babel occasion actually arose as a result of conflicts among the gods. Sitchin believes one intervention (about 3450 B.C.E.) was to foil Marduk's attempt, using human labor, to achieve his own agenda described above.[14] Another language-confusion event (about 2850 B.C.E.), he believes, reflected AB Ishtar and Enmerkar disputes over who would control kingdoms in Mesopotamia and the Indus Valley.[15] If these interpretations are correct, then disputes among ABs (not humans) had significant language consequences for their human subjects.

Recent human history offers an unnerving parallel of dividing and controlling by the imposition of different languages. European colonists forced indigenous peoples to adopt French, English, Spanish, German, Dutch, or Portuguese in Africa, Asia, and Latin America. Given the effectiveness of their manipulation in a period of a few generations, imagine what the Anunnaki could have done in a few hundred years.

Linguists believe it takes about a thousand years for a new language to evolve, based on the assumption of a natural process without external imposition of pre-developed languages. Thus, something similar to Babel-like events is required to account for the rapid pace of numerous language splits in the Middle East during a relatively brief period. Humans under the hegemony of a god and needing to master his or her language to be able to enjoy AB "protection" would have considerable inducement to learn a new language quickly. As in modern human colonies, speaking the ruler's language may have been a matter of survival.

Implications

This chapter demonstrates that languages and writing systems are inextricably woven into the evidence for AB intervention in human history. In cultures where historical and metaphysical materials point to significant AB involvement in human affairs, we discover earlier, more highly developed languages and writing systems. Likewise, where we find more advanced human cultures we find more references to the role of ABs. The two phenomena seem to go hand in hand.

The record is clear that cultural and linguistic imperialism spread from the alleged centers of AB presence on Earth.[16] Historical events like the diaspora from Eden and the post-Flood repopulation of a wide region by Noah's descendants exemplify an early sense of "manifest destiny" by a superpower culture. With further research I believe we can trace this historic process of globalization. The following examples illustrate the kinds of research that would help test the AB-intervention hypothesis.

Combining DNA analyses and language maps, we find that for all Indo-European language speakers in Europe, about 85 percent of their genetic stock has been in place for 50,000 years.[17] This phenomenon could correspond to the diaspora from Eden. It suggests that Anunnaki influence from the heart of its Earth colony in Mesopotamia had already extended to Europe well before the Cataclysm. The AB colonial philosophy would have shaped European language, measures, and commerce.

But not everyone in Europe arrived from the Middle East. For instance, the Basque, Hungarian, Finnish, and Estonian peoples and languages do not fit in the Indo-European family. Neither do other peoples (possibly including the Celts, Berbers, Etruscans, and some Nordics) who may have migrated to coastal areas during the disintegration of Atlantis described in chapter 3.

When one does this sort of comparison over those of religious, political, and other institutions, a general correlation with the AB story appears. The correlation of language development with reported AB activities is further strengthened when one maps the spread of specific areas of advanced knowledge such as astronomy and mathematics. While such correspondences do not prove or disprove the AB-intervention hypothesis, the evidence reviewed to this point tends to support it.

17 Who Introduced the Alphabet?

A spoken language can be used and orally transmitted from generation to generation without a written form. Many such languages have existed for millennia without a written version, but most have disappeared from human memory. However, the advent of writing made it possible to more effectively propagate and preserve the communications of a culture. It is very difficult to imagine what our history would have been without it. Unfortunately, evidence of the earliest writing systems is almost as elusive as the history of speech. The stories of how the various peoples came to have writing attribute it to a god or Advanced Being.[1] Following are a few samples of these stories.

A Sumerian scribe recorded on a clay tablet that he had been taught to write by the "god of the scribes." Egyptian writing was attributed to the god Thoth, who allegedly provided nearly all advanced knowledge to humans. Nebo, the son of the god Marduk (an Anunnaki AB), reportedly gave the Babylonians writing.[2] On stone tablets, Moses received a script from *YHVH* (an invisible AB).

The Greeks trace their writing to the god Hermes (who was the Greek version of the Egyptian AB Thoth). The Phoenicians ascribe theirs to the god Taut (again another form of Thoth). Chinese historians attributed their ideographic system to divine origins. The Vedics gave credit to AB Sarasvati for their writing. As mentioned earlier, *devanagari*, the name of the Hindu script used in Sanskrit, means "from the gods." Tellingly, the word Sanskrit itself means "polished or perfected," suggesting an already established system.

Evidence of Antediluvian Writing

Samples of sophisticated precataclysmic writing systems have not yet been discovered—presumably they were all destroyed or possibly because we have assumed that they don't exist. Only some primitive systems of hash marks and simple runes have been "officially" dated to more than 12,000 B.P. It is possible that some writing we now consider postcataclysmic may have existed more than 12,000 years ago.

In fact, historical claims of the existence of antediluvian writing have survived in various cultures. Druids said writing (attributed to Pridian) and books (written by Pheryllt) existed before the Flood. Hindus say the god Vishnu became a fish and retrieved their "holy books" from the bottom of the ocean, taken there by the demon Haya-Griva before the Cataclysm. Chinese and Spanish legends report writings before the destruction of an earlier race. Hebrews assert that genealogical records from Adam to Noah were recorded prior to the Deluge. Phoenicians and Egyptians claimed their writing came before the Cataclysm. Egyptians claimed AB Anubis wrote "annals" before the Flood.

A Sumerian tablet found in Nineveh records King Ashurbanipal saying he was "initiated into the secrets of writing . . . by the god of scribes . . . and that he could read Sumerian (and) . . . understand the stone carvings of the days before the flood." The phrase "stone carvings" may suggest it was not the cuneiform system used in the Nineveh clay tablets.

Egyptian and Sumerian king lists clearly cover antediluvian rulers. They included gods and demigods (the human kings and pharaohs came much later). Retaining such chronologies for thousands of years on both sides of the Cataclysm would have required permanent records in some durable form and a safe location.

Analphabetic Writing

Before humans knew of an alphabet, various graphic systems were used to keep records, preserve descriptions of events, and symbolize spoken language. In widely separated cultures in the Near East and Eastern Mediterranean areas, in China and elsewhere, various versions of pictographs, ideographs, and symbolic scripts appeared. The characters in these systems represented a particular thing, action, or abstract idea.

Pictograms visually represented objects or concepts and were most useful to keep records of specific items or events. The Aztecs' highly pictographic script reportedly came from their ancestors, created by an AB known as Zanna.[3] The Toltecs credit AB Quetzalcoatl with the origination of their writing. The Mayan writing system appears full-blown in the archaeological record (as does Mayan knowledge of astronomy and mathematics). Combining elements of pictographs, ideographs, and syllabic characters, some believe the Mayan system to be alphabetic and related to the Indo-European alphabets.

A combination of pictograph and symbolic writing occurred around 4,000 years ago on the island of Crete and in places on the Greek mainland. Early versions employed Egyptian-like hieroglyphs. A later system of 88 signs was deciphered in 1952 by British scholars. It revealed an early form of the Greek language and documented economic matters such as land ownership, cattle, and slaves. References to ABs appeared with frequency in this era of god-cults.[4]

The most widely known of these earlier systems currently in use is the ideograph system used for the Chinese, Japanese, and Korean languages. A few Chinese characters have been found that analysts now date to about 6600 B.C.E.,[5] but officially accepted evidence of formal use does not appear in the record until after 4000 B.C.E. In either case, they are older than the alphabet.

The Chinese-based ideograph system uses a character (each with its own unique pronunciation) limited to one concept, like a whole word in English. So, it requires almost as many characters as a language has words. In contrast, English and most other languages now use an alphabet where each letter stands for a single sound. The alphabet provides for much greater flexibility as the letters can be infinitely recombined into complex words.

Fragments of pottery and other objects found in the ruins of Harappa (in the Indus Valley) have an unknown script dated by carbon-14 to 3300 B.C.E. It may have been one of the first widely used postcataclysmic systems designed for administrative operations and simple record-keeping purposes. The two most generally known were the Mesopotamian cuneiform and the Egyptian hieroglyphic systems.

These last two were explicitly described as AB-inspired systems, which suggests the contemporaneous Indus Valley script was, too.

Both cuneiform and hieroglyphs evolved from the pictographic systems. They evolved from clearly representational characters to more abstract symbols. They were almost syllabic, in the sense that symbols could be combined to create a new word with its own meaning. With improved human skills and writing equipment (pens, clay, wedges, paints, etc.), proficient scribes using cuneiform or hieroglyphs could convey almost any information or concept they desired.

The most widely preserved archives of such systems contain Sumerian or Akkadian cuneiform covering hundreds of thousands of clay tablets and date between 3200 B.C.E. and 75 C.E. In this system, one symbol (e.g., a wedged cone) represented a small word (e.g., NI), root, or suffix/prefix. Each of these symbols could be combined with others to form a more complex word. This Sumerian system's shortcoming was its cumbersome nature, requiring as many as 600 common characters and 2,000 unusual characters.

The cuneiform system—with more than 100,000 excavated tablets still untranslated and many more buried in the sands of Iraq—recorded the well-known *Epic of Gilgamesh*, Hammurabi's legal code, business records, medical prescriptions, and historical texts. These historical texts have provided us with convincing details of what can only be interpreted at least as a form of Anunnaki hegemony over, and perhaps a colonization of, the Middle East. The volume of details about specific humans and ABs and concrete events susceptible to verification makes a strong case for one group of flesh-and-blood ABs that had a lasting impact on human history.

The Egyptian hieroglyphics comprise the second-most pervasive ancient writing system. It, too, preserved for posterity records not only of concrete items and events, but of the nuances of religion and personal emotions. The wealth of information that survived in tombs and ruins up and down the Nile River portrays a highly developed intellectual and emotional culture. The records reveal that the structure of consciousness of the ancient Egyptians would not appear to be beyond the comprehension of modern tourists who visit their land.

The Alphabet Appears

All the fields of advanced knowledge described in part 5, from astronomy and mathematics to codes of justice and medical practice, were documented in cuneiform, hieroglyphic, and other scripts. This happened during the reputed AB colonial era in the Middle East described in the Sumerian and Egyptian texts themselves. However, a quantum leap in both the fragmentation of human consciousness and the ability to manipulate its symbols occurred near the end of that era. Widespread sharing of both actual human experience and human wishful thinking were facilitated by the unprecedented "introduction" of the alphabet into Indo-European culture.

The word "introduction" seems appropriate. The alphabet did not naturally evolve from the Mesopotamian cuneiform and Egyptian hieroglyphic systems which overlapped with the alphabetic system for more than 1,500 years. We do not know exactly when and where the introduction occurred, but the current "universal alphabet" appeared full-blown in human records between 3,000 and 4,000 years ago. The term "universal alphabet" applies because all ancient and modern alphabets derive from the exact same concept and structure discussed below.

Sanskrit, the oldest known and most complete version of the alphabet, may have appeared in South Asia as early as 4,000 years ago. It contained almost twice as many letters (16 vowels and 34 consonants) as any subsequent versions. The 50 precise symbols found in Sanskrit represented a range of mutually exclusive sounds. Each letter indicated one specific sound that can be made through the human mouth, using air from the lungs against parts of the voice box from the throat to the lips.

About 300 years later, a less sophisticated version (22 letters of consonants only) appeared in Phoenicia (peopled by proto-Canaanites who lived in the coastal areas of what is now Lebanon, Syria, and Israel/Palestine). The earliest Phoenician version had 18 letters from the Sanskrit system that can be found in all the more recent major alphabets. The Phoenician model has been associated with two Canaanite towns. One, Qiryat Sepher, means "city of the letter," and the other, Byblos, means "book town."[6] Byblos has been associated with Osiris (one of the AB gods who may have favored technology transfer for humans).

The process of the alphabet's transmission from India to Phoenicia remains a mystery. Some believe the Hyksos people may have known of the original alphabet at least a century prior to the Phoenicians.[7] A proto-Semitic group whose history has them ranging from beyond Mesopotamia to Egypt and the Aegean Sea, the Hyksos were positioned to serve as a cultural conduit from India to the Middle East, and vice versa.[8] If the *devanagari* alphabet predated all the others, the Hyksos could have been the connecting link between East and West.

This possibility is reinforced by the close resemblance (shape of the letters) of the Phoenician (Canaanite) alphabet script to the Sanskrit one. A few words also illustrate the links between Sanskrit and Western languages. "Angel" is *Angelos* in Greek and *Angiras* in Sanskrit. "Eucharist" is *eu-kharistos* in Greek and *su-haritas* in Sanskrit. The Celtic word for "priest" is *druid* and the Sanskrit word is *dru-vid* (meaning "knower of the word").[9]

During the period from 1500 to 500 B.C.E., several adaptations of the "universal alphabet" can be documented in the Middle East. In addition to the above-mentioned Phoenician, Hebrew and Aramaic versions were also developed for those languages. Sinaitic, Byblian, and Canaanite attempts at working models of the Middle Eastern alphabet have been discovered. But, like pharaohs who later tried to emulate AB-constructed pyramids, most such efforts resulted in feeble copies. Egyptians late in their pharaonic culture may have tried to adapt hieroglyphics to the alphabet. Their Meroitic characters (less pictorial) became almost alphabetic.

Both the Hebrews and the Greeks adopted the Phoenician model using the same number of letters in the same order. The Hebrews named each letter; each name was encoded with several meanings (see discussion of Kabbala). The Greeks modified the Hebrew names and added vowel endings to their letters. They claim to have received the original version from Kadmus (meaning "ancient one") and used it unchanged for centuries. The poet Simonides of Ceos was credited with increasing the number of Greek letters to 26 prior to 400 B.C.E.

Linguists have several theories of which alphabet came first and which one derived from the other. Debate swirls around Phoenician and its morphing into a northern Semitic version and a southern Semitic one. Did the Ethiopian version come from the Semitic north or south? Which was the progenitor of versions in Aramaic, Hebrew, and Greek? How did the later Arabic and Cyrillic (used in Russia) versions evolve? Was the Greek alphabet responsible for the Latin used in the Etruscan and Roman cultures? Was the Phoenician really a derivation of the Sanskrit? Did it come from Atlantis?

Whether it came from the East or West, or regardless which came first, the alphabet bore no relationship to indigenous writing systems.

Like the gap between Sanskrit and the Indus Valley script (a mixture of pictographs and ideographs still undeciphered from the 6,000-year-old cities Harappa and Mohenjo-daro), the chasm between cuneiform and hieroglyphics and the alphabet is unbridgeable. Such a virgin birth of the alphabet requires an extraordinary explanation. Could it have been the same gods who accounted for biblical claims of "virgin birth" when no human father could be identified? Tantalizingly, all the cultures involved in the early development of the "universal alphabet" have a history of Anunnaki patronage just prior to its appearance. Is there a link?

Genius of the Alphabet

The origin of the alphabet remains among the greatest unsolved mysteries of human history. Who could have possessed the scientific knowledge to understand that the 50 precise symbols found in the Sanskrit could represent a range of mutually exclusive sounds made by the human voice box? They had to have analyzed the human body's speaking capacity and fully understood how it could be consciously manipulated. Who had the imagination to recognize that those sounds could be joined in various arrangements to create spoken words that could communicate the inner and outer reality of all aspects of human experience? Let's consider the alphabet's underlying principles.

In the Sanskrit alphabet, each letter represents one specific sound that could be made through the human mouth. Vowels were the "open" sounds, and the consonants were the "closed" sounds. The former could be used alone, but the latter always had to be combined with a vowel. For instance, "A" could be independent, but "J" had to be combined with "E" (or another vowel) to be pronounced. In most current versions of the alphabet, separate letters do not exist for each possible vowel. Some, especially the Hebrew and Arabic, combine vowels with particular markings to indicate whether they are long or short, or how they should relate to the consonants in the context of a given word.

In addition to the abstract word, all humans understand the power of the spoken word. Its sonic energy can be harnessed to motivate, to heal, to manifest phenomena within, and to manipulate the physical and energetic worlds. Claims have been made for both the original Sanskrit and Hebrew alphabets that they represent the primal (and creative) sounds of the universe. Both are considered to be gifts from the gods who understood that vibration and sound comprise the fundamental energy of the universe. Acts of creation in the physical universe, in this view, come through the manipulation of sounds or words. Thus, the Bible says "in the beginning was Logos [Word]," whence all else came into physical form. In his theory of the universe, Plato used "idea" instead of "word" for the hidden force that gives form to objective reality.[10]

Jewish Kabbalists and Hindu esoterics believe letters and words created from their alphabets have several levels of meaning. Vedic scholars believe the original words in Sanskrit had four levels of meaning. First was the physical spoken word. The second was its inner meaning. The third was its vibrational force that was transmitted telepathically through prana (a subtle energy that permeates space). The final was its transcendental significance.[11] Scientist and mystic Itzhak Bentov described the Sanskrit letters as shapes "that impart certain tendencies to consciousness, making it vibratory."[12]

The Hebrew letter was considered to have at least three levels of meaning. The first level dealt with the inner structure of reality, of the universe itself. The second involved nature, the physical level of reality. The third was for individual understanding and social communication.[13]

From the perspective of these esoteric schools, if a written word evokes the appropriate sound frequencies, its subtle energy or emotional meaning is conveyed along with the mental concept. They believe that if a spoken word comprises the root sounds that energetically correspond to its referent, it will more accurately communicate with the receiver. Kabbalists and others worry that modern language usage has been artificially severed from its energetic roots. (For instance, English speakers no longer employ the full range of nuanced pronunciations. Thereby, we lose some of the emotive power of the words.)

If they are correct, the result is a confusion of sounds and energies that creates serious gaps in transferring knowledge and maintaining successful communications, even among people who speak the same language. With the arbitrary introduction of artificial new words, we may add to the already socially destructive "Tower of Babel" phenomenon caused by many different tongues.

Other traditional cultures had similar views about the power of language. Priests and shamans used primal sounds, producing an appropriate word to cause manifestation or action in the physical realm. In Western religions, incantations and chants are examples of this belief, as are mantras in Hinduism and Buddhism. The ancients believed names have power to affect the material realm and the actions of all organisms, including humans. That is why so much emphasis was traditionally placed on selecting the name for a baby—or a new initiate: Master teachers in the Eastern tradition (and in Christian monastic orders) seek to intuitively discern the right name for their students.

On a more mundane level, modern singers can shatter glass with the appropriate note, in the manner that particular sounds brought down the walls of Jericho in a familiar bit of Bible history. The process works very much like a suspension bridge in Colorado that vibrated so much at certain wind speeds that it had to be taken down. Tibetans have been reported to lift stones through the use of certain combinations of sound frequencies. Perhaps the Arab word "Abracadabra" pronounced correctly really did cause something to open.

If the above views have any validity, the inventors of the alphabet did not merely create an arbitrary set of symbols to go with just any spoken sound. They meant it to be used to create written, and thus pronounced, words that accurately communicated and purposefully affected ordinary reality. To fulfill this purpose, it stands to reason that the successful use of words and sentences requires that the alphabet and languages have an inherent order. Perhaps this is why nouns have verbs that connect them to a predicate in a sentence to infuse the situation with the subtle energy of the speaker's intention.

As physicists rediscover the creative power of focused intent (for healing, psychokinesis, manifestation, etc.), multidisciplinary linguists can help sharpen our understanding of the "power of the word." Perhaps we can learn to use only words whose frequencies resonate with the energies of the desired effect. For instance, we cannot talk peace into existence using the words of war. Neither can we elicit love from another using the terms of threat.

Devolution of the Alphabet

Its more precise and nuanced structure makes it very likely that the *devanagari* Sanskrit was the pattern from which devolved the other alphabets. As already mentioned, it contains almost twice as many letters as any other and captures the full range of sounds that can be made without stress on the voice box. History suggests that cultural inventions that redirect human history start with a peak of clarity and refinement that subsequently becomes distorted by their transmission through various cultural filters. Comparisons of Sanskrit to Hebrew and of Hebrew to English illustrate their progressively diminishing representation of the full energetic potential of the voice, and thereby, the deeper levels of human communication.

An ancient Anglo-Saxon runic alphabet contains more of the Sanskrit's longer vowel sounds than the more modern alphabets. Does this suggest that early Indo-Europeans retained some of the original alphabet, with its perceptual and expressive depth, that was lost under the influence of Greco-Roman culture?

Is it possible the Western progression toward what we consider a more highly "civilized" language actually resulted in the loss of some of the older, more nuanced sounds? For instance, Greek and Latin lost some of the aspirated (accompanied by a release of breath) sounds found in the earlier Hebrew. And the original Hebrew had already lost many of the Sanskrit sounds. English has become even less nuanced in sounds as the vocabulary has expanded. This may mean that the cultures now dominated by Indo-European supernaturalism speak less of the "language of the gods" than in ages past.

Using the Alphabet

The association of each letter in an alphabet with its exclusive sound provides the most flexible of all speech-related writing systems in human history. By its nature, the alphabet is phonetic. Its correct usage depends on correct pronunciation. Debates about the current use of phonics in teaching someone to read should take this into account. All of the sounds in the 50-letter Sanskrit alphabet can be pronounced naturally if the student learns how to use the voice box, along with the breath, tongue, teeth, and lips. When the student learns how to make the sounds, only two more steps are required for accurate reading and speaking. Students must only learn to arbitrarily relate each symbol (letter) to its sound. These sounds will occur naturally in normal speech if the student has been exposed to the pronunciation of words that accurately reflects their written form. Then the student just needs to memorize the meanings of written words (through oral explanations or the dictionary).

Sound-based alphabets are now used throughout the world in various forms, with the notable exceptions of China, Japan, and a few other cultures that still use ideographs. An ideographic system means a person must learn thousands of characters to read a newspaper and several hundred thousand to read a scholarly text. Compare that to the intellectual flexibility made possible with the rearrangement of simple letters in an alphabet for the creation of new words. Even spoken Chinese, Japanese, and Korean (as distinct from the written ideographs) can now be phonetically converted into alphabetic words. Based on an understanding of the particular alphabet used, a person can reproduce the sound without knowing what it means in the Chinese or Japanese culture. (One must know each sound's connotation to actually converse in the language.)

We can now create words to represent iconography (picture writing) from cave walls or petroglyphs dating 30,000 B.P. or earlier. Words can replace mnemonic devices like knotted cords (in Peru and parts of Asia, for example) or notched sticks (in Australia and all other continents). With an alphabet, crude symbols standing for physical objects and ideographs representing ideas instead of things can be translated into English, or any other alphabet-based language. (A Cherokee in North Carolina named Sequoia did just that in the nineteenth century for his native spoken, but unwritten, language.)

The universal alphabet has the potential to facilitate the adoption of a universal language. (Just the opposite of what happened in Babel.) However, for its full impact on consciousness (a combination of emotions with ideas) to be realized, we would probably need to go back and recapture all the nuances of universal sounds provided for in the Sanskrit. A pell-mell rush to make standard English the world norm may result in more of a "dumbing-down" of global consciousness than having no universal language at all.

Implications

The alphabet is a key piece of the "jigsaw puzzle" being assembled to identify the role of ABs in human development. The timing and places of its introduction and development coincide with the regions and cultures that have documented most extensively the presence of ABs in their history. Its use in translation of the AB-based culture's religion and history helped its diffusion in the diaspora of humans from the core of the Anunnaki civilization in the Fertile Crescent.

The dispersion of Caucasoids from West Asia 50,000 years before the Cataclysm put in place the ancestors of 85 percent of modern

Europeans. If they carried with them the archetypes of an Anunnaki-focused culture, they would have been predisposed to the social developments of the post-Flood AB culture. The remaining 15 percent of European ancestors who arrived from the Middle East after 10,000 years ago carried with them more than agricultural crops and practices.

Taking advantage of common cultural roots established in the pre-Flood era, their migration routes served as the first "information highways" for god-cults and supernatural religion via the revolutionary technology of the alphabet. This dispersal pattern would have been similar to the way modern English-language trade routes have transmitted the modern version of that same dominating culture to the world.

Possible Agenda behind the Alphabet

Even if ABs introduced the alphabet, at this point we can only infer their motivations. Was it to facilitate the teaching or introduction of a new spoken language? Was it to make humans better prepared professionally to serve in an AB priesthood (as the Brahmin in India)? Or was it simply a gift to provide humans with another tool for intellectual and social development?

Such a gift would have enhanced the access of humans to all advanced knowledge. It could have been the result of the generosity of a benevolent AB-god (perhaps known variously as the Serpent, Thoth, or Hermes) who wanted to empower humans. Whatever the motivation, its acquisition helped humans transcend limitations of local languages and writing, and it may eventually help us escape the still-heavy legacy of the Anunnaki culture.

Of course, independent and aboriginal societies outside the AB hegemony were disadvantaged by the absence of the alphabet in their cultures. Much later, when they were exposed to alphabets, they learned to phonetically convert their spoken or more cumbersome writing systems to letter combinations. Unfortunately, by then, the first beneficiaries of the alphabet had already about taken over the world.

The identity of the benefactor remains hidden. In India, the likely point of any AB transfer of the alphabet, the AB Sarasvati has been credited with providing the Vedic peoples much knowledge, but no mention was made of the alphabet. This suggests to me that the source may not have been one of the well-known AB rulers in the universal pantheon of gods. If *YHVH* was not involved in the introduction of the alphabet to the Hebrews, he appears to have taken advantage of it to shape the written history of the Semitic and Caucasian people. The Hindu Vedic hymns (Rig Vedas) were preserved in the same universal alphabet as the Jewish Pentateuch, replete with stories of AB exploits and their interactions with humans. Thus, the source of the alphabet (literally a "Deep Throat"[14]) ensured that humans would have an accessible record of the reality of their involvement with ABs.

I speculate that our benefactor was one of those beings more advanced than we, who wanted humans to know the truth and, knowing the truth, set themselves free of the limiting legacy of the Anunnaki era. It may have been one god's way of clearing the karma (or absolving himself of guilt) for his species' violation of the "Prime Directive" (the principle of noninterference in the integrity of other beings made popular in the *Star Trek* television franchise). By giving humans the tool that would help them escape the punishment of Babel, he or she may have made restitution for generations of servitude.

18 Does Language Shape Consciousness?

Which came first, mental concepts or words to describe them? The answer to this conundrum is as impossible to solve as that involving the chicken or the egg. We simply don't know what happened during that seminal interplay between the first humans' evolving consciousness and their first words. Helen Keller, blind and deaf from 18 months of age, wrote, "She brought me my hat, and I knew I was going out into the warm sunshine. This thought, if a wordless sensation can be called a thought, made me hop and skip with pleasure."[1] Keller then learned that everything had a name and that each name gave birth to a new thought. But what was it like for the first human before someone gave something a name to be learned by another?

We cannot recapture the species' first moments of knowing that it knows. The best we can do today is to sometimes glimpse with an imaginary third-eye perspective the ongoing, mutually shaping interaction between our inner sensations and our language. Most of the time we unthinkingly swim in a swirl of words, images, and feelings like a fish in its sea. Let's illustrate this situation.

I felt a warm, inner opening response to—let's call her Betty— when we first met. Later, I told her I felt love for her (associating my response with the word). She told me of feelings of love for me. This caused us to experience our subsequent meetings in what seemed a more profound way. As we continued to verbally describe the aspects of love we felt for one another, our feelings grew stronger and more subtle. Did use of the love-words influence our feelings or merely describe them?

Such situations reveal what appears to be a continually reciprocating influence between belief (defined by words) and experience (felt at an emotional level). We search to find the right word for our experience, and using it may either reinforce the feeling or cause it to shift a bit. To determine which one exerts more influence on our overall consciousness is probably as difficult as attempting to decide whether environment shapes personality more than genetics. However, social scientists have some insight into how language can expand or constrain the way an individual sees reality.

Noam Chomsky wrote that "the syntax and structure of sentences people speak suggest the existence of a universal grammar . . . [that] is part of the intrinsic biological inheritance of every human being." He said that language "serves as an instrument for free expression of thoughts."[2] Other experts believe children come equipped with a variety of language skills, which may be associated with various genes, that unfold in clearly definable stages.[3]

It has been suggested that with fewer words for the nuances of colors, ancient Egyptians actually did not see as many shades as modern artists. Researchers have noted that Eskimos have many words for snow and South Sea islanders have many words for the state of the sea, and believe the larger vocabulary actually enhances the acuity of their visual perceptions. People in high-tech societies hear more distinct mechanical sounds than agrarian folks, who are more sensitive to natural sounds. Each group has more terms for the nuances of its own environment. In these examples, one can argue the external reality does not change while the individual's experience of it does.

What does this have to do with the influence of Advanced Beings in human history? If we could grasp the impact of language on human consciousness, we might better understand why some people attempt to shape the language we use to communicate about the human experience of ABs. We might become concerned about the psychological implications of the words we use. Obviously, some people intuitively sense how important it is.

Many political and religious groups try to exercise various controls over their society's language. For instance, Muslim clerics fight forcefully to keep their followers from learning English and its foreign concepts. Americans afraid of losing their exclusive definition of truth use all possible means to prevent the United States from becoming a multilingual society. Chinese political leaders suppress the Fulun Gong movement with its new words suggesting meditative routes to truth. Such groups fear people having access to other interpretations of reality.

Acceptance of a term like AB for all Advanced Beings will frighten people who know the use of natural words will undermine their "divine" authority. For that reason, many religious leaders will likely try to repress this book's introduction of the AB terminology. Authoritarian political and economic interests will fear its power to expose false claims about the "anointed" or "chosen people" basis of authority.

Elements of Consciousness

Given how little we know about the way this universe actually works, it would be presumptuous to try to pin down something as elusive as human consciousness. But perhaps we can identify some of its elements and trace the impact of words and concepts on them. We may also be able to discern some of the words' connections to human behaviors. The following paragraphs set forth one way to view the processes of consciousness.

Self-reflection seems to suggest that consciousness has two complementary functions: knowing and thinking. *Knowing* is the state of being aware of oneself within the larger picture of reality and its many dimensions. It is a passive, interpretative (yin) mode. *Thinking* is the active, expressive (yang) mode. Thinking considers or analyzes what we "know" and puts it into concepts or words.

Combining our thinking and knowing functions energizes our actions. So our behavior reflects both what we know about something *and* what we think about it. Behavior comprises the actions (mental, emotional, and physical) we take vis-à-vis our environment. However, this is always a reciprocal process of give and take; each action (remember thoughts are actions) elicits a reaction. What we learn (know) from a reaction may change our thinking. This is the learning process.

As we've seen, limits to our vocabulary may limit both how we perceive and think, thus reducing the range of our potential perceptions and behaviors. Conversely, restricting our range of behaviors reduces our potential for knowing. (Obviously, having no limits at any level would be dysfunctional.) This reciprocating process provides the mechanism for testing what we think we know against the more extensive, less subjective reality. Testing our beliefs through experience either confirms them or shows we need to modify them, resulting in conscious learning.

Energy Memories and Archetypes

The naturalist school of thought (see chapters 7 and 23) operates on the assumption that the influence of language on consciousness and behavior goes more deeply than simple terminology. It recognizes at least three mechanisms by which the use of language has an effect on our consciousness. First, the vocabulary actively used by the individual establishes her range and levels of perception of phenomena. This process was introduced by the above comments on colors, snow, and water.

Second, the sounds themselves (pitch, frequency, and amplitude) transmit energetic stimuli to the receiver that evoke a particular emotional response. (The act of making the sounds has a similar feedback effect on the speaker. We can literally talk ourselves into a different emotional state.) Third, words energized by the human attention they have received over time become archetypes. Verbal use of archetypal words activates conditioned emotional responses and physical behaviors in the person who hears them.

These three processes may be referred to in shorthand as "vocabulary effect," "energetic effect," and "archetypal effect." Human consciousness can be reshaped by any one of these through fundamental changes in language. These processes take time because of the inertial weight of individual and collective habits bound to each word or phrase, but they provide the potential mechanism to change the course of human history. Let's look at the theoretical basis for energetic and archetypal effects.

The Energy of Words

Noted consciousness researcher and author Gary Schwartz has analyzed the living energy nature of our universe.[4] He says all forms of communication involve an exchange of energy. Physicists would use such terms as "energy transfer" or "phase change," indicating that an energy state in each body changes with any communication. Thus, a one-way communication is an oxymoron and cannot happen.

Even if the one who hears another's word does not overtly respond, an energy shift still occurs.

According to this view of our universe, even the thinking of a word causes vibrations in the mind. Words, whether written or spoken, when perceived by a person stimulate a subtle energetic reaction. An internal shift occurs whether one sends or receives the word. Test this for yourself. Attempt to imagine a noun, verb, or modifier and avoid feeling it in your emotional energy field.

Power of Archetypes

An archetype is an idea (image, word, or concept) that resides in the collective memory of a people and contains the emotional energy of their historical experience with it.[5] So, in addition to their vibratory impact, words that have become archetypes affect an individual's behavior by tapping into one's cultural conditioning. The activation of an archetype's emotional power through the individual's conditioned response results from a long process of energetic exchanges between the word and its users. Thus, when one hears words like "mother," "hero," or "villain," the response is automatic and conditioned.

An archetype's name continues to activate the conditioned response until its energetic memory has been completely erased. Attempts to redefine a word result in a period of transition when the new connotation changes the intellectual use of the word, but the original energetic basis continues to influence the user. This subconscious process results in an inconsistency between perception and emotional reactions. Clever use of archetypal words like "god," "evil," and "love" provoke emotional and behavioral responses not necessarily intended by those who speak or hear them.

Leaders in the U.S. government in the 1950s wanted the phrase "under God" added to the American pledge of allegiance to evoke a supernatural religious archetype. Repeating the phrase on a regular basis energizes the sense of a chosen people whose leadership is blessed with divine power to carry out God's destiny for the country. People now resist the idea of removing it because they don't want to give up the feeling of psychological security or superiority evoked by the archetype.

Natural Thinking

What would be the character of language in the natural, realistic culture described in chapter 7? In these circumstances its role would be primarily to integrate all the facets of human experience into a singular reality. It would be a language of "is-ness," with each noun reflecting as accurately as possible the human experience of whatever is being named. The structure of a phrase or sentence would again reflect as accurately as possible the direct relationship of the speaker to the subject. Action words would convey a sense of the event being observed or experienced by the human reporter. And so on. The function of language would be close to the language of science or mathematics.

In a culture with magical thinking, much of the language would distance the speaker (subject) from the verb and the object being described or explained. The terminology would categorize unexplained phenomena as magic, but the speakers would believe that they had the potential to understand how it works. The vocabulary would provide for, as J. R. R. Tolkien would say, "sub-creations" (magical realms beyond human experience) of obvious fiction. Adults would be able to identify the difference between reality and magic (recognizing that Santa Claus falls in a "sub-creation") and act accordingly. That perception of the difference between external reality and human projection does not exist in a supernaturalist culture.

The language of supernaturalism goes one step further and describes a realm that by definition lies beyond hope of human understanding. Such descriptive words (like the Christian or Muslim's "heaven" and "hell") are treated as real but have no basis in human experience. Their meanings are arbitrary. Created as artificial terms, with no soul of their own, they energetically become over time what authorities want them to be. Thus, words of fiction have become archetypes, and people no longer remember why.

This chapter attempts to illustrate the distinctions in the use of language in these three types of culture. The reason for distinguishing among natural, magical, and supernatural ways of thinking becomes more clear in chapters 20, 21, and 22. They illustrate how each mode of thinking results in its own mode of consciousness-based emotions and actions. They point out how magical and supernatural thinking can retard human development.

Culture and Word Choice

The alphabet appears to have been designed to be culturally neutral, so it should function in all three cultures. Therefore, taking words from different eras of Indo-European culture, we should be able to trace the culture's evolution from naturalism to magical thinking, on to supernaturalism. Looking at the same words used at different times and looking at different words referring to the same thing, we should be able to infer the basic experiences that led the society to its choice of words. Chapters 20, 21, and 22 illustrate that process.

We assume that in the process of creating new words in each society people had to agree on some basic assumptions about the nature of their lives and experiences. In the normal stages of language development, words that would describe something that has not been experienced did not get created. Thus, the resulting language should comprise a map of the group's actual history.

As an illustration, let's look at what could have been involved in the creation of a word, using the universal alphabet, to describe the human sense of original creation. The inventor of new words (a wordsmith) would wish to energetically express appreciation of this awesome source. Working with the universal alphabet (Sanskrit), the wordsmith would start with the first *devanagari* character, the unaspirated[6] sound "ah" (written in the Sanskrit as अ and represented by the Latin letter A). This human sound stands for the universal sound of full potential, before the physical act of creation (or aspiration). This vowel sound encompasses the potential of all other sounds not yet expressed.

Starting with infinite potential (the continuous sound from the deepest "ah" at the base of the throat) additional letters/sounds would represent the breath or wind moving to and reaching the point of creation. This can be done by starting with "ah" and moving it through the voice box to its exiting through closed (completed) lips. It would go something like this "ah . . . oo . . . mm" (ॲं in Sanskrit). It is Sanskrit's fifteenth vowel and the AUM sound of various chants. For the naturalist this could energetically convey the ultimate-in-one-beingness.

This may explain why most Indo-European languages have a word that starts with their version of "A" to refer to the supreme beingness or force that could account for all creation. Hinduism with its Sanskrit chose Atman. Ahura was chosen by Zoroastrianism. Islam much later in the Indo-European tradition chose Allah. By the time Judaism committed its sacred texts to writing, the personal appellation *YHVH* for their most high god had been adopted.[7] The more majestic Hebrew word Abba (father) or El-ab (high one) might have been used, but they too would have been anthropomorphic.

To be more consistent with a natural cosmology Genesis could have begun with the first Hebrew letter (*aleph*), as in *Ab-reshit bara Elohim* (suggesting that the Father-of-Beginning created the Elohim *and* the Heaven and Earth).[8] This would have recognized that even the Elohim arose from a single unnameable source of creation. *Ab-reshit* would be more comparable to the other Indo-European "A"-words. In English, one could use Almighty or All-in-One to convey the natural connotation. Use of *Breshit bara Elohim* (suggesting the Elohim created the Heaven and the Earth) in Genesis 1:1 gives credit to a group of ABs for creation of the whole, of which they are by definition only a part.

Inner and AB Communications

In the next six chapters, we must keep in mind that, in a natural culture, humans would have treated inner-sense communications as part of the natural world. In other words, they would have accepted telepathy, precognition, remote viewing, etc., as normal, even if poorly understood, phenomena. The same would have been true for encounters with Advanced Beings, whether in material or energetic form. Although not fully understood, such phenomena would have been accepted as part of the same reality of which humans perceived themselves to be parts.

The objective reality of human experience in all three types of cultures is the same; the different interpretations given to that experience depend on whether people see some of the experiences as magical or supernatural. It is the naming or labeling of natural events as either "magical" or "supernatural" that distorts the person's emotional and behavioral response. Naming involves the thinking mode of consciousness described earlier.

As we go through the developmental stages of Indo-European culture, we see that the way humans named or thought about external events produced changes in consciousness. Changes to magical and supernatural thinking resulted in different human reactions to natural events. While humans perceived the gods walking on Earth with them, their language reflected a sense of the ordinary, even when faced with an awe-inspiring reality. When they realized that the gods also operated out of human sight, in a space that humans did not understand, they engaged in magical thinking (we can't see how it works because we are not the magicians).

When the gods disappeared for a long time, people began to think of them as being in a realm to which humans could never aspire on their own. However, this projected supernatural reality was a product of their own thinking (based initially on a primitive understanding of space and space travel) from which they had excluded themselves. Today, humans react to ABs and other dimensions with the assumption dictated by their dominant belief system: natural, magical, or supernatural. (Recall the earlier section on Robert Monroe's work in other dimensions and with ABs.)

By now the reader probably understands that I suspect such a metamorphosis can be traced through the words used to describe flesh-and-blood ABs, then to imply absentee (but tangible) ABs, and finally to connote supernatural ABs. Chapter 4's discussion of the etymology of the word and concept of "angel" followed just such a progression. The next several chapters give examples of this progression of words and archetypes relating to the idea and experience of gods.

Magical versus Supernatural Thinking

The word "magical" derives from the Magi,[9] ancient Persian priest-scientists who were believed to have access to secret knowledge and technologies. During the medieval era such people were considered to be sorcerers. Common people did not understand their skills, like the reported prediction and location of Jesus' birth, and thus were a little frightened of them. Today magicians usually do tricks involving only sleight of hand and illusions.

Adolescents at a magic show probably illustrate the intellectual and psychological elements of ancient magical thinking. Things happen on stage that surprise and shock and otherwise titillate them. Their eyes and brains are at odds; they see things happen that their experience tells them should not happen. They are confused about what to believe. The magician, whom they recognize as a person like them, has a bag of tricks that break the rules of ordinary reality. Somehow the magician has learned to circumvent the laws of nature or fool them. Either way, they understand they have the potential to learn the tricks of the trade and be like him.

This kind of thinking seems to have occurred during the time of the AB-cults. Even though beings more advanced than humans could perform feats that surprised and shocked them, the humans were ready to learn. (Remember that at the time of Babel, humans seemed ready to help construct a way to ascend to the skies.) The existence of the ABs themselves was taken for granted. People did not imagine the activities of the ABs; they just didn't understand some of them. That is the crucial difference between magical thinking and supernatural thinking. The connection between the magician and the magic is known. In supernaturalism, the "magician" is *imagined,* as is his connection with effects that he is thought to have caused. And there is no way to demonstrate the assumed links to others.

The different cultures (natural, magical, and supernatural) have different ways of describing or interpreting three aspects of any situation. The aspects are: the effect, the assumed cause of the effect, and the connection between the two. Let's illustrate this. In a natural culture the crop needs rain. The farmers and their families do a dance with energetic movements and sounds asking the clouds to pour. And the rains come. They don't understand the principles involved, but they know from experience that such focusing of intent gets rain more often than not. They have learned that they can work with nature. Their vocabulary treats all this as ordinary.

In a magical culture rain is needed, too. The local people ask the AB in the ziggurat to have his angels cause rain to come. An emissary flies over the fields in a small "fiery chariot" spraying a mist into the clouds. And the rains come. The farmers don't understand what happened, but they see the direct connection to the AB and his craft. It's magic that they don't understand, but they believe someone can ask the "magician" how the trick works, and it can be explained. Their magical vocabulary provides for the temporarily unknowable.

In a supernatural culture, the farmers pray for rain to an invisible god they have *been told* exists. The rains come, but they can't know for sure whether it is a result of the unknown god's actions or the energy they put into their prayers. They have to take on faith both the assumed cause and the connection, with no way to be sure, except that the priests said so. Their vocabulary places them outside the process, except just to pray for the will of another being to happen.

When I engage in supernatural thinking and a "good" thing happens in my life, I assume it was my unknowable god's blessing and that I must have been good. When a "bad" thing happens (if I believe in an equally powerful devil), I can blame the evil supernatural being or I can blame myself for displeasing my god. I am devastated and immobilized. I'm "damned if I do and damned if I don't." Either my god has chosen to use this negative event to teach me a lesson (that I'm ashamed to know that I needed), or he has decided not to give me the protection that would have precluded the devil's act. Either way I come out a diminished, undeserving being who still has not measured up in some way.

The natural-thinking person who does not assume that a supernatural god was controlling his life thinks what happened to him was a natural event, perhaps even one that he helped to precipitate. As a natural-thinking person he can only feel that the event was part of the natural order of learning by trial and error. Thus, whatever the outcome, he sees it as a contribution to his life experience, perhaps even a way to learn to what degree he can have some control over it.

As we look at the phenomenon of god-cults from 1500 B.C.E. to the fifth century C.E., we can see the results of magical thinking that developed when humans were exposed to advanced knowledge and technologies. For instance, the post-Exodus Hebrews, producing the earliest versions of the Pentateuch, were already under the sway of a now-invisible AB who had demonstrated his magic to get them out of Egypt and defeat the Canaanites. They expected the magician to return to Earth and resume his performance to restore the glory of his chosen people.

This kind of magical thinking may account for the fact that the Old Testament scribes did not fully develop the concept of a universal creative force like the Hindu Atman. Their ideal was still that of their god demonstrating he was more powerful than his competitors. Thus, they were not able to evolve beyond monotheism (belief that one's own definition of god represents the only real god) to embrace the "A-word" (Atman) which had the implication of a force beyond a god limited by anthropomorphic traits.

While magical thinking can be a natural response to an encounter with one or more Advanced Beings, forever worshiping the magician is not. To create new words that set the magician off in a divine realm (divided from us) moves humans from the consensus of their collective experience to individual blind faith. They must believe their god is both hypothetical cause of and connection for every effect.

The unconscious incorporation of supernaturalism into one's worldview can be illustrated with a contemporary example. A well-educated investigative reporter who had taken a research trip wrote a private account to a few friends and colleagues explaining why she thought it was so successful. Her account indicated no awareness of how her religious assumptions had conditioned her thinking and behavior. For this reason, I must respect her anonymity.

Describing several stops along her itinerary, she said, "God spoke to me through other people. God spoke to me with the flash of what to do in my head. God spoke to me by making my current situation not work because he had something else better for me. God spoke to me by making clear that something in the current situation revealed what I should do next. God made me realize that I had to plant seeds and wait to see what he would send me."

By using the word "God" to express her experiences of the trip she, perhaps unwittingly, evoked the supernatural Christian archetype associated with it. Doing so stimulated the conditioned emotions of dependency and self-deprecation. This meant she could neither give credit to her friends for having good advice (based on learning from experience) nor to herself for having the intelligence to see its merits. It meant she did not trust in her own capability to have intuitive or precognitive flashes into possibilities for appropriate action.

It further meant that she did not recognize that she had the capacity to learn from a seemingly negative situation and confidently depend on her own ability to find a better option. She did not feel her own inherent power of discernment, her ability to see the cause-and-effect relationship between something in the present situation and what happens in the next. (She assumed that the god she believed in was independently controlling the cause and effect in both situations.)

In other words, she "learned" from the trip that God directed each step of her journey but learned nothing about her own capabilities. She only reinforced her faith in a supernatural being who operates outside the laws of nature. This circular thinking characterizes the psychological and emotional bind of supernaturalism. Of all industrialized nations, the United States today represents this supernatural perspective more than any other. According to a University of Michigan survey[10] Americans in general are closer to the Turks, Indonesians, and Iranians in this respect than to any of the European nations.

Need for Self-Conscious Language

A mature society, like mature individuals, recognizes that its future progress depends on increasing self-awareness and conscious self-development. A society that wishes to improve itself must identify and assess its blind spots. All nations wishing to exercise leadership for the duration of the twenty-first century now face this challenge. This chapter has focused on the need to understand the way a culture's language can circumscribe a people's view of reality.

Most humans speak only one language, assuming it is the "real" way to communicate. When we consider our own language special (divine or otherwise superior), it has an implicit, but significant impact on our emotions and behaviors. It diminishes any inclination to transcend the barrier of different languages to grasp common fundamental truth. Supernaturalism by its very nature, regardless of the religion, leads to artificial divisions (another way of saying alienation) among cultures. With no way to universally test its hypothesis of a supernatural god, each subculture creates its own god in the image it desires. This results in as many gods (on a spectrum from the most humanoid to the most abstract) as there are cultural groups. Conflicts and wars easily follow.

Christianity and Islam both settled on the Jewish AB-*YHVH* model for their supernatural god, a god antagonistic to all other gods. It is no wonder that the Judeo-Christian-Islamic tradition has had difficulty making the memory of the AB god of Abraham big enough to encompass all beings and a multidimensional universe. They have been emotionally inhibited by a name and archetypal image of a far-too-humanoid figure for such a big role.

Centuries and many generations later, they still have not outgrown their limited and mutually exclusive concepts of what should be seen as one supreme and primal force in the universe. The most virulent cultural conflict in the world today springs from such antagonistic terms and their effects on consciousness.

How can we escape this self-imposed myopia and develop a universal vision? I believe we must start with reconsidering the most central words. For instance, God in the Anglo-Saxon world and some form of *deos* in the Latin languages are both Indo-European derivatives, respectively of *guo* and *deus*, which originally meant simply one of any number of ABs from the sky (as did Elohim, meaning more than one AB, including *YHVH*). Using the framework developed here, later chapters will explore the impact of such words on the evolution of human consciousness.

Rending the Human Psyche

Introduction to Part VII

A majority of humans today wear modern religious assumptions as if they were as natural as their skin. Christians, Jews, Muslims, and many others exclaim, "The Lord/Allah/*YHVH*/God wants me to do this," "He would be angry at that," "Many times He has helped me in trouble," "He will answer my personal prayer," "He would forbid that," and on and on. When asked how they know such statements to be true, they reply, "I believe them because I believe my religion." When asked if they know how such beliefs first got started, they resort to even more circular logic: "It has been that way since the religion was established by the Lord, Allah, *YHVH*, or God."

To grasp just how much people unquestioningly assume that such beliefs are normal, let's speculate about how the notion of an invisible male god first surfaced. Imagine yourself around a Neolithic campfire. One of the men announces that an invisible male god had told him he had been designated to "interpret for the god, stop his normal work, and rule over the tribe on the god's behalf." The likely response from the others, male and female, would have been incredulity and a request that he carry on his share of the work. We find in the Old Testament where similar claims generated that sort of disbelief.

When Joseph reported he had dreamed of one of his sheep standing up and his brothers' sheep bowing to it, implying that an unseen god gave him special status, his brothers' reaction was to throw him in a well and sell him into slavery. The same skepticism prevailed at the time of Moses, when *YHVH* had to demonstrate his technology (a magic staff, engraved commandments, and bio-weapons) to the Egyptians and Israelites to prove Moses represented a real AB.

Earlier sections of this book describe an era of 3-D human encounters with beings possessing expansive knowledge and high technology. Humans, in awe of them, learned to worship these beings more advanced than they. Now, chapter 19 suggests some humans had a profoundly dependent relationship with these flesh-and-blood ABs. Chapter 20 focuses on how those relationships apparently turned into cult worship of the memories of departed ABs. Chapter 21 postulates how continued worship of invisible AB-gods can split or rend human consciousness, with one part hoping that gods will provide "salvation" from Earthly perils, while another believes humans are responsible for living within a natural system. Together these scenarios show how humans may have gone from the above-described skepticism of the hypothetical Neolithic campfire scene to today's worshiper's unquestioning beliefs.

19 Have ABs Abused Humans?

Abuse, like beauty, often depends on the beholder. Hundreds of current "ET encounters," like the sample given in chapter 5, reveal a range of views. Many experiencers see themselves as unwilling victims, at the mercy of more powerful beings. Many others see themselves as subjects in examinations and experiments that are intimidating and uncomfortable, but not intentionally abusive. Others see themselves as co-participants in a grand interspecies project of mutual benefit. We do not know how many Advanced Beings, in physical and noncorporeal states, have deliberately and directly intervened in human history over the last half-million years. I suspect, however, that the range of human perspectives on the encounters has always existed.

Some ABs now speaking through human channels (recall chapter 1) claim to have had the long-term, best interests of humans at heart. The Anunnaki would likely consider their influence the same. *YHVH*, for instance, claimed to have been supportive of the Hebrews long before he met with Moses. He said he was the god looking out for the Hebrews back to Abraham's time in Sumeria.

Chapters 11 through 14 focused on how humans benefited from AB assistance following the worldwide Cataclysm of 11,500 B.P. This present chapter looks at the possible downside to this "assistance." Were humans abused by the very ABs who helped them to recover from the disasters of the worldwide Cataclysm?

I will risk starting the chapter with my answer. With the benefit of 4,000 years of hindsight and more knowledge of ABs in general, I believe the evidence suggests the Anunnaki in the Fertile Crescent and its contiguous areas did not intend to abuse the humans associated with their rule. Perhaps not coincidentally, the word "abused" can be written "AB-used." The second variation may be closer to the truth. The ancient texts amply referenced in earlier chapters give the impression that the Anunnaki simply used the humans for the services they needed for their own tenure on this planet. The record suggests the Anunnaki treated humans with more respect than humans have treated some of their own species.

Colonial Analogy

The world has learned over the last 500 years of colonization of more primitive human societies by more advanced ones that even well-intentioned interventions can have negative consequences, even for both sides. This chapter considers the proposition that humans, and possibly the gods, may have suffered psychological trauma due to the Anunnaki-human entanglement described in Mesopotamian and Hebrew texts. Even though the Bible and other texts describe an AB-human relationship that is not exactly like that of a modern colonial one, I believe colonialism is the best analogy to relate to that ancient experience in terms we can appreciate.

To infer something of the mental, emotional, and behavioral conditions under which humans may have lived at that time, we can use the experimental but rational process described by Jared Diamond: ". . . historians are . . . able to evaluate related hypotheses by retrospective tests."[1] Using this process we can identify reflections of the Anunnaki-era practices in modern religions and colonies. We see similar comparisons in human reactions to current AB-human encounters. Such parallels support the hypothesis of negative emotional and mental (and sometimes physical) effects from AB interventions.

AB attitudes and behaviors that support the "colonial analogy" include the Anunnaki view that humans, whom they had a role in creating, could be forced into labor. Emotionally remote, the ABs generally kept humans at a distance, similar to that between the King or Queen of the British Empire and indigenous people in colonies. They had no compunction about using force to obtain the behaviors they desired from humans. Under the penalty of corporeal punishment, humans learned to respond as the ABs demanded. As beings of heavenly origin, they appeared to be the ultimate source of wisdom and power to a naïve human perspective. All ABs, even the female ones, assumed what we now see as patriarchal roles. Even the ABs who taught humans science and technology and promised to protect them appeared to act like stern fathers.

The first such "father figure" recorded in the Sumerian tablets is Anu, the in-orbit commander of the Anunnaki colony. His Earth-based sons Enlil and Enki formed with him the first example of a ruling troika. All the leading Anunnaki required and received subservience, service, support, and sacrifice from the less-developed humans. They required deference and homage and acts of obeisance. For the most part, the dependent humans saw no option but to be docile and tractable, amenable to the instructions of their colonial rulers.

The Anunnaki Colony

This chapter deals with the period from about 6500 B.C.E. (marked by obvious evidence of high culture in Catal Huyuk on the Anatolian plain in Turkey[2] and other sites) to about 2000 B.C.E. During these four and a half millennia, the AB-dominated culture achieved its broadest reach, from Kurdistan to Egypt, from India to Asia Minor. City-states proliferated under the rule of various Anunnaki gods. This region accounts for the essential directions of social and intellectual development that came together to form the basis of what we call Western Civilization. It set the stage for the religions, political institutions, and economic powers that now dominate the world.

The AB Perspective

The Sumerian, biblical, and other ancient texts suggest that each god had a unique personality with his or her own personal agenda. From those sources, we discover the AB-gods' attitudes toward humans apparently ranged from a remoteness toward or disdain for humans to a paternalistic benevolence, from feelings of physical attraction to concern for their welfare. Some ABs simply wanted to take advantage of human brawn and products, while others desired to see the humans receive some personal benefits from their services to the masters. A few gods wanted to give knowledge and training to the humans where possible.

Enki, the second son of the Anunnaki colony's commander, epitomized the last category. Pro-human in every policy debate, he opted to warn Zuisudra/Noah (Utnapishtim) of the impending cataclysm so that he and his family could prepare for survival. After the flood waters subsided Enki convinced the other gods to help the human survivors restart civilization. The other gods agreed, but they behaved toward humans as they were apparently accustomed to treating less elite Nibiruans.

Each city-state with a surrounding support community was ruled by a god, with each kingdom seen as a separate people (or tribe). For instance, the Hebrews have been thought of as such a tribe, although they were not very genetically or culturally different from other Semitic peoples. All rulers treated humans under their regime as colonial subjects, but their respective personalities tempered the way they exercised power (as the French, British, and Belgians differed slightly in their administration of African colonies in the twentieth century).

We have a lot of information about the perspective of one personality: *YHVH*. He does not appear in history under that name until about 3,500 years ago, when he chose Moses to rally the Israelites in Egypt around him. This god, who kept himself invisible, may have personified the naturally arrogant Anunnaki view of less-developed beings. He demanded absolute obedience and loyalty, and impeccable service. He viewed his relationship to his "chosen people" as:

> "And they shall know that I am *YHVH*, who rescued my people, giving them the covenant. . . ." And how shall they be rewarded for their loyalty [asked Ezekiel]?[3]
>
> ". . . I will strike them with a great [blow] in the midst of the land . . . when all the curses happen to them and strike them until they die and until they are destroyed."[4]

From the Anunnaki perspective the primary function of the city-state was to support the needs of the god and his/her immediate circle of AB staff[5] and demigod dependents. Thus a city's life focused on the god's palace and its environs. Human labor raised the buildings, produced the food, and provided life-support services required by the few-score resident ABs. Humans were required to entertain the "royals" and carry out elaborate rituals of homage when a more senior AB visited or on special occasions. They had to be careful not to offend the gods and served as soldiers when called.

Ziggurats: Symbols of Power

Perhaps the ziggurat and its monumental style of architecture can help us understand the nature of the god-human relationship. The ziggurat first appears in Sumerian history as the precataclysm E.KUR (meaning "house which is like a mountain") in Nippur. Anunnaki leader Enlil reportedly lived there and, with access to the DUR.AN.KI (meaning "Link Heaven and Earth"), commanded the AB colony's mission control center.[6] The control center was reserved for the gods. Other inner areas were limited to the gods and their chosen priesthood. Anyone encroaching was punished. The ziggurat's size and magnificence showed who was king and lord.

After the Cataclysm, the Anunnaki who were assigned to rule Mesopotamian city-states had their headquarters in personal ziggurats. These were constructed and maintained by humans under AB supervision, but access was controlled. Archaeologists in the 1940s counted 33 ruins in 27 Mesopotamian cities. Babylonian texts mention active ziggurats, as in Lagash, as late as 2200 B.C.E.[7] (This is compatible with the 2024 B.C.E. date mentioned elsewhere as the end of Anunnaki presence in many cities.)

Conflicts among the Gods

Near the end of the Anunnaki era, the original conflict between Enlil and Enki (about who would be senior on Earth) was still being played out by their progeny. The Enlil lineage (Ninurta and Nannar) still ruled in Sumer when Abraham was born the son of Tera (a Sumerian priest) around 2125 B.C.E. Shortly thereafter, Babylon, the capital of Sumer, was given to Marduk (Ba'al) of the Enki lineage (which favored human self-control). Ninurta opposed this and supported action to reduce Marduk's power.

Enlil's faction of the Anunnaki had only reluctantly reconciled itself to Enki's warning to Noah and allowing for the revival of human civilization. Perhaps as *YHVH*, Ninurta tried to organize the Hebrew nation to circumvent the Anu decision to give Marduk hegemony (favoring human independence) over West Asia. (A bit of evidence supporting this hypothesis was that *YHVH*'s plan for his Jerusalem temple, to be built by King Solomon, duplicated that of Ninurta in Lagash.)[8]

Such struggles among the ABs for control of territory and groups of humans fostered a xenophobic mentality. Humans came to understand they were protected by the ruling god as long as they stayed within his area and under his auspices. Thus, they avoided behavior that would get them banished from the homeland by priestly or administrative officials. Subjects of an AB considered his war against another god to be a holy war, establishing the basis for modern concepts of "holy wars" as fought by the followers of one god against those of another god. Worshipers of another god were assumed to have no rights and could be enslaved, sold, or slain. *YHVH* gave this law to the Hebrews.

Given the amount of information we have in the Hebrew Pentateuch about the attitudes toward humans held by *YHVH*,[9] he illustrates a range of behaviors that is consistent with the stern, authoritarian colonialist model. He showed himself to be a vindictive god against the enemies of Israel, but it was a trait he also turned on his own people. When the Hebrews after 600 B.C.E. grew rebellious and brazen in their defiling of his temple, *YHVH* reportedly somehow instigated its destruction by the Babylonians in 586 B.C.E.

While the leading Jews were exiled to Babylon, their prophet Ezekiel went into trances seeking to communicate with *YHVH*. He revealed to the leaders of Judah that *YHVH* had been upset because they participated in activities like those of the secret societies of Egypt which knew about the AB king-making procedures. (Remember Egypt was the domain of AB Enki, who was always on the opposite side of Enlil and his son Ninurta/*YHVH*.) Ezekiel channeled the message that *YHVH* expected a reuniting of Israel and Judah, rejection of any relationship with the other gods, and a reconstruction of his Jerusalem temple.

YHVH's reach exceeded the Hebrew people. He apparently did not hesitate to enlist others in supporting his chosen Israelite followers. Cyrus, king of Persia, said he had been ordered by *YHVH* to rebuild the temple of Jerusalem. The Book of Ezra (chapter 1) reports that Cyrus declared *YHVH* had anointed him king of "all the kingdoms of the Earth." This indicates that although the Hebrews had been selected by *YHVH* to implement his vision of a post-AB human culture, he did not hesitate to order others to support his agenda.

From such experiences, humans learned to adapt to domination by these superior beings. Their survival depended on obedience. The initial authority of the gods (based on naked power) was later transferred to their designated representatives. Later, human kings and priests who successfully cloaked themselves in the authority of the gods could dominate people who had been trained to be psychologically dependent on such external authority.

Sacrifices to the Gods

One of the techniques used by powerful beings to maintain a sense of subservience and control was the requirement of some sort of sacrifice. The rituals in many traditions included the practice of offering sacrifices to the gods. However, the item offered was mostly symbolic. These practices contrast greatly with later practices that used volunteer sacrifices or violent sacrifices of captives, slaves, criminals, and even children to propitiate the gods or gain their blessing.[10] I know of no evidence that the Anunnaki gods required human sacrifices. I believe explanations for such practices can be found among the many devious means various groups of priests invented to enhance their psychological control over a naïve populace during the era of god-cults (see next chapter).

Biblical evidence indicates that the Elohim and *YHVH* (the Anunnaki) did require the preparation of roasted meat for the gods to eat. The first three chapters of Leviticus go into great detail on the selection and preparation of the food to be presented to a god. Meat was to be male and unblemished; fowl was to be of a special kind. The method of cutting is described, indicating the parts to be left out and burned with the wood on the altar. That which comprised the actual offering was to be properly cut and made by fire to be "of a sweet savor" for the lord. (Sound familiar to modern-day fathers put in charge of the backyard barbecue?)

We are told in Genesis 8:21 that when the lord smelled a sweet savor from Noah's roasted offering that he had a change of heart and vowed to never again curse man's land nor smite another living being. Such was the influence on ABs of well-roasted meat. It is no wonder that when humans felt abandoned by an AB god, they resorted to the tried and true method of sacrifice to regain his attention.

When Abraham (in Genesis 22) was commanded by his god to go to the land of Moriah and make a sacrifice, such an act appeared normal; Isaac asked his father where the sacrificial animal was to be found. *YHVH*'s demand that Isaac be sacrificed appears to have been a symbolic test of Abraham's faith, where he did not expect to see a human killed.

As we'll see later, religious cults set new standards for sacrifices in frantic attempts to induce the gods to return, or at least to direct their powers to the aid of the worshipers. In supernatural religions, the ritual of sacrifice has become increasingly symbolic. Even though the Eucharist may have roots in the archetype of cultist human sacrifice, it has no basis in what the AB-gods required of humans. Humans are responsible for their own inventions to manipulate the human psyche, even though they blame it on the gods.

Psychology of the Colonized

From sacred-text reports of human reactions to their experiences with the gods, we can infer something of the psychological syndromes they must have engendered. Descriptions of the obedience and deference required by the ABs reigning on Earth can be found in the early books of the Old Testament and other religious texts.

Such self-deprecating syndromes have been prevalent on every continent during the past two centuries, as colonial powers have crushed technically weaker civilizations. With more primitive technology, the less-developed perceive themselves as lacking in material comforts and prowess. Depending on the conquerors to provide better "goodies," they devalue their own social and cultural principles. These same mental, emotional, and behavioral patterns displayed by the recently colonized were evident among humans in the time of the gods.

For instance, the ritual of worship required by the ABs, particularly involving self-abnegation, would not appear in the natural societies described in chapter 7. (Note the word "abnegate" can be written "AB-negate.") Seeing themselves as vassals, at the mercy of the alien colonists, indigenous people would come to believe that their way of life did not measure up. In the AB-focused culture, the worship/followship mode of behavior had to be learned by humans if they wanted to benefit from the AB assistance.

The societies most addicted to the worship/followship syndrome seem to be the ones most affected by the Elohim and Nefilim of the Bible during the formative years of their civilizations. Priests and kings subsequently used Anunnaki symbols (*mitre du pape*, gowns, crowns, etc.) to take advantage of this psychological conditioning. Humans who had learned what the ABs expected, when in positions of power, turned on their fellow humans. They assumed the roles of AB lords and ladies, claiming special status and demanding a hierarchical pecking order among humans.

In a recent book,[11] noted independent scholar and author Riane Eisler reports on many ways in which that "dominator model" of society has hampered human development. The persistence of the dominator model depends on the existence of its polar opposite: the "dependency syndrome." Whether god or goddess-oriented, psychological deference to "divine" authority appeals to two types of humans: those who want to dominate and those who want to be dependent.

The latter find comfort in having someone else in control of their destiny. Conversely, the dominators also have their psychological needs met by docile humans. Belief that one is being ruled by gods so advanced that one cannot even grasp the scope of their powers naturally reinforces this two-way syndrome. The nature of the colonial setting was conducive to the development of a dysfunctional dominator/dependency syndrome in both ABs and humans.

Humans tending toward the dominator model would have curried the favor of the "royal" ABs by learning to effectively control other humans.[12] The symbiotic god/priesthood institutions described in chapter 15 would have nicely fulfilled the needs of both groups. The patriarchal priests arrogated for themselves the role of explaining the AB perspective to other humans, and those satisfied to be followers choose to believe whatever answers the priests gave them.

Historians had considered this patriarchal tradition in history to be natural until well into the modern era. In the late twentieth century, writers like Merlin Stone began to point out that history was written by males who skewed their interpretation of artifacts, documents, and legends.[13] She and others suggested that men wrote history the way they did in order to justify the supremacy of male humans and gods, labeling rituals dealing with natural phenomena as "pagan, sinful, cultist," etc.[14] Some tried to substitute a matriarchal fiction for a patriarchal fiction. Both groups failed to deal with the possibility of influence by primarily male gods on human institutions.

The Final Blow

After several millennia of an AB colonial regime, during which a partial transfer of political power to human kings had occurred, an unplanned-for and traumatic end apparently came to the symbiotic AB-human experiment. The gods up and left humans to fend for themselves. No evidence has been discovered to pinpoint exactly when and why that face-to-face contact ceased. However, it turns out that this may have been the most lasting form of abuse. Its scars are still evident in the separation anxiety inherent in modern religions.

The Bible gives no reason for the gods' withdrawal, but accounts from other cultures suggest one. A Patagonian tribal legend states the AB god El-lal's battles with other gods in his family caused him to decide to leave Earth and let humans look after themselves.[15] Quetzalcoatl was said to have departed in sorrow after a war with or among other ABs.[16] A myth from what is now Liberia says the human creator god, after a period of quarrels on Earth, wanted his AB sons to return to their sky home. The Mende tribe says its god Ngewo returned to a place far away that he made for himself, after humans became too dependent on him.[17] Bushman tales suggest the god Kang deserted his terrestrial home after battles among ABs on Earth.

Sitchin believes portions of Sumerian, Akkadian, and Assyrian texts translated during various periods of the twentieth century suggest a time frame and reason for the conflicts that led to the Anunnaki withdrawal.[18] As recounted in Sumerian lamentations texts, the struggle involved brother against brother (Marduk versus Nergal) and cousin against cousin (Ninurta and Marduk representing the Anunnaki families and human allies of Enlil and Enki, respectively). Battles had reached such a stalemate that a council of senior AB leaders, with Anu from Nibiru breaking the tie, voted to permit the use of nuclear weapons to settle it.

According to Sitchin's calculations, the attack came in 2024 B.C.E., reflected in the Bible as the story of Abraham bargaining with Ninurta/*YHVH* on the behalf of "righteous people" before the "upheavaling" of Sodom and Gomorrah. The attack caused the vaporization of these and other targets by nuclear "fire and brimstone." Humans, and apparently some ABs who stayed too close, were quickly killed by the heat and radiation. The southern end of the Dead Sea was blasted open (where the springs remain contaminated to the present).

Descriptions in various Sumerian lamentations texts (The Uruk Lament, Lamentation Over the Destruction of Ur, Lamentation Text Over the Destruction of Sumer and Ur) of the aftermath of the AB use of awesome weapons that might have been nuclear read like eyewitness accounts of early U.S. nuclear blasts: storms preceded by gigantic flashes of light, deadly clouds, unseen death-rays, the Earth trembling, and an evil wind that killed all life it touched. Plants, animals, and humans died, buildings were destroyed, waters were poisoned. Chaos reigned as the gods left in various craft to save themselves.[19]

The radioactive fallout was blown eastward and destroyed people, livestock, and vegetation all the way to the Tigris and Euphrates Rivers. All of Sumer was decimated, and the gods withdrew from their temple-homes now filled with deadly radiation. Human kings were left to rule the wasteland. The scorched Earth left by the fiery blasts remains visible in the Sinai even today, an ancient reminder of the dangers of nuclear war. There is some evidence that the conflagration may have changed the climate of the entire region.[20]

Only Enki and Marduk reportedly agreed to provide assistance to rebuild human civilization in the devastated region. Enki undertook a massive decontamination effort, and after 70 years Sumer and Akkad were declared habitable. However, as soon as the new cities began to arise, more squabbling broke out among the gods. They no longer exercised effective control over the now human-led land of Sumer.

According to the *Shurpa* (Sumerian "purification" texts), the resumption of something like normal life in Ur, Larsa, Nippur, and several other Sumerian and Akkadian cities had occurred by 1953 B.C.E.[21] However, little evidence remains of further direct AB intervention in mundane human affairs. Some human kings may have had communications with the Anunnaki, but they appear to have been channeled through priests or prophets. If the gods physically stayed on Earth much past this period, they had withdrawn to facilities dedicated to space travel. (This development could account for *YHVH's* practice of remaining out of human sight.) According to some legends, for many centuries humans like Alexander the Great allegedly tried to gain access to the gods' facilities but were apparently unsuccessful.[22]

Finally, Anu and Enlil reportedly agreed that Marduk would be the one to watch over (rule from orbit) Babylon, whose newly powerful king Hammurabi recorded:

> Lofty Anu, lord of the
> gods who from Heaven came to Earth,
> and Enlil, lord of Heaven and Earth
> who determines the destinies of the land,
> Determined for Marduk, the first born of Enki,
> the Enlil-functions over all mankind,
> Made him great among the gods who watch and see,

> Called Babylon by name to be exalted,
> made supreme in the world;
> And established for Marduk, in its midst
> an everlasting kingship.[23]

Marduk's hegemony from space was not to last. Babylon would have to fight for its existence on human terms. Hittites, Hyksos, and Kassites would vie for supremacy in the region. Much later Assyria would rise to overshadow them. The Chaldeans would in turn overthrow the Assyrians. The descendants of Noah were given their independence, prepared or not, only to fight among themselves. The absence of records seems to suggest that the final AB pullout was precipitous, leaving not only huge structures unused, but also a large power vacuum. Without an effectively planned transfer of power, rapid societal decline resulted.

In summary, this chapter portrays a plausible set of psychological effects on humans during a long period of subservience to beings much more advanced, both technically and intellectually, than they. It suggests that even if the goal of the ABs was to assist in human development, their superior culture had the unintended effect of weakening the human sense of self-reliance. The great gap in levels of power created anxiety, insecurity, and a sense of dependency among humans. This left them ill-prepared to cope with independence from AB rule.

20 When Did God-Cults Arise?

This chapter reviews an historical period that is fairly well documented in many respects by research placing cultural upheavals and physical events into a known timeline. However, the reasons for this chaotic era in Middle-Eastern history have not yet been understood. I believe the AB-intervention hypothesis set forth in this book can help explain that epoch's political and social developments. Thus, I wrote the scenario in this chapter with the Sumerian Anunnaki materials woven into its presentation as credible evidence.

The Anunnaki internecine battles of 2000 B.C.E. described in Sumerian texts and the gods' apparent withdrawal from human society led to what historians have called the Dark Ages of Mesopotamia. The former AB-god centers of technical prowess, along with their associated pomp, had fallen on hard times. Science, philosophy, and culture entered a period of decline. Institutions began a slide into decadence. By 1500 B.C.E., Sumerian supremacy in Mesopotamia had ended, and the Babylon of Marduk was fading. Pharaonic Egypt fragmented as the Old Kingdom dissolved into the Middle Kingdom. Hebrews fled the chaos in Egypt and began 40 years in the Sinai desert (led to a new home by an unseen AB known as *YHVH*). Troy was destroyed again; the Minoan kings of Crete no longer had cultures to rule. The Indus Valley civilization sank into oblivion.

Exacerbating the human mental and emotional despair, adding impetus to a call for help from the departed gods, a natural disaster occurred about the time of the Hebrew Exodus from Egypt.[1] Historian Immanuel Velikovsky described the Middle East at that time: "Cities were overturned; epidemics left the dead piled in common graves; the pursuit of arts and commerce came to an abrupt end; empires ceased to exist, strata of earth, dust, and ashes yards thick covered the ruined cities. In many places the population was annihilated, in others it was decimated; settled living was replaced by nomadic existence. Climate changed."[2] The Greek island of Thera's volcano exploded as earthquakes shook the cradle of civilization.[3]

During a period of 1,000 years, all of West Asia became embroiled in border wars among the former AB city-states (Babylon, Elam, Medes, Sidon, Tyria, and Phoenicia). By 538 B.C.E. Babylon fell, the Persian Empire was founded, and, by 510 B.C.E., the Indus Valley was part of it. What remained of city-states was no longer controlled by the direct descendants of the AB-designated demigod rulers. Human kings attempted to maintain the lifestyles demigods had developed for themselves, but the AB-originated royal palaces and temples deteriorated even further.

Breeding Ground of Despair

Accustomed to help from the gods since their recovery after the Flood, humans now bereft of such support were frightened. Historic declines in social conditions would have disturbed anyone, but among psychologically dependent peoples the distress caused by such conditions must have reached extreme levels. This anxiety was even more traumatic for people who thought they had been "chosen" by the gods.

The Hebrews were not the only group to have believed they were a god's chosen people, who would be given special protection and treatment in return for loyalty. In another part of the world, the Modoc people believed that their god Kumush, like *YHVH*, had promised his people to defeat all who came against them. But he, they said, broke this promise to humans when he departed for a new home in the sky, where he could live with his daughters.[4]

People suffering from separation anxiety or a sense of being deserted would have been psychologically ready for the promises of

AB-god cults. The Bible and other texts suggest people thought that the gods had only gone temporarily. The departing gods might even have made promises that fostered the idea. Belief in an imminent return would certainly have encouraged frightened people to continue rituals and offerings in former temples. In such circumstances, the formation of cults focused on absentee gods would have been easy.

Individuals who saw an opportunity for amassing power over people or resources—the same motivations behind cults today—likely encouraged them. Greek historian Xenophon (ca. 431–ca. 352 B.C.E.) is said to have pointed out that cult leaders created images of their gods to meet their own needs (a reversal of the Sumerian and Hebrew creation stories of gods creating humans in their images). While it may not rationally justify it, the AB-colonial experience of dependency on AB leadership could perhaps explain why humans turned to the worship of their own idealized images of departed gods.

Bizarre acts of all types would have been predictable as the cults failed to bring back the AB regime. After the traditional offerings of roasted meat and other delicious foods did not entice the gods back to their altars, some could even have turned to human sacrifice. By ceding their power to the departed gods, the cult members absolved themselves of accountability and responsibility. The excuse of being under the control of an imagined scapegoat (a god's will or the wiles of the devil) met the AB-colonized human's need to be cared for. Thus, it is no surprise that the Hebrews had a word *(azazel)* for scapegoat. It connotes an abstract entity who excuses sin or responsibility for human actions.

Addicted to Bad Habits

Why did humans not relish freedom from their subservient, dependent relationship to more Advanced Beings? Why did they not leap to pursue a uniquely human path of development?

Perhaps maintenance of complex institutions had required AB input or policy decisions. Removing AB technology, communications, and control systems could have left humans unprepared to maintain the institutional infrastructure and fend for themselves. But the most likely reason was that the "colonial" experience had made humans too psychologically dependent on external authority. In this regard, they would not have been very different from twentieth-century citizens in recently liberated colonies appealing to their former rulers to bail them out of later difficulties.

Origins of AB-Cults

This chapter deals with what I would call Stage II in the evolution of human consciousness. If one starts from the natural perspective described in chapter 7 as Stage I, the next step fragments our collective and individual consciousnesses to include magical thinking. Magical thinking involves the temporary suspension of belief or judgment, to say, "I don't know how it works but it does." Stage III requires becoming convinced that an imaginary world is real.

These three stages of conscious evolution roughly correlate with three eras of history (which may overlap chronologically). Stage I represents the natural human setting, including the ordinary experience of Advanced Beings and nonphysical dimensions. Stage II represents the period of worship of absentee ABs (who may or may not still be involved in human affairs). Stage II comprises magical religion and may be called the era of AB-god cults. Stage III involves human worship of imagined gods (supernatural religion). These gods may be based on human traits (anthropomorphism) or details known about particular ABs, or some combination of the two (as in the Christian notion of a supreme god modeled on the AB called *YHVH* by the Hebrews).

How does one stage evolve into the other? This chapter offers a view of history that explains how Stage II god-cults sprang from Stage I naturalism.

During the period of chaos described earlier, humans forced to cope with unanticipated independence sought to keep the AB-gods involved in human affairs. They organized ongoing worship at the temples or shrines of the now absent gods, with ceremonies and sacrifices that they hoped would entice the gods to return, or at least continue to care for them.

Priests who had served in the AB temples might have tried to keep up the charade of ongoing interest by the ABs, now very distant in physical and social terms. To reinforce the memories of the now absent AB rulers, priests perpetuated worship by their former human subjects and gained new converts. They helped the devotees to transfer their psychological dependencies from departed flesh-and-blood ABs to memories of them. Thus, god-cults emerged.

From shortly after 2000 B.C.E. until the fifth century C.E., AB-based cults proliferated in the area we now think of as the primal Indo-European culture. They reached from the Straits of Gibraltar to the Indian continent, extending across Southern Europe and Central Asia to the north and down to Saharan North Africa. (Some cults may also have started this way in Meso-America and the Andes if they experienced a precipitous departure of local gods. Alternatively, cult worship may have been exported to these areas from West Asia within the last 2 to 3 millennia. More comparative analysis of these traditions with the AB-cult era in the Eastern Mediterranean and West Asian regions is needed.)

Cults Gave Meaning and Emotional Stability

The formation of cults would have given intellectual meaning and emotional stability to humans who had never known life without the gods. They may have believed that these very powerful ABs could still exercise intellectual, psychological, and physical control over human behavior and events on Earth. They probably hoped that the gods at a distance would aid humans who behaved appropriately, or dispense justice when humans broke their rules.

These colonized humans likely still believed in the AB promises of protection and special benefits for their followers. Though now invisible, an ingrained fear of AB use of distant weapons perpetuated the previously enforced obedience to AB expectations. Promises of their return could be seen as a threat or salvation, depending on whether the individual felt "marked" by the gods.

Definition of a Cult

A cult starts with a self-defined circle of individuals who share devotion or allegiance to a particular being—alive or dead. (The object of veneration can be a human or an AB.) Members share a system of beliefs, and their rituals honor or worship that being. The human leader proclaiming the cult's dogma has special status. He helps the members to define themselves as different from anyone outside their circle and purports to interpret the being's intentions. Exclusive beliefs and membership, not the group's size, determine its cultist nature. (Many large religious groups in the world today still fit these criteria.)

Throughout this book, the reader must remember the word "cult" as used here does not have the negative connotation usually associated with it in contemporary society. It was originally a neutral term that simply applied to groups meeting the definition just given. The reader will note that it has become an archetypal word with considerable energy attached. In this book, try to avoid that emotional reaction.

Evolution of Cults

The first AB-god cults to be organized after an AB's departure probably formed around people with connections to the actual ABs or people who claimed to have known them. The human staff of the former AB rulers had more credibility as potential channels; devotees assumed they knew the true views and requirements of the departed masters. They probably also hoped that requests delivered to the god by intercessory prayers of a previously trusted servant, i.e., the priest, would have a better chance of a favorable response.

Fanatics, said to be communicating through inner channels with absent ABs, tried to keep the human rulers and their subjects in line. In Israel, known as "prophet," "seer," or "one who sees visions" (respectively *Nabih, Ro'eh,* and *Hozeh* in Hebrew), they included Elijah, Elisha, and Isaiah. Despite the prophets' efforts, Israel split into two kingdoms. One leaned toward the gods of Sumeria, while the other remained faithful to *YHVH*. In Sumeria, Queen Jezebel (pledged to AB Baal) had her own prophets who advised opposition to the Israelites. Such "prophecies" may have in fact come from absentee gods through human channels to perpetuate control of, or simply to help, their former human subjects. Or, the prophets may have acted on their own, making "prophecies" they thought would serve the former AB ruler's interests.

Over time, the cults had to raise the ante to maintain public support. As a drug addict has to keep increasing the level or frequency of his fix, so the cults had to come up with something new and dramatic to survive. Their biggest problem was that the gods had gone and ceased involvement with their human devotees. It became increasingly difficult to claim that the worship activities produced any results beyond the good feelings of the participants. Thus, many cults began to focus more and more on orgiastic rites or suspense-filled initiations, sometimes including various levels of sacrifice. Let's describe some.

Selected AB-God Cults

We cannot easily retroactively differentiate between groups originally involved in natural celebrations that evolved into AB cults and ones directly resulting from human experience with actual ABs. Given biblical documentation, one can say the *YHVH* cult falls in the latter category, as does its contemporary cult of Baal; the cults of Mithra, Demeter, and Dionysus appear to be in the former category. The cults devoted to Isis and Osiris, two of the oldest, probably evolved from groups of Egyptians who served them during their actual reign.

Cults of Demeter and Dionysus

Two examples of AB cults co-opting nature ceremonies are probably those of Demeter and Dionysus. They appear to have originated in practices designed to achieve psychological harmony with the natural transformations of an individual life and the Earth's seasons. For instance, the Greeks celebrated Spring with rites that symbolized nature's awakening from winter. Their celebrations honored the fertility of plants, animals, and humans, focusing on sexual energies that animate conception and birth. They likely served an educational purpose, illustrating the principles of agriculture and animal husbandry (and perhaps human reproduction), ensuring the transmission of this knowledge to the young.

Demeter (daughter of Cronos and Rhea) and Dionysus were the Greco-Roman names for Anunnaki. Demeter was likely a sibling of Zeus (Enlil, "first among equals" in charge of the Earth colony) and Hades (Enki, in charge of Abzu), involved in the creation of humans (as Ninhursag) and the science of agriculture. Dionysus or Bacchus was sometimes identified with Hermes. Demeter and Dionysus were among the "twelve great Olympians."[5] Their Greek cults were later adopted by the Romans and attracted many followers.

Cults of Isis and Osiris

These two of the most ancient AB-god cults were active well into the Greco-Roman era. They probably originated in Egypt from the period of physical AB rule, before the eras of demigods, kings, and pharaohs. Over the millennia, the emotional fervor of their members created archetypes that energized large groups of Mesopotamian and Egyptian peoples. One powerful archetype associated with their lives was that of physical resurrection.[6] This may have been stimulated by the accounts of Osiris' resuscitation (with AB medical technology) after his mutilation by Seth.

To prepare for a hoped-for resurrection in the AB heavens, the pharaohs, and many other Egyptians, practiced eating "divine" foods and observing other rituals, including mummification of the body after death. Devotees who hoped to follow the same path flocked to one of the cults associated with the power of resurrection: Tammuz, Mithra, Balder, or Christ.

One Orphic song goes, "Say, 'I am a child of Earth and starry Heaven, but my race is of Heaven'. . . ." It continues to say the initiate desires to assume his role with the other ABs. The greeting desired by the initiate from an AB in heaven was "Happy and blessed one, you have become divine instead of mortal." They were prepared to give up Earthly life to rejoin their AB relatives in the skies.[7]

Mithraism

The Persian culture that gave birth to Zoroastrianism is vague regarding the identity of Mithra (around 600 B.C.E.). He reputedly had a "virgin birth," a term sometimes used to signify the child's father was an AB "watcher." In another version, he was an AB subordinate to Ahura Mazda, the AB ruling Persia.

Mithraism included beliefs in a physical resurrection and a judgment after death. The horns of the bull became a symbol that identified its followers throughout West Asia and into the Roman Empire. Its influence was great among men of action (soldiers, tradesmen, and financial officials) and had fraternal relations with the female cult of Cybelle.[8] It absorbed certain symbols of the older Osiris cult, including the seamless robe representing universal light.

Mithraism was eventually subsumed under the politicized Roman Christianity, but it provided archetypal symbols that helped to energize the Christian movement. Mithraist contributions to Christianity included the substitution of Sunday for the Sabbath as the most holy day, the adoption of December winter solstice rituals as the birthday celebration of Jesus, the sacraments of bread and water (later wine), observance of 40 days for Lent, Easter (Eastra in Latin after an AB known as Astarte in Phoenicia and Ishtar in Mesopotamia), and the 12 stations of the cross.

YHVH and Baal Cults

The cases of Baal and *YHVH* seem to represent a very direct evolution from allegiance to a specific Anunnaki AB to religious cult worship. Baal (which means Lord, and who is referred to in the Hebrew Pentateuch) is portrayed in many sources as an AB who ruled a large region of West Asia. His Ugarit temple in part of the old Canaanite Empire was discovered in 1928, where he was identified as the son of a more senior AB (perhaps Enlil, known in the Canaanite cuneiform clay tablets as El). His legacy is honored in Lebanon's ruins of Baalbek, still awaiting scholarly explication.

As for the story of *YHVH* (covered in chapter 12), the Bible does not clearly describe his motives for initiating his relationship with the Hebrews. That he was one of the Anunnaki is suggested by the moral and ethical standards promulgated in the books his angel dictated to Moses, similar to the behaviors of the Anunnaki described in the Sumerian literature. *YHVH* called for an eye-for-an-eye system of justice, bloody warfare against those who opposed his regime, harsh penalties for citizens who disobeyed him, patronizing views of women, rigid social behaviors, and exclusive worship by his followers.

By providing the intellectual and social cohesion to keep a large percentage of the descendants of the Abraham-Moses-David lineage together, his intervention established the perfect cult. His followers were convinced they had been chosen for a special mission and that their AB would return soon to begin the reestablishment of a "society of the elect."

The Hebrews had to contend with Baal's followers when they followed *YHVH*'s instructions to take over Canaan as their new home. In the long struggle to conquer local rulers and establish the land of Israel, the Hebrews slaughtered scores of local kings and their followers, all of whom were loyal to Baal. Yet, Hebrews continued to be drawn to the worship of Baal, with *YHVH* and his prophets and judges for generations fighting a war against cultural co-optation of the Hebrews by local followers of Baal. In fact this conflict grew more intense as the centuries passed and became symbolized as an eternal struggle between good and evil in the Jewish mind by the time of the Essenes.

Enduring Cult Hostilities

Hostility between the AB-cults, epitomized by followers of *YHVH* and Baal, became so ingrained in human societies that the resulting hatreds outlasted the Persian Darius, Alexander the Great, the Roman Empire, the Muslim Empire, European colonialism, and modern efforts to find peace in the Middle East. Hitler's Aryan cult atrocities against the twentieth-century descendants of the Hebrew cult were the most despicable perpetration of this historic animosity between religious cults, but not the last.

Fifty years later, religiocide spanned the turn-of-the-millennium globe. Christian Orthodox Serbs and Muslim Albanians engaged in mutual genocide. Russian Orthodox Christians and Muslims waged a deadly struggle in Central Asia. Muslims and Christians carried on bloody decades of religiocide in the Sudan. Intra-Christian (between sects) hatreds spilled blood on a regular basis in Northern Ireland. Muslims and Hindus fought for a disputed region between India and Pakistan. Christians slaughtered believers in native cults in Guatemala and other Latin American countries and suppressed followers of indigenous religions in North America. And the flames of a worldwide conflagration were being fanned by the actions of extremists on both sides of the Jewish/Christian-Islam split in the followers of *YHVH*.

What kind of god would not only sanction, but require such fratricide of his followers? Who would want to promote the killing of one's brothers and sisters? The answer seems to me to clearly lie in the internecine battles of Anunnaki gods that have been unwittingly taken on by naïve humans. Human religions still blindly wage war among themselves thousands of years after the reasons vanished.

During the active period of these cults, other AB cults sprang up throughout the Indo-European region. For instance, the Radha-Krishna cult was a strong movement in the Hindu Bengal. Personal devotion to the absent god was pledged, expressing a yearning for reunion with the departed AB. Devotees desired to experience the bliss, and sometimes erotic ecstasy, they or their forebears had enjoyed when the ABs inhabited Earth.[9]

An Unintended Cult

When one reviews *The Lost Gospel Q* (edited by Marcus Borg and a best estimate by biblical scholars of what is believed to be the shared source from which the gospels of Matthew and Luke drew material, and which may be what Jesus actually taught)[10] and the Nag Hammadi material discovered in 1945, one cannot assert that Jesus attempted to form a new religion. In the Gospel of Thomas, he made it clear that all humans were part of the creative consciousness of the universe that had manifested itself through humans.[11] "We came from the light, the place where the light came into being on its own accord and established [itself] and became manifest through [our] image."[12] This quotation suggests Jesus believed the original light (life) was self-creating and that humans were direct manifestations of it.

By stressing each individual's direct linkage to a self-manifesting creator, Jesus dethroned the idea that *YHVH*, any other AB, or their demigod and human lieutenants could be intermediaries between individuals and the ultimate source of consciousness (light). After his political execution, different groups felt empowered to establish communities of belief and lifestyle independent of the self-perpetuating priesthood that had served the AB rulers. Jesus' life story was adapted and used as the basis for the Christos cult that grew from some of his Greek followers and evolved into Roman Christianity.

Ironically, as seen in chapter 22, Jesus' efforts to preach human responsibility and promote a region-wide movement of self-determination in political and social matters ended up with the opposite result. Early Christian theology reinforced the ABs' authoritarian, other-world-oriented model of society. (Even though Greco-Roman Christianity espoused the Gospels' ideas of love and peaceful service, it used *YHVH*'s stern wrath and punishment as the preferred model of social control.)

Cults and Religion

Religion is a modern social invention, taking on its current, Western supernatural form in the Roman Empire less than 2,000 years ago. *Merriam-Webster's Collegiate Dictionary* defines religion as "The service and worship of [a] God and the supernatural. The commitment or devotion to a particular faith or observance. . . . system of beliefs held to with ardor and faith." The word religion comes from Latin *re* + *ligare,* meaning to re-bind or reconnect. This etymology implies that humans had to have already been separated from their gods and wanted to reconnect with them.

Thus, the AB-cults were the first religions, worshiping gods who were no longer present with their human subjects. Each cult/religion offered specific beliefs and practices purported to re-bind "left-behind" or "fallen" humans with its now departed AB.

When we use the term "god or goddess cults" to imply people worshiping only an idea, it is important to keep in mind the correct chronology of words. The English *god* came from Old German *got* that corresponded to the Latin *deus*, which was in turn based on the Greek word *deos* that originally meant a *being from the sky*. Thus, "god cults" were originally groups devoted to ABs who had descended from the skies and later returned to the heavens.

Outside the Cult Culture

It is very difficult if not impossible to trace the evolution of consciousness in traditional societies that escaped the Indo-European cultural experience of god cults. After all, it is we "moderns" who have collected the stories and translated them into our language *after* our advanced cultures have influenced those very societies. Many have traditional practices that respect the power of or honor a particular AB. But they never confused that limited being with the supreme or universal creator, as Western religions learned to do. In fact, up until the time of the Dead Sea Scrolls, most Hebrews kept the distinction between *YHVH* (the most high of the gods they knew) and the Lord of the Universe.[13]

Avoiding the period of AB-cults and the AB-modeled deism (described in parts 7 and 8) allowed traditional people to maintain a clear distinction between the universal "creator god" and ABs from the skies, at least until Western missionaries arrived.[14] For instance, the Nyamwezi people of Tanzania believed in Mulungu, a supreme god (our term) who was remote, although not necessarily indifferent to humans. They also believed a hierarchy of nonmaterial ABs existed between Mulungu and humans. They had no conception of the universe's creator being directly involved in human affairs in the manner that cult worshipers did.

Humans outside the West Asian colonies were nonetheless intimidated by early exposure to the power of the Advanced Beings. They learned to seek to gain favor or goodwill through the Anunnaki messengers *(dyinyinga)*. For instance, the Mende of Sierra Leone believed a senior god originally met with humans and tried to meet their needs but that the supplications became so burdensome that he shut himself off, leaving humans to deal with his subordinates.

The Lotuko (Sudan) and Lugbara (Uganda) peoples, like many others, developed the practice of offering sacrifice and prayers to gain the favors of AB-gods.[15] This perhaps reflected the apparent Anunnaki practice of requiring humans to provide food for the gods' tables in exchange for protection or support. When the gods didn't answer, some people may have concluded that greater sacrifice on the part of humans might win favorable attention. For instance, the Makoni of Zimbabwe turned to strangulation of a human victim when all else failed.[16]

Impact of Cults on Consciousness

The advent of AB-cults filled a psychological need created by the departing ABs. Unfortunately that served to perpetuate the dysfunctional ways of thinking and behaving among humans under colonial rule. Cults provided humans with a scapegoat, letting them escape the opportunity and responsibility to develop an independent, human, Earth-based sense of psychological security.

Humans under AB rule had become conditioned to looking to the ABs for direction and help. With the gods no longer there, they turned to a cult leader who would do everything possible, using threats as well as inducements, to maintain the illusion that his cult's god was still in control. As long as people believed the AB-gods would play the same role from a distance, the psychologically demeaning behavioral traits were reinforced. The priests' mastery of inner senses and subtle energies, gained from study with the ABs, gave them an advantage in predicting or manipulating natural events. Any success in their prophecies or forecasts would have made gullible followers believe the AB still loved them.

Eventually large groups among the Egyptians, Israelites, Philistines, Phoenicians, Assyrians, Babylonians, Persians, Aramaeans, and even the Greeks succumbed to magical thinking. The miracles or illusions performed by the cult priesthoods "proved" the distant ABs still watched over them. As we'll see in the next chapter, general acceptance of this "magic" by large groups led to internal contradictions in human consciousness. Experience-based knowledge became pitted against beliefs based on faith in the priests' dogma.

21 What Fragmented Human Consciousness?

Over the last three millennia, humanity has gradually developed mutually inconsistent and antagonistic modes of interpreting its experience of the universe and hypothesizing about the unknown. Perhaps without stretching the metaphor too much, the species *Homo sapiens* can be said to have developed an extreme multiple personality disorder. Two modes of thinking—materialistic and supernaturalistic—make up the extreme polarities of this spectrum of human consciousness. Their manifestations, fundamentalist religions and dogmatic scientism, inhibit human learning and species self-realization.

Most people vacillate somewhere between the two extremes as they attempt to understand and explain events and experiences in life to themselves. Flexible forms of skepticism and temporary uses of magical thinking fall somewhere along the spectrum. Continuing with the multiple personality disorder metaphor, we can say that different groups of humans have developed fundamental definitions of self that are antagonistic to the personalities of other groups. These personality fragments struggle with each other for control of species consciousness. This internal conflict inhibits the emergence of an integrated, reality-oriented, problem-solving *Homo sapiens* consciousness.

Multiple Personality Disorder As a Metaphor

A few definitions at this point will facilitate distinguishing among the groups in the following discussion. First, a caveat—no label is intended to clinically characterize any given group. Each psychological term implies only relative tendencies in interpretative thought. A second caveat—the reader should not ascribe any term to him/herself or anyone else. Every individual combines the modes of consciousness described here in various ways.

In this chapter "multiple personality disorder" applies to the collective consciousness of the human species, not to individuals. Thus, the species "personality" comprises various "subpersonalities" (groups with primary tendencies in the directions suggested by the psychological terms used here). The tendencies fall into basically three categories: psychosis, neurosis, and authenticity. In clinical usage, as they refer to individuals, psychoses affect the whole personality, while neuroses affect only part of the personality.

For that reason, the "psychosis" category encompasses the two extremes identified in the opening paragraph. "Paranoia" refers to the exclusively materialist orientation (scientism). "Schizophrenia" refers to fundamentalist supernaturalism. Under the "neurosis" category we include magical thinking and other psychological syndromes where maturation has been retarded by the AB intervention experience. "Authenticity" refers to progress toward or the achievement of a realistic human perspective on the natural order.

Chapter 7 articulated a plausible path of authentic development (naturalism) in human consciousness. This present chapter provides one explanation for the transition from naturalism and flexible skepticism to a neurotic primary focus on magical thinking in the Indo-European culture. The next chapter speculates on how magical thinking led to the schizophrenic worship of an imaginary supernatural realm. Chapters 22 and 23 show how the influence of supernaturalism caused a paranoid reaction on the part of natural science.

These four chapters together demonstrate how historical factors may have caused humans to go from a unified consciousness to a fragmented one (or how the species personality dissociated into multiple subpersonalities). A unified consciousness (personality) sees the universe as one integral organism with all beings and phenomena interdependent and governed by the same principles. A fragmented species consciousness includes various psychotic and neurotic "group personalities" which arrive at different and often mutually antagonistic interpretations of reality.

Perhaps the following will help explain why I think it does not stretch the terms psychosis and neurosis too far to apply them to fragments of species consciousness. For instance, I apply the term schizophrenia (a form of psychosis) to the dualistic thinking necessary in supernaturalism. In individual schizophrenia, the person vacillates between functioning in "tested" reality and mentally inhabiting an "imagined" reality, as in the movie *A Beautiful Mind.* On this basis, I apply the term schizophrenia to groups with mutually exclusive ways of thinking about reality. One group develops and modifies its beliefs on the basis of experience and public "testing," while another group projects an "imagined" explanation of the world and tries to make the facts fit its beliefs.

A distinction must be made between the way most psychologists view schizophrenia and its usage here. The psychologist would label anyone who says he hears voices and sees beings that others cannot perceive with the five senses schizophrenic. Given a multidimensional universe that includes other conscious entities, the term schizophrenia in this book would *not* include people whose inner senses give them access to other beings or other levels of consciousness that can be confirmed by group experimentation.

In this discussion, certain other distinctions become important. The involuntary psychotic imagining of another reality and the voluntary creation of a phantasm are quite different from the creation of an imagined but plausible explanation (hypothesis) for a previously unexplained event. With a hypothesis, one has the intention of testing it against other knowledge, while one who psychologically needs to hold on to his fantasy will avoid putting it to someone else's test.

What I have called "naturalism" in earlier chapters includes groups that relate to the universe as an aspect of one conscious organism (including other levels of consciousness) and test their assumptions against collective human experience. In the "personality" model of species consciousness, it is called "authenticity."

What I have called "supernaturalism" involves the acceptance of a projected, nontestable divine realm (the equivalent of hallucinations in the psychiatric definition of schizophrenia). In effect, the supernaturalist has fixated on an imaginary version of our universe with an anthropomorphic heavenly father and his minions ruling over mankind outside the laws of nature. As a result of this assumption, the supernaturalist has taken magical thinking to its extreme.

The "paranoid" materialist on the other hand suppresses and denies aspects of his own experience. Fearful of anything that lies outside his own concrete experience, he limits his consciousness to the realm of the five senses. This polarity alienates individuals or groups from each another, just as multiple subpersonalities dissociate within an afflicted individual's personality.

A devoted materialist and a fanatical supernaturalist can agree on neither the nature of any problem nor its solution. The former says humans must abide by what they see and touch. The latter says the outcome is ultimately in the hands of one's god. Thus, consensus about even the basic facts becomes impossible. An individual schizophrenic, as I defined the terms (part materialist and part supernaturalist), is continually torn between self-management and absolving himself of accountability for what happens. He can never distinguish between what his god causes and that for which he has responsibility.

At the level of species consciousness, supernaturalists tend to look to their gods for "the solution," while the materialist depends exclusively on the physical sciences to provide solutions to all human problems. In between, the realist believes in learning from human experience but does not ignore information from other beings or other dimensions of consciousness. While the realist believes he is responsible for the choices he makes and their implications, both the materialists and the supernaturalists have an external scapegoat.

The materialist believes he can ultimately blame genes, random selection, the environment, or accidents for everything that happens. The supernaturalist believes a higher power will ultimately compensate or punish him for any mistakes he might make. The struggle for dominance by these different "subpersonalities" has fractured human consciousness for millennia, shaping social institutions to conform to one perception of reality and then reshaping them to fit another.

How Did This Struggle Come About?

Assuming that humans originally had a propensity to authenticity (developing a natural and experience-based conscious awareness of their universe), how did mankind develop this set of obvious internal contradictions? This chapter seeks an explanation for the split from naturalism to magical thinking. We should be able to identify historical events contributing to the split that divided humans into those who primarily worship anthropomorphic gods and those who mainly see themselves as integral parts of nature. Chapter 22 is devoted to that search. Similarly, historical events should explain why modern science and supernatural religions have come to avoid each other's intellectual territory. Chapters 23 and 24 look at that issue.

An inborn human impulse to discover the fullness of the species' involvement in the universe at large seems to characterize the development of human consciousness.[1] Each individual has an innate need for experimentation and learning. The nature of life itself and the survival of the species require that individuals—and the species as a whole—continually expand their awareness of the levels and consequences of the species' interactions with its multidimensional environment. This process would seem to lead to an appreciation of the awesome power and magnificent design of life in a dynamic universe. If successful, perhaps a highly conscious species could learn to deliberately and constructively participate in the ongoing process of creation.

This concept of an authentic Stage I in the historical process of conscious evolution has not been included in conventional models of social evolution. Scholars generally espouse the notion that early humans must have engaged in fantastical thinking, attributing a magical character to the world. However, we must remind ourselves that we have no historical evidence to support that. On the contrary, chapter 7 set forth an argument favoring the view that a unified consciousness grew out of the primal natural experience.

If that argument has merit, what could have derailed this natural, ever-deepening process of learning about one's own nature and the nature of the universe? Significant numbers of people would have had to become convinced that their tentative understanding of reality was absolutely wrong. What experience would be powerful enough to cause a young species to abort its natural learning process?

The most plausible cause would be an encounter with a species so much more advanced that the naïve humans would accept that the ultimate answers lay in this advanced culture. They would give up their own search for knowledge in deference to the ABs' information and technology.

The need for "a-ha" experiences of learning or insight seem to be a built-in part of human nature. Recent imaging technology that captures pictures of brain activity, or lack thereof, reveals that when humans open themselves to a-ha experiences of poetry, prayer, meditation, and other ecstatic states the body has a pleasant and satisfying response.[2] Anticipation of this state is highly motivating, perhaps as essential to human survival as the sex drive. The particular experience or practice does not seem to matter; what is important is the experience of one's shift in states of consciousness. If one is exposed to a new culture that offers more frequent and more powerful a-ha experiences than one's normal environment, that culture gains great influence over that human's behavior.

The AB-intervention hypothesis suggests that *Homo sapiens sapiens* encounters with a highly advanced culture would have provided for just such an altered state. The natural progression of physical, mental, and spiritual development in the human species would have been shocked off its track by the seemingly all-powerful AB presence. This chapter provides material that tends to confirm this hypothesis.

The Unified Mind

During the last two centuries, Western scholars collectively created the notions that pre-modern humans operated with a simple consciousness and that their minds were occupied by superstitions (mistaken beliefs about the universe). However, when we look at historic artifacts and traditions without interposing our relatively recent ideas of "gods" on them, a different picture emerges. Early human consciousness may have been closer in its understanding to our current scientific insights about the inner workings of the universe than our supernatural, nonscientific suppositions of the past two millennia.

Reports from the few extant "unconverted" aboriginal and traditional cultures give some insight into how our ancestors communicated with departed spirits, linked with natural energies, and exchanged information with other species. If they had an abstract idea of a universal power, it was just that, a realm of universal life, energy, or consciousness in which they lived unquestioningly.

What would the cosmology of groups unaffected by modern religious developments be? One of America's leading cell biologists, Ursula Goodenough, makes a persuasive case for a universal cosmology that would resonate with all humans fully exposed and sensitive to nature. She writes that dealing with the cycles of birth, life, and death—making sense of the elements, the seasons, other species, and the reality of an ever-changing landscape—evokes "awe and wonder at the grandeur, the poetry, the richness of natural beauty (and) fills us with joy and thanksgiving."[3] Such a cosmology must have preceded religion.

Prior to the intervention of ABs, humans would have had only their direct experience of nature with which to formulate notions about the universe in which they were embedded. As a part of this direct experience, early humans would have used their inner senses to access the multidimensionality of our universe. Still experienced by some current traditional societies, modern science has now rediscovered this skill. Jeremy Narby's wonderful description of how Amazonians access information about the medicinal values of rain forest plants through an altered state of consciousness illustrates such a way of knowing.[4]

Like present-day shamans, traditional peoples lived in multiple realms, using their inner senses as well as their physical ones to perceive different aspects of the world. For these humans, there were no artificial divisions between other levels of consciousness and mundane existence. They were sensitive to the life in all things, relating to the energetic fields of natural phenomena and other beings as they lived in harmony with their own nature and in nature.

Geographer and cultural historian James DeMeo has presented substantial proof that our ancient forebears living in a more natural world were nonviolent and far more social and loving than most humans are today. He writes, "With very few exceptions, there is no clear and unambiguous evidence for warfare or social violence on our planet Earth prior to around 4000 B.C.E. and the earliest evidence appears in specific locations, from which it firstly arose, and diffused outward over time to infect nearly every corner of the world."[5] The date and locations highlighted by DeMeo correspond with my estimated time (see chapter 20) for the AB pullout and the ensuing period of chaos in the Indo-European region.

Most anthropologists have assumed that such ideas about inner realms and invisible realities came from a primitive dream world of totally subjective experience.[6] However, recent consciousness studies have confirmed that inner senses transfer information energetically and through as-yet-unknown channels. So, for instance, we have reason to believe that early humans could have perceived a subtle energy departing a body after death, as reported in ancient texts. After all, many people report seeing it today. Early humans could also have been as aware of the auras of living bodies as any modern psychic or other sensitive human. Modern Kirlian photography was not necessary for them to sense the biofield of a leaf or body limb.

To continue to dismiss traditional human stories about such natural beings and forces as the result of an overactive imagination ignores their basis in current scientific research. To accept unconfirmable psychological processes such as Freud's theoretical "obsessional neurosis"[7] as explanations for religious thinking is equally ill-founded. Scrupulously dealing only with the available *evidence* would help us avoid projecting such modern assumptions on the past.

We must try to transcend our own Western cultural conditioning, steeped in the notion of an anthropomorphic God, which assumes artifacts found at a burial site represent god-worship. There is no evidence that early humans shared the anthropomorphic idea of God that permeates all our current patriarchal and authoritarian religions. In fact, there is no reason to believe that the thinking of early humans would have naturally arrived at the notion of "gods" or "a God" as we define those terms today.

Mythologists have extensively debated the origin of concepts about Advanced Beings, but their conclusions have been based more on presuppositions than evidence. We have no record of early languages that included comparable terms. When we find prehistoric symbols or artifacts, we have no idea of the assumptions underlying their creation. We certainly have no basis for concluding that a 35,000-year-old stone carving was used to worship or appease a god.

Most Westerners are not cognizant of the theological blinders through which they look at ancient material. We forget that transition humans did not have the accumulated cultural baggage of two thousand years of *YHVH*-based religions. Even scholars who are not strong supernaturalists assume earlier people were. They unthinkingly mislabel many concepts or objects in other languages. For instance, we have labeled many natural, emotionally charged archetypes in ancient or foreign cultures as "gods." To do so mistakenly implies the users believed the archetypes were "divine beings to be worshiped."

A brief look at Japanese Shinto myths illustrates how we can mislead ourselves and others.[8] The following, called "gods" by Western translators, would more accurately be labeled the characters ascribed to natural events and forces: Diakoku would be translated as a "field of prosperity" instead of a god. Inari would be called "the essence of rice" instead of the god of rice. And so on with Ebisu, the energy of fishing, and Hotei, the zest of joviality. The Japanese use many such Shinto affirmations when thinking of natural phenomena. By misinterpreting them, the naïve Westerner concludes they worshiped many gods, i.e., were pagan and less advanced than we. I believe it was the Indo-Europeans who regressed into magical thinking.

In another instance, early Teutonic peoples (Scandinavians, Germans, and some Anglo-Saxons) seem to have developed a set of labels for natural phenomena before their exposure to the supernatural perspective.[9] They included Woden, symbolizing the wind; a warrior, Thor, for thunder; and Freyr, the life force animating crops. Anunnaki gods probably did not become associated with such local concepts until after the post-Flood diaspora. By 1000 B.C.E., names for natural forces were likely to have been replaced by gods venerated by the AB-cults.

It stands to reason that the ABs would have had their own natural perspective. Not seeing the universe from the lesser-developed humans' misperceptions, they would have seen more accurately how humans fit into the overall schema of life. If humanity were able to identify the areas of knowledge, information, or technology we have received from ABs, we might grasp something of that more-balanced view of ourselves. With the help of a nonhuman take on human progress, we could perhaps see ourselves more clearly.

Magic from Misunderstanding

No basis exists to assume that magical thinking and supernaturalism develop from natural human evolution. People don't start fantasizing about the "lottery god" smiling on them until they have knowledge of and experience with an actual lottery. Neither is there any reason to believe humans would naturally develop visions of a magical or divine realm full of beings who maintain personal relationships with humans unless they had some basis in experience. Magical thinking only evolves after one has observed what appears to be magic (outside of one's personal experience). Children do not believe in Santa Claus until parents or others produce the goodies allegedly left by him.

The anthropologist's concept of "cargo cults" offers a reasonable explanation of how magical thinking could have appeared in the AB-god cults of the last chapter. The film *The Gods Must Be Crazy* was a popular illustration of a cargo cult. In the movie, aboriginal people took any item that came from the skies as something to be worshiped, including a Coke bottle tossed from the plane of overflying moderns. The original idea actually came from a group of Melanesian islanders who thought World War II parachute drops of supplies came from gods. They did various rituals in hopes of securing more "goodies" from the airplane gods. Early humans might have reacted similarly to AB landings.

An important example about the Anunnaki that resembles the cargo-cult/Coke-bottle phenomenon has to do with physical immortality. The ABs lived longer lives than humans could imagine (possibly due to their planet's long orbit around the Sun). They were able to resuscitate their apparently mortally wounded cohorts by seemingly magical means. They disappeared for long times and then reappeared on Earth. All these things could have caused naïve humans to develop several misunderstandings of AB reality. An understandable mistake, from the human perspective, would be to believe that death did not exist for those who came from the heavens.

Many texts refer to humans who tried to escape Earth's constraints and gain access to what they thought to be physical immortality. Gilgamesh, one of the early demigod kings anointed by the Anunnaki, thought his AB maternity would qualify him for life as an immortal. *The Epic of Gilgamesh* recounts his many attempts to find the plant of eternal youth. After battles, hardships in travel, travails that would have killed an ordinary man, and personal sacrifice, he finally discovered that all his efforts could not gain him his wish. Only the "Gods in Assembly" could make a decision to extend man's longevity, and they apparently never decided to attempt it. Some followers of Jesus, desiring immortality, wanted him to provide the secret for travel to the heavens where the chief AB-god lived, but he responded, "For men this is impossible." Only a god could grant admittance, according to the Gospel of Matthew.

Some humans believed if they took an AB "injection" they would gain eternal life. Others sought to enter the AB shuttles between Earth and the deep-space ships to travel to a place of immortality. Such magical thinking does not die easily; in 1997, more than two dozen members of the Heaven's Gate community in California committed suicide with the expectation that a spaceship (in conjunction somehow with the Hale-Bopp comet) would pick them up. Today members of a vast "ascension movement" believe they have the key to achieving immortality.

Magical Thinking Today

I trust the examples given here clarify how human misunderstanding of the advanced AB technologies could have led to magical thinking. This was likely the first dissociation within the naturally unified human consciousness. Magical thinking became the "neurotic subpersonality." The next chapter searches for the causes of humanity's next fragmentation, the appearance of what I have metaphorically called society's "psychotic subpersonalities."

On the cusp of the millennium, polls in the United States were conducted about many priorities, values, and attitudes. One *USA Today*/CNN/Gallup poll in December 1999 dealt with issues of religion, spirituality, and faith. It found the nation still largely Christian, but less tied to the specifics of any church. Denominational lines were blurred as many people claimed allegiance to a church-free spirituality, with the idea of God not attached to a particular religion. Thirty percent chose the label "spiritual, but not religious."

However, the amazing finding for the most scientifically based, industrially developed society on Earth is that more than 86 percent reported the magical belief that their special god was personally interested in the minutiae of their daily lives. Regardless of apparent natural laws of cause and effect and mutually inconsistent results, people believed their private prayers would be magically answered. Lotteries would be won, sports teams would prevail, accidents and injury would be escaped, etc. Their gods were expected to do tricks for them.

To paraphrase another author, I would conclude this chapter by arguing that "until we better understand how [human experience with ABs] resonates deep within ourselves, we have little hope of understanding how our most basic fears and desires manifest themselves in the external world and how we can learn to live with them."[10]

PART VIII

A Bipolar Legacy

Introduction to Part VIII

What would modern society be like if there had never been institutions of kingship and priesthood? How would humans behave without their supernatural religions? Try to imagine how much these institutions have shaped human history for the last six thousand years. Earlier chapters have attempted to ferret out the origins of these institutions and speculate how humans came to believe that self-anointed kings had divine rights and that self-appointed priests spoke for invisible gods.

We have seen how naturally developing human consciousness confronted with Advanced Beings would have been likely to perceive them. Our most logical inference is that humans, from either physical or nonmaterial contact with ABs, would have seen them as natural entities, i.e., would have taken them at face value.

When ABs encountered by humans appeared and disappeared at will, made things seem to materialize in mid-air, and performed other feats beyond human comprehension, they were likely to have been seen as magicians. Whether the actions had occurred in 3-D space or in other states of consciousness, they would have been called magical (in the terminology of the times). Performing these magical acts, the ABs would have been perceived as being from some dimension of the universe, unknown or unreachable by humans.

Part 8 sets forth a process by which magical thinking could turn into what we now know as supernatural consciousness. It then reviews how supernaturalist institutions have interacted with natural and authentic movements in society. Their effect on human thinking and behavior has been the creation of a somewhat bipolar mind.

Chapter 22 postulates how recognizing an AB as an elusive being with powers or technology beyond those of humans could evolve into defining the same AB as a being beyond nature and human comprehension. In other words, how the magical thinking described in the previous chapter could cause a bifurcation of human consciousness, in which one lives partially in a consensual, experienced reality and partially in an imaginary one. Chapter 23 looks at how the force of dogmatic supernaturalism has often overwhelmed the natural impulse to authentic development and an integrated consciousness. Chapter 24 defines materialistic science as the defensive, extreme opposite reaction to the institutional power of supernaturalism and explains how it came to be.

22 Why Did AB-Worship Turn Supernatural?

Worship is a learned behavior, not a natural emotional response. Extensive cross-cultural research by the internationally respected neurophysiologist Manfred Clynes identified seven universal, mutually exclusive human emotions. Each one (anger, hate, grief, joy, sex, love, and reverence) gives off a distinctive energetic profile that can be electronically measured.[1]

Reverence, one of these seven emotions, involves feelings (inner responses) that we describe with words like awe, adoration, and deference. While the act of worship may be based on or evoke feelings of reverence, it requires focusing one's attention on a specific object. The object may be anything we deem worthy of esteem: natural phenomena (including Advanced Beings) or supernatural concepts. Thus, while reverence is a universal emotional response, how and what to worship must be learned.

What Is Natural Worship?

Natural worship focuses one's attention on an aspect of or an object in nature that evokes any of the emotions of joy, sex, love, or reverence. A man experiencing the emotion of love may worship the woman who evokes the feelings within him. A young girl learning to play soccer, in awe of high performers, may worship the women's national team. A farmer revering their power may worship the sun and rain that make his crops grow. An early human may have worshiped an AB who helped him rebuild his city or an angel who gave him a prescient warning. All these forms of worship are natural; their objects fall within the natural universe of the worshiper.

Early humans, keenly aware of their interconnectedness with all aspects of the universe, could have naturally worshiped the life energies of various plants, creatures, and weather or seasonal phenomena. Such worship was not directed to a higher, separate, supernatural realm. Living the Vedic concept of "oneness with the One," they had no Western sense of being "fallen" or separate.

In North America, among tribes that seem to have escaped the postcataclysm system of West Asian, multiple AB-gods, we find at least three examples of worship of an all-pervasive spirit. The Maidu in California, the Algonquins in the Midwest, and the Selish in Canada all carried the concept of a single creative spirit throughout nature. While plants, animals, and other natural phenomena were apparently perceived to be conscious, potentially a source and object of communication, no anthropomorphic gods were identified in their worship.[2] Their beliefs were compatible with scientific models of a self-generating universe where all beings and all nature are considered manifestations of a single creative force.

A number of African cosmologies include a similar nonhuman-centered assumption of an ultimate force at work in the universe. This concept does not encompass a separate supernatural, divine realm; the gods and any other Advanced Beings, including spirits, belong with humans in a natural system. This pre-supernatural notion of god as the "ultimate source" can be seen in some African peoples: Chiuta the self-creator in Malawi, Chuku in Eastern Nigeria, Imana in Rwanda, the Bantu Khuzwene, Jok in Uganda and Zaire, the Bushman's Kang, and many others. Although their science was not on a par with today's, their cosmology is more elegant and compatible with twenty-first-century science than the AB-based religions that came later.

Steps to Supernatural Thinking

Not all philosophers will agree with my view that supernaturalism represents a retrogressive step in human development. One of the most progressive modern views of the evolution from god-cults to an intellectually defensible notion of a "supreme mind with freely choosing parts" goes as follows: Primitive man believed in many gods until the Hebrew idea of *YHVH* as the one all-powerful god prevailed in Western culture. Over time Christians and Muslims adopted the view that this invisible god was a transcendent being (outside nature). Later theologians transformed him into an immanent god (pervading the universe). Next the one god was seen as "god-is-everywhere" (pantheism) but not of it. The next concept, panentheism, implies "everywhere-is-god."[3] This leads us back to the early African and Vedic cosmology that all is in one and one is all.

If this book accurately portrays early humanity as already conscious of "everywhere-is-in-and-of-god," then two important questions follow: Why did a large segment of the collective mind (mainly the so-called Western part) develop a dualistic sense of reality? And, how did the "universe-is-one" mind-set become so highly evolved in the East (particularly India), eschewing the Western concept of a divine dichotomy between gods and humans? Answers to these questions appear to be found in the development of supernatural religion in what we call the cradle of civilization, beginning less than 3,000 years ago. Here religions that grew out of absentee-AB-cults that described their gods as immortal, magical beings took the next step toward supernaturalism.

What Is Supernatural Worship?

Supernatural worship is the worship of something that does not fit into any dimension of the universe accessible by human consciousness. By placing an object of their worship in this imagined supernatural realm, humans have concluded it lies *beyond* their comprehension and acts according to its own rules. It acts on our world unilaterally, and we can only appeal to it.

This supernatural realm in Western religions includes a god, its subordinates, and its unknowable laws in whatever dimension they exist. While there are slight differences in the various god images, all deities depicted possess human-like attributes; monitor and judge the behavior of individuals; and may act in response to personal invocations, prayers, or other expressions of human needs or desires. The god is responsible for both the good and bad things that happen to humans, according to its own logic. Each religion, even when granting the possibility of other paths to this supernatural realm, believes it has been given special access to the one god, requiring its own beliefs and forms of worship.

Many people will concede that the current image of their god may have evolved through succeeding generations of believers. But they no longer remember how or when this god attained the level of truth in the minds of their ancestors, nor why their own participation in a particular form of worship produces the emotional charge it does. Yet, three-fifths or more of the world's people act on the faith that this imagined being will take care of them, if they worship it and place responsibility for their destiny or personal fate in its hands.

This global supernaturalism (as expressed through orthodox Judaism, Christianity, and Islam and their derivatives, such as new thought, new age spiritualism, and various sects) appeared relatively recently in historical terms. A confluence of historical events (some already discussed) during the declining era of the Roman Empire provided the basis for the consolidation of the notion of supernaturalism:

- The development of absentee-AB-cult worship in the Middle East.

- The existence of a Hebrew cult whose members claimed to worship the most powerful of the departed gods (*YHVH*).

- A fresh and compelling myth that developed around the Jesus who attempted to reform the Hebrew cult.

- The organization-building skills of Roman citizens, including Saul/Paul, who appropriated Jesus' name and reputation[4] to create a Greco-Roman cult devoted to the concept of Christos as its god.

- Enough political power left in a waning government to elevate that cult to the status of an empire's religion.

- A council of bishops decision (Nicea) to cull from competing texts a Bible that largely excludes references to the reality of other ABs and Jesus' humanity.

Supernaturalism Based in AB Experience

This book postulates that a group of humans over time developed supernatural theology due to two experiences. First, humans misunderstood the intellect and technologies of physical and/or ethereal ABs and assumed their role was to take care of humans. (Humans became psychologically conditioned to worship their superiority.) Second, the emotional impact of separation from those beings after a long period of dependency reinforced magical thinking (the "neurotic subpersonality" described earlier). The people left behind for what seemed an unbearable length of time went into denial, causing the final split into dualistic or schizophrenic thinking. Denial is a refusal to see the reality of a situation and the creation of an imaginary, but more palatable, interpretation of what had happened. (Counselors assist modern individuals to work through their denial of the real causes of their problems in therapy.)

The Anunnaki had apparently decided to go about their own affairs, but humans felt bereft at being deserted. So supernatural theology was the defense mechanism created to help cope with the pain and anxiety of an obvious separation of humans from their gods. One of its purposes was to assure humans that the religion's rituals would either bring the departed gods back to Earth or reconnect the humans to them in the supernatural realm.

This defense mechanism was the creation of a mind-set conditioned by the exposure to the highly advanced AB culture. Natural humans, attempting to live an authentic life, would have had no need to reconnect with something considered *divi*ne. In the natural view, humanity never *divi*ded from its creator. Forming the word *divi*ne (or its equivalent in any language) was a definitive step in the *divi*sion of human consciousness from its natural source. Humans, not the gods, took that step.

This group denial and formation of the defense mechanism didn't happen instantaneously. The first and maybe second generations of left-behind humans would have remembered they were mourning the departure of one of the previously present AB-gods. Subsequent generations would have imagined the metamorphosis of the physical beings into energetic beings who had gone back to the skies. They may have thought of the now-absent ABs as beings who could magically shift dimensions, returning to some ephemeral state. After a few more generations the ABs may have been thought of as beings who were essentially ethereal but had taken on physical form to survive on Earth. Even later, the metamorphosis in human imagination, not in objective reality, would have made the AB-gods into what humans think of as divine beings.

At the height of the cult era (described in chapter 20), competition to have one's god known as the true and supreme god was keen. It involved missionary programs, psychological warfare, and military battles. The cults struggled for membership just as religious organizations do today. In Western civilization, the adoption of *YHVH* the Jewish god by the new religion of Christianity in the Roman Empire won the battle for historical supremacy. This possibly helped Judaism, alone among the cults, to maintain its status into the modern era.

Supernaturalism's Hebrew Roots

The history of the Israelites following their settlement in Canaan, after 40 years in the Sinai desert, illustrates the early stages of supernaturalism. (One can find similar stages in Zoroastrianism and other cults.) The first phase involved efforts by the gods (or at least by their followers) to maintain the allegiance of their respective regions. The second involved competition among the gods (or their followers) to determine who was the most powerful. For almost a thousand years the Hebrews were caught up in these two stages of cult worship. The Bible tells us they vacillated in their faithfulness to *YHVH*. The nation broke into two sections, factions of which were always attracted to Baal or some other god. Jerusalem was defeated, and many of its leaders and citizens were exiled to Babylon.

Similar cognitive fragmentation (confused beliefs) characterized the societies of Egypt, Mesopotamia, Palestine, Greece, and Rome, resulting in cultural chaos in the region. In 539 B.C.E., the Persian king Cyrus, who had just broken up the Babylonian Empire, released Jews from their Babylonian captivity. They were free to depart with the treasures taken by Nebuchadnezzar a half-century earlier from the Temple in Jerusalem. With their return to Jerusalem, and some measure of local self-determination within the Persian Empire, they began to believe that *YHVH* might truly be the first among all the gods. By 500 B.C.E., they had reintegrated with the Jews who had not been taken into captivity and built the New Temple of Jerusalem (led by the King Zerubbabel, heir to David's throne).

Back in the land designated for them by *YHVH*, they gave thanks and rededicated themselves to the law of their unseen god who seemed to have triumphed over the others. They set up a new priesthood, severely restricting the role of women in the temple—they could no longer be priests. Strict dietary laws were enforced. Social customs to set themselves apart from those who were not followers of *YHVH* were strictly enforced, including a ban on marriages to non-Jews. The idea of *YHVH* as the most powerful AB-god gained adherents.

But neither such social cohesion nor exclusive AB loyalty lasted. As *YHVH* from a distance appeared to manipulate the actions of other cities to protect his flock, the Jewish society again fragmented from within (while other "watcher" AB-gods may have pursued their own agendas with their cult followers). Sects began to splinter from the mainstream temple culture. The Dead Sea Scrolls show that 2,000 years ago *YHVH* was still seen as just one powerful god among many. By then Judaism was in disarray under the Roman emperors.

While a wide variety of god cults still competed with each other in Indo-European culture, among the Hebrews, schisms even more fundamental than the political split of Judah and Israel had fragmented the vision of a *YHVH* nation. The disunity had become so great that the Romans had little difficulty controlling this province of their empire. *YHVH*'s grand vision for his people had dissipated, and various sects continually squabbled among themselves. Some Hebrews were still devoted to Baal's cult. Quarrels among the Sadducees, Pharisees, Essenes, Zealots, and others added to the dissension among the Israelites. In the views of the Essenes and others, the Sanhedrin (leading the Jewish quasi-state) were turncoats collaborating with Roman procurators for their own personal gain.

As *YHVH*'s absence became more extended, the desire for restoration of his direct rule grew stronger. Jews had the impression that before he disappeared, *YHVH* had promised that he would return in some form or the other to politically and spiritually reclaim his followers. Prophets claimed that those who kept the faith during his absence would be reunited with him and enjoy his protection. (Remember this was still only magical thinking.)

Hebrews were not alone in expecting their god to return. The Blackfeet tribe of the United States believe that their AB, Napi, had promised to return one day. The AB Gluskap was expected to return by the Algonquins, and Quetzalcoatl had apparently left the same impression in Mexico.[5] When the Spanish conquistadors arrived in their sailing ships in the sixteenth century, Aztecs welcomed them as their returning god. Such expectations could have led to widely accepted prophecies, like the Hebrew one that caused many to believe Jesus was the promised messiah.

Some Jews expected a new political leader (*misphat* or Davidic king of justice); others wanted a new spiritual leader (*tsedeq* at the temple); and yet others called for a return to basic *YHVH* values and simple living (the Essenes), awaiting a *mashiah* (anointed one) to give order to the religious chaos in Jerusalem. More orthodox Jews hoped the appearance of a *mashiah* (messiah) would gain *YHVH* the attention he deserved. None of them anticipated the arrival of a reformer named Jesus. It would take a few centuries more before Roman Christians adopted *YHVH* as their own and promoted him to the world, not only as the most powerful AB, but as the supreme god of the universe.

The Christos Cult

Most historians now credit the formation of the Christos cult to Saul, a Pharisee, Roman-Jewish tentmaker from Tarsus in Asia Minor, who recruited from among the splintered followers of Jesus and welded them into a new religion.[6] (Christos is the Greek word for "messiah," a title that no record shows Jesus ever claimed.) Taking on the new persona of Paul, Saul divorced budding Christianity from Judaism, developing the idea that Jesus had been both human and divine.

Using the appearance of Jesus as an explanation for the non-reappearance of the AB *YHVH* drew anxious followers to the new religion, steeped in the AB-god cult tradition. By claiming Jesus was a recently returned messiah (thus renaming him Christos) who came as a substitute for *YHVH*, Paul and other writers gave people a new and fresh personality to worship. Combining several attributes of other AB-cults (Osiris, Horus, and Mithra) made the Christos cult attractive to many groups. Ironically, co-opting the powerful martyrdom of an anti-cult Jewish teacher, the early Christians animated a religion that emerged as the strongest AB-cult ever.[7]

Given the longevity and strength of devotion in two cults (those of Isis and Osiris), the architects of the Christos cult attempted to coopt their members by espousing some of the same beliefs. The widespread belief in resurrection central to the Osiris cult helped strengthen the promotion of the same belief about Christ. Osiris the god was believed by some to have been reborn in his son Horus, so Christian evangelists taught *YHVH* had been reborn in Jesus.

Due to the fact that the Isis cult had declared for centuries that she was supreme among all the other gods (responsible for inventing human language, arts, agriculture, medicine, government, etc.), associating her with the Mother Mary helped to reinforce the Christian trinity as that of the supreme god's family. Followers of Isis who had believed their faith in her would gain them a heavenly home were susceptible to converting to Christianity when told Mary could also intercede with the Supreme God to gain them immortality.[8]

By the end of the second century after Jesus, Christianity had garnered a following rivaling any other cult. It was persecuted by the Roman authorities (Christians refused to pay allegiance to the Emperor) until emperors like Galerius and Constantine began to realize the growing numbers in this new group could bolster the crumbling Roman Empire. Constantine first decided to tolerate growing Christian groups (313 C.E.) along with other AB-cults. He later convened a council of Christian bishops (at Nicea in 325 C.E.) to define their orthodoxy and centralize control, effectively allying the church with the state.

Later Emperors (Julian and Theodosius I) decided to further co-opt Christianity, progressively making it into the state religion (by 392 C.E.). Eventually emperors exempted Christian clergy from taxes, built churches at government expense, authorized independent ecclesiastical courts, made Sunday a legal holiday, and began to suppress worship of other gods and goddesses.[9] This most energetic of supernatural religions helped to shore up the authority of the Roman Empire, even with its imperial capital in Constantinople. The 438 C.E. Theodosian Code required all citizens of the Roman Empire to be members of the official Church.

What had started out as natural worship of the demonstratively AB *YHVH*—who apparently returned to the heavens and became the object of cult adoration—came to be seen as prophetic of a new form of worship. That form was anthropomorphic supernaturalism, a synthetic combination of Jewish and Greco-Roman ideas. Three-plus centuries after the Old Testament vision of *YHVH* as most-powerful-among-local-ABs (held by Jesus' contemporaries, the scribes of the Dead Sea scrolls), the new Christian church needed a single supreme being. That was long enough during a period of language barriers and unreliable communication channels to allow the council at Nicea in 325 C.E. to efface *YHVH*'s connection with the Anunnaki and designate him the only true God. To reinforce that claim, they tried to censor all references to the history of other ABs in officially recognized texts. They banned Hebrew, Aramaic, and Greek texts that revealed too much historical realism.

The Nicean manufacturing of this new church produced an institution with its heart and its head in competition. The *YHVH* tradition of the Old Testament emphasized blind faith and obedience to so-called temporal representatives of the divine. It promoted the use of force and ritual to inhibit the realization of individual and community experimentation. Incorporation of the New Testament message of Jesus emphasized individual responsibility based on values of peace, love, mercy, and forgiveness. Struggles within the church and within individual members have revolved around the differences in these two modes of being from the beginning.

AB-Channeled Islam

A few centuries later, Christian supernaturalism would find an unanticipated supporter in the Arab world. Mohammed's linking of the concept of Allah to the Roman-redesigned *YHVH* would implicitly strengthen the claim that the Western world had found the only real and supreme god of all creation. Christianity's incorporation of the *YHVH* tradition also benefited Islam, which could then claim histori-cal roots in the by then widely respected Hebrew Pentateuch. Islam may exemplify how the fates of cultures peripheral to the Anunnaki colony were determined by the growing psychological attraction of supernaturalism.

Given the cultural chaos during the last phase of AB-cults, local cultures could have gone in many different directions. The proto-supernatural models of Mithraism and Zoroastrianism had lost their emotional appeal after a few centuries. As people gave up hope for an early AB return, the psychological control enjoyed by various AB-cult priesthoods diminished. It is arguable that even the nascent, monotheistic supernaturalism of Judaism would have dissipated without the creation of the widespread emotional appeal of the Christos cult. While a few groups in the region tried to find a natural way out of the cognitive chaos, most fell under the sway of Greco-Roman supernaturalism. Islam would likely never have arisen had it, and Judaism, not reacted to and drawn from the energetic field (emo-tional archetypes) of Christianity born in the Christos cult.

While the Mediterranean region was being consolidated by the Roman Empire and Christianity, Arabia remained in the post-AB period of political chaos. Just as it had remained largely untouched by the empires of Darius (Persian) and Alexander (Hellenic), the region escaped Roman domination. Centuries later Arabia was still peopled by a few urban communities (such as Mecca and Yathrib, now Medina) and nomadic (Bedouin) tribes. Various cults, some based more in naturalistic traditions and some more associated with AB gods, had no common following. Some Arabs—linked with the Abrahamic lineage of Ishmael, born of the handmaiden Hagar—believed in Allah, their version of *YHVH*.[10]

The region could have progressed in an independent direction (with its strong intellectual and scientific bent) instead of succumbing to the supernaturalism of Greco-Roman Christianity had it not been for one man's encounter with another invisible AB: Mohammed's visitation by the Archangel Gabriel. This AB, like *YHVH*, apparently remained invisible but dictated sacred documents that would be the foundation of a new religion.

From their earliest memories, peoples of the Arabian Peninsula had venerated a black meteorite ("sent down from heaven") enshrined in the Kaaba of the town of Mecca. Mohammed understood from his revelations that Mecca was to be the worship center for the anthropomorphic god Allah (perhaps so named after Alalu, the first Anunnaki god who had once ruled planet Nibiru and visited Earth).[11] Since Mecca was not associated with an AB who would have had his "priests," Allah's religion would have no hierarchical priesthood between man and god.

Mohammed believed he had been called to organize a new religion under Allah to bring order and progress to the Arabian peoples. To motivate them he prophesied a coming "day of judgment" with future rewards and punishments, to be administered by a loving Allah.[12] He channeled the Koran to complement the Old Testament and other religious texts. Mohammed had probably been exposed to the Ebionite and Nestorian followers of Jesus and saw Jesus as one of a line of prophets, like himself.

Thus, Islam ("Muslim" originally meant "traitor," a name given Mohammed's followers by members of his own tribe) did not originate as an AB-cult, deriving from the relationship of one flesh-and-blood AB with its human subjects. Mohammed incorporated some of the beliefs associated with Judaism and Christianity and gave it a cultural flavor that would make it acceptable among the nomadic tribes. He, like Jesus, gave up on the aristocracy as a means to social reform.

Where Supernaturalism Did Not Develop

The Indo-European world of 3,000 years ago extended from northwestern India to the Mediterranean basin. While the complete process of transformation from naturalism to modern supernaturalism ensued only in the Judeo-Greco-Roman-Arabic nexus, developments in India opened a window to its early stages. The Hindus went through the AB-god-cults era but did not throw out the already existing pantheism. There we can see the progression from natural worship of ABs to worship of absentee ABs as magical beings. However, this way of thinking about multiple ABs did not replace the original Vedic idea of Atman as the expression of the one source from which the universe manifests itself.

The earliest forms of the Vedas (sounds and practices to communicate with universal consciousness), the Brahmanas (prose), Aranyakas (rituals), and Upanishads (speculative concepts), were progressive extrapolations of the naturalist perspective described earlier.[13] But as contacts with the Anunnaki culture expanded, epic poems like the Ramayana and the Mahabharata portray a more concrete view of gods, based on experiences in the Anunnaki colonies.

We can be fairly certain that between 2500 and 1500 B.C.E., male and female gods from the Anunnaki leadership began to be worshiped as Shiva and Devi. Hindu writers began to identify Vedic archetypes (such as Usas symbolizing the dawn and Surya the Sun) with ABs who played roles in the proto-Indo-European Anunnaki civilization. Such cultural borrowing reflected the AB-cult era, but no one AB was assigned the same supreme position as the anthropomorphic *YHVH*.

A Dichotomy within Supernaturalism

Not only did the creation of supernaturalism split a part of human consciousness from its natural whole, but supernaturalism split itself into the false dichotomy of good versus evil, and with deleterious effect.

When the religious came to believe in two separate realms (natural and supernatural) that could not be bridged by humans, they became susceptible to believing in other absolute polarities. The acceptance of such labels to distinguish ABs (God versus Satan, etc.) in the divine realm made it easy to categorize human events in the same manner. Humans could be tagged with the label "evil" and become associated with God's opponent Satan. Under this logic, any self-labeled "god's people" could feel justified in carrying out their interpretation of their god's justice against anyone they labeled evil. (See chapter 4 for insight into the AB protagonists whose conflicts precipitated divisions among humans.)

Supernaturalism's Staying Power

Whatever its origins and earlier manifestations, history records that supernaturalism reigned supreme in the West as Roman Catholic dogma, and that its offshoots held sway from the fourth century throughout the so-called Dark and Middle Ages. Naturalists hid in esoteric schools and secret societies, a necessary practice due to church persecution and the Inquisition that began in the thirteenth century. The human creation of a new persona for the AB *YHVH* was transmitted by fluctuating empires to large parts of Europe and limited areas of the continents of Asia and Africa until 500 years ago.

In the fifteenth century, the campaign for global supernatural hegemony began in earnest, carried by Spanish and Portuguese maritime exploration and British-led intercontinental trade. By then, everyone except a few esoteric societies had forgotten that the supernatural god of Indo-European culture had originated as an ordinary AB in a family of ABs from the planet Nibiru.

Spread effectively by military might and trade buttressed by modern shipping and European religious/political institutions, supernatural Christianity—the European flag-bearer of the *YHVH* tradition—took over both American continents, Australia, large sections of Africa, and much of Asia. As a result of the modern era of colonization, this supernatural religion and its assumptions about reality have been insinuated into almost all cultures on the planet.

It Couldn't Happen Today

In the world of today's communication systems and with our appreciation of the technological potential of conscious beings, it is unlikely that an AB landing on Earth today would have the same destructive impact on human consciousness. A public exposure to more advanced species today would likely accelerate the expansion of human consciousness. However, humans are still mired in the institutional legacy described earlier and in the "multiple personality" fragmentation we have metaphorically called neurosis and psychosis.

In order to achieve any sort of reintegration of these fragments, humanity must be willing to reexamine its past. Each religion must develop in a public process a reassessment of its origins and review them with all other religions. Only then can humans collectively operate from a common perspective and consciously choose a coherent planetary future.

23 What Happened to Naturalism?

What distinguishes a 1,700-year-old, institutionally contrived supernaturalism from a perennial, naturally developing spiritual perspective? Here is an illustration.

Supernaturalism treats a tragedy like a fire or physical disaster, something that leaves random survivors scattered among the dead and wounded, as an event choreographed in heaven. The survivors feel blessed by the unfathomable wisdom of their god, and they vow to be more faithful to him in the future. Relatives of the deceased seek comfort for their loss by believing that the same god made personal selections and took only those he needed in heaven. Or, he made judgments that determined who deserved to die. Regardless of the outcome, those who lost family and loved ones and those who felt guilty about surviving can decide to move on because they believe a divine plan was at work. And the learning stops there.

In the natural perspective, humans admit they can't see all the factors that played a role in who died and who didn't, and that they may never understand. They realize that many circumstances come together to produce an outcome, and they try to discern as many connections as possible. However, they recognize that nature is very complex and that life includes risk and accident as well as room for the effect of conscious intentions. They accept uncertainty as the crucible that forges stronger and wiser beings. And the learning continues.

Philosopher Rudolf Steiner called the natural perspective Anthroposophy (from the Greek phrase meaning "wisdom in Man"), suggesting that "man's [natural] intelligence was derived from a more spiritually perceptive form of consciousness."[1] Such a continually expanding form of spiritual awareness can incorporate all human experience into its naturally knowable universe. In contrast, by defining part of their experience as "supernatural," humans forever place it beyond their ability to understand.

When fourth-century bishops in Nicea concluded the topic of ABs belonged in a supernatural (divine) realm, they officially gave up the search for natural explanations of the AB presence in history. As later Christian followers accepted the assumptions of supernaturalism, they made themselves susceptible to psychological manipulation by clever humans who created compelling images of the divine. As ordinary people projected the god(s) beyond their intellectual reach, they accepted the authority of the priesthood to interpret reality for them. Thus began one religion's campaign for control of the human soul.

The ensuing conflict pitted people who wanted to protect the perennial wisdom of collective human experience against the Church that wanted to rewrite history and gain control over a mass social movement. The so-called perennial wisdom placed humans squarely in a natural reality, along with any other conscious beings who might exist anywhere in the universe. The promoters of supernaturalism determined to prevent humans from learning about ABs and the inner dimensions. We can only assume the motivation was to gain control over the course of human thinking and behavior ("by their fruits shall ye know them").

Using the multiple-personality metaphor, the primal *Homo sapiens* personality had now split off another subpersonality, one more malignant than the neurotic one of magical thinking. The schizophrenic subpersonality of supernaturalism would become strong enough to temporarily overpower the natural one and distort human consciousness. This chapter reviews examples of the resilience of the "core personality" and suggests why it has temporarily lost control.

The history of the core personality has been nurtured by esoteric groups for thousands of years. This shows some humans have always been cognizant of their natural relationship to all beings and all facets of the universe. Aspects of this natural perspective can be found in the Vedanta materials, parts of Hebrew prophecy, the Tao Te Ching, the Platonic dialogues, some of the apocryphal Gospels, the Mahayana theology, the works of Plotinus and the Areopagite, Sufi sayings, writings of some Christian mystics, and various scientist-philosophers of the Renaissance and later.[2]

This body of insights regarding the multidimensional nature of the universe and universal consciousness, to our knowledge, first appeared in the historical record in the Vedic literature. The following represents what appears to be the deepest level of understanding humans (and perhaps the ABs who taught us what they knew) have been able to fathom about the nature of our universe:

- All aspects of the phenomenal universe—the world of things and all beings, even the gods—are a manifestation of one Source.

- The human mind is of the same substance as the Source and is a local manifestation of that universal consciousness.

- Human beings are capable of directly accessing knowledge of the multidimensional universe through physical and inner senses.

- Conscious life must increase its knowledge of the whole and develop new skills to grow in harmony with nature.

Given that new insights in physics and biology and research in consciousness now confirm much of that perennial wisdom,[3] the question remains: How did supernaturalists with their assertion of a separate realm succeed in pushing this perennial wisdom (natural science and philosophy) aside? Given the history described in this book, much of the answer appears to have been *psychological manipulation and intimidation backed up by the threat and use of force.*

Some part of the human mind seems to abhor internal conflict. It wants to know the "truth" and may even be hard-wired to question incongruences within any dogma or inconsistencies between dogma and personal experience. To suppress such an innate, self-learning nature would require a powerful effort. So, why did one group of humans determine that they would use whatever force was necessary to condition humans to accept the unprovable assertions of their new religion?

Many theories of elitist conspirators, evil cabals, and even AB manipulation have surfaced in the past few decades. It is beyond the scope of this book to satisfactorily deal with that issue. However, the material reviewed for this book does make it clear that the imposition of supernaturalism (in all of its forms) has been accompanied by many types of force against unwilling converts. It is also clear that political use of supernatural archetypes has made possible the motivation of whole societies for military and economic benefit to the manipulators.

Once supernaturalism is officially established, a small group can gain control of the resources of society's central institutions and marshal them to solidify and perpetuate its unnatural view of reality. The identity of who has been behind the imposition of supernaturalism and for what ultimate purpose remains elusive.

The previous chapter looked at some of the events that led to the triumph of the supernatural movement over naturalism. This chapter reviews some efforts during the era of AB-god cults made by some individuals and groups to prevent society from succumbing to an otherworldly mentality and the control of its political and religious advocates. Although they failed to hold back the supernaturalist tide, they maintained a base of knowledge (described in this chapter and the next) that can still challenge it.

A Natural Resilience

Ancient Greece provides a good example of the innate impulse of people living beyond the AB sphere of influence to challenge magical and supernatural thinking. At the beginning of the decadent AB-cult era in the Middle East, the early Achaeans—probably Aryans from the plains north of the Black Sea—had a sophisticated civilization about 4,000 years ago. Moving into the Aegean region over 3,000 years ago, the Dorians (apparently Alpine or Nordic peoples along the Danube River) joined the Achaeans.

Natural science and human reason blossomed in their combined Hellenistic culture prior to and after the local "dark ages" from 1200 to 800 B.C.E.[4] These Greeks refused to humble themselves before the Mesopotamian AB-gods or submit themselves to the dictates of their representatives, including the "divinely" anointed kings of Persia.

They stressed rational inquiry and placed their faith in tested knowledge instead of asserted truths, and they saw the gods as beings to be dealt with directly. They kept a detached perspective on tales of the ABs (see the naturalistic treatment of ABs in the writings of Homer and Hesiod). They did not lose sight of humans' responsibility to think for themselves. Instead of worshiping ABs, they used AB legends as material for dramas (Aeschylus) and even comedies (Aristophanes).

This rational worldview tried to take away the mysteries of the material world, account for human behavior and its self-control, and learn how to live well with nature. These Greeks were not concerned about being saved from sin or blessed by otherworldly beings as a result of blind faith. They had no commandments, dogma, complicated ritual, or sacraments. Their freedom "from fear of the supernatural was one of the most important factors contributing to the intellectual and artistic progress of the Greeks."[5]

The second rise of rationalism occurred in the seventh century B.C.E., remembered in the scientific and philosophical works of Thales of Miletus (in modern Turkey), Anaxamander, and Anaximenes. These Ionian intellectuals espoused ideas similar to those in the Vedic East. By the sixth century B.C.E., Pythagoras (550 to 500 B.C.E.) taught along the natural lines reflected in the Vedanta principles.[6] (He reportedly studied the teachings of the Egyptians, Assyrians, *and* Brahmins.)

By this time the AB-god cult movement had become stronger in Greece. Perhaps to attract followers, Pythagoras mixed some mysticism (such as belief in the transmigration of souls) with his powerfully rational concepts, and his followers slipped more toward magical thinking in the following century. Socrates attempted a similar balancing of the natural and supernatural, but his intellectual progeny, Plato and Aristotle, edged more toward the mystical side. Plato abandoned the Greek idea that truth could be proven only with the five senses and embraced the conception of a supernatural world of which this one is only a shadow. Aristotle's retrogressive astronomy provided a basis for the Christian Earth-centered universe that lasted until the sixteenth-century Renaissance.

Ambivalent Cults

In the early days of the AB-cult era, religious groups were ambivalent about the nature of the gods. Zoroastrianism, dated by historians at various times from around 1200 to 500 B.C.E., had a somewhat humanistic perspective but had an anthropomorphic god as its centerpiece and gave the edge to supernaturalism. Yet, its texts clearly documented the "flesh and blood" nature of the ABs (known as the Sons of God) who consorted with and corrupted humans.

From Zoroaster's period until the Nicean Council, advocates of the supernatural view resorted to selective censorship to suppress memories of the Anunnaki gods as physical beings. For instance, the pre-Christian era Jewish hierarchy omitted several "sacred texts" from the Septuagint, including the Book of Noah and the Book of Enoch, with their explicit accounts of physical intercourse between the gods and humans. This version of the Old Testament was adopted by the new Christian religion as it developed in Greece. Such acts of censorship culminated with the church's codification of acceptable theology at the Council of Nicea, where it attempted to efface all evidence of realistic views of ABs.

At other times, physical force was used to suppress views that would undermine the theology of supernaturalism. Two individuals who met similar fates were Jesus (see later) and Mani.

Mani, whose views made him a third-century competitor to Christianity, was a descendant of the rulers of Babylon/Persia, and he founded Manichaeism. Although influenced by Zoroastrianism, he was strongly disposed to portray the nonhuman beings who played such an important role in human affairs as corporeal entities with appetites like those native to Earth. His religion, combining parts of the other major traditions, was seen as a huge threat to the leaders dependent on their claims that they had direct channels to the supernatural god. His realistic interpretation of the Zoroastrian accounts of ABs who disobeyed orders and slept with human females earned him the enmity of the Persian Zoroastrian and Christian leaders of Asia Minor. They slaughtered his followers and tortured him before subjecting him to a gruesome public death.

This price has been paid over the subsequent 1,700 years by many whose personal encounters with ABs threatened institutions whose power depended on people's blind faith in a human-projected anthropomorphic heavenly father. Any who press for public disclosure of government-held evidence of ABs and human inner ways of knowing become enemies of all these institutions. Thus, the suppression and cover-up reaches way beyond the government, to all organizations who benefit from the fragmentation of human consciousness.

Attempts at Natural Reform

About 1000 B.C.E., the pharaoh known as Akhnaten made an attempt to move the Egyptians away from the god-cult mentality. He attempted to gain acceptance for the idea that humans should relate to the natural order of the universe. He tried to get worship to focus on the Sun as the symbol of that universal power. His Egyptian experiment was very short-lived, a totally unsuccessful effort at transcending the era of AB-god cults, but its seeds may have survived in esoteric circles.

By 500 B.C.E., teachers with a more natural, realistic conception of reality were trying to bring the increasingly popular god-cults back to a human focus on Earthly life. For instance, Orpheus, in a cult that honored the AB Dionysus, did not support the idea of an anthropomorphic god. His concept was closer to Eastern thought, an immanent power that is also inherent in humans (similar to the teaching of Jesus).[7] He distanced himself from the popular cult belief that man might become a physical AB (like Ezekiel being physically taken up into heaven) through certain rituals. Rejecting the notion of physical resurrection, Orpheus believed consciousness (soul) lives before and after an incarnation.

The Orphic philosophy had several parallels with other contemporary Hindu beliefs, including the Vedic vision of creation from a cosmic egg (or seed bed) existing in "timeless time," similar to Kronos, the Greek idea not antithetical to modern cosmology. Orphic rites also tended toward the Buddhist practices of discipline and inner focus, the desired result being purity of thought and deed (as taught by Jesus a few hundred years later).

Buddha himself had attempted to reform the increasingly supernatural and ritualistic practice of Hinduism. He appears to have wanted a return to the Vedic view that the Almighty is immanent in humans and all of nature (not a being separate from its creation, but a force pervading it)[8] and humans are aspects of the creator— Brahman is Atman and vice versa. He spoke against taking the symbols (names and images from Vedic literature) that represented aspects of the natural universe to be divine beings.

Jesus—Reformer and Martyr

Borg's *Lost Gospel "Q"* and other analyses suggest that Jesus attempted to pierce the veil of the AB-god cults and bring people to an awareness of their own "divinity." This man represented a synthesis of the East and West (including various Hebrew concepts) but primarily taught the perennial wisdom summarized herein.[9]

So much confusion surrounds Jesus' often reinterpreted history that the truth now eludes us. His Hebrew name suggests he was the offspring of Mary (whose husband was Joseph) and an angel of *YHVH*. The Bible calls him Yeshua ben-Yussef (born of *YHVH*, son of Joseph). It is possible Joseph had descended from the demigods of the AB "royal lineage" even as Noah reportedly did. Such a diluted blood tie would have justified the label *ben-Elohim* reportedly given him (it means "Son of the Gods" like the AB "Sons of the Gods" in the Old Testament). Some reports suggest he also used the title *ben-Adam*, making the point that he was descended from Adamu, the humans created by the Elohim (AB-gods).

Regardless of his family tree, Jesus' message included the view that every son of mankind (Adamu) is equally a son of the gods (ABs). (This could be interpreted as placing stress on the universal nature of consciousness in all beings, or it could mean recognition of the mixing of AB and human genes.) A Hebrew teacher with such progressive ideas would have had to receive an education outside the radical Essene community with which he has been linked. Metaphysical sources report Jesus learned a natural perspective during youthful training in esoteric schools in Babylon, Persia, India, and Egypt.[10]

Jesus' message was clearly intended for a wider audience than the Hebrews alone.[11] He opened his ministry to all people, inviting the "unclean" to a wedding, visiting the homes of people who had defied religious tradition, treating women as equals in religious discussions, and preaching forgiveness of sinners. Reflected in comments like the following in parentheses, he is believed to have stressed several principles of the perennial wisdom tradition: the power of one's own intentions in healing ("stand up and walk"), the role of self-judgment in determining moral behavior ("do unto others as you'd have them do unto you"), and conscious survival of the spirit after death, as after his crucifixion ("they thought they were seeing a ghost").

This revolutionary message was rightfully perceived to threaten both Temple and Roman authorities. To keep it from spreading, the local Roman ruler Pontius Pilate and the Temple leadership in Jerusalem conspired to have Jesus tried and crucified. He reportedly appeared afterwards in a ghostly body to demonstrate that consciousness could survive physical death.

The close associates of Jesus went away with varying interpretations of his calls for reform and other teachings. On the basis of his martyrdom, his name and message energized a number of groups to spring up in Greece and Egypt as well as Palestine. They represented schools of thought ranging from a more natural orientation to just a new form of cult worship. Most lost sight of his truth.

One group, the Gnostics, appeared to remain close to Jesus' democratic and humanistic approach.[12] They gained many supporters in the Hellenistically influenced Egyptian culture. Perhaps Jesus' ideas on resurrection (survival of the ethereal or subtle energy body after death)—first seen as a ghostly figure by Mary Magadalene and then by the other disciples—and reincarnation found resonance there. But the Gnostics alone split into at least sixty sects.[13]

With no common language, little literacy, and historical enmities, Jesus' followers remained fragmented and underground. Eventually, Jesus' reform message succumbed to a supernaturalism requiring less human responsibility than he called for.

Resolution in Rome

Near the end of the Roman Republic, the expanding AB-god cults of the Near East, with their emotional escapism, had overpowered Greek naturalism and shaped local cultures from the Indus River to Egypt and the Greek Peninsula. A natural scientific and philosophical perspective that was mature in Greece by 600 B.C.E. had been discouraged by mobs 150 years before Jesus' birth.

Distant enough from Mesopotamia, the early Roman culture apparently never experienced direct rule by the AB-gods or their demigods. During the roughly 500 years of the Republic (until Julius Caesar), the Roman cosmology was similar to that of the early Greeks. It focused on a natural universe, not a supernatural one, and saw AB-gods as real entities to be negotiated with as with any other parties. It had no "dogma or sacraments or beliefs in rewards and punishment in an afterlife."[14] Initially, their celebration of natural events invoked the *numina* or essence of the phenomenal world. Only with the later influx of cult influence from Greece and the eastern Mediterranean did worship of personal deities (Roman names given to the Anunnaki gods) become popular.

By this time, would-be leaders and demagogues had realized that manipulation of supernatural beliefs gave them emotional power over credulous citizens. Democratic principles in Greece and republican institutions in Rome gave way to various autocrats who, with cult-energized support, established various forms of dictatorship. Over the course of the Roman Empire from 27 B.C.E. to 476 C.E. one can see the full transition from naturalism to the magical views of AB-cultism, then to the official supernaturalism described in earlier chapters.

That Rome, the last major Western society to lose its independent natural philosophy, institutionalized supernaturalism reveals it was imposed from the top down. Leaders of a failing empire needed a mechanism to regain control of a fragmented nation. As an act of last resort, a series of weak emperors committed the established powers of government to the support of the newly defined (in 325 C.E.) supernaturalism of Christianity. Based on such artificial foundations, it is no wonder that the threat and actual use of force became the method of preference for recruitment as the church spread into new areas.

In a religion where fundamental tenets must be held on faith, members are not psychologically free to test their view against a non-believer's perspective. To keep them from being exposed to contradictory evidence, leaders of cults and religions use various methods to inoculate their members' minds against other worldviews. These range from blatant assertions that their god has controlled everything that is written in their church's texts, but not in others, to labeling other views as satanic or otherwise trying to discredit the source. Even raising the possibility that the church's dogma is not self-sufficient may be the basis for excommunication. When these methods do not work, some religions turn to force.

Bastions of Naturalism

As most of the "civilized world" succumbed to the magical thinking of supernaturalism, small, learned communities tried to preserve a sense of emotional independence and freedom of thought. They attempted to keep a "here-and-now" perspective on humanity's place in the universe. Their orientation stressed the acceptance of personal responsibility and the inherent value of each individual. They have been fighting an uphill battle.

In the early days of Roman Christianity, small groups had to go into hiding as supernaturalism gained control of cities and states. These became known as esoteric (inner) or occult (covered) groups who did not go along with the increasingly supernaturalist cults. Groups with varying degrees of a natural human perspective included the Hermetics, Magis, Kabbalists, Gnostics, Rosicrucians, and, later, the Templars and Freemasons.[15] Some focused on guarding documentation of the true role of the AB-gods and maintaining records of the knowledge gained from them. A few of the esoterics retained proficiency in the science of consciousness and use of the subtle energies. The alchemist tradition partially reflects this science.

The discovery of lost documents like the Sumerian and other pre-biblical texts, the Nag Hammadi library, and the Dead Sea Scrolls (which were not available to the church when it attempted to rewrite history) has finally confirmed the "secret" guarded by these groups: descriptions of tangible ABs that would reveal the artifice of supernaturalism.

Hermeticism

An esoteric scientific perspective grew out of the intervention of Egypt-based Thoth (known as Hermes in Greece), an AB contemporary of Osiris, Seth, Isis, etc. (The Sumerian and Egyptian texts suggest he was a son of Enki, the chief scientist of the Anunnaki.)[16] He reportedly provided much advanced knowledge and technical assistance to humans. Elements of this knowledge were guarded and selectively disseminated over the years by protective groups of scientist-priests originally trained in its applications by AB teachers.

The Hermetics believed that consciousness pervades all beings in the universe and that the material universe derives from it (as quanta of matter in modern laboratories arise from an unseen energy field). The goal of conscious life was a sort of "re-cognition" of an individual's connection to and participation in the universal.

While Hermeticism cannot be described as a natural human tradition, it did appear to involve an AB transfer of "knowledge for knowledge's sake," not tainted by the emotions and credulity of cult worship. Much of the knowledge was probably degraded and lost over time in the destruction of great libraries and temples. Some metaphysical sources suggest that Jesus had access to Hermetic initiates for part of his training in the East and in Egypt.[17]

For self-preservation, Hermetics, like Kabbalists, developed a public facade of supernaturalism around their secret knowledge. Thus, Hermeticism sometimes appeared like a cult focused on the AB

Hermes (Thoth). In Greece, for instance, while scientific principles from Hermeticism appear to have found new life in people like Pythagoras and Empedocles, its superficial followers became engaged in worship of the departed god. However, much of the esoteric knowledge survived and fired the imaginations of groups currently identified in history as Templars, Freemasons, and Rosicrucians.

Freemasonry

The organization popularly known in America as the Masons officially traces its origins to Freemasonry in fifteenth-century Scotland. The collective of state and national lodges now publicly portrays itself as "secret and fraternal organizations . . . descended from the craft guilds of stone masons. These groups, open to men only, represent no single religion or ideology but instead try to foster spiritual development and fraternal charity among all classes and creeds."[18] However, the truth lies much deeper, with greater significance for human history. Two English writers, Christopher Knight and Robert Lomas, claim to have traced the roots of Freemasonry back to the building of Solomon's Temple in Jerusalem almost 3,000 years ago.[19]

For reasons of competition, the Hebrews wanted to create the impression that their god was the most powerful. King Solomon, in the line of Moses and King David, wished to keep up the facade (through the temple) that *YHVH* was still active in the region. The research of Knight and Lomas suggests the associates of master builder Hiram Abif must have known the connection between the real Anunnaki Ninurta (opposed to Enki's human independence policy) and the Hebrew god named *YHVH*. They must have learned that Solomon's Temple duplicated the "Ninurta temple" constructed in Lagash almost 1,100 years earlier.[20] (Abif had been recommended to Solomon—who had no Hebrew architects or master builders—by Phoenician King Hiram of Tyre. King Hiram had been taken to visit the ABs abode and knew the truth of their existence.[21])

After the temple's completion, Abif was murdered, possibly to keep him from contradicting the Hebrew claim that *YHVH* was something other than one of the now departed Anunnaki. Associated with Abif, Freemasonry's founders must have known the millennia-old AB practices of temple construction (for use of ABs and their consorts to interact privately with their human priests and priestesses). They would have also known how the ABs anointed demigods and their human descendants as kings. They could have vowed to protect and pass on to subsequent generations the truth of AB-human relationships.

The earliest Freemasons (meaning they were not subjects of any so-called "divine king") apparently established as core priorities: the search for increasing knowledge of the universe; recognition of the worth of the individual; the practice of self-determination over AB-oriented, autocratic government; and social equality. They believed people should rise to positions of leadership on the basis of effort instead of through family bloodlines. Through the late 1700s and the early 1800s, Masons, dedicated to these values, helped shape the institutions of the new United States of America.[22] These values are now mainly implicit in Masonic lesson, ritual, and practice.

Rosicrucians

This group's origins go back to the Egyptian well of knowledge (in the Enki-controlled sector of the Anunnaki colony) that fed Freemasonry. Its official history links the group to the pharaoh popularly known as Akhnaten, who attempted to counter AB-cult worship by focusing on celebration of the natural power of the Sun. Under various guises over the centuries, the brotherhood of the Rosicrucian order has promoted expansion of human consciousness, self-healing, scientific research, and support for the foundations of a civil society. Rosicrucians have been an important bastion of naturalism in a supernatural world, promoting independent human development and self-responsibility.

This and preceding chapters have identified some of the teachers and groups dedicated to maintenance of a naturalistic perspective in the face of the overwhelming forces that benefit from the divisiveness and manipulation made possible by supernaturalism. The examples suggest ample evidence of actions by political and religious interests to distort the history of AB interactions with humans. Suppressing the truth about historical and current human experiences with other forms of consciousness makes it possible to set groups with their untestable illusions against one another.

One theme of this book holds that the greatest obstacle to reintegrating humanity's "subpersonalities" (each with a god of its own creation) resides in unquestioning acquiescence to the assertions of authority figures about their religion's institutional history. In order to objectively examine the underpinnings of our blind faith, we must learn to escape the emotional manipulation made possible through the use of loaded code words. The following discussion illustrates how difficult it is to think such forbidden thoughts.

The Challenge

Despite the efforts of such groups as those just mentioned and many natural scientists and philosophers to heal the fragmentation of human consciousness, the divisions still remain. Given the defensive reactions institutions mount to possible threats to their interests, the best hope for their reform lies with the individual members. Within the religious community some have made recurring efforts to adapt traditional dogma to new scientific and historical knowledge. Others have tried to come to grips with the new evidence concerning the origins of their religion and treat the subject as a historical phenomenon. They want to keep the religion, but make it consistent with today's knowledge.

In the twentieth century, the discovery of Jesus' all-too-human life and naturalist beliefs undeniably revealed the artifice of the organizers of Christianity. Up to this point, those who believed important documents had been ignored or destroyed to support the church's distortions of history had to depend on circumstantial evidence. But, with the discovery of the Nag Hammadi Codices (loose documents bound together) in 1945 and the Dead Sea Scrolls in 1947, the charade was exposed. In addition, the recent piecing together of the putative lost "Q" gospel counters the assumption that Jesus himself had promoted the founding of a supernatural religion.[23]

In acknowledged pre-Christian material, Jesus is neither the Greek Christ nor the Jewish Messiah. He tells his listeners they have the Kingdom of God within them. His vision of the future is a Heaven on Earth, possible if people live according to their inner wisdom. All beings are equal in his schema, with direct access to ultimate truth. Each individual is responsible for his or her own behavior. He gives simple and direct advice for peaceful and joyful living in harmony with others. Neither the vitriol of the old Hebrew god nor the authority of priests is evident. Faced with this unveiling, many "inside reformers" would like to redefine the traditional concept of Christ.

Some want to honor Jesus as a great teacher but still take advantage of the archetypal power of the name Christ. They attempt to draw a distinction between its historical origin and the use of the word Christ to represent an ideal being. For them, a "Christlike" person (or a person with the Christ within) is a highly evolved human. They promote the "Christ nature" as a potential but special state achievable by everyone to motivate people to live more spiritually.

Other Christian reformers have tried to square their more generic spiritual perspective with traditional beliefs by giving new meaning to existing church symbols or sacraments. Unfortunately, as we saw in chapter 18, the use of any current religious archetype as a new metaphor continues to activate the historical emotions associated with it. The Roman Church used the same techniques when it redefined symbols such as the midwinter Saturnalia celebration as the birthday of Jesus and the spring fertility rites as Easter. It worked for the church because they wanted the emotional energy of the traditional symbols.

Based on the earlier discussion of the power of archetypal words I would counsel reformers to avoid trying "to pour new wine [concepts] in old bottles [words]." The supernatural words are now too emotion-laden, still embedded in the separation anxiety complex of magical thinking. To recapture natural thinking we must use natural terms that release individuals from a sense of dependency on an imaginary realm and from external manipulation through emotionally charged words.

Continued use of archetypal words in order not to offend other believers or somehow capture their emotions cannot facilitate humanity's efforts to become free of distorted thinking associated with ABs. For instance, Protestant theologian Paul Tillich said in a private exchange with the author that he wanted to get rid of the "bearded-father-in-the-sky" image when people think about the ultimate creator of the universe. He redefined that creator as "the ground of being" but continued to use the word God for it. Unfortunately, his usage of the traditional word God continued to reinforce the anthropomorphic illusion identified by Freud that Tillich wanted to leave behind.

24 Has Modern Science Failed Humanity?

As the logical outgrowth of the natural path of human development described in this book, "metascience" melds the advantages of scientific experimentation and metaphysical insight.[1] A holistic learning process that requires input from all ways of knowing, metascience uses the inner and subtle senses as well as the ordinary physical senses. What we today call the scientific method comes from the innate self-learning process required of all conscious species to survive and mature in a changing environment. Conscious beings must continually engage in experimentation that tests their hypotheses about the nature of the inner and outer worlds in which they live. Absent such fundamental learning, species atrophy and eventually disappear from the scene.

In the terminology already established in this book, metascience in society corresponds to the metaphorical authentic personality in humanity's current state of conscious fragmentation or multiple personality disorder. Unfortunately, as earlier noted, modern institutional science corresponds with the paranoid subpersonality. Along with supernaturalism (the schizophrenic subpersonality) it comprises the two psychotic aspects that have rent the collective human mind. The schizophrenia element comes from the supernatural resorting to projections of a divine realm to assuage our existential anxiety. The paranoia found in scientism derives from a mode of thinking that fears and denies the intangible dimensions of human life.

This chapter attempts to demonstrate how modern science differs from metascience's natural approach to learning and how its exclusively materialistic focus was a psychotic reaction to the growing power of supernaturalism. (Without being facetious, one can say that schizophrenic behavior by one segment of society caused another to become paranoid.) It traces natural science through the eras of cult worship and supernatural religion to the point of direct confrontation during and just after the European Renaissance. It identifies the Faustian bargain that allowed unfettered growth of materialistic science as long as it did not challenge the key assumptions that underlie religious authority.

The failure of eighteenth- and nineteenth-century institutional science to empirically challenge the assumptions of supernaturalism meant that the more holistic natural view of reality had to go underground again. Limiting itself to the obvious material aspects of the universe, modern science failed to benefit from much knowledge already well developed in earlier phases of civilization. Its limited focus abetted the forces of authoritarian manipulation in religion, politics, and economics. By leaving largely unchallenged the history of religion that the religions themselves constructed, science in effect reinforced the cover-up of their false claims to intellectual and moral legitimacy.

This standoff between religion and science has left the global society fragmented and alienated from its authentic potential. The failure of modern science to help integrate all aspects of human consciousness into its self-defined purview has indirectly affected the character and quality of modern life. One result of separating the physical world from inner wisdom has been the aggrandizement of high-tech consumption for a few sectors of global society (including the military-industrial complex). Another effect has been the stagnation of progress in physical, psychological, and societal health. The most egregious negative side-effect has been the swath of habitat destruction for all species in the Earth's web of life.

Just as the supernatural church, stressing human domination over it, separates humans from nature, so does materialistic science. By ceding human experience in nonmaterial dimensions and with other beings, science abdicated responsibility for the development of human consciousness to the supernatural "priesthood." To use a blunt metaphor, the shepherd who must keep the sheep dumb to have a job is left in charge. As a result of its agreement to experiment only with the material realm, modern science lost its heart, conscience, and consciousness.

In the previous chapter, we noted the temporary surrender of the natural human scientific impulse in Greece during the height of the AB-god cult era 2,000 years ago. The explosion of experimentation and creative thought that characterized the earlier Classical Greece had been overwhelmed by the dogma and emotionality of otherworldly cults. It was in this environment that supernaturalism was institutionalized. No scientific expansions into new areas of thought were forthcoming. Men like Ptolemy, Lucretius, and Celsus only recapitulated knowledge (astronomy, physics, and medicine, respectively) from earlier periods. The great storehouse of natural wisdom in the library at Alexandria would be partially burned (in the year 265 C.E.) and then totally destroyed (in 389 C.E.). Carl Sagan's "candle" (his metaphor for science) was engulfed in darkness.

Church Strengthens Its Hand

Strengthening its psychological hold on human consciousness through political, economic, and military force derived from its status in the waning Empire, Roman Christianity would become a monolithic power in its own right. For instance, Emperor Valentinian III, from Constantinople in 455 C.E., decreed all Western Bishops must submit to the jurisdiction of the Pope. This extensive hierarchy would 500 years later continue in the Holy Roman Empire (962 C.E.) that would serve the joint purposes of the economic and military elite. The Roman Church's creation and control of universities would limit education to dogma for hundreds of years. Its long hegemony forced would-be scientists underground.

From about 400 C.E. until 800 C.E., Western civilization was truly in the Dark Ages of medieval society. The light of universal knowledge only glimmered in scattered redoubts of scholars and scientists hiding from the scrutiny of the Church. With the Carolingian Renaissance of the ninth century, flashes of perennial wisdom and new creative thought appeared in literature, philosophy, and art. With expanding economic freedom, prosperity increased in certain locales.

This upward spiraling of human creativity, lasting until the twelfth century, would be cut short by the age of Crusades (1095 to 1281 C.E.) and Inquisitions.

During that period of about a thousand years, the supernatural mentality of the Byzantine Empire (infused with Eastern Orthodox Christianity) and the Islamic world (a new brand of supernaturalism) maintained control of the rest of the cradle of (AB-influenced) civilization. These three religious regimes, with varying overlapping boundaries, held sway in the lands bounded by the Mediterranean Sea, Europe's North Sea, the Caspian Sea, and the Persian Gulf. Thus, Indo-European culture, jump-started by AB intervention and shaped by the human reaction to that legacy, would arrive in the second half of the second millennium as the dominant force in the shaping of the global human psyche.

Underground Science

Naturalism kept its head down throughout the 1,500 years during which supernaturalism ran rampant over Europe and the other regions under its control. Few, like Boethius in the sixth century, who dared write a naturalist volume called *The Consolation of Philosophy* and was burned for it, would risk speaking out. Preserving the track of Egyptian and Greek science, the European alchemists, epitomized by Roger Bacon and the Nominalists of the thirteenth century, kept the naturalist perspective alive. (The word "alchemy," derived from a similar sounding Arabic word, implies an "art from Egypt.") The alchemists believed all matter was animated with a life force and stressed independent thinking and the need to prove truth for oneself.

During this period, the Kabbalists also preserved some of the ancient understanding of natural science, some of which was lost in their parsing of supernatural treatises. Some researchers believe the Rosicrucians assisted in the survival of a natural perspective well before the fourteenth century. Others consider the Freemasons, although not publicly organized until the seventeenth century, to have been a repository of perennial wisdom throughout the Dark and Middle Ages.

The Kabbalists had been an integral part of Hebrew culture from at least the third century B.C.E. The Zohar, known as the Book of Splendor or Wisdom of the Mysterious Truth, is associated with Rabbi

Shimon Bar Yohai. He and a long line of subsequent Kabbalists had the difficult task of keeping alive the natural wisdom in Hebrew culture as its popular supernatural religion became more authoritarian and dogmatic. This split between the superficial and the essential was reflected in the use of the Talmud and Mishnah by a credulous public, while the Kabbalist material was for those who wanted the deepest knowledge available.

The Kabbalists believed that prayer and ritual, devoid of meaning and spirituality, are like straw; they don't nourish the spirit.[2] Contradicting the very essence of *YHVH*'s approach to social control, Kabbalists ruled out all forms of coercion, saying threats and force to compel any form of behavior are not justified. They taught that humans had the inner light of creation at birth and that an encircling light could be gained by individual control over desire. This light would liberate humans from ignorance. They saw the Hebrew concept of a Messianic era (later transmuted by Christians into a second coming) as a time of unprecedented enlightenment, when hope and optimism would triumph. These views were at odds with orthodox Judaism and the opposite of the way Christians interpreted the Hebrew Bible.

This underground stream of a naturalistic orientation must have animated people like Copernicus, Bruno, Galileo, Newton, and others who catalyzed the European Renaissance during the sixteenth and seventeenth centuries. Their impact, rooted in the natural science tradition, resulted in a limited liberation of individuals, institutions, and society. Yet, alone, it was not enough to push back the veil of simplistic supernaturalism that still shrouded human consciousness.

Schism in Church

Help for the survival of human authenticity came from within the church. Over time, new orders of Christian devotees had arisen (monks and friars like the Franciscans and Dominicans). Some disliked the affirmation of centralized papal authority and wanted more group decision-making. By the sixteenth century, the public had many areas of complaint against the abuse of power by many clergy. Reformers like Wycliffe and Huss wanted to turn back to the teachings of Jesus. They were persecuted by the church (Huss was burned), and the church still influenced every level of society.

However, the decision to build a new cathedral in Rome (St. Peter's) would result in the first major theological split in supernatural Christianity. To raise money, preachers were authorized to sell indulgences on commission (with Rome getting its share for the building fund). Indulgence meant papal assurance the subscriber would be "let off for a certain amount of time in Purgatory . . . in which the soul was believed to be purged and cleansed of its worldly wickedness."[3] This stimulated Martin Luther's protest (1517 C.E.) that led to the Protestant Reformation. These religious and political conflicts fostered opposing ideas. The resulting cracks in church controls permitted a resurgence of natural science.

Limited Renaissance

While the fragmentation within the church gave a sense of freedom, giving birth to a scientific renaissance, it was to be limited, and one whose potential was aborted. The revitalization of the naturalist tradition was preceded by the Italian renaissance in the arts.

From the 1400s intellectual ferment in the city-states of Italy was innovating new forms of literature and art. The fiction of Petrarch and Boccaccio made the transition from medievalism to a more humanistic perspective. The orientation of classical (pre-supernatural) Greece and Rome animated poetry, drama, and history. The comedies of Machiavelli and others helped shift the emphasis from divine, otherworldly thinking to a more humanistic, natural orientation. Painting and sculpture reclaimed Greco-Roman naturalism. The unfortunately increasingly superstitious Neo-Platonist philosophy hindered Italian science.

However, by the sixteenth century, when Copernicus (1473–1543) studied and worked in Italy, Italian scientists began to make breakthroughs, represented by the likes of Galileo (1564–1642) and Leonardo Da Vinci. Astronomy was escaping the Ptolemaic error and going back to Greek understanding of the solar system. Galileo's work confirmed posthumously Copernicus's heliocentric view of the solar system. Giordano Bruno (1548–1600), an independent-thinking former priest, developed one of the most naturalist cosmologies *(Magia Naturalis)* of the day. His astronomical discoveries preceded those of Galileo and Johannes Kepler (1571–1630). His cosmological vision was of "the infinite multiplicity and unity of the universe." He was burned at the stake for it in 1600.

Contributing to and reinforced by the religious ferment in Germany, the Renaissance began to take root there. German astronomers (Kepler et al.) and physical scientists (Libavius, Glauber, et al.) added to the expanding field of knowledge. However, the trinity of Rene Descartes, Isaac Newton, and John Locke (joined by Thomas Hobbes) was largely responsible for reintroducing the rationalistic path to knowledge last seen in Classical Greece. They had a mechanistic view of the universe as governed by inflexible laws and the notion that five physical senses are the only route to the truth. They and others emphasized reason, concrete experience, and individuality. A human was deemed to be born a *tabula rasa* (blank slate) to be written on by the experience of his environment.

Up to this point mathematics was a disparate collection of disciplines. Three people conceptually brought the field into a coherent whole: Fermat, Descartes, and Leibnitz. They are responsible for the coordinate system which became useful in expanding the theoretical grasp of physics. Three others—Kepler, Galileo, and Newton—contributed scientific discoveries that required the integration of all the disciplines. Kepler applied plane geometry to his work on the orbits of the planets around the Sun and initiated use of trigonometry in the process.

Galileo was the first experimental physicist. He actually tried to verify Aristotle's principles on the motion of planets and stars and found them to be false. Doing so upended a belief system that had prevailed for almost 2,000 years and had supported the theology of the Christian church for 1,500 of them.

Kepler used mathematics to prove the Copernican heliocentric view of the solar system. Newton, living up to his reputation as the greatest scientist of all time, made use of all the mathematics known in the seventeenth century: arithmetic, algebra, geometry, and trigonometry. He used them both to demonstrate his own theorems and to support his theories of physics.

Descartes, on the surface a dilettante and adventurer, had an inspirational dream (insight from the noumena) that implied the key to understanding nature lay in mathematics. He concluded he was supposed to apply algebra to geometry to unlock the secrets of the universe.[4] The result was analytic geometry. On the physics side of his work, he hypothesized that all of space was a continuous plenum. (The argument as to whether or not the idea was true has been only recently settled by quantum mechanics; the plenum of space is now understood to be a field of positive and negative charges.)

Isaac Newton invented "the calculus," which totally changed the course of mathematical and intellectual history. His claim to fame was the introduction of universal principles that could be proven with mathematics. He started the field of theoretical physics when he used algebra to formulate the laws of motion and gravity. He built upon the work of Galileo to identify the role of inertia in moving bodies (correcting and moving beyond Aristotle and his colleagues). Newton's work provided a rational and predictable basis for dealing with the universe.

The research and insights of these and many other innovative scientists of the period did not stop with the physical and material discoveries like those found listed in today's science textbooks. Many of them pursued research into the inner meaning of alchemy, numerology, astrology, divination, and spiritual matters. In fact, Newton spent more time and wrote more on these matters than about the mathematics and physical sciences for which he is known today. The key unanswered question regarding the history of the Renaissance is: Why did these fields of study not become an integral part of eighteenth- and nineteenth-century science?

The answer is found in the most powerful institutions of the day. The universities were still almost completely under the control of the church (which founded them). A few private individuals funded centers for scholars (like Gresham College in London), but these financiers were part of the small circle of royalty and religious leaders whose agenda was to maintain the institutions of kingship and priesthood based on the AB model described in chapter 15.

Science and Church Stand-Off

The ideas in this next section will not be found in any history book. No meetings like the Councils of Nicea or Trent were held. No covenants were signed. Nevertheless, the live-and-let-live, post-Renaissance history of modern science and supernatural religion cannot be explained without postulating some sort of implicit division of territory—even if it was only mutual recognition of the common value of avoiding a mortal attack by either one on the other.

What would the church have most feared from a more expansive and aggressive science? What if it discovered evidence that the church had falsified documents to support its assertions about the life of Jesus and the history of *YHVH?* What if science had recognized the inner senses and the ordinary nature of human communications with other beings? What if it had provided natural explanations for the miracles claimed to be interventions from its supernatural god?

Such information would have been devastating. Destroying its claims of exclusive access to divine truth would have eliminated the need for the church.

If this knowledge were potentially available (and the church leaders knew it was), what would be the logical thing to do? Work out a deal to keep it secret! The playing out of a Faustian bargain between financiers and science researchers was the most likely way it was handled. The implication was "you can have the funds you need for scientific research *if* you don't question the church's basic assumptions."

Science Limited to Materialism

The powerful families to whom church leaders listened, if such family members were not already leading the church, clearly began to finance scientific research and establish businesses to exploit its products. By encouraging the church, by means including economic contributions, to keep the populace passive and fearful, the economic elite assured themselves a ready labor force and a consumer market.

The Industrial Revolution was built upon the power accumulated by these wealthy capitalists during the "commercial revolution" from around 1400 to the 1700s, largely as a result of religious-oriented global exploration and colonization. Beginning in the late 1700s, about the time the possible inner and external implications of Renaissance science began to be recognized, the leaders of the Industrial Revolution were interested in the application of mechanical power to agriculture and industry. They wanted to harness new fuel sources, develop factory and bureaucratic structures, speed up transportation and communications, and use their capital to gain as much control as possible over most sectors of society.[5]

The seventeenth-century centralization of capital made it possible for a relatively few people to design and implement a "church/science nonaggression pact," muting the inherent antagonism of the scientific method to the delusions of supernaturalism. All that the historian of today can see are the effects; the secret negotiations were never recorded.

It took only one or two centuries for this narrow approach to science to completely fall prey to the seductions of money and politics. By dismissing human metaphysical experience as "anomalous" and denigrating crucial aspects of consciousness as "paranormal," officially recognized science became the handmaiden of industrial power rather than a route to personal empowerment.

The resulting industrial focus of materialist science can be seen in its devastating long-term external effects. Examples include the impact on our natural ecosystems of internal combustion engines, oil drilling rigs, refineries, urban sprawl, highways, box-like buildings, belching factories, boilers, power grids, strip mines, dumps, and noisy flying machines.[6]

By the twentieth century, institutionalized science would no longer be free to challenge the dogma of its economic masters. Knowledge essential to a self-sustaining planet would be suppressed or ignored. Environmental degradation caused by industry would outstrip its ability to correct its errors.

The fact is that both educational and religious institutions have benefited from the ongoing psychosis. It helped each avoid confronting the buried secrets of human experience. Science has had free rein to play in the physical realm, without concern for the moral or ethical implications of its activities. The church avoided having the standards of rational analysis applied to its dogma. Both sides were able to divert the attentions of their respective participants from questions about their founding assumptions and who stood to benefit most.

That implicit covenant constrained the work of Western science for almost 400 years, until the early twentieth-century relativity theories of Einstein and Planck. The revolution in physics they started changed the Newtonian principles underlying all the important concepts about the nature of the universe. Concepts of space, time, motion, matter, and energy were revolutionized along with the very process of progression inherent in nature. The division between matter and energy was erased. The particle and wave polarity required a different mathematics. So did the idea of an electromagnetic spectrum that behaves through a range of frequencies. Quantum mechanics, with the notion that everything continually shifts into and out of existence, required new concepts of algebra. Apparently contradictory behaviors of subatomic particles and wave functions required new thinking.

As we entered the twenty-first century, quantum thinking had challenged some academic disciplines. Physics had rediscovered consciousness. Biology was being re-visioned in terms of information theory. Psychology was being forced to rediscover its whole human focus. Medicine was confronting the fact of self-healing and losing its grip on the patients who were taking charge of their own health.

Independent science was made possible by individuals determined not to be stifled by institutions. A glimmer of hope for a reintegration of natural science and spirituality (not religion) motivated a new focus on metascience.

New Opportunity

Despite the physical-world focus of the large majority, a growing number of individuals now support a metascientific approach to knowledge and values that incorporates the perennial wisdom of natural science and natural philosophy. Support for its resurgence comes, to the surprise of many, from the unintended discoveries of industrial science.

Physicists attempting to manipulate smaller and smaller subatomic particles came face to face with the effect of consciousness on their experiments. Medical researchers trying to prove the efficacy of one consumer drug over another could not escape the evidence of the power of mind in healing. Geneticists searching for the keys to human differences found a few common ancestors unrelated to the species they had deemed to be our evolutionary ancestors. These common ancestors could be dated to a period already associated in historical materials with AB genetic engineering. Scientists themselves experienced consciousness outside the body and communications with other conscious beings. Reports of ET encounters and inner voices grew.

All these developments provide exciting pieces for a new model of humans in the universe. A few innovative and independent thinkers now envision the possibility of putting them together in an interdisciplinary cosmology, one that no longer keeps the human focus of traditional science and religion, but places humans squarely in a multidimensional and multiple-being universe that is conscious, alive, and well.

The final section of this book suggests how such initiatives can help facilitate a reintegration of human consciousness. The time has come for a recrudescence or renewal of the natural science and philosophy tradition—metascience—long suppressed by supernaturalism.

PART IX

The Current AB Agenda

Introduction to Part IX

This book has synthesized evidence from different kinds of sources that humans are not now alone in the universe and have never been. It has reported significant interactions that have occurred between humans and various groups of other conscious beings. Self-evident historical shifts in human conceptions about their experiences with these beings, whether physical or ethereal, have been identified.

Now a majority of the world's people has accepted the supernatural model. It believes conscious beings exist in two realms, a divine one limited to their god and his helpers and another limited to humans (and perhaps some other beings inhabiting distant planets). A scientific minority believes humans (and possibly some star races light years away) are alone with their brain-based minds. This dichotomy has coexisted for several centuries because the members of both groups saw no conflict between the two models. The five-sense oriented scientist just assumed the divine realm was a figment of the supernaturalist's imagination. Both are now being challenged as never before by the obvious existence of conscious beings that transcend their neat dualism.

Many people see other conscious entities as a physical or psychological threat to humanity. Use of the term "alien agenda" has taken on ominous connotations. In the context of this book, I think terms like "AB threat" should imply more concern about the *impact* of their reality on a fragile human consciousness than about AB intentions to inflict physical harm. In effect, at the beginning of the twenty-first century, we find ourselves with exactly the same dilemma that faced the Indo-European cultures of 2,000 years ago.

Will we ignore the presence and influence of Advanced Beings in human history and bury our heads in "supernatural sand"? Or will we attempt to realistically deal with the self-evident reality of a multidimensional and multiple-being universe? Will we reintegrate our fractured species personality into a natural whole or continue to let our "multiple personality disorder" subject us to manipulations by devious groups of beings, human or otherwise?

Chapter 25 reviews the mixed legacy of both the contributions of ABs to human development and the ways in which humans have reacted to them. Chapter 26 takes a different approach to assessing the AB threat to human society. Chapter 27 closes the book proposing a unique strategy for resolving the hidden historical and current issues that set human groups in conflict with one another.

25 A Mixed Legacy

This chapter begins with some general observations and conclusions from the historical material of the first eight parts of this book. The concept of an AB as a generic category has enabled us to compare the "apples and oranges" terminology used in different reports of human contacts with other entities. It makes it clear that subcultures use different labels to speak of the same reality. The AB concept has also helped us to see the similarity between historical and current human interactions with nonhuman entities, for instance, the similarity between "god/angel events" and "ET/higher-being interactions." It has also provided a useful way to see that the same set of inner senses that facilitates conscious communications with beings in various dimensions works for modern psychics as it did for the prophets of the Old Testament.

Taking advantage of the AB concept has made it possible to describe different cultures and belief systems without prejudgments about "chosen people" and "the ultimate truth." The expanded definition of Advanced Beings used here has included all historical and contemporary entities with whom humans have communicated. It has made it evident that human history, like the fish in the ocean, is "swimming in a sea" of ABs.

In the future, if anyone asserts that a category of nonhuman beings should not be included under the rubric AB, we would have to consider certain issues. Do they consider that group of beings too powerful, too malignant, too pure, or too special in some way to be included in the assessment? The choice of such qualifiers would expose that particular individual or group's assumptions. Would it be fair to exclude one person's AB and not someone else's? What would make a category so different that its ABs deserve exclusion?

If we exclude one being from this universal category, we in effect reestablish the notion of a dualistic universe where one part is separate from all else. By doing so we would be declaring to everyone else that we do not wish to give up a split consciousness, preferring the "beautiful mind" of our own imagination.

Different AB Mentalities

Both the ancient stories and current reports of AB personalities and activities have amply demonstrated the variety of conscious perspectives. Because of such variety, humans now know they must exercise good judgment in reacting to any particular source of knowledge or advice. Just because it comes from a being who is more advanced than we are in one way or another does not mean everything they say and do must be taken as ultimate truth.

Most ABs have appeared to be benevolent in their approach to humans. Some have become engaged in serious relationships, beyond the physical labor and sexual contacts mentioned earlier. Some seem to have taken humans into their confidence, revealing profound knowledge about the nature of the universe and its physical, energetic, and more ephemeral properties. Their technical training and knowledge transfers went far beyond what was necessary for the humans to do the "grunt work" required by spacefaring colonists. These deeper exchanges have enhanced the psychological and mental development of some human circles (likely leading to so-called mystery schools) and even entire cultures (possibly some Atlantean[1] centers or the early Vedic society).

A strong case can be made that humans have benefited from much AB technical assistance. But much of the technology transfer, particularly involving equipment relating to warfare, has had destructive influences on human development. Humans have apparently gained access to some forms of technology before the species was mature enough to consider the implications of their use. Until we show more maturity of purpose, some species may wish to keep us on a short leash. Some people believe such AB interference would explain why some of our space exploits on the Moon and Mars have run into strange roadblocks.

Many social influences, both positive and negative, have been identified. The evidence reviewed for this book seems to have demonstrated that AB intervention has had its most deleterious effect in the realm of emotions or human psychology. This area has been the most thoroughly covered in this book due to its profound impact on the development of human consciousness.

The ABs' Perennial Message

One other general conclusion to be drawn up to this point is that AB messages have remained fairly consistent over several millennia. Comparisons of present-day "visions" or "angelic voice communications" with some of those now accepted as holy writ in past eras reveal they do not differ in substance. Humans still receive admonitions to live peacefully, to take care of the Earth, to love one another, etc. Sometimes one group of ABs urge humans to beware of another AB group. Some of the messages from metaphysical sources or remote viewing encounters are as apocalyptic in terms of both content and tone as Revelation in the New Testament. Only the metaphors have been updated.

This suggests the ABs interested in humans have a more extended time perspective than we normally have. We could likely benefit from mentally taking on their longer time frame when thinking about the implications of some of our current behaviors. Some traditional cultures who remain close to the original AB teachings still think in terms of "seven generations."

Channeled texts circulated by various spiritual groups give a general cosmology, identifying the place or role of humans in the overall order, and some history. They may (like the Seth materials channeled by Jane Roberts) explain aspects of the universe in scientific concepts. They may introduce us to other dimensions and levels of beingness. All of them focus on ways for us to live more successfully. When studying them, as with records of historical AB communications, one must take into account the channel and his or her culture, language, and religion.

Given the diverse content and approaches to knowledge and understanding of the universe afforded humans from all these AB sources, it is conceivable that they already provide a general picture of the "whole elephant." In the metaphor of the blind men touching various aspects of the elephant, they had to pool their individual perceptions in order to understand something of the whole beast. Humanity may be at that point today, where cross-cultural and inter-AB sharing of information could provide the basis for a quantum leap in knowledge about the universe (the elephant) and its implications for human development.

An AB Balance Sheet

As this book makes clear, there have been both constructive and destructive implications of AB intervention in human history. Regardless of whether we dismiss one or more aspects of the AB story told here, there can be no doubt that humans have done some terrible things to one another and the Earth in the name of ABs. However, I believe humans on balance are much farther along the path of species development having had the different AB influences in our history than we would have been if left on our own. We may have to do a good bit of damage control before our global society can function like one species again, but the lessons from AB intervention have been valuable.

We now recognize the need to better balance the interests of small groups in favor of species *Homo sapiens* interests. We know more about how interrelated our lives are with other species. We have some understanding of how to work in accordance with natural principles instead of against them. Our technologies are far beyond where we would be today without having had some AB jump-starts. Conversely, our stage of moral and ethical standards may have been retarded by some of us feeling so favored by the gods—as spoiled children, we haven't yet learned to "share the sandbox" with others.

Regardless of our judgment about one aspect or another of this history, it cannot be changed. We can only change our perception of it, by doing the kind of analysis done here. With a different understanding of our past we will be able change the future from its currently projected path. The choice will be up to us.

Mixed Legacy

This book argues that while the form or content of many AB contributions to human history has undergone important changes over the last few centuries, their psychological and intellectual implications still shape the core of human consciousness. Many of these effects were very likely unintentional, simply the by-products of AB actions to meet their own needs. Even *YHVH* asked only to be seen as the best, most appropriate god to become protector and benefactor of his chosen nation, and look what we did with the story of his intervention in the life of one tribe. We extrapolated from it to explain the entire universe.

Earlier parts of the book devoted to possible evidence of a physical AB intervention and material corroborating it were divided along functional lines. Starting with the physical (part 3) implications of intervention, we proceeded to social impacts (part 4), then technology transfer (parts 5 and 6), to institutional (part 5), and psychological (part 7) effects. Let's continue this assessment of the AB legacy (particularly that of the Anunnaki) in a similar manner.

A Hybrid Species

Chapter 9 and historical accounts mentioned in other chapters together present a fairly persuasive case that transition humans may have been the product of genetic engineering, and that modern humans reflect subsequent interbreeding with ABs. Reviewing the evidence of human development available to us from the fossil record and genetic studies, in the context of other Earth species, the AB-intervention hypothesis makes more sense than others.

This may cause some to think of themselves in negative terms. However, we can choose to see ourselves as either half-breeds (negative connotation) or mixed-breeds (positive connotation). Many people in former European colonies have chosen to see their mixed racial and cultural heritages as getting the "best of both worlds." Operating from this assumption, their self-confidence has enabled them to exceed the performance of their respective parents. Such a positive perspective may help us realize more of our potential.

Social Divisions

One of the most troubling aspects of the AB-intervention legacy is its divisive effects on the social fabric of the world culture. Some would say that division is based in selfishness. No less an AB than Alice Bailey's spirit guide Master D. K. (the source of her numerous books) said, "There are adequate resources for the sustenance of human life [that] science can increase and develop. . . . Man is the controller of it all, and they belong to everyone and are the property of no one group, nation, or race. It is solely due to man's selfishness that . . . thousands are starving whilst food is rotting or destroyed; it is solely due to the grasping schemes and the financial injustices of man's making [sure] that the resources of the planet are not universally available under some wise system of distribution."[2]

That answer is descriptive, not explanatory. The AB-intervention hypothesis may offer an answer that gets at the historical roots of behavior not evident in other species. Perhaps a sense of god-given inequality makes it easy to justify why you have more right to the good things in life. If you believe your own family's ancestors were blessed with special treatment, and became accustomed to it as a "matter of right," do you feel that you have legitimately inherited the birthright? You would not be alone. That sense of being more deserving than others seems to be a part of the assumptions passed on from generation to generation among the groups who identify with an AB heritage.

Often a sense of being deserving or deprived correlates with one's race. To the extent that the interbreeding referred to in the Bible and Sumerian texts resulted in racial differences between those given special treatment and those left out, this AB intervention has had unforgivable implications for human unity. (The species-wide issue of a racial hierarchy is somewhat analogous to the shades-of-blackness issue among African-Americans. Resolution of this is helped by understanding that historical miscegenation and the resulting social advantages were not under the slaves' control.) Modern humans will be able to transcend such a superficial sense of difference when they better understand the historical (and likely AB) origins of so-called racial differences.

Over the centuries, the god's-chosen-people myth has become so strong in certain cultures (well known to the reader) that it has become unconsciously subversive. At a psychological level, the "select" and "elect" archetypes derived from the AB colonies still resonate. When people believe a god has chosen them, they respond with a divisive sense of arrogance and disdain for others. (Millions of books are sold today that play on the traumas of people who will be left behind, according to fundamentalist Christians, when the elect are saved.)

The sense of inherent inequality could have also resulted from AB preferential treatment after the Cataclysm. If we look at the unintended negative consequences of our own aid programs (domestically as well as abroad), perhaps we can understand how a similar "luck of the draw" mentality arose from AB programs in human history. Human groups may have mistaken simple AB allocation of attention (and perhaps affection) for some cosmic judgment about their merits. Being chosen by the ABs to receive special aid after the Flood was likely a function of AB interests and needs, unrelated to human qualifications. It's time to give up the notion of superiority that has resulted.

Technology and Nature

Evidence supporting the probabilities of AB introduction of various technologies into human society is almost universal. The human applications of much AB technology can be considered to be valuable and useful to human development. On the other hand, we cannot calculate the impact on human behavior of a premature introduction of inappropriate technology. Artificially losing our sense of place in nature may account for humanity's very poor record in keeping its use of technology consistent with the natural habitat. It means we skipped a crucial stage of understanding the interdependence between humans and other Earth species, to the detriment of all.

The weakening of the energetic connection between humans and trees and birds and earthworms has removed an essential link in the organic processes of planetary life. The breaking of any links among species ultimately leads to the disintegration of social cohesion within the human species. Without sufficient appreciation of the need for mutual support, we have contributed to the shrinking of the life force holding together all creatures large and small.

Religious Legacy

By definition, religion is a direct result of human experience with ABs. Without exposure to and subsequent separation from them, there would have been no impulse to re-link with them. Without the AB experience humans would have very likely still been celebrating their sense of awe and reverence for natural forces and the natural principles that govern life. They would have developed other social bonding rituals to honor the passages in human life and the natural cycles of the Earth and the stars.

Thus, religion, like all other effects of an AB presence, has a mixed legacy. While it engendered the social and psychological problems already amply covered and summarized in the following discussion, it has in many ways also expanded human horizons. Whether one stands in the throng in a great Catholic cathedral of Europe or in an evangelical revival tent in the American South, one's spirit soars in a sense of communion borne aloft by the music and ritual. Joined together in common purpose, humans have been motivated to sacrifice and serve others. Great community deeds have been accomplished in the name of religion.

At the same time, the dark shadows of alienation and dependency are fed by unsupported beliefs in an authoritarian divine order. In the supernatural religions self-sacrifice and service to others have their poles of tyranny and treason. Mind-numbing obedience counters creativity. Dependency counters self-responsibility. However, lacking a more progressive communal institution, traditional religion has kept alive the sense of humanity's inner spirit in an age of industrialism and the aggrandizement of individual, external power.[3]

We must remember the great cathedrals that inspire the visitor today served a different function in medieval Europe. As the church moved to distinguish itself from the cult temples of Greece and Rome, it chose to focus humanity on the alleged heavenly abode of its god. In contrast to the nature sites of many groups and the Earthly perspective of Greco-Roman temples, the soaring edifices that eventually evolved into the Gothic cathedral emphasized religion's otherworldly focus. Its vertical character stressed the hierarchy of concepts on which the church was organized and by which it was controlled.

The organizing principle drew attention toward a level over which humans had no control,[4] stressing their dependence on the AB-god who had returned to the skies. Places of worship were designed to exclude the natural habitat, denying any human dependence on its nurturing womb. Control of the ritual by the priesthood eliminated spontaneity or input from the individual's experience of the cosmos.

It is a great irony that within the institution that has served to limit human aspirations, constrain self-development, and control social behavior, individuals have found ways to demonstrate their natural powers of compassion and service and artistically express some of the creative aspects of the human potential. By following an inner standard of quality and excellence, individuals have often kept their authentic power. In effect, people who have ignored the notion that they are fallen beings and taken the responsibility to be the best person possible have outwitted the would-be controllers of the human spirit.

Had supernaturalism managed to totally subsume every culture, all humanity would now be poised for a return of the ABs in one guise or the other. Fortunately, the human natural impulse to independence reasserts itself, and friendly ABs have helped keep alive alternative perspectives. Even Jesus has allegedly spoken to us through human channels in recent years to straighten out human misperceptions and false attributions regarding his teachings.[5]

Even though the current practices of supernatural religion dominate human consciousness in a majority of the world's citizens, it has failed to become the all-encompassing matrix of mental and social control that it may have been designed to become. Hope for humanity lies in developing a replacement institution of natural worship that builds on the positive aspects of its legacy.

Good versus Evil

One of the most pernicious influences to have come out of the cults of West Asia was the arbitrary labeling of people as good (of the god) or evil (of the devil) based on their allegiance to different ABs. That polarity has now been applied to anyone who is considered different for practically any reason. It has "justified" every conceivable form of man's inhumanity to man.

As we saw in chapter 4, this social stereotyping or religious profiling goes back to the internal conflicts between the Anunnaki gods, first described in Sumerian and then Persian texts, and later adopted by the Hebrew culture. To solve this problem, the strongly archetypal words "good" and "evil" should be excised from ordinary conversation. When speaking of cultural or religious differences we should use the names by which others call themselves. When we need to describe behaviors that are disruptive or destructive (or conversely helpful or constructive), we should use terms that *neutrally* describe the acts.

Eliminating the misuse of good and evil as adjectives pales in comparison to another implication of these archetypal terms. As we learned in chapters 4, 20, and 22, the labels satan/demon/evil and god/angel/good initially simply implied two groups of ABs. One group favored sharing their knowledge with humans to help them develop their own potential, while the other group wanted to keep humans less intellectually developed and more emotionally subservient.[6]

Within the Anunnaki circles, the hard-liner group prevailed in that policy debate. The gods and angels who wanted to help humans to, in effect, join the privileged circle were punished and banished. They were given the satan/demon/evil labels—not because what they wanted to do was bad (it would have helped the humans), but because they lost the Anunnaki council's vote. The winners, who always write history, portrayed these human-lovers as rebels, deserving to be deprived of their rights in the heavens.

Although this group of ABs has apparently continued to offer positive support to humans, human religions have perpetuated the bad rap given them by the Enlil-oriented "keep-the-humans-down" camp of ABs. The negative energy associated with these terms has been used by religions to urge humans to suppress their own creativity and potential. In effect, supernatural religion has adopted the AB policy that opposed independent human development. (This makes one wonder if the odds of Roman Christians prevailing over the other followers of Jesus, and the successes of Islam, were helped by AB support.)

The challenge of reversing this age-old, double-talk tactic and its role in keeping humanity fragmented and oppressed seems formidable. How does one go about demonstrating to a majority of the human species that its crucial interests have been subverted by religions' adoption of reverse psychology (calling something evil to keep people from doing what's good for their own development)? Reformers, like Jesus of 2,000 years ago, have been adopted and falsely represented by the same religion and its demeaning consciousness that they sought to change.

Psychological Traits

Much has already been said in chapters 21 and 22 about the effect of AB influence on human thinking and emotions, but a few traits merit recapitulation here. They are the polarities and implications of the sense of being a special or chosen people.

Dependency Syndrome

That we have not outgrown the dependency syndrome of the AB colonial era is still evident today in the passive acceptance of behaviors unnatural to a conscious species. We see unquestioning group subservience to specious claims of "divine" authority. Individual suffering continues under a self-imposed fallen-being ("original sin") complex. Widespread self-limiting worship of a projected humanoid god diminishes the human sense of potential.

Abdication of self-responsibility for the human impact on the planet and future generations caps this syndrome. Placing our destiny in a distant and unreachable source of power (supernatural gods or ABs we expect to return to save us) has permitted society as a whole to elude psychological accountability for our destructive behavior internally, interpersonally, and against nature.

Quotes from the sermon of a well-educated, sophisticated priest help illustrate the dependency syndrome. "You need a belief in God so strong that it will sustain you in a personal crisis, when you're facing a dark night of the soul." "When you are healed, be sure to give credit to God." "Without God there is no order, no hope. We don't know how to live. God makes order out of chaos."[7]

Existential Fear

The AB-instilled fear of authority has resonated down through the millennia. A members-only e-mail list exchange of personal concerns makes this point.

> Person One: "I think one of the greatest fears I had to deal with was the fear of God. Later in life I learned fear was used in terms of respect rather than being afraid . . . by then it didn't matter! I'd already internalized FEAR!"
>
> Person Two: "The fear of God originated from respect and secondly from my insecurity of [sic] what I was doing and how I was doing things in my life. I was in the beginning very afraid not to make a mistake, according to God's rules. . . . So, for years I've been very careful about what I think."

Divine Destiny

These self-deprecating thoughts and emotions are not questioned because people feel they have no choice over their destiny. They see themselves as creatures of an AB who has a record of being capricious and over whom they have no influence. Even many of the "new thought" or religious science persuasion see their lives as part of some master design, where external forces intervene to establish an individual's destiny. The use of the word "destiny" implies the external definition of outcomes for one's life that are independent of personal choices/decisions.

This view is not very different from the fundamentalist Christian who believes that his god has a detailed blueprint for each human life and that the human purpose is to discover and "follow the plan." This view promotes far too little self-responsibility and self-learning.

Humanity's Challenge

Now that ABs may have left humans free to deal with their own challenges, groups who oppose one another in many ways still prefer to choose the same *azazel* (scapegoat). Scapegoating has led humans to a point where we may be approaching a suicidal alienation from nature severe enough that it provokes an intra- and inter-species breakdown. Instead of accepting responsibility for their own contributions to *Homo sapiens'* self-destructive behaviors, most people look to "outsiders" to eventually bail us out. Religious people, new-age groups, ET/UFO cults, and materialistic scientists have left the ultimate responsibility for our survival up to external forces (god, higher beings, the mother ship, or genetic forces beyond our control). Such is the unfortunate AB legacy.

Psychiatrist Immanuel Velikovsky, in his research during the 1940s and 1950s on the Earth's cataclysmic past, pondered why, if the Earth had suffered such trauma in its history, did humans not recall these events. Given his experience with human psychology, he called the process of forgetting "collective amnesia." If individuals are able to submerge painful personal memories from normal recall, as they obviously do, it appears feasible that the species as a whole can do the same with regard to AB influence in the distant past.

The debilitating effects of post-traumatic stress syndrome in individual lives are well known. We do not yet understand all the effects of species-wide Cataclysm trauma, followed by an AB departure trauma, but the material in this book suggests they are profound and have far-reaching implications for humanity's future, and perhaps its survival. We need this book and others with its thesis to help piece the real human story together from partial artifactual and legendary sources. We must first understand the nature of the trauma before it can be dealt with.

Thus, the most important story of this book is not AB interventions (both past and present) in human affairs, but how humans have reacted to and made use of such events for their own purposes. Ultimately, humanity must take the responsibility for how it responds to this central part of our history. How we choose to interpret it and what we do with this information will determine our future development.

We cannot change the past, but we can change our future possibilities by changing the way we see history. From this point on, the most important thing is not what ABs might have previously said or done to us, but how we are going to consciously deal with that past. We are like the adolescent getting ready to leave home. We must decide how much of the baggage of childhood we want to take with us into maturity. We are like the person whose past lives have been illuminated by hypnotic regression. We may better understand why we behave as we do, but we have to choose what we want to do about it.

The first step in the process of owning our past and choosing our future is to distinguish reality from illusion. Much historical work is required to decipher the reality of the Anunnaki and other ABs and their intentions. With our current scientific capabilities and research base we should be able to correct our ancestors' naïve interpretations of ABs, what they said and did, and why.

In order to look at our AB-filled past and present more realistically, we must begin with two processes. The first requires self-release from the delusion (held by a vast majority of humans) that a limited notion of the universe's supreme power and purpose, based on one historical AB, is the true one. The second requires the psychological healing of the dysfunctional complexes (described earlier) left over from an era of AB worship and dependency. We need to address the reasons for our suppression of the AB-human dimension and ask why we have not yet purged our collective consciousness of its "colonized mentality."

If humans choose to stay intellectually and emotionally stuck on centuries-old misinterpretations of encounters with other conscious beings, they will fail to realize their own potential and Earth will likely remain a backwater society in our galaxy. Freud stated the same conclusion in his own way. "I shall assert the view that civilization runs a greater risk if we maintain our present attitude to religion than if we give it up."[8]

26 Do ABs Pose a
Current Threat?

An old bureaucratic cliché applies to this chapter's question: "Where one stands depends on where one sits." Almost daily I receive articles, reports, and books purporting to offer the latest "true story of alien abduction," the just-uncovered facts about the cover-up, the hidden AB agenda, mind-control experiments, ETs and spirituality, military-AB cooperation, covert or psychological "psy-ops" projects, crash investigations, attacks on believers by debunkers, etc. Some claim a threat comes from ABs while others believe human organizations pose the threat.

A number of researchers believe some wars or terrorist acts and political disputes over trivial issues have been deliberately manipulated solely for the purpose of distracting people's attention from the subversion of basic rights and civil institutions. They say creating confusion on these issues makes it easier to divide and control the nation's activists and to reallocate tax money. Evidence in the book *Disclosure Project* suggests that some covert agencies have actually staged abductions and hoaxed other alleged AB events as a part of this strategy. The popular TV program *The X-Files* has portrayed fictional versions of this premise.

If such a covert strategy exists, it may be having success; large segments of the population are still passive in any kind of AB-oriented discussion. Much inaction may be due to such a bewildering cacophony of conflicting material. People may also be preoccupied with the demands of making a living and distracted by simultaneous media diversions. Such diversions mean few have time and energy left to think very deeply about such complicated issues.

I take the presence and involvement of multiple ABs, or at least the belief in their influence on us, as a given. Thus, I believe the large discrepancies among human reactions to AB issues in general should perhaps be of greater concern to us than the actions of the ABs themselves. Citizens should be concerned about what their leaders believe about and do with the many channels of AB information.[1] Individuals have a right to know to what extent, if any, their friends and colleagues use AB information or support. We ought to be concerned if unknown advisors provide information to or tell government officials what they should do.

An Attempt at Synthesis

Space does not permit here the comprehensive review necessary for the reader to create a synthesis of all the perspectives people have on a possible AB threat. The reader may wish to review chapters 1 and 6 for some relevant comments. The following paragraphs summarize selected points of view and give my tentative, very personal assessment of where we stand.

Many fundamentalist Christians expect heavenly hosts to arrive any day now to take the "elect" away and leave the rest behind to suffer the consequences of sinful behavior. Best-selling books tout this message across America. Some ET analysts seem convinced the ABs are already here in humanoid form walking among us, subtly taking over control of social institutions. Others believe a star fleet stands waiting for the right moment to descend and save representative life-forms from another cataclysmic upheaval caused by a passing planet or star.

According to reports of recent AB contactees and abductees, certain "ET visitors" are here to take advantage of human genetic stock to strengthen their own species. In this case, humans are not slave labor, but guinea pigs for ABs searching for ways to heal themselves or overcome biological deficiencies. Some ABs reportedly use the expression of strong human emotions to energize or "feed" themselves. According to this view, they even stir up conflicts among humans to harvest more abundant energies from our difficulties. In both cases, humans serve the role of AB livestock and lab animals.

The Internet circulates thousands of claims and counterclaims about the intentions of ETs and other ABs regarding humans. Some look to the ABs as the ultimate saviors of humans from their own faults, while popular UFO/ET authors Jim Marrs and David Jacobs (mentioned earlier) present a diametrically opposite point of view. Their books, *Alien Agenda* and *The Threat* respectively, paint a picture of ABs who will use their superior technology to manipulate and enslave humanity for their own ends.

Material received from metaphysical sources provides some evidence that other intelligent cultures intend humans no harm. Remote viewer Courtney Brown's impression of Martians who wish to immigrate into the United States and other nations is that they wish to become ordinary citizens and peacefully meld into our society. The "revelations" experienced by Steven Greer (founder of CSETI) support this position. In addition to the positive interventions of *YHVH* and Jesus, Christians believe an active Virgin Mary, a Holy Spirit, angels, and various saints (now-departed humans in an ephemeral AB form) are being helpful to humans.

What Do ABs Say About ABs?

The Verdants introduced by Phillip Krapf in chapter 5 represented this interesting view: "While the Verdants do not interfere in the internal affairs of any species on their home planets, they do have strict regulations in matters involving the stellar community with regard to weapons. They are not tolerated, period. The cardinal rule is that space is only for the peaceful."[2] Countering these reassuring words is Barbara Marciniak's Pleiadian voice (mentioned earlier) contending that humans are manipulated by current governments, a "world management team," and some ABs in space.

Krapf reported that the Verdants intended no harm to the thousands of humans who were monitored and studied by them. He said it was done to determine if humans were suitable to become galactic citizens. We have been deemed suitable, if we give up our space weapons. If we don't, they and the "Intergalactic Federation of Sovereign Planets" (IFSP) will gently disable our capability to go off-planet. We will be isolated until we become more morally mature. Verdants believe, "Species resort to war and conflict when they lack the intellect to resolve their differences through peaceful means."

These conflicting AB voices (not unlike conflicting human voices) raise two questions regarding AB intervention: How much can we count on the veracity of a noncorporeal source, and how does the consciousness of the human channel distort the message (whether it is a valid communication or not)?

The only logical way to deal with such questions is analysis of each category of AB reports in interdisciplinary/cross-cultural forums, with the members having minimal vested interests in a particular answer. In this setting groups can assess the material in a larger context of historical and contemporary reports that tend to confirm or refute it. Such comparisons should make it possible to judge the merit of both the AB source and the channel.

This type of effort cannot now be undertaken due to the refusal of major institutions and special groups, and many individuals as well, to submit their material to such public scrutiny. The development of a reliability index for various messages and their AB sources continues to be undermined by the commercial world of publishing and the free-for-all Internet. Thus, the individual with little time has no objective guidance as to whom and what to believe.

The Question of a Cover-Up

That there is a long-standing U.S. government cover-up of its interests in AB activities is beyond doubt. U.S. agencies refuse to allow public access to any information beyond the most peripheral documents concerning discussions of ABs. They suppress any reference to direct AB evidence and their various programs dealing with the AB issue.

The more important issue for citizens today is *why* the cover-up is in place. For decades the putative rationale was that the government wished to avoid public panic, pretending that private citizens were not mature enough psychologically to handle the truth. (This was likely one reason given by the church's early bishops when they censored the various sacred texts.) Given the current widespread rational interest in and professional experience with AB encounters, that is no longer a credible excuse.

I believe this book sets forth the "real reasons" behind the censorship of not only government agencies, but that of the church and related institutions. First, admission that ABs exist would cause a collapse of the entire "card house" of divine rights and powers. Second, insitutional authorities do not wish to reveal that their predecessors wittingly or otherwise supported the Anunnaki who had opposed the natural development of humanity. To admit having been on the "wrong side" of that early choice between human freedom and further AB control (whether real or projected) could hardly be justified in the twenty-first century.

While their personal motives may have evolved over the centuries, the leaders responsible for maintaining the split in human consciousness fear "the revolt of the masses" that would occur if the truth became known. The perpetrators of our species psychosis feel threatened by the reassertion of natural rights for everyone. In constant fear of their own duplicity, powerful groups keep holding "the lid on" until they amass psychological control over enough people and enough physical control over resources to weather a revolution in consciousness. This damage control effort has many guises but its focus is self-preservation.

From the power elite's perspective, a three-track strategy of denying the AB past, discrediting inner ways of knowing, and covering up current AB realities makes sense. It explains the observation made by noted abductee counselor Leo Sprinkle[3] in Fiore's book mentioned earlier. He concluded that both the ETs and the U.S. government seem to have an interest in covering up the number and nature of AB-human encounters. Their combined efforts, Sprinkle wrote, have created a climate in which individual experiencers voluntarily suppress their own stories in fear of negative repercussions. From his perspective, the ABs committed to the cover-up can be assumed to share the human elite's objective: manipulation of humans in the elite's and ABs' own interests.

Many officials in American security agencies and members of defense industry corporations have a career interest in proving AB forces pose a threat to our national security. Some may actually believe we face imminent attack. Others seem motivated by the power and profit that go with the U.S. government's space-oriented and space-based defense initiative. They waste taxpayer dollars on technologies that neither apply to potential threats from rogue states nor offer protection against the high-tech ABs encountered by our military forces. But this is only a means to an end. The objective is to focus so much attention on a "today scenario" that humans will not pay attention to historical truths.

Some people believe that selected official projects may have a dual purpose. For instance, NASA scientists launched two pairs of spacecraft in the 1970s that, according to this perspective, could have been intended to signal to the inhabitants of Nibiru (home of the Anunnaki) that we had emerged into the Space Age. In addition to transmitting photos of the outer planets back to Earth, the trajectories[4] of *Pioneer 10* and *11* and *Voyager 1* and *2* would be visible physically and electronically to Nibiruan scientists on their planet's 3,600-year voyage back from its orbit[5] around the Sun's brown dwarf.

Many people, including current and former government officials, believe that secret parts of the U.S. government wish to demonize the nonhuman realm of beings and frighten citizens into handing over power to those who claim they can protect us against ABs. They believe that if citizens are convinced of the reality of an off-planet enemy (or global terrorists), we will provide the taxes to fund the trillion-dollar military-industrial complex of which President Eisenhower warned America when he turned the reins of power over to John F. Kennedy. In an irony enjoyed by covert planners, they use fear of current ABs to frighten off citizens who might discover they owe who and what they are to ABs of old.

The contrived threat of a potential ET attack has been a ploy since the early 1960s, as the most recent iteration of the 2,000 year-old cover-up. It will be impossible to get Department of Defense leaders to show proof that threatening ETs require defensive preparations. They already know that the friendly ABs (those unfortunately tagged with the Sin/Satan label) pose no threat, and that the hostile ABs (those who want to control human development) are in effect using them. Honest and committed career officials and UFO activists know nothing of the charade in which they are pawns.

The problem is not so much a question of a particular AB threat, but the human use of any evidence of AB activity to frighten humans away from exploring the entire AB realm. Part of the divide-and-conquer rule involves keeping people from putting all the pieces of the puzzle together in the direction this book points. Those with covert agendas want us to see only one part of the picture, and a negative part, even if they have to fabricate the negative.

Fabrication on Top of a Cover-Up

Some researchers suggest that we must be careful to distinguish between actual contacts/encounters with ABs and hoaxed AB activities. They assume the latter come from covert human agencies as part of a psy-ops project that manipulates the attitudes of citizens vis-à-vis other conscious beings. The project reportedly takes individuals who believe they have had a genuine AB encounter and abduct them. In this fabricated abduction, they make sure the person has a negative experience that he or she will always associate with ABs. (See mention of Angela Thompson-Smith's account in chapter 5.)

By creating fear among people who have been mistreated in a "false abduction," the project seeds fear throughout society and motivates people to support high defense expenditures and new controls on individual freedoms. (The use of a purported alien threat may be as effective as the use of an exaggerated terrorist threat.) It also frightens them away from the covert, three-point strategy described above.

Further public assessment of this charge is obviously needed, but the fact that most humans (except those who appear to have been frightened by hoaxed government UFO/ET abductions) who encounter ABs come away with a view that their intentions are at least benign if not positive. This is further evidence that some core units of the present American government, and perhaps others, side with the Enlil tradition of keeping humans subdued and dependent. This alignment of interests helps to corroborate the finding that the secret of the ages is the "double-speak" used by the supernaturalists when they attempt to brand humanists and naturalists with a false image of the AB named Sin.[6]

As part of this apparently ongoing struggle between opposing factions of one group of ABs, it appears that some may have tried to make amends for past harm done to humans. Through various channels, they have offered humans their advice and insights into the larger universe. While appearing to be constructive, this act of "helping" humans actually reflects ongoing divisions among ABs. Toward the end of the twentieth century, the number of such "helpful" communications (through both physical contact and interdimensional channels) increased dramatically. With twenty-first-century hindsight, perhaps we can see such activities as an aspect of a nonhuman agenda in which we are secondary.

We are no longer threatened! I here abandon the attempt I have made in the rest of this book to stick close to evidence that, at least, if not interpreted by other analysts as I do, has been carefully examined by them. Taking an intelligence officer's approach, I now extrapolate speculatively from a cross-section of modern ufology and metaphysical sources. On balance, I believe from hundreds of books, reports, and personal interviews that humans are *not* currently directly threatened by an advanced species. This does not preclude ongoing communications between some human groups and ABs, where I believe positive cooperation now likely offsets the demeaning objectives of some ABs in the past.

It appears to me that the recent accounts of so-called "hostile" AB encounters can be reasonably explained by the "observing and experimenting" mode of a technically advanced species conducting "laboratory" exercises with a lesser species. Many human doctors and scientists do things to children (and disenfranchised humans and others species) in the guise of "helping" them or future generations. Regardless of the experimenter's intention and how careful he or she tries to be, it scares the hell out of the subject.

In many instances physical or psychological harm is done (sometimes resulting in death) without raising ethical or moral concerns on the part of the experimenter. If we get outside our human-centered consciousness and look at the process objectively, the many abduction books written over the last 40 years by frightened humans could all be written by the lucky animals who survive in human labs. Thus, I conclude the preponderance of evidence suggests the Anunnaki and others have withdrawn from any colonial roles they may have filled in ages past. They now await human action on their legacy.

Since we can't be sure we can read the AB mind, perhaps we can infer something of what has happened from their actions or indirect communications. For instance, Pleiadians channeled by author Barbara Hand Clow have said that various AB groups (Anunnaki, Maya, Sirians, and Pleiadians) have all pulled back from direct involvement on Earth because they got sucked into our level of reality, and it detracted from their own evolution. This reasoning makes sense to humans who have tried to help others who were not able to respond to the level of knowledge or training offered. At some point any good AB teacher would come to realize that the human students were not ready to learn what they had to teach.

Perhaps a "Prime Directive" Exists

The *Star Trek* television series popularized the notion of a Prime Directive: A moral imperative of noninterference observed by intelligent beings exploring space and encountering lesser-developed beings. This concept has roots deeper than a screenwriter's fanciful creation. Psychic Edgar Cayce's readings on the nature of soul incarnation and free will suggest such a principle came with the universe. His reading of original intentions was that no god or AB at any level—including the creator itself—sat "in judgment, mete[d] out punishment, . . . cajoled by lip-service, nor award[ed] special dispensations to a favored few."[7]

If such a principle characterizes the universe as a whole (incorporated into the primal-design DNA), then it must apply to all its creatures. In fact, only in a system with a Prime Directive can every soul have the freedom of choice to become aware of its impact on others, learn from its mistakes, and make truly unique contributions to the whole. Is such a principle hard-wired (instinctual) in all life, or is the nature of life such that it creates conditions in which it must be learned to avoid failure? If it has to be learned, then only a species with a self-aware level of consciousness (the ability to teach oneself) could be expected to gain that insight.

When a species gains the ability to consciously harm another species, if it does not recognize the moral imperative of the Prime Directive, it will suffer the consequences. Perhaps the self-recognition of a species' power to be destructive as well as constructive incurs the obligation to use that power responsibly. In a self-learning universe, violating the Prime Directive would subject a species to the possibility of self-destruction as a consequence. Planetary life-support systems appear to be designed to ensure that if one species runs amuck, it may destroy itself by the destruction of its own nest.

How can the Prime Directive be self-enforcing? The violator has to live with the naturally resulting consequences of its actions, whether intended or not. If humans interfere in the life cycle of a "lower animal," bacteria for instance, they must suffer the consequences of that species' adaptation to the intervention. In a world where identity is based on one's tribe or nation, a colonial state should not be surprised at the terrorism unleashed in reaction to its acts of colonization (military, economic, or cultural).

In a self-learning universe, a species desiring to survive must learn to cooperate with other species. Conscious beings learn that successful changes in the natural relationship between any two species have to be reciprocal and beneficial to both parties. This comes with awareness of one's own dependence on the well-being of the whole system, recognizing that violating any part of the web of life degrades one's own lifelines. Traditional societies, which understand such interdependence, stress that humans must listen to the wishes of all species and respect them. If a species does not learn to work in harmony with these principles of nature, the ultimate price may be its death.

The Prime Directive Breached

This book suggests that the Prime Directive has been violated, deliberately or accidentally, one or more times during human evolution on Earth. The historical reports of Anunnaki activities possibly involving genetic and social engineering and the reported instigation of several religions by invisible ABs would certainly be examples of this violation. Such breaches of the Prime Directive would suggest we need a better understanding of how and why ABs might intervene in human development. Was it done with good intentions, but unintended consequences? Was it simply a mistake of AB immaturity? Was it only a function of the hubris of a group able to travel through space and wield their technology in new worlds? Or was it an intervention with a covert agenda?

Whatever earlier intentions or motivations may have existed, the current situation seems to suggest that ABs are operating only in an observation or research mode. Did they learn from the Anunnaki or other AB projects on Earth? (Perhaps ABs have made more moral progress in the interim than humans.) Has the group of beings interested in Earth made a joint decision to forego further direct manipulation on Earth but to continue communications and advice-giving? Such a decision would explain why humans have recently been receiving plenty of unsolicited advice from a multitude of angels, guides, ETs, and other realms.

The current record of inner AB communications may be the highest in recorded history. We have more modern-day prophets than ancient Egyptians and Hebrews could have imagined. Scientists get hints for new discoveries from angels, dreams, or visions. Observation visits within Earth's airspace by ABs are reported somewhere on the planet practically every day. Studies of humans and other species, even including experiments on some of us and our livestock, appear to be continually ongoing. In other words, a lot of AB attention is now focused on Earth life and human progress. But, even with painful experiments on individuals as described earlier, it appears to be of a research nature. For the time being we seem to be left alone to determine our own fate.

Illustrating the "hands-off" character of current AB policy, one abductee, Jim Sparks,[8] was told ABs had received promises from some Earth leaders that they would correct environmental practices the ABs told them were threatening the planet. Although the promises have been broken, the ABs did not take direct action and have turned to advising "average" people to stimulate corrective action.

Some observers speculate that the strange formations in plants commonly called crop circles may be a gentle nudge from ABs to humans to clean up their act and save the planet along with themselves.[9] Such unobtrusive messages would fall within the Prime Directive, representing advice but not a bailout.

Remote viewer Courtney Brown believes he learned that more advanced civilizations ("the Galactic Federation," he called it) did not intervene in the demise of the Martian culture when it encountered a cataclysm. He also believes that no AB action will be taken on Earth even if we undermine its ecological system. The Martians reportedly had to learn from their experience, and Earthlings are expected to do the same.

We Are Our Own Worst Threat

Still living with the AB-colonial mentality described in earlier chapters, we are not yet prepared to act as a single species to resolve the current threats to our survival. It appears that we still prefer to depend on the possibility of absentee AB rulers for favors or attention, physical goodies, and frequently for life itself. Humans are still psychologically fragile, subject to manipulation by anyone claiming access to AB views. Now that the gods are gone, most people still cede their personal authority to a few inner-circle priests and kings who seem to have hijacked communal institutions for their personal agendas.

The present state of human development is analogous to the personalities of children who grew up under alcoholic or abusive parents. People subjected to slavery or groups oppressed by colonialism share the same pathological dependency syndrome. Its following characteristics describe far too many humans: diminished sense of autonomy and high state of insecurity; passive-aggressive personalities, easily provoked; a low sense of self-worth, very other-directed; and psychologically defensive, with sado-masochistic tendencies.

To overcome these traits, now inculcated from birth, humans

must join together and collectively reexamine their past. When one understands the AB phenomenon has been with us throughout a significant portion, if not all, of human history, much of the current fear of the unknown will dissipate. Embraced by our acceptance, the AB loses the strangeness that alienates or mesmerizes us. Losing some of our own sense of insecurity will help us take advantage of knowledge and advice now available to us from many AB sources.

Confirming this assessment, the Pleiadians assert through Barbara Marciniak that humans could be much more than we have become thus far, but we have let ABs hold us back in earlier times. They urge humans to stop turning to them as the "boss" (whether we conceive of them as God or aliens) and assert our own sovereignty. The nature of this Pleiadian advice suggests that if ABs have any unwanted influence on human progress at this stage, it is our own fault.

As we'll see in the next chapter, this means shedding the veil of supernatural religion. Ostensibly created to keep humans in contact with the realm of the ABs, it has actually separated *Homo sapiens* from the community of Advanced Beings of which we are members. Instead of offering a route to universal wisdom and experience, it has made most humans dependent on the few who have pretended to represent the *only* channel to the gods. Fooled by the pretenders, we have been deprived of the nourishment and enrichment of ideas from conscious beings far more experienced than we.

27 A Public AB
Discussion Project

Popular Christian fundamentalist Billy Graham says, "Angels are just as active today as they were in Bible times."[1] On any given morning in Washington, D.C., groups of the most powerful politicians, lobbyists, and representatives of interest groups from all over America gather and pray for guidance from the imaginary ABs to whom they pledge allegiance. Then they beseech those beings (defined in the human mind) to intervene in the affairs of the nation to make what they prayed for happen. Each goes about his business all day acting as if he had the support of his god and its angels. This delusion strengthens their resolve to push the policy they have come to believe their AB wants of them.

These believers may be willing to sacrifice personal comfort or social approval and even die for their image of a god of human fabrication. Such is the present schizophrenic state of human consciousness. In this book I have tried to identify the causes of this fragmentation of the human psyche or species soul.

On a natural path of conscious development humans saw themselves as part of a unified nature. Exposure to beings more advanced than they (whether physical or ethereal) caused them to develop a mode of magical thinking, resulting in cult worship. During a period of lack of contact with the real ABs whom they had come to worship, some humans began to revise the story of their AB experience. The fabricated story provided for supernatural beings, created by a few humans and imagined as being beyond nature so other humans could not validate their existence. Religions grew up on the promise that their faithful could unite or reunite with those anthropomorphic figments of a fragmenting human consciousness. Much of modern history involved campaigns to impose that supernaturalism to keep humans psychologically dependent on those who manipulate the belief system.

The belief in personal access to some religion's god—illustrated in this chapter's opening paragraph—comprises an example of far-reaching, indirect AB influence on the life of the United States. Its national impact greatly exceeds that of any alleged ET reverse-engineering project underway in a place like Area 51 in Nevada. It touches more lives than a dozen beings channeling relationship advice to workshop audiences on the West Coast. Its effect on the nation's psyche may be more negative than all the previous night's UFO abduction experiences.

Despite its significance, the continuing impact of this misunderstanding of the AB phenomenon (past and present) gets glossed over in the media-based national discussion. Not only do we underestimate the importance of present-day human experience with real ABs, we ignore continuing misrepresentation of earlier AB involvement in human history. *Twisting reality inside out, we deny the self-evident nature of ABs and worship an AB fiction.*

It is immaterial that network television has not yet broadcast the landing of an AB spacecraft on the White House lawn. As the following pages indicate, a great variety of beliefs in ABs already influence many of the decisions made in the White House and throughout Washington every day. You may question this assertion, but I remind you of the religious practices of presidents and their advisors. The current president and his predecessor are evangelical Protestants, while another recent president is a born-again Christian. They and others have attended church and born witness to their beliefs in a transcendent god, invoking his name and promising to act in accordance with their interpretation of his will. Some admit to a belief that they receive guidance through prayer to their idea of a personal AB.

There can be no question that they, like most supernaturalist Americans, make some decisions on the basis of words they believe have come from one or more ABs.[2] And, they rely on advisors (including people like Billy Graham) who operate from the same level of consciousness.

I do not suggest that people in Washington should be forbidden to behave this way because they serve the public. After all, "conversations with God" are going on all across America. I am only suggesting that all of us who are voting taxpayers have a right to know of the AB influence on our leaders in the nation's capital. Remember the public relations flap at the White House when it was revealed that Ronald and Nancy Reagan had been consulting an astrologer for advice prior to making decisions about affairs of state. The public issue should not have been whether the president was seeking advice from an ancient form of divination, but whether or not the citizens knew of it. After all, astrology has probably played a role in most voters' decisions at one time or another. The concern should be the extent to which officials' belief in, or inner communications with, other conscious beings shape their decision-making.

False Separation of Church and State

In the schizophrenia of modern society (described in chapter 21), we have concluded that religious beliefs and contacts with other levels of consciousness should be considered private. That is an illusion when one recognizes the magnitude of the influence the historical AB phenomenon has on individual decision-making. Such an important factor in people's lives, particularly those making important decisions that affect many others, should be known to those affected. For instance, when policy studies are published on the pros and cons of a course of action, with supporting documents from various experts, they should include the ideas or principles attributed to a god or other levels of consciousness.

When a president decides to go to war, we have a right to know whether he thinks an AB has influenced his thinking. We need to be able to talk about the input other people are getting from ABs on a proposed war. Just as we compare the positions of human experts, we need to compare the positions of any AB advisors. Keeping this crucial part of the political and social process hidden subjects us to covert manipulation. The advantage of Billy Graham's published statement is that you know "where he's coming from." Only with full disclosure about the alleged direction people have received from their AB-gods can we make informed choices.

In important meetings, people sometime dare to say, "I'm going to do this because I have a gut feeling about it" or "My intuition tells me" so and so. Sometimes they are willing to say, "I had a dream about this that triggered my thought." Few people go beyond that in revealing how they have been influenced by communications or inspiration from an AB. (The publisher of this book is willing to say, "I talked to The Gentlemen Upstairs about this," but he is a rare exception.) I am suggesting that we attribute knowledge or advice to the source whence it came, to the best of our ability. The sources should include all the AB categories covered in parts 1 and 2, and any we have forgotten.

In the interest of full disclosure, I must state that several of the concepts in this book came to me through some inner channel unknown to me; they popped into my head full-blown and unexpectedly seemed to fit into the research or writing of the moment. I must also explain that those thoughts did not get included in the text before I had looked for corroborating material from other people. I then tried to make these flashes of inspiration from that well of universal consciousness as compatible as possible with the related things I knew about. I appreciate the conscious source whence they came, and without that assistance the evidence and logic described here would be incomplete.

The fact that we hide such a source from others indicates just how much value it has to us. If its impact on us were insignificant we would not mind casually sharing it with others. We do not share it because we would be embarrassed to do so or because it gives us an advantage. The latter may lead us to being accused of having a hidden agenda, but a hidden agenda may be less important in the long run than having hidden advisors or sources of information.

Transparency Called For

In ancient times, when the king or high priest consulted the oracle or read tea leaves or prayed for guidance from a nonmaterial being, the public knew about it and may have taken part in the process. They knew and trusted this source of information. Modern people still use it but do not talk about it. As one effort to break this silence, a group called the Center for the Study of Extraterrestrial Intelligence (CSETI) has launched a "disclosure project" to press for release of information about the U.S. government's UFO/ET-related activities. While there is a crucial need for this public campaign, we need to go even further.

We need a policy beyond the disclosure of ET materials, one that brings back the ancient practice of open discussions of and with "the gods" on key questions relating to a society's threats, challenges, and possible directions.

It seems as if individual leaders these days generally receive advice from ABs consistent with their own previously held positions. I wonder how often the ABs who advise them give opinions contrary to what the person might have been expecting. (Of course the personal position may be held due to the god's earlier guidance.) It would considerably increase public confidence in political decisions if officials would reveal what their gods or angels have told them. A private citizen could contrast what the Congressman's god told him to do with what the citizen's god recommended to him. People could compare notes and openly decide which god's advice they ought to take, maybe based on his track record.

The Urgent Need

Why make what some might consider a seemingly tongue-in-cheek or simply outrageous suggestion? In a world that appears suicidally divided against itself, new and untried measures seem called for. Such a blatantly different approach to this most fundamental of society's unaddressed issues may be the best way to stimulate "outside-the-box" thinking about the role of ABs in public life. Perhaps this probable description of a day in our nation's capital will gain your support:

While the Washington prayer breakfast ritual unfolds, some demonstrators in front of the Supreme Court yell that their AB says it is a sin to murder unborn children. People on the other sidewalk yell back that their AB gave the individual the right to the integrity of her own body. Up around DuPont Circle two other groups square off in front of each other. A loudspeaker blares that homosexuality is a blasphemy toward their AB. The group supporting free choice of gender orientation screams back, "[My AB] made me this way." A response comes back saying, "[Our AB] ordained marriage to be only between a man and a woman."

On the Mall, marchers wave placards proclaiming that "the people of [AB ___] seek peace in his name." Their AB is one of love and harmony, they say, while the AB advising the Administration has a mentality of "hate and smite-thy-enemy." Inside the White House, the president assures another group of religious leaders that he will fight only "a just war, for a just cause," and receives resounding applause.

One of them tells the president that his war is necessary because the enemy worships a false AB (although it is historically the same one the minister worships).

Somewhere in Asia a group of devotees of the same AB under another name rouse themselves in fervent praise of martyrs who died smiting the infidels (worshipers of the White House AB). Over at Georgetown University some scholars admit to one another that "a just war" is a relative concept, depending on which AB's truth and enemies one accepts.

On the Pentagon steps a group of citizens against UFO secrecy has come to pressure the military and intelligence agencies to reveal what they know about ABs. The Pentagon spokesman denies that there are any such things as ABs and says even if there were, the military would have no interest in them. Up on Capitol Hill a delegation of former military and intelligence officers plead with their Congressmen to provide a forum to tell the public what they did relating to ABs in their government jobs.

Outside of the District of Columbia, in Maryland and Virginia, U.S. government employees and military officers deliberately relax their minds and send aspects of their consciousness to roam other dimensions and meet disembodied ABs. Others of them probe the thoughts of unsuspecting foreign officials and domestic dissenters. Some travel through the noumena to survey hidden areas and then sketch what they saw for U.S. policy makers. Some intelligence contractors experiment with technologies that replicate AB voices inside the heads of troublesome opponents, while others work on holographic images that can be projected into the sky over Muslim troops simulating the AB Allah's heavenly hosts.

At the end of the day, Senate hearings are still going on comparing whose AB said what about the difference between humans and animals and why we can clone one and not the other. Over in the Department of Education, an internal debate is taking place regarding whether AB so-and-so made the different races for different reasons and whether humans should use quotas and affirmative actions to give them all an equal opportunity. And, as millions sit down for the evening meal, they explicitly or implicitly thank their own AB for choosing them to receive the blessings they enjoy, which most of the world goes without. . . .

What can we make of this daily cacophony involving the gods' views? There are two explanations, both of which warrant that the public beware. First, the speakers falsely claim to have the words of a god to support their position. They have had no communications from any AB and have made them up assuming their imagined god would have said them. Second, if the speakers have actually communicated with an AB they have no right to claim that it represents the ultimate truth. Each AB's view can only represent that AB's view, and not the perspective of the universe on the political or social question being debated. Whether one imagined a communication with an AB or actually had one presents the same problem: The view must be seen as only one finite (human or AB) being's idea, which should be judged on its own merits.

Seen from the definition of ABs in this book, the array of voices, each presuming to speak for the god of the universe, uses false pretenses to manipulate the feelings and actions of others. To bring our societal debates down to Earth, we have to become aware of the source of claims made by people who interject the "views of gods" into conversations that affect us.

I can think of no better way to deal with this babble of conflicting AB advice than the kind of public AB discussion project suggested here. The source and channel must be identified for any important or unique communication tagged as representing nonhuman consciousness. To achieve a common basis for evaluation of such communications, only a bold and robust effort will work. It should have four objectives: *community*—to develop a vocabulary that transcends culture and religion; *exclusion*—to eliminate communications purported to be from the level of universal creator; *inclusion*—to include all other categories of relevant AB messages; and *equality*—to give everyone's declared AB communication equal respect.

A Public AB Discussion Project

What would such a project look like? It might look something like the South African truth and reconciliation process designed to heal the divisions wrought by apartheid. All the parties, those who had been wronged and those who did the wronging, met face-to-face and agreed to exclude no questions and to give their honest answers. Without the ability to change the past, they had to forgive, or at least accept, the wrongdoing for what it was, without justification or retribution. It effectively wiped the slate clean and allowed for starting over.

Such a project would require that we think of all humanity as one family. In discussing the difficulties of dealing with family trauma, psychoanalyst David Shaver wrote in a private e-mail exchange: "The first rule of highly dysfunctional families is that nobody talks about the dysfunction. The second rule of dysfunctional families is that nobody talks about the first rule." And further that the "dysfunction arises partially from and is maintained by demands for respect of the authority figure (no matter how arbitrary and unfair the authority figure) as well as demands that truth not be spoken."

Shaver's comments highlight the difficulty we face as a species in any attempt to deal with such profound issues buried so deeply in the human family's past. Humans have spent the last two thousand years covering up the AB "skeletons in the closet" that led to the fragmentation of the human psyche. Now that we have the different subpersonalities, each locked into its own partial reality, we fear admitting to our dysfunction. Further, no group wants to admit to the fact that they aren't talking; this is what the institutional cover-up is all about.

Shaver's final point is also relevant to the AB cover-up. The very authorities responsible for the suppression of truth are the ones in a position to ignore the demands that the truth be spoken. There is no external mediator who can command the participation of the parties. This calls for new methods for uncovering the truth. The time is ripe for an entirely different strategy.

The Disclosure Project organized by CSETI and animated by the efforts of Steven Greer seeks to stimulate public debate concerning the reality of ABs and upper-level attempts to keep citizens from having access to secret information about it.[3] Launched in 2000, the project has identified 400 witnesses (formerly in official government roles) who are prepared to testify about their personal involvement with U.S. government UFO/ET research programs, reverse AB engineering, psy-ops, intimidation of AB contactees, etc. They would like to get the U.S. Congress to give them immunity from prosecution for telling their story in public hearings. The problem is that the Congress is part of the cover-up (although many members do not know it) and is not about to act.

Direct confrontation has never proved to be the most effective way to bring about social change. So protest and other challenges to the authorities (just as in the case of challenging the abusing father) will only elicit stronger denial. Only a bottom-up approach will work. Since maintenance of the status quo depends ultimately on the acquiescence of ordinary people, their withdrawal of support is the quickest way to challenge any regime. Security comes from large numbers participating in public events organized to let people with so-called "secret" information bring it out in the open. Visibility and the transparency of the process provide protection for the participants.

Therefore, the starting place should be a grassroots effort to find and display all the pieces in the AB jigsaw puzzle,[4] perhaps somewhat along the lines suggested in this book. The project would invite the participation of knowledgeable people with experience dealing with any category of AB phenomena. Its first step would be to demystify the subject of ABs by placing all definitions and relevant evidence on the table with no deference for divine, sacred, or official labels.

We must do as the Greeks and Romans did and treat all ABs as appropriate subjects for tragedies, satires, or comedies, including everyone's favorite AB in one natural framework. They knew it was a perfect way to demystify the gods and bring them down to Earth. A public effort to naturalize the whole area of AB-human interaction is necessary if *Homo sapiens* are to assess that part of our history more realistically. It will require that we consider all ABs as only aspects of one ordinary reality. This "de-deification" is essential to dispassionate assessment of the impact of various Advanced Beings and their messages on human history.

Interdisciplinary teams of researchers ought to begin with issues like early religious decision-making (who decided what and why). Equally important will be the discoveries regarding the foundations and covert control of political institutions. The question of differentiation into races would be immediately relevant to current social conflicts. All the findings from historical and scientific analyses should be shared in the broadest forum possible. Although many might consider much of this new knowledge threatening, it must not be withheld.

Serious collection and compilation efforts must be undertaken to ensure that all information be available to analysts and the public. Data banks, organized like the best library retrieval systems, need to be set up for rapid processing and dissemination of AB-related materials. People having contacts with and information from ABs must be encouraged to speak up and given recognition for doing so. Gone must be the days of prophets crying in the wilderness, with no one to hear their message. Ignoring such information can result in the loss of valuable wisdom known to other beings that humans could use.

The Challenge

As a child must be weaned from its mother's breast, so must our adolescent species be weaned from magical and supernatural thinking. That which was comforting and perhaps even necessary for some people during our youth is not robust enough for the rigors of cosmic adulthood. Even when the muscles are strong enough, the capacity to run is hampered if one continues to hold on to his crutches. Enough metaphors—I am sure you get the point.

The most difficult challenge is to be honest with ourselves. First, we must recognize the existence of nonhuman entities or levels of consciousness. Second, we must achieve wide public understanding of the artificiality of supernaturalism. These steps can lead to a serious attempt at assessment of the psychological import of the suppression or denial of individuals' reports of their encounters with ABs. The objective must be to discern which of humanity's current social and psychological illnesses result, even partially, from magical or delusional consciousness. Only then can we take corrective action.

Two issues for participants in the Public AB Discussion Project are two sides of the same emotional coin: to overcome the fear of giving up one's dependency on an AB and to accept responsibility for one's own actions.

In American society we are taught to fear any idea that would call into question the conventional concept of god or to admit to fallacies in the official scientific story. That's because most of us have bought into the same Faustian bargain as the church and eighteenth-century science. To enjoy the fruits of industry and commerce, science has deferred to the church/synagogue/mosque when it comes to questioning history, morality, and deeper meaning. Most of us are willing to go along with the cover-up to get the "goodies" dualism can bring.

The reason scientific materialism has run rampant over nature and had such disastrous side effects in many areas of life (particularly the health of the planet, including that of humans) has been its self-exclusion from the moral and spiritual implications of dualism. Avoidance of such fundamental questions in both the scientific and religious communities has become so culturally ingrained over the centuries that we are not even aware that we could have made other choices. If we move a little intellectual distance away from conventional dogma, psychological fear kicks in.

Overcoming that fear will be a major obstacle to widespread discussion of the AB phenomenon. However, as more people realize that uncontrolled technological advances may threaten our own existence, the fear of questioning dogma may be overcome by fear of species extinction. The hope for immediate survival may gain priority over untested religious assumptions about some future immortality. Facing uncertainty may heal our fragmented consciousness.

As many humans will not be favorably disposed to open-ended discussions of ABs, some ABs may also not be in favor of full communication. (Although, as noted in parts 1 and 2, a number of species seem to want to help us.) So we should expect resistance to this discussion among some of them and not be deterred by suggestions that this is not the business of humans. Everything possible must be done to avoid another Tower of Babel that inhibits full communication.

Many humans and some ABs may also wish to stifle a discussion of multidimensional communications because it would highlight the human capacities for inner access to information. Exclusive focus on speech and physical symbols weakens human use of the inner senses, such as telepathy and remote viewing. To the extent that we ignore or deprecate inner communications, we become less able to access the intentions of other humans and ABs and become more alienated from one another.[5] Being deprived of our inner sense makes us more susceptible to psychological operations and propaganda programs launched by "authorities."

Evaluating Past Actions

An effort to heal humanity's multiple personality disorder, whether through this Public AB Discussion Project or another, will only be successful if it declares the purpose of the search for truth to be reconciliation of all the fragments of human society. Its retrospective reexamination of history must be as neutral as possible, avoiding the moralizing casting of blame that perpetuates divisions. Blame differs from the assignment of responsibility. Understanding that beings may have acted in accordance with their perception of what was right and appropriate at a given time, we can still judge those actions' effect and hold people accountable for them.

This will require that we not only consider the reasons people did what they did, but the unintended consequences of their actions. Thus, there are two different levels of responsibility, one for intention and one for lack of attention. We only learn of the unintended consequences after the fact.

So, I suggest that in evaluating history and its makers it would be appropriate to keep in mind certain assumptions about how we got into the mess we are in. First, we can recognize that things were probably handled as they were due to the historical context (people did not know what we now know). This minimizes casting of blame. Then, we should assume that humans did not invite ABs into their lives. We should also give some benefit of the doubt to ABs; they probably did not intend all the effects they had on us. The AB-human encounters probably resulted in negative impacts on both sides.

Psychological conditioning occurs whether one intends it or not. The development of particular traits occurs over long periods of time, and in unanticipated directions. For instance, there should be no blame for the "worship/followship syndrome" developed in the AB-human relationship. Humans faced with such an advanced species as the Anunnaki would naturally look up to them, and develop the subordinate mentality they did. It serves no purpose to say they should have done otherwise.

Another caveat is that no phenomena exist in absolute, black-and-white terms. There are pros and cons in every situation. The overall AB legacy is mixed, including that of *YHVH*, for instance. The light and dark sides of Christianity must be seen as a result of embracing conflicting archetypes. The choice of *YHVH*'s authoritarian, top-down mind-set contrasted with Jesus' bottom-up, inwardly directed mind-set. The church itself embodies a mix: builders who seek to control its members and influence outsiders, versus servants who place the needs of members and outsiders first. Such contradictions are natural, and we are only now learning that they must be consciously managed.

The same nuancing must be applied in our assessment of the Anunnaki and other ABs. For instance, the previously described policy conflicts between Ninurta and Sin that led to the unfortunate human misunderstandings about god versus the devil were legitimate differences of perspective and priorities about the Anunnaki role. In a similar vein, we cannot blame *YHVH* for the damage done humanity in his name. We have to assume his actions were well-intended, representing the best understanding he had of the human situation at the time.

In thinking about recent history and current events, we must remember that the structure and energetic force of institutions do not necessarily represent the present motivations and aspirations of their members. The Queen of England seems an unlikely candidate to represent the "imperial nature" of the early Indo-European institution of kingship. If modern humans come to understand their institutional legacy, they can make considered judgments about how to shape it in the future.

In other words, the current generation of humans is not responsible for the past. Long-standing dysfunctionalities in society have shaped today's individuals. No interest is served by castigating those who made poor choices in ages past. Given the chance, I believe most individuals will want to look to the future as they focus on doing something constructive about these issues so deeply rooted in our AB history. They will see the greater opportunity that awaits all of us after we free ourselves from a self-imposed but ill-founded legacy of supernaturalism and rediscover our natural spirituality.

A Natural Spirituality

In the event that the reader has gotten the impression that everything associated with current religious organizations should be left behind in the new era, let me clarify my view on that. If local community churches, temples, and mosques did not exist, something like them would have to be invented. Most of the social functions performed by local religious organizations fill crucial needs. They provide stability and cohesion in a society faced with daily challenges to its well-being. They provide a rallying point for emotional expression and problem-solving. Millions of their dedicated staff and volunteer members provide emotional and material support to their fellow humans in need.

Humans need rituals that reinforce their confidence when faced with the practical matters of life, particularly the essential passages of birth, illness, death, grief, marriage, and other periods of transition. Appropriate rituals, without any supernatural meaning, can serve to give order to human emotions in such times of stress or celebration. Without them, individuals miss out on the richness of human experience and local tradition.

In the transition from supernaturalism to natural spirituality, local churches, temples, synagogues, and other centers of worship could take two steps that would permit them to discover for themselves the appropriate role to play for their members. As members came to understand that supernaturalism no longer had a hold on them, they would rejoice in their direct and natural connection to all the universe. The tenets of belief that produced fear, shame, guilt, etc., would be jettisoned without looking back. As beliefs in an authoritarian, patriarchal, or matriarchal god were severed, so would official ties to authoritarian, patriarchal, or matriarchal organizational structures be severed. Each community organization would assume responsibility for its own survival and take actions to carry out the programs its members desired.

People would be free to design their own activities to meet their own intellectual, emotional, and social needs. The spirit of connectedness and inclusivity toward all other beings striving to live an ethical and responsible life would fill psychological needs for a sense of place and purpose in the universe. Just think how much energy now devoted to coping with the supernaturally derived feelings of unworthiness, sin, and guilt, and reliance on a vengeful god would become available for joyful service to humanity.

Such positive spiritual experiences could lead people to envisage a larger perspective, one that includes actual beings willing to communicate with humans. Rather than being anxious that one is not doing God/Allah's will, individuals could freely take advantage of advice from what Frank Demarco calls "upstairs." Doing so would help them discover, as Neale Donald Walsch suggests, that when we talk to god under any guise, we are really talking with some part of ourselves. If such experiences convince us that we must take responsibility for our own actions, we will recognize our oneness with the creator.

Instead of worshiping a diminutive vision of an anthropomorphic cultural god, spiritual societies will naturally rejoice in a vision of the supreme power that encompasses all beings, all forces, and all dimensions. Seeing ourselves as conscious parts of such a grand enterprise will enhance our own sense of power and potential. Petty issues from the AB-influenced past will quickly fade from our focus.

Postscript

Obviously one book attempting to cover the full sweep of human origins and history falls far short of definitively establishing the "new myth for the twenty-first century" called for in the introduction. Nevertheless, its expansive scope has the merit of illustrating that sufficient input from enough separate disciplines can begin to fill the gaps that now prevent us from seeing the whole picture. This approach requires a synthesis that cannot be satisfied by conventional piecemeal approaches to making and disseminating new discoveries. Continuing efforts to confirm or deny the tentative conclusions set forth in the preceding chapters will automatically make connections among facts from many fields of study.

The introduction of such an interdisciplinary approach to producing the "new myth" was the reason I started with the AB-intervention hypothesis as I did. It requires input from all fields of study with any relevance to possible AB activities on Earth. A first effort could never include all that is available. But I believe this book has demonstrated that enough evidence of AB involvement in human history exists that no responsible student of the human past and present can dismiss it in good conscience. To further study the issue would not be divisive, but would contribute to healing the now fragmented human soul.

Even a process to disprove the AB-intervention hypotheses would stimulate the human imagination to bring new perspectives to old information and create new attitudes toward human institutions. With such breaking of traditional mind-sets, I am confident that we would forge new directions in the conscious self-development of our species. And take our rightful place among all beings.

Endnotes

Preface

1. The *Encyclopedia of Gods* by Michael Jordan (Facts on File, 2002) identifies over 2,500 deities worshiped at one time or another around the world.

2. Mark Matousek, "Up Close and Transpersonal with Ken Wilber," *Utne Reader,* July/August 1998, pp. 50–55, 106–107.

3. From the cosmology of "heretic priest" Giordano Bruno, who was burned at the stake in 1600 for thinking more broadly than the Catholic Church.

Introduction

1. To identify the manipulators, one needs only to identify those who consistently receive benefits from the turmoil regardless of the nations involved and whether they win or lose.

2. See www.cseti.org or www.disclosureproject.org for information on the Disclosure Project headed by Steven Greer.

3. As we entered the twenty-first century, polls showed a majority of Americans believe intelligent life exists in the universe beyond Earth, and a third of them believe some of those life-forms have visited Earth. Almost half believe that reported UFOs are real, and half think the government is withholding information on them. (Nationwide poll by Yankelovich Partners, January 12–13, 2000.)

4. An August 23–25, 2002, Roper ASW Poll found "72 percent of Americans believe the government is not telling everything it knows about UFO activity and 68 percent think the government knows more about ET life

than it is letting on." Strong majorities say the government does not share enough information and should share more about extraterrestrial life.

Introduction to Part I

1. See Barbara C. Sproul, *Primal Myths: Creation Myths around the World* (San Francisco: HarperSanFrancisco, 1991) and Arthur Cotterell, *A Dictionary of World Mythology* (Oxford: Oxford University Press, 1990).

Chapter 1

1. Dolores Cannon, *Conversations with Nostradamus* (Huntsville, Arkansas: Ozark Mountain Publishers, 2001).

2. Walter Russell, *The Universal One* (Waynesboro, Virginia: University of Science and Philosophy, 1974).

3. *YHVH* himself reportedly used an angel as a channel to dictate the first books of the Bible. "And he told the angel . . . to dictate to Moses from the beginning of Creation until my temple is built in their midst." Genesis Apocryphon, page 239 of Dead Sea Scrolls document (1Q20).

4. José Argüelles, *The Mayan Factor: Path beyond Technology* (Santa Fe, New Mexico: Bear & Company, 1987).

5. Robert Siblerud, *In the Beginning: Mysteries of Ancient Civilizations*, The Sacred Science Chronicles: Vol. 1 (Wellington, Colorado: Sacred Science Publications, 1999).

6. Barbara Marciniak, *Bringers of the Dawn: Teachings from the Pleiadians* (Santa Fe, New Mexico: Bear & Company, 1992).

7. Barbara Hand Clow, *The Pleiadian Agenda* (Santa Fe, New Mexico: Bear & Company, 1995).

8. Amorah Quan Yin, *Pleiadian Perspectives on Human Evolution* (Santa Fe, New Mexico: Bear & Company, 1996).

9. Robert Ellwood, *Theosophy: A Modern Expression of the Wisdom of the Ages* (Wheaton, Illinois: Quest Books, 1986).

10. Donald Johanson and Blake Edgar, *From Lucy to Language* (New York: Simon & Schuster Editions, 1996).

11. Robert McDermott, *The Essential Steiner* (San Francisco: Harper & Row, 1984).

12. Rudolf Steiner, *Cosmic Memory* (San Francisco: Harper & Row, 1959).

13. David Morehouse, *Psychic Warrior* (New York: St. Martin's Press, 1996).

14. Joseph McMoneagle, *Remote Viewing Secrets* (Charlottesville, Virginia: Hampton Roads Publishing, 2000).

15. Courtney Brown, *Cosmic Voyage* (New York: Penguin Books, 1997).

16. Noel Langley, *Edgar Cayce on Reincarnation* (New York: Warner Books, 1967).

17. Website: www.awakening-healing.com.

18. Dolores Cannon, *Legacy from the Stars* (Huntsville, Arkansas: Ozark Mountain Publishers, 1996).

19. Jess Stearn, *The Search for a Soul* (New York: Doubleday, 1972).

20. Eric Klein, *Crystal Star: A Guide to Ascension* (Livermore, California: Oughten House Publications, 1994).

21. Gordon-Michael Scallion, *Notes from the Cosmos* (Chesterfield, New Hampshire: Matrix Institute, 1997).

22. Deborah and Jack Bartello, *We the People Are the Messiah* (Mount Shasta, California: Project Enlightenment Press, 1999) p. x.

23. Charles C. Wise, Jr., *The Magian Gospel of Brother Yeshua* (Penn Laird, Virginia: The Magian Press, 1979) p. 305.

Chapter 2

1. Interdisciplinary scholar Jean Houston has written several books on this subject and has developed training programs using mythic material and its archetypes to assist individual self-empowerment.

2. Cotterell, p. 3.

3. Ibid., pp. 2–3.

4. The Old Testament text we now use came from a collection of oral and written pieces collected by the Hebrews over several millennia. Probably first written down in a form now recognizable 2,600 years ago, the oldest existing partial manuscripts in classical Hebrew date from just over 2,000 years ago. See *The Dead Sea Scrolls Translated* (New York: E. J. Brill, 1994). The present so-called Massoretic text, probably created from such manuscripts as survived the destruction of Jerusalem in 70 A.D., is about 1,900 years old.

5. Zecharia Sitchin, *Divine Encounters* (New York: Avon Books, 1995).

6. John R. Kohlenberger III, *The NIV Interlinear Hebrew-English Old Testament: Vol. 1/Genesis–Deuteronomy* (Grand Rapids, Michigan: Zondervan Publishing House, 1979).

7. Moses Aberbach and Bernard Grossfield, *Targum Onqelos to Genesis* (Center for Judaic Studies, University of Denver, 1982).

8. The Aramaic Bible: Vol. 6 (Wilmington, Delaware: Michael Glazier, Inc., 1987).

9. Mary Phil Korsak, *At the Start: Genesis Made New* (New York: Doubleday, 1993).

10. Jan Knappert, *Indian Mythology* (London: The Aquarian Press, 1991).

11. Cotterell, pp. 97–104.

12. Albert Churchward, *Signs and Symbols of Primordial Man* (New York: A & B Book Publishers, 1903) p. 218.

13. In one legend, King Arthur is associated with Arcturus (Keeper of the Bear), the brightest star in the constellation Boötes, pointed to by the last two stars in the tail of the Great Bear, Ursa Major. John Michell, *New Light on the Mystery of Glastonbury* (Glastonbury, Somerset: Gothic Images Publications, 1990) pp. 16–18.

14. Cotterell, p. 240.

15. Ibid., p. 240.

16. Ibid., pp. 237–45.

17. Ibid., p. 136.

18. Ibid., p. 172.

19. Ibid., pp. 200–202.

20. John Mack, *Passport to the Cosmos* (New York: Crown Publishers, 1999) p. 160.

21. According to a Sumerian tablet translated by W. G. Lambert. See Zecharia Sitchin's *The Wars of Gods and Men* (New York: Avon Books, 1985) p. 115.

Chapter 3

1. The scholarly work of Zecharia Sitchin in this area over more than three decades has established a body of knowledge that must be reckoned with by all future researchers. The findings of a number of scholars, including my own efforts, have provided complementary and corroborative support for the general themes of Sitchin's analysis. His name throughout the text indicates his "fingerprints" in this field.

2. Examples of this concept include the Hermetic Principles from Egyptian antiquity, writings of twentieth-century artist and metaphysician Walter Russell, and the ancient Vedanta tradition of India. Physicists, biologists, and psychologists meeting under the auspices of the University of Science and Philosophy have documented the correlation among these various sources.

3. Sitchin, *Divine Encounters*.

4. Cotterell, pp. 203–21.

5. Ignatius Donnelley, *Atlantis: The Antediluvian World* (New York: Dover Publications, 1976) p. 171, and Plato's *Critias*.

6. Shirley Andrews, *Atlantis: Insights from a Lost Civilization* (St. Paul, Minnesota: Llewellyn Publications, 1997).

7. Alexander Marshack, *The Roots of Civilization* (New York: McGraw-Hill, 1972) p. 34. See also Riane Eisler, *Sacred Pleasure* (San Francisco: HarperSanFrancisco, 1995).

8. Cotterell, pp. 197–214.

9. The theme of hybridization of the human DNA pool with alien DNA has also surfaced, published in modern reports of alien encounters (see ET abduction references in other chapters) and in allegations of secret government projects. The latter theme was popularized in the television series *The X-Files*.

10. Zecharia Sitchin, *The 12th Planet* (New York: Stein and Day, 1976).

11. Sitchin, *Divine Encounters*, p. 14.

12. Genesis 2:21, in an early Hebrew version, says Adam was "cast into a deep sleep" when Eve was being fashioned from part of him. This may suggest unconsciousness from anesthesia that involved some form of surgery. See The Pentateuch: Vol. 1, Genesis translated by Samson Rafael Hirsch (New York: The Judaic Press, 1971).

13. Zecharia Sitchin, *Genesis Revisited* (Santa Fe, New Mexico: Bear & Company, 1991).

Chapter 4

1. Cotterell, pp. 246–51.

2. Sitchin, *Divine Encounters*, p. 272.

3. Andrews, *Atlantis* and James M. Robinson, *The Nag Hammadi Library* (New York: Harper & Row, 1978).

4. Robert Siblerud, *Keepers of the Secrets: Unveiling the Mystical Societies* (Wellington, Colorado: Sacred Science Publications, 1999).

5. I and II Enoch and the Book of Jubilees (also known as the Apocalypse of Moses) provide more detail on this subject than the Genesis accounts.

6. The Book of Enoch (I Enoch), translated by R. H. Charles (London: Hollen Street Press, 1917) chapters VI–VII. Enoch was known as the seventh generation after Adam and reportedly walked with the angels and learned secrets of the natural order from them. He knew of the angels' decision to take earthly wives and tried to intercede with the AB-gods on behalf of the "fallen angels," but the petition was rejected. See Margaret Barker's *The Lost Prophet* (London: SPCK, 1988). "There was no suggestion of any threat [by the angels] to God's authority, beyond rebellion in the [sharing of knowledge with humans and marrying human females] . . . , and no mention of any direct confrontation with God's authority." Maxwell Davidson's *Angels at Qumran: A Comparative Study* (Sheffield, England: Sheffield Academic Press, 1992) provides additional insight.

7. See the story of conflict between Sin and Ninurta and their respective AB descendants and human followers pieced together from several Sumerian texts in *The Wars of Gods and Men* by Sitchin. This story is consistent with other examples of Ninurta's opposition to AB support for human self-determination. For instance, he reported to his father Enlil that Enki had given warning and plans for a "submersible" to Noah before the Flood.

8. Elaine Pagels, *The Origin of Satan* (New York: Random House, 1995) p. 61.

9. Ibid., p. 58.

10. *The Scroll of the War of the Sons of Light against the Sons of Darkness*, edited by Yigael Yadin (Oxford: Oxford University Press, 1962) p. 15. This scroll includes very detailed instructions on how to wage war and remain consistent with Jewish religious practices.

11. Andrew Collins, *From the Ashes of Angels* (Rochester, Vermont: Bear & Company, 2001) p. 5.

12. Knappert, pp. 40 and 239.

13. Collins, p. 105.

14. Dead Sea Scrolls, Pseudo-Ezekiel, Document (4Q385), p. 286.

15. In more recent history, demagogues who want to control their fellow citizens have resorted to reverse psychology, calling other people by the names that might just as well be applied to themselves. If they wish to hide their own agendas, they divert attention by calling others liars. If they want to distract their people from knowing the truth about their own underhanded dealings, they label their opponents followers of the devil.

16. William Bramley, *The Gods of Eden* (New York: Avon Books, 1993).

17. *The Gospel of Mary Magdalene,* Jean-Yves Leloup [translation and commentary] (Rochester, Vermont: Inner Traditions, 2001) p. 4 and the Gospel of Philip in the *The Nag Hammadi Library* (San Francisco: Harper & Row, 1981) p. 134.

18. Leloup, pp. 7–9.

19. In St. Augustine's *De Civitates Dei*, XV, 23 the Book of Enoch was considered contrary to and potentially dealing a death blow to the orthodoxy being established by the fourth- and fifth-century Christian Church. See Margaret Barker's *The Lost Prophet* in reference 6, this chapter.

Chapter 5

1. A notable cross-cultural study is Gordon Creighton's *Angels, Men, and Jinns: The True Nature of UFO Entities* (Kent, UK: FRS Publications, 1983).

2. Edith Fiore, *Encounters* (New York: Ballantine, 1990).

3. Budd Hopkins, *Intruders* (New York: Ballantine, 1987).

4. Ibid., p. 280.

5. Mack.

6. Ibid., pp. 64–5.

7. Jacques Vallee, *Confrontations: A Scientist's Search for Alien Contact* (New York: Random House, 1990).

8. Ibid., pp.18 and 89.

9. Vallee points out that several technologies demonstrated by the aliens seem to precede official military developments by a short period, suggesting that they may be playing with humans. In this regard he lists weapons like energy pulsing or microwave beams that aliens allegedly used before the military developed them. This symmetry could lead to other conclusions. The military could have gotten the technology from aliens (directly or through reverse-engineering) or hoaxed an "alien event" to cover-up the fact that they had already developed the weapons.

10. Vallee, p. 18.

11. Raymond E. Fowler, *The Watchers: The Secret Design behind UFO Abduction* (New York: Bantam, 1990).

12. Ibid., pp. 372–73.

13. Fowler's identification of ET/angel references in the Bible include the following:

- Nocturnal lights: Exodus 13:21–22 and Matthew 2:9.

- Daylight disks: Exodus 12:21–22, Isaiah 60:80, and Acts 22:6.

- UFO: Genesis 15:17.

- UFO with physical effects: Exodus 14:19–29.

- UFO with occupants: Exodus 3:1–5 and 33:9–10, Ezekiel 1:1–28, Matthew 28:2–3, Mark 9:4 and 7–8, Luke 2:8–9.

- UFO abduction: II Kings 2:11, Acts 1:9–11, II Corinthians 12: 2–4.

- Descriptions of various physical effects that have also been associated with modern UFO/ET events: Exodus 16:4 and Psalms 78:25 (artifacts); Genesis 19:11 (blindness); Exodus 14:19 (fog); Genesis 19:13 and 24–38 (heat); Exodus 14:22 and 29 and Ezekiel 3:13–16 (levitation); Exodus 34:29–30 and Matthew 17:2 (luminescence); Daniel 8:15–19 and 10:4–9, Matthew 28:2–4, Revelation 1:12–17 (paralysis).

- Descriptions of paraphysical effects: II Corinthians 12:2–4 (out-of-body-experiences); Matthew 17:1–9 and Mark 9:1–8 (transfiguration or shape shifting).

- References to genetics: Genesis 6:2–4 (hybrid births); Genesis 18:2, 9–10, and 21:2, Luke 1:7, 11–13, 24, 26–34, and 57 (anomalous births).

14. Angela Thompson-Smith, *Diary of an Abduction* (Charlottesville, Virginia: Hampton Roads Publishing, 2001).

15. Phillip H. Krapf, *The Contact Has Begun* (Carlsbad, California: Hay House Inc., 1998).

Chapter 6

1. Carlos Castaneda, *The Teachings of Don Juan, A Separate Reality,* and *Journey to Ixtlan* (New York: Pocket Books, 1971, 1974, and 1974).

2. Collins.

3. Rick Strassman, *DMT: The Spirit Molecule* (Rochester, Vermont: Park Street Press, 2001) pp. 21–22.

4. Castaneda, *Journey to Ixtlan*, pp. 225, 251, and 255.

5. Castaneda, *The Teachings of Don Juan*, p. 236.

6. Robert A. Monroe, *Far Journeys* (New York: Doubleday, 1985) p. 20.

7. The Monroe Institute, 62 Roberts Mountain Road, Faber, VA 22938, phone: 434/361-1252, fax: 434/361-1237, e-mail: monroeinst@aol.com, website: www.monroeinst.org.

8. Monroe, p. 94.

9. Ibid., p. 100.

10. Rosalind McKnight, *Cosmic Journeys* (Charlottesville, Virginia: Hampton Roads Publishing, 1999) p. 42.

11. P. M. H. Atwater, *Children of the New Millennium* (New York: Three Rivers Press, 1999) p. 187.

12. P. M. H. Atwater, *The Complete Idiot's Guide to Near-Death Experiences* (Indianapolis, Indiana: Macmillan USA Inc., 2000) p. 65.

13. Dannion Brinkley with Paul Perry, *Saved by the Light* (New York: Harper Paperbacks, 1993).

14. Raymond Moody, *Life After Life* (New York: Bantam Books, 1976).

15. Frank DeMarco, *Muddy Tracks: Exploring an Unexpected Reality* (Charlottesville, Virginia: Hampton Roads Publishing, 2001) p. xxi.

16. Ibid., p. 17.

17. Ibid., pp. 339 and 342.

18. Neale Donald Walsch, *Conversations with God: An Uncommon Dialogue,* Books 1, 2, and 3. Book 1 from Putnam Publishing Group (New York, 1999), Books 2 and 3 from Hampton Roads Publishing (Charlottesville, Virginia, 1997 and 1998, respectively).

19. Walsch, *Book 2*, p. 237.

20. See groups.yahoo.com/group/AncientMelchizededk/messade/582.

21. *Hildegard von Bingen's Mystical Vision*, Bruce Hozeski (translator) (Santa Fe, New Mexico: Bear & Company, 1995).

22. Edward Carlos, "Fomentation in the Creative Process: Metaphoric Effigies of Mystical Consciousness," Sixth Annual International Society for Phenomenology, Aesthetics, and Fine Arts, Harvard Divinity School, May 12–14, 2003.

Chapter 7

1. A combination of sequential Earth changes and other as yet unknown energetic and/or electrochemical factors may be assumed to have given rise

to genus *Homo*. However, we have not yet identified the precipitating factors related to the emergence of this new category of primates. Only a few gross geological/climatic measures have been correlated to the dates of species. For instance, the appearance of several distinctive hominid groups three to six million years ago seems to have occurred after a significant shift in climate zones, atmospheric gases, and vegetation. These genera are now known as: *Ardipithecus, Australopithecus, Kenyanthropus,* and *Paranthropus.* Since the geological record points to shifts in the Earth's magnetic field between five and ten million years ago, the notion of magnetic influences on these specific DNA structures should not be dismissed.

2. See a discussion of the evidence for a self-learning cosmology in the author's book *Our Solarian Legacy: Multidimensional Humans in a Self-Learning Universe* (Charlottesville, Virginia: Hampton Roads Publishing, 2001).

3. Marshack.

4. Ibid., p. 109.

5. Jeremy Narby, *The Cosmic Serpent: DNA and the Origins of Knowledge* (New York: Putnam, 1998).

6. Legends quoted in the Museum of Cherokee History located in Cherokee, North Carolina.

7. Richard Klein, *The Dawn of Human Culture* (New York: John Wiley & Sons, 2002).

8. Craig Stanford, *The Ape-Human Continuum and the Quest for Human Nature* (New York: Basic Books, 2001).

9. Eugene Linden, "The Wife Beaters of Kibale," *Time*, August 19, 2002.

10. Cleve Backster, *Primary Perception: Biocommunication with Plants, Living Foods, and Human Cells* (Anza, California: White Rose Millennium Press, 2003).

11. Ingo Swann, *Natural ESP* (San Francisco: J. P. Tarcher, 1991).

12. Belinda Gore, *Ecstatic Body Postures* (Santa Fe, New Mexico: Bear & Company, 1995).

13. William Collinge, *Subtle Energy* (New York: Warner Books, 1998).

14. Heretical cosmologist Giordano Bruno, burned at the stake by the Church in 1600, is considered by some to have been both a Hermetic magus and a Kabbalist mystic. See Giordano Bruno, *The Cabala of Pegasus* (New Haven, Connecticut: Yale University Press, 2002).

15. Persia had several teachers known as Zoroaster. This one probably lived centuries before Moses. He spoke of the Hermetic Principle of Polarity as it was understood in esoteric circles, before it turned into the rationale for the good/evil dichotomy of later Zoroastrian fame. See Paul Roland's *Revelations: Wisdom of the Ages* (Berkeley, California: Ulysses Press, 1995).

16. David B. Ruderman, *Kabbalah, Magic, and Science* (Cambridge: Harvard University Press, 1988) p. 161.

Chapter 8

1. E. G. Garrison, "Physics and Archaeology," *Physics Today*, October 21, 2001.

2. Rick Gore, "New Find," *National Geographic*, August 2002.

3. Johanson and Edgar.

4. The radiocarbon method (introduced in the 1940s) was used on bone and other organic matter. It measures the rate at which carbon-14 decays after the death of an organism. With its half-life of 5,730 years, scientists can compare the amount of carbon-14 to the amount of carbon-12 (a stable form of carbon) and deduce when death occurred. However, given its half-life rate, carbon-14 decays beyond measurable levels in 50,000 years and cannot be used to date items older than that. A newer approach to radiocarbon dating, using accelerator mass spectrometry (AMS), has now extended the technique's viability to about 75,000 years.

5. Three methods involve the counting of electrons trapped by flaws in the structure of materials and organic remains (electron spin resonance, thermoluminescence, and optically stimulated luminescence). Other methods that can provide corroborating measurements include X-ray fluorescence, paleomagnetism, fission-tracking, uranium-series, and amino-acid racemization.

6. Johanson and Edgar.

7. The fossil was discovered by a French team led by paleontologist Michel Brunet in a desert area of Chad that was a lush forest long ago. Dated at 7 million B.P., according to *Nature* it is the oldest currently known hominid or prehuman fossil.

8. See article by Craig Feibel et al. on dating by the magnetic orientation of metal fragments settled from water in sediments: "Pleistocene Milestones on the Out-of-Africa Corridor at Gesher Benot Yalaqov, Israel," *Science* 2000, pp. 944–947.

9. In the flurry of nineteenth-century excavations, many of the bones discovered were of creatures that no longer existed, but some of them appeared to be related to modern species. The presentation of Charles Darwin's and Alfred Wallace's views on the origin of species in 1858 offered a natural explanation for evident variations between groups of skeletons, including those assumed to represent humans. The theory that became known as Darwinism postulated that modern species (plants and animals) had evolved by a gradual process of development from one-celled organisms, through intermediate stages randomly mutating from one species to another. This assumption caused scientists to arrange their fossils in an ascending order of refinement. Since the validity of that practice has now been called into question by many scientists, this chapter addresses only the correlation of dates imputed to various fossil types without asserting that they accurately represent the human family tree.

10. Mesopotamian texts included the *Atrahasis*, the *Enuma Elish*, and the *Myth of the Pickax*.

Chapter 9

1. DNA phylogenetic studies are based on extrapolations backwards in time of a hypothesized rate of change for incremental genetic variations (called *alleles*). This means that since current genetic differences among ethnic or racial groups can be calculated, an assumed rate of change permits

one to estimate their ages on branches of the human tree. MtDNA and Y chromosome studies introduced in this chapter base their estimated dates on such hypothetical calculations.

2. The human body's external appearance, organs, and brain and nervous system result from its DNA patterns. The information coded in our DNA includes the blueprint, construction drawings, and assembly instructions for every aspect of the organism. About 34,000 genes in DNA segments, encoded on 23 chromosomes, are defined by a "code" of only four nucleotide bases known by the abbreviations A, G, C, and T arranged in more than 3 billion sequences of "words." Comparisons of selected areas of these sequences identify the variations used in this research.

3. Sitchin, *Divine Encounters*, p. 14.

4. Rebecca L. Cann, Mark Stoneking, and Allan C. Wilson, "Mitochondrial DNA and Human Evolution," *Nature*, January 1, 1987.

5. Studies have suggested mutations in a strain of human mtDNA occur about once every 10,000 years. This factor helps date the original maternal group but cannot fix the location.

6. Jonathan Marks, *Human Biodiversity: Genes, Race, and History* (New York: Aldine de Grutyer, 1995).

7. Hugh Ross, "Neanderthal Takes a One-Eighty," *Facts & Faith*, 3rd Quarterly 1997 (Vol. 11, No. 3).

8. Douglas Wallace et al., "Global mtDNA Variation and Origins of Native Americans," Origins of Man conference paper, Center for Molecular Medicine, Emory (Georgia) University, and Alan R. Templeton, *Nature*, March 7, 2002.

9. Chris Stringer, Department of Palaeontology, Natural History Museum, London. www.NewScientist.com/news/news.jsp?id=ns99993814.

10. Bryan Sykes, *The Seven Daughters of Eve* (New York: W. W. Norton, 2002).

11. Gina Kirchwager, "Black and White," *Discover*, February 2001, pp. 32–3.

12. Jared Diamond, "Race without Color," *Discover*, November 1994.

13. Ross.

14. Sitchin, pp. 90–92.

15. Luigi Luca Cavalli-Sforza, *The Great Human Diaspora* (Reading, Massachusetts: Addison-Wesley, 1995).

16. Peter J. D'Adamo, *Eat Right for Your Blood Type* (New York: Putnam, 1996).

17. Cavalli-Sforza, pp. 131–49.

18. M. Baigent, R. Leigh, and H. Lincoln, *Holy Blood, Holy Grail* (New York: Dell Publishing Company, 1983).

19. Carlo Suares, *The Cipher of Genesis* (York Beach, Maine: Samuel Weiser, 1992).

20. *I Enoch*, chapters CVI and CVII.

21. The first mtDNA tests on Neanderthal remains were conducted by a team of German and U.S. scientists in 1997 (July 11, 1997, report in *Cell* by Mark Stoneking of Pennsylvania State University). "The results indicate that Neanderthals did not contribute mtDNA to modern humans . . . (and) . . . are not our ancestors."

22. Some serious researchers maintain that descendants of Neanderthals, or even *Homo erectus,* may still exist as Bigfoot, Sasquatch, etc. Some very convincing evidence suggests these beings have a fairly high level of intelligence, have survived against tremendous odds, and employ a basic language. In addition, some reports indicate a fairly sophisticated level of telepathic communication with humans. A part of our unraveling of human history will require us to officially engage in this area of research that has been long ignored.

23. An Australian abductee reports having been forcibly "seduced" by a Nordic-looking being he did not consider human. (She and a companion allegedly appeared mysteriously on his bed and vanished when he resisted.) Afterwards he allegedly found two blond hairs under his foreskin. Analysts found that, although patterned like human DNA, five of the blond hair markers were judged not to have come from humans with Caucasian, blond features. On the basis of the current human genome, they could have only come from a Chinese Mongoloid with black hair. Had the hair sample been bleached blond it would have destroyed its DNA material. (Michael Linderman, editor, "Alien DNA Alleged," *CNI News,* June 16, 1999, Vol. 5, No. 8.)

Introduction to Part IV

1. A number of people believe Planet X is due to pass near Earth in the very near future. Some charge a U.S. government cover-up of its projected trajectory. They point to several hints that might suggest the government is slowly preparing the public for a warning: On September 13, 2001, NASA alluded to a Pluto-sized object in chilly outer reaches (swarming with thousands of dark and mysterious objects) of the solar system. On July 14, 2002, the discovery of Asteroid 2002 NY40 was published. It measured 800 meters in diameter and passed in sight of Earth on August 18. A little earlier (July 9), Asteroid NT7, with a 1 in 250,000 chance of hitting Earth in 2019, was announced. (For instance, see National Optical Astronomy Observatory Press Release NOAO 01-10, dated July 2, 2001. NOAO is supported by NASA and the National Science Foundation.)

Chapter 10

1. David Frawley, *Gods, Sages, and Kings: Vedic Secrets of Ancient Civilization* (Salt Lake City, Utah: Passage Press, 1991).

2. D. S. Allan and J. B. Delair, *Cataclysm: Compelling Evidence of a Cosmic Catastrophe in 9,500 B.C.* (Santa Fe, New Mexico: Bear & Company, 1997) p. 242.

3. Excerpts from Genesis, chapters 7 and 8.

4. Cotterell, p. 229.

5. Ibid., p. 212.

6. Sitchin, *Divine Encounters.*

7. If Nibiru (the home of the Anunnaki mentioned earlier) was split into fragments in the Kuiper Belt collision, the AB colonists of Sumer may have had no home to go to after the Earth cataclysm. Such a disaster could explain why the Anunnaki had to return to Earth and re-establish their settlements, a decision that led to working with humans to rebuild civilization.

8. Allan and Delair, p. 206. The change in rotation could have been caused by an axial shift that reconfigured the Earth's continental and tidal profiles. Some researchers speculate the opposite may have occurred on Mars.

9. Rand and Rose Flem-Ath, *When the Sky Fell: In Search of Atlantis* (New York: St. Martin's, 1995).

Chapter 11

1. Jared Diamond, *Guns, Germs, and Steel* (New York: Norton, 1999) p. 52.

2. Frawley.

3. Cotterell, p. 212. (This was the third flood in the Mayan recorded history.)

4. Ibid., p. 204.

5. Zecharia Sitchin, *The Stairway to Heaven* (Santa Fe, New Mexico: Bear & Company, 1992) p. 86.

6. Maria Gimbutas, *The Language of the Goddess* (San Francisco: Harper & Row, 1989) and Bryan Sykes, *The Seven Daughters of Eve* (New York: W. W. Norton, 2002).

7. Oral traditions, written down in Egypt and later preserved by the Greek Solon, suggest the Phoenicians and early Hellenes also had access to knowledge from beyond the Anunnaki colonies.

8. Frawley.

9. Cotterell, p. 258.

10. Marshack, p. 25.

11. Maurice Chatelain, *Our Cosmic Ancestors* (Sedona, Arizona: Temple Golden Publications, 1988) pp. 105 and 130.

12. "Farm History Retold," *Research in Review* (Florida State University, Vol. XII, No. 3) p.4.

13. One such group advertising in national media is Christ's Soon Return, P. O. Box 1464, Bloomington, IL 61702.

Chapter 12

1. Sitchin, *The Wars of Gods and Men*, pp. 118–19, and Genesis 6–8.

2. Genesis 8:21.

3. Sitchin, *The Wars of Gods and Men*, pp. 120–22.

4. Ibid., p. 118.

5. This chapter is based on accounts in the Old Testament, various Sumerian cuneiform texts, and other ancient documents. Commentaries of other historians on this material have been used appropriately, with considerable weight being given to the analyses of Zecharia Sitchin. I have personally verified selected primary documents to ensure their interpretations reflect the sources. I understand that some researchers may not agree with my conclusions, but I have tried to ensure that they represent a responsible reinterpretation of historical documents in the light of new knowledge.

6. J. M. Roberts, *A Short History of the World* (New York: Oxford University Press, 1997) p. 44.

7. Sitchin, *The Wars of Gods and Men*, p. 125.

Endnotes

8. Sponsored by the International Association for New Science based in Fort Collins, Colorado, an international forum convened on October 6, 1996, in Denver, Colorado, facilitated the first such gathering of scholars researching the AB thesis in Sumerian history.

9. Roberts, p. 58.

10. "Ancient City Found in India Irradiated by Nuclear Blast," excerpt from *World Island Review*, January 1992; and Sitchin, *The Wars of Gods and Men*, pp. 331–32. The first reference describes a heavy layer of radioactive ash in Rajasthan, India, that covers a three-square-mile area, ten miles west of Jodhpur.

11. E. M. Burns, *Western Civilizations* (New York: W. W. Norton, 1963).

12. Sitchin, *The Wars of Gods and Men*, p. 290.

13. Genesis 12:1–4.

14. Sitchin, *Divine Encounters*, p. 20.

15. A careful reading of the oldest versions of Genesis reveals that different appellations were used to refer to "the gods," "the Lord," and "one God" at various times in the chronology of events. Moses's encounter described in Exodus is the first time the Hebrews appear to have actually heard the name *YHVH*. It was not a name or the cognate of a name in Sumerian or Akkadian (mother tongue of Assyrian, Babylonian, and Hebrew) that referred to the gods. Therefore, it is likely that after the Exodus the Hebrews inserted *YHVH* in lieu of previously used AB names in their oral and written history.

16. The Bible's description of the Ark suggests it might have involved some electromagnetic forces dangerous to humans. Exodus 19:17–19 makes it sound like a loud amplifier. *YHVH* forbade people to approach or touch him and prohibited access to his "holy of holies."

17. It should be noted that an AB struck the pharaoh's family with "grave diseases" centuries earlier for taking Abraham's wife Sarai into his household (Genesis 12:10–20).

Chapter 13

1. Cotterell, pp. 216–17.

2. Collins, pp. 109 and following.

3. More detailed discussions of this scenario can be found in Lloyd Pye's book *Everything You Know Is Wrong* (Madeira Beach, Florida: Adamu Press, 1997), Bruce Smith's *The Emergence of Agriculture*, and Zecharia Sitchin's books *The Wars of Gods and Men* and *The 12th Planet*.

4. Cavalli-Sforza, pp. 131 and following.

5. Cotterell, p. 223.

6. Ibid., p. 244.

7. Cavalli-Sforza, pp. 131 and following.

8. Several articles—reported over time in the journal *Science*—have pointed out that dogs, like humans, have an "Eve": genes from one to three females from whom 95 percent of all dogs descended.

9. Pye, pp. 289–90.

10. For the reader unfamiliar with such "unexplained mysteries," metaphysical sources like psychic Gordon-Michael Scallion's "intelligences" report

that the construction of the Great Pyramids of Giza took place in 12,553 B.P. or earlier.

11. Bruce Cathie, "Acoustic Levitation of Stones," chapter 8, *Anti-Gravity and the Unified Field*, D. H. Childress (editor) (Kempton, Illinois: Adventures Unlimited Press, 1990).

12. See the Andean Explorers Foundation website at www.aefose.org and www.genesavoy.org.

13. Thomas Brophy, *The Origin Map: Discovery of a Prehistoric, Megalithic, Astrophysical Map and Sculpture of the Universe* (New York: Writers Club Press, 2002).

14. Chatelain.

15. Ibid., pp. 32–35.

16. Ibid., p. 210.

17. Ibid., p. 126.

18. L. K. Green, *The Astrologer's Manual* (Sebastopol, California: CRCS Publications, 1975) p. 219.

19. Dead Sea Scrolls, Document (4Q186).

Chapter 14

1. A. Hellemans and B. Bunch, *The Timetables of Science* (New York: Simon & Schuster, 1988).

2. Michael Cremo and Richard Thompson, *The Hidden History of the Human Race: The Condensed Version of Forbidden Archaeology* (Los Angeles: Bhaktivedanta Book Publishing, 1999).

3. Hartwig Hausdorf, *Ancient Skies* (Beabemburg, Switzerland: German Edition, 1998) p. 5. Also author of *The Chinese Roswell* (Boca Raton, Florida: New Paradigm Books, 1998).

4. Eudoxus made his calculations with the Earth as center, as was generally believed at the time. With his calculations based on a false premise, he suggested a calendar of 365 days for three years followed by one year of 366 days. This model was accepted by Julius Caesar 300 years later and remains our current calendar.

5. Due to Euclid's text *Elements*—which stood for almost 2,000 years—he has been mistakenly known as the father of geometry. Now we know the Anunnaki had already mastered geometry and much more in their space voyages.

6. See Shirley Andrews and others in bibliography.

7. Marshack, p. 135.

8. James Mellaart, *Catal Huyuk: A Neolithic Town in Anatolia* (New York: Bacon, 1960).

9. Writers like Charles Berlitz, author of *Atlantis: The Eighth Continent* (New York: Fawcett Crest, 1984) and Javier Cabrera, author of *The Message of the Engraved Stones* (Lima, Peru: Servicio Grafico, 2000, 1989), have collected lists of such anomalous artifacts.

10. Cotterell, p. 241.

11. Ibid., p. 220.

12. Joseph R. Jochman, "Top Ten Out-of-Place Artifacts," *Atlantic Rising*, Issue No. 5, September 2000.

Chapter 15

1. We must dig deeper under current excavations to determine if post-cataclysm structures were built on top of previous ruins. We know by dates from some religious sites in Europe that precataclysm sites were reoccupied. We should hope that it is not one of the objectives of the turmoil in the Middle East to prevent comprehensive exploration of the ruins that lie beneath the sands of Iraq, Iran, Palestine, Israel, and other countries reported to have sites that could validate AB activity in their prehistory. Heavy bombing could serve the purpose of permanently obliterating structures and artifacts left over from antediluvian civilizations.

2. Sitchin, *The 12th Planet*, p. 110.

3. David Kalakaua, *The Legends and Myths of Hawaii* (Rutland, Vermont: Charles E. Tuttle Company, 1972) p. 53.

4. Cotterell, p. 199.

5. Sitchin, *Divine Encounters*, p. 109. Sitchin believes the number of Anunnaki on Earth never reached more than 600.

6. See Genesis 19 regarding the AB-angels sent to discipline the citizens of Sodom and Gomorrah.

7. Sitchin, *The 12th Planet*, p. 119.

8. M. Baigent, R. Leigh, and H. Lincoln.

9. Genesis chapter 5, and Sitchin, *Divine Encounters*, pp. 45–47.

10. Sitchin, *Genesis Revisited*, p. 204.

11. *The* (Akkadian) *Fable of the Tamarisk and the Date Palm*, and Genesis, chapter 10.

12. Sitchin, *The Wars of Gods and Men*, pp. 33–35. Reference corroborated by the Tablet of Abydos ordered produced by Pharaoh Seti I.

13. After the surrender of Japan at the end of World War II, Emperor Hirohito renounced his claim to divinity.

14. Cotterell, p. 244.

15. H. V. Guenther and L. S. Kawamura, *Mind in Buddhist Psychology* (Emeryville, California: Dharma Publishing, 1975) p. xv.

16. Michael Harner, *The Way of the Shaman* (New York: Harper & Row, 1980) p. xii.

17. Gerald L. Berry, *Religions of the World* (New York: Barnes & Noble Inc., 1958).

18. Frawley.

19. Cotterell, p. 246.

Chapter 16

1. Of interest in this regard is the use of the Hebrew term "a spirit uttering speech" in reference to the just-created human in Genesis 2:7. Its use there "emphasizes man's faculty of speech as his pre-eminence over the beast . . ." where both man and beast are called "living beings." See *The Aramaic Bible: Vol. 6* (Wilmington, Delaware: Michael Glazier Inc., 1987).

2. Johanson and Edgar, p. 106.

3. *Language Families* by Kryss Katsiaviades at www.krysstal.com/lang fams.html.

4. All languages change with time. If two groups of people speaking the

same language separate, their languages will develop along different paths. First, they develop different accents; next, some of the vocabulary will change (due to influences from other languages or gradual changes from generation to generation). Such changes create different dialects, but the two groups can still understand each other. If the dialects continue to diverge they become mutually unintelligible, with the two groups now speaking different languages.

5. Cotterell, p. 206.

6. The term "aboriginal," used to describe the most primitive people in Africa, derives from Latin's *ab+origine,* meaning "from the beginning." Maybe it is not inappropriate to describe these people as "AB-originals."

7. Some researchers (on the basis of common physical characteristics, similar art forms, parallel rituals, and overlapping oral traditions) believe these Africans are members of a worldwide family of aboriginals and pygmies whose remnants still survive in places in Australia and parts of Asia (see Churchward and Donnelley). The Khoisan (actually made up of two groups, the Khoi and the San, sometimes known as Bushmen and Hottentot) and the Pygmies are different from the other blacks in Africa, but they are also different from each other. The Khoisan actually have yellowish skins and tightly coiled hair. The Pygmies have small bodies, with somewhat reddish skins and more body hair.

8. Katsiaviades.

9. Joseph Greenberg, *Language in the Americas* (Stanford, California: Stanford University Press, 1987).

10. Sykes.

11. "In Search of the First Language," a Nova Production for public television by BBC-TV and WGBH/Boston, 1994.

12. Several dark-skinned groups now in North Africa could have in effect migrated to their present location from Southern Africa, but via a detour in Mesopotamia. This would account for their physical differences from groups who remained in Africa. The evident genetic variations could have developed by direct AB-human interbreeding in Mesopotamia.

13. Andre Parrot, *Tower of Babel* (New York: Philosophical Library, 1955). The ziggurat in Babylon was described in historical times by Herodotus in 460 B.C.E. and Diodorusbiculus in the first century, but where it stood is now a hole in the ground filled with Euphrates river water.

14. Sitchin, *The Wars of Gods and Men,* pp. 197–99.

15. Sitchin, *Divine Encounters,* p. 130.

16. John Philip Cohane, *The Key* (New York: Ballantine, 1988). Cohane discovered evidence of key words common to many languages on different continents, suggesting a proto-language rooted in the god-oriented Semitic cultures.

17. Luigi Luca Cavalli-Sforza, *Genes, Peoples, and Languages* (Berkeley: University of California Press, 2001).

Chapter 17

1. David Diringer, *The Alphabet: A Key to the History of Mankind* (New York: Philosophical Library, 1948).

2. Babylonian is similar to Akkadian, another Anunnaki-oriented language and culture.

3. Diringer. In this regard, discovery of 600 B.C.E. Olmec writing near Mexico's Gulf Coast has been claimed by Florida State University's Mary E. D. Pohl to be the oldest known writing in the Western Hemisphere (*Los Angeles Times*, December 6, 2002).

4. Pierre Leveque, *The Birth of Greece* (New York: Harry N. Abrams Inc., 1990) pp. 140–41.

5. Roberts.

6. Diringer.

7. Ibid.

8. Burns.

9. Frawley.

10. Plato's *Phaedo,* on a "theory of ideas."

11. Michael Poulos, *First Lessons in Sanskrit Grammar* (Beersheba, Tennessee: Stone Door Yoga Center, September 2002).

12. Itzhak Bentov, *A Cosmic Book* (Rochester, Vermont: Destiny Books, 1988) p. 62.

13. Philip S. Berg, *Kabbalah for the Layman* (Jerusalem: Kabbalah Research Center Press, 1981).

14. Deep Throat was the name given to the unknown official in the Nixon administration who helped reveal the cover-up that eventually forced President Nixon to resign.

Chapter 18

1. Helen Keller, "The Day Language Came into My Life," *Reflections on Language*, S. Hirschberg and T. Hirschberg (editors), (New York: Oxford University Press, 1999) p. 4.

2. Noam Chomsky, Ibid., pp. 9–10.

3. Steven Pinker, Ibid., p. 34.

4. Gary Schwartz et al., *The Living Energy Universe* (Charlottesville, Virginia: Hampton Roads Publishing, 1999).

5. Carl Jung's usage as in *Merriam-Webster's Collegiate Dictionary* and *Dictionary of Theories* (London: Gale Research International Ltd., 1993).

6. An aspirated sound is closed off by the expulsion of air, as in pronouncing "D." All consonants pronounced alone are aspirated or completed.

7. Exodus, chapter 20.

8. In *Divine Encounters*, Sitchin mentions this phrase begins with the first Hebrew letter *Aleph* instead of the second letter *Beth*, but he does not point out that other references in the Old Testament include *YHVH* among the Elohim.

9. I find it interesting that the way of thinking I call "magical thinking about ABs" may have begun in the same region from which sprung the modern word magician—West Asia, which includes modern-day Iran, the land of the ancient Persians.

10. *Newsweek*, February 24, 2003, p. 37.

Chapter 19

1. Diamond, p. 405.

2. Mellaart.

3. Pseudo-Ezekiel, Document (4Q385), p. 286 of the Dead Sea Scrolls.

4. Pseudo-Moses, Document (1Q22 [1QDM]), p. 276 of the Dead Sea Scrolls.

5. Sitchin estimates the largest number of off-planet colonists was never more than 600. (Oral presentation on "Sitchin Studies Day" at IANS 1996 International Forum on New Science, October 9, 1996, in Denver, Colorado.)

6. Sitchin, *The Wars of Gods and Men*, p. 140.

7. Parrot.

8. Christopher Knight and Robert Lomas, *The Hiram Key: Pharaohs, Freemasons, and the Discovery of the Secret Scrolls of Jesus* (Rockport, Massachusetts: Element Books Inc., 1998).

9. Who was *YHVH?* Evidence found in the Sumerian accounts indicates he may have been known as Ninurta. Ninurta, son of Enlil, had a Lagash temple that contained facilities for his spacecraft—the "Divine Black Bird"—and telecommunications. It had characteristics of the pyramids of Giza and could have been built only with Enlil's permission. The human king Gudea reportedly constructed the temple E.NINNU in the Girsu (sacred) precinct of Lagash for Ninurta but received the temple plans from AB Ningishzidda (possibly aka Thoth). They were inscribed on a lapis lazuli stone tablet (remember the Ten Commandments given Moses on stone tablets) and gave information on design and materials. Ninurta (in the *Erra Epic*) and *YHVH* (in the Bible) are both associated with the establishment of dikes and irrigation systems and the destruction of Sodom and Gomorrah. (See Sitchin, *Divine Encounters*, p. 186.)

10. M. A. Green, *Dying for the Gods* (Charleston, South Carolina: Tempus, 2001).

11. Riane Eisler, *The Power of Partnership* (Novato, California: New World Library, 2003).

12. The most powerful instrument for reshaping consciousness is the direct experience of a contravening reality. Mini-epiphanies and psychic or transcendent experiences are also powerful modifiers of consciousness. Dominators will use any means to prevent access to such ecstatic states. They outlaw mind-expanding substances, tranquilize individuals who have these alternate states, and distract people from independent meditative practice.

13. Merlin Stone, *When God Was a Woman* (New York: Dial Press, 1976).

14. Eisler, *Sacred Pleasure*.

15. Cotterell, p. 208.

16. Ibid., p. 224.

17. Ibid., pp. 236 and 252.

18. Sitchin, *The Wars of Gods and Men*, p. 327.

19. Possible evidence of nuclear devastation in historical times:

1) Scientists reported in 1992 the discovery of radioactive ash (depleted uranium) covering a three-square-mile area in Rajasthan, India (ten miles west of Jodhpur), dated to between eight and 12 thousand years ago. The area had been long associated with high rates of birth defects and

cancer. The ash covered an ancient city of perhaps a half-million people that appeared to have been destroyed by an atomic blast (comparable to that over Nagasaki or Hiroshima in 1945). Such a horrific event is described in the Hindu Mahabharata where "a single projectile . . . (caused) an incandescent column of smoke and flame. . . . a gigantic messenger of death which reduced to ashes an entire race." (Lee Hunley, *World Island Review*, January 1992).

2) Glass found in the Libyan Desert (and in King Tut's tomb) is considered to be comparable to the trinitite (a green, glass-like substance) formed as a result of atom bomb tests at the Trinity Site in New Mexico in 1945. (Posted at www.rense.com/general3/8000.htm on June 2, 2002.)

20. Geographer James DeMeo wrote, "A massive climate change shook the ancient world. . . . The vast Sahara Desert, Arabian Desert, and the giant deserts of the Middle East and Central Asia simply did not exist prior to circa 4000 B.C.E." He goes on to postulate that this drying out created social and emotional havoc among human societies in the region. See James DeMeo, *Saharasia: The 4000 B.C.E. Origins of Child Abuse, Sex-Repression, Warfare, and Social Violence in the Deserts of the Old World* (Ashland, Oregon: Orgone Biophysical Research Lab, 1998) pp. 209–12.

21. Sitchin, *The Wars of Gods and Men*, pp. 343–44.

22. Charles Mercet, *Alexander the Great* (New York: Harper & Row, 1962) p. 17.

23. Sitchin, *The Wars of Gods and Men*, p. 344.

Chapter 20

1. Apparently only a regional event, it may have been caused by the near miss of an outer-space object somewhat farther from the Earth than the Phaeton/Nibiru pass of 11,500 B.P.

2. Immanuel Velikovsky, *Earth in Upheaval* (New York: Doubleday & Company, 1955) p. 275.

3. "Volcanoes and Earthquakes in History and Myth," *National Geographic*, July 2000, pp. 59-80.

4. Cotterell, p. 216.

5. J. E. Zimmerman, *Dictionary of Classical Mythology* (New York: Bantam Books, 1972) pp. 84 and 88.

6. Physical resurrection is often considered the same as immortality, but there is a difference. In the latter one never dies. That possibility apparently captured the human imagination when they observed that ABs seemed to live forever. (There was no evidence that the Anunnaki were actually immortal; they just lived several thousand times longer than humans.) People apparently believed that if the gods took individuals (like Ezekiel and Daniel in the Bible) into space they, too, would never die. This would feed into later religious belief in immortality.

7. John Ferguson, *Encyclopedia of Mysticism* (New York: Crossroad Publishing, 1982) pp. 136–37.

8. Ibid., pp. 120–21.

9. Ibid., pp. 154–55.

10. *The Lost Gospel Q: The Original Sayings of Jesus,* edited by Marcus Borg (Berkeley, California: Ulysses Press, 1996).

11. See *Our Solarian Legacy* for elaboration of the self-manifesting and self-directing nature of the universe.

12. Robinson, *The Nag Hammadi Library,* p. 123.

13. The Genesis Apocryphon statement ". . . I offered to the God Most High and invoked the name of the Lord of the Universe" suggests the worshiper distinguished between *YHVH* as his most important god (and an AB from space) and a universal creator. While he gave an offering to *YHVH*, he prayed that his action was in accord with the Universal One. Genesis Apocryphon, Dead Sea Scrolls Document (1Q20), p. 230.

14. Knappert, Cotterell, Sproul, Ferguson, and Zimmerman.

15. Cotterell, p. 239.

16. Ibid., p. 241.

Chapter 21

1. In our self-learning universe, this seems to characterize all species to some degree, from the bacteria who learn to evade human antibiotics to the coping mechanisms of humans themselves.

2. Andrew Newberg, Eugene D'Aquili, and Vince Rause, *Why God Won't Go Away: Brain Science & the Biology of Belief* (New York: Ballantine, 2002).

3. Ursula Goodenough, *The Sacred Depths of Nature* (New York: Oxford University Press, 1998) p. xvi.

4. Narby.

5. DeMeo.

6. Lewis Spence, *The Outlines of Mythology* (New York: Fawcett Publications, 1961).

7. Sigmund Freud, *The Future of an Illusion* (New York: Anchor Books, 1964) p. 71.

8. Paul Von Ward, "Rediscovering Our Natural Heritage," *The Cosmic Light,* University of Science and Philosophy, Autumn 2000, Vol. 2 No. 4, pp. 18–21.

9. Eleventh-century manuscript from Iceland. *The Prose Edda: Tales from Norse Mythology,* translated by Snorri Sturlson (Los Angeles: University of California Press, 2002).

10. Richard Kearney, *Strangers, Gods, and Monsters* (New York: Routledge, 2003) Frontispiece.

Chapter 22

1. Manfred Clynes, *Sentics: The Touch of Emotions* (New York: Anchor Books, 1978) p. 33.

2. Cotterell, p. 197.

3. C. Alan Anderson and Deborah G. Whitehouse, *New Thought: A Practical American Spirituality* (New York: The Crossroad Publishing Company, 1995) pp. 53–4.

4. Baigent et al., p. 78.

5. Cotterell, pp. 21–24. Some metaphysical groups believe Quetzalcoatl did return in 1987 at the time of the Harmonic Convergence.

6. Berry, p. 71.

7. Most scholars today understand that the institutionalization of Christianity in the Greco-Roman culture involved the incorporation of symbols and rituals from earlier religions to make it more palatable to less sophisticated folks. By co-opting the practices of natural celebrations and social rites of passage, as well as the accoutrements of the AB-god cults, Christianity attracted the emotional energy and intellectual commitment of converts. For this reason, its founders accepted many pagan rituals to gain adherents for the new religion.

8. Ferguson, pp. 88–89.

9. Berry, pp. 72–3.

10. Sitchin, *Divine Encounters*, p. 20.

11. Sitchin, *The Wars of Gods and Men*, p. 84.

12. Berry, pp. 60–1.

13. Frawley.

Chapter 23

1. *Dictionary of Theories*, edited by Jennifer Bothamley (London: Gale Research Int'l Ltd., 1993) p. 26.

2. Swami Prabhavananda and Christopher Isherwood, *Bhagavad-Gita: The Song of God* (New York: Mentor Books, 1954) pp. 11–12.

3. Von Ward, *Our Solarian Legacy*.

4. Leveque.

5. Burns, p. 147.

6. Ferguson, p. 152.

7. Radhakrishnan, pp. 135–37.

8. Plato used the term *Khora* (a placeless place) to connote the primordial origin from which all things come in *Timaeus* 48e–53b.

9. See Gnostic documents from *The Nag Hammadi Library* and Borg's *The Lost Gospel "Q."*

10. Wise.

11. Jesus' message made it obvious that he was not representing *YHVH;* he was preaching against the hierarchical system that *YHVH* has commanded the Hebrews to establish 1,500 years before his ministry.

12. Robinson, *The Nag Hammadi Library*.

13. *Encyclopedia of Mystical and Paranormal Experiences*, edited by Rosemary Ellen Guiley (New York: HarperCollins, 1991) p. 236.

14. Burns, pp. 212–13.

15. Siblerud, *Keepers of the Secrets: Unveiling the Mystical Societies*.

16. Sitchin, *The Wars of Gods and Men*, p. 267.

17. Wise, *The Magian Gospel*.

18. Guiley, p. 215.

19. Knight and Lomas.

20. Ibid., p. 23.

21. Ezekiel 28.

22. Gordon Davidson and Corinne McLaughlin, *Spiritual Politics* (New York: Ballantine Books, 1994) pp. 246–47.

23. Borg.

Gods, Genes, and Consciousness

Chapter 24

1. Metascience integrates all fields of study into a comprehensive science of humanity's experience of its universe. See the author's *Our Solarian Legacy* for a complete discussion of this multidisciplinary search for knowledge.

2. Berg.

3. Roberts, p. 291.

4. Rene Descartes (1596–1650), too, rediscovered the truth of a heliocentric universe. But when he learned that the Inquisition had forced Copernicus to declare his heliocentric theory false, to escape burning at the stake, Descartes decided to have his *Le Monde* published after his own natural death.

5. Burns. Also see article "Science for Sale" by Tinker Ready of the *Boston Phoenix* in the *Utne Reader,* November-December 1999, pp. 60–2.

6. Brian O'Leary, *Reinheriting the Earth* (Ridgeway, California: Brian O'Leary, 2003).

Chapter 25

1. The limited material available on memories of life in Atlantis suggests that although ABs retained supreme authority for most of its existence, humans enjoyed intellectual and technological progress. Some of that may have found its way into postcataclysm Egypt, as hinted in Egyptian accounts.

2. Alice Bailey, *The Externalization of the Hierarchy* (New York: Lucis Publishing Company, 1939). See also *Rays and the Initiation*, 1971.

3. See Gary Zukav's book *Seat of the Soul* (New York: Fireside, 1990) for a clear distinction between external power and inner power.

4. Linda E. Olds, *Metaphors of Interrelatedness* (Albany, New York: State University of New York Press, 1992).

5. See such works as *The Magian Gospel, We the People Are the Messiah,* and others.

6. Readers familiar with twentieth-century world history will recognize that similar debates took place among leaders of the more powerful nations after World War II as they tried to make policy on aid to defeated and backward nations. To freely help the lesser developed might have resulted in future competition for the winners. Therefore, decisions (sometimes secretly) were made to minimize the level of knowledge and technology transfer and to develop international institutional controls that would ensure the continued domination of the world by the victors.

7. Spoken by an Episcopal parish priest near the author's home.

8. Sigmund Freud, *The Future of an Illusion* (New York: Anchor Books, 1964) p. 57.

Chapter 26

1. This is the rationale for an organization called Citizens Against UFO Secrecy based in Washington, D.C.

2. Krapf, p. 78.

3. Fiore, preface by Sprinkle.

4. In February 2003, 31 years after launch, *Pioneer 10* had traveled far enough away that NASA could no longer receive its transmission.

5. Some believe spacecraft in this program (sent in pairs to ensure one each made it beyond Pluto) evidenced the expectation by "those in the know" of the imminent return of Nibiru at the end of its 3,600-year orbit. [See Mark Hazelwood's *Blindsided: Planet X Passes in 2003* (Orlando, Florida: First Publish, 2001).] (If correct, this would mean the Nibiru orbit last placed it near Earth at the time *YHVH* may have tried to help the Hebrews organize a society that could survive a period of AB-rule in absentia.) According to Hazelwood's logic, the NASA probes demonstrated how far the former human subjects had evolved in about 3,500 years. They may have signaled a readiness by humans to engage the Niburians as "more equal" than when they last were on Earth. Recent preparations for a missile defense system could indicate that some humans intend to defend their territory. [Refer to Angela Thompson-Smith's book discussed earlier.]

6. This psy-ops technique involves taking a term that means one thing and giving it the opposite connotation, building up negative emotional energy around the use of the term. This happened when the church taught that anything associated with the words sin or satan is evil (as did earlier Hebrews, the later Essenes, and others before the advent of Christianity). The purpose was to inoculate future humans against taking an interest in any historical references to an actual Advanced Being named Sin/Satan and the idea that he and his AB friends wanted to help humans.

7. Langley, p. 125.

8. Mack, pp. 106–07.

9. *Crop Circles: Harbingers of World Change,* edited by Alick Bartholomew (Bath, England: Gateway Books, 1991).

Chapter 27

1. Billy Graham, "Angels Are Still Active," Tribune Media Services, December 14, 2002.

2. For examples see news articles like "Bush and God" in *Newsweek*, March 10, 2003.

3. See www.cseti.org and www.disclosureproject.org.

4. Katharina Wilson, *The Alien Jigsaw* (Portland, Oregon: Puzzle Publishing, 1993).

5. Ingo Swann, *Penetration: The Question of Extraterrestrial and Human Telepathy* (Rapid City, South Dakota: The Twiggs Company, 1998).

Suggested Reading

(Note: Books are listed alphabetically by the last names of authors, editors, or translators. Multiple books by the same author are indicated by ———, in place of the name in the preceding listing, as in the two works under Atwater listed below. Hebrew, Gnostic, and Christian texts are listed alphabetically under the common name of the work, as the *Aramaic Bible* listed in the A section.)

Aberbach, Moses and Bernard Grossfield, *Targum Onqelos to Genesis* (Center for Judaic Studies. University of Denver, 1982).

Allan, D.S., and J. B. Delair, *Cataclysm: Compelling Evidence of a Cosmic Catastrophe in 9,500 B.C.* (Santa Fe, New Mexico: Bear & Company, 1997).

Anderson, C. Alan, and Deborah G. Whitehouse, *New Thought: A Practical American Spirituality* (New York: The Crossroad Publishing Company, 1995).

Andrews, Shirley, *Atlantis: Insights from a Lost Civilization* (St. Paul, Minnesota: Llewellyn Publications, 1997).

[The] Aramaic Bible: Vol. 6 (Wilmington, Delaware: Michael Glazier Inc., 1987).

Argüelles, José, *The Mayan Factor: Path beyond Technology* (Santa Fe, New Mexico: Bear & Company, 1987).

Atwater, P. M. H., *Children of the New Millennium* (New York: Three Rivers Press, 1999).

———, *The Complete Idiot's Guide to Near-Death Experiences* (Indianapolis, Indiana: Macmillan USA Inc., 2000).

Backster, Cleve, *Primary Perception: Biocommunication with Plants, Living Foods, and Human Cells* (Anza, California: White Rose Millennium Press, 2003).

Baigent, M., R. Leigh, and H. Lincoln, *Holy Blood, Holy Grail* (New York: Dell Publishing Company, 1983).

Bailey, Alice, *The Externalization of the Hierarchy* (New York: Lucis Publishing Company, 1939).

Barker, Margaret, *The Lost Prophet* (London: SPCK, 1988).

Bartello, Deborah, and Jack Bartello, *We the People Are the Messiah* (Mount Shasta, California: Project Enlightenment Press, 1999).

Bartholomew, Alick, ed., *Crop Circles: Harbingers of World Change* (Bath, England: Gateway Books, 1991).

Bentov, Itzhak, *A Cosmic Book* (Rochester, Vermont: Destiny Books, 1988).

Berg, Philip S., *Kabbalah for the Layman* (Jerusalem: Kabbalah Research Center Press, 1981).

Berlitz, Charles, *Atlantis: The Eighth Continent* (New York: Fawcett Crest, 1984).

Berry, Gerald L., *Religions of the World* (New York: Barnes & Noble Inc., 1958).

Borg, Marcus, ed., *The Lost Gospel Q: The Original Sayings of Jesus* (Berkeley, California: Ulysses Press, 1996).

Bramley, William, *The Gods of Eden* (New York: Avon Books, 1993).

Brophy, Thomas, *The Origin Map: Discovery of a Prehistoric, Megalithic, Astrophysical Map and Sculpture of the Universe* (New York: Writers Club Press, 2002).

Brown, Courtney, *Cosmic Voyage* (New York: Penguin Books, 1997).

Bruno, Giordano, *The Cabala of Pegasus* (New Haven, Connecticut: Yale University Press, 2002).

Burns, E. M., *Western Civilizations* (New York: W. W. Norton, 1963).

Cabrera, Javier, *The Message of the Engraved Stones* (Lima, Peru: Servicio Grafico 2000, 1989).

Cavalli-Sforza, Luigi Luca, *Genes, Peoples, and Languages* (Berkeley: University of California Press, 2001).

———, *The Great Human Diaspora* (Reading, Massachusetts: Addison-Wesley, 1995).

Suggested Reading

Cannon, Dolores, *Conversations with Nostradamus* (Huntsville, Arkansas: Ozark Mountain Publishers, 2001).

——, *Legacy from the Stars* (Huntsville, Arkansas: Ozark Mountain Publishers, 1996).

Castaneda, Carlos, *Journey to Ixtlan* (New York: Pocket Books, 1974).

——, *A Separate Reality* (New York: Simon and Schuster, 1971).

——, *The Teachings of Don Juan,* (New York: Simon and Schuster, 1973).

Chatelain, Maurice, *Our Cosmic Ancestors* (Sedona, Arizona: Temple Golden Publications, 1988).

Childress, D. H., *Anti-Gravity and the Unified Field* (Kempton, Illinois: Adventures Unlimited Press, 1990).

Churchward, Albert, *Signs and Symbols of Primordial Man* (New York: A & B Book Publishers, 1903).

Clow, Barbara Hand., *The Pleiadian Agenda* (Santa Fe, New Mexico: Bear & Company, 1995).

Clynes, Manfred, *Sentics: The Touch of Emotions* (New York: Anchor Books, 1978).

Cohane, John Philip, *The Key* (New York: Ballantine, 1988).

Collinge, William, *Subtle Energy* (New York: Warner Books, 1998).

Collins, Andrew, *From the Ashes of Angels* (Rochester, Vermont: Bear & Company, 2001).

Cotterell, Arthur, *A Dictionary of World Mythology* (Oxford: Oxford University Press, 1990).

Creighton, Gordon, *Angels, Men, and Jinns: The True Nature of UFO Entities* (Kent, UK: FRS Publications, 1983).

Cremo, Michael, and Richard Thompson, *The Hidden History of the Human Race: The Condensed Version of Forbidden Archaeology* (Los Angeles: Bhaktivedanta Book Publishing, 1999).

D'Adamo, Peter J., *Eat Right for Your Blood Type* (New York: Putnam, 1996).

Davidson, Gordon, and Corinne McLaughlin, *Spiritual Politics* (New York: Ballantine Books, 1994).

Davidson, Maxwell, *Angels at Qumran: A Comparative Study* (Sheffield, England: Sheffield Academic Press, 1992).

[The] Dead Sea Scrolls Translated, edited by D. Dimant and U. Rappaport (New York: E. J. Brill, 1994).

Gods, Genes, and Consciousness

DeMarco, Frank, *Muddy Tracks: Exploring an Unexpected Reality* (Charlottesville, Virginia: Hampton Roads Publishing, 2001).

DeMeo, James, *Saharasia: The 4000 B.C.E. Origins of Child Abuse, Sex-Repression, Warfare, and Social Violence in the Deserts of the Old World* (Ashland, Oregon: Orgone Biophysical Research Lab, 1998).

Diamond, Jared, *Guns, Germs, and Steel* (New York: Norton, 1999).

Diringer, David, *The Alphabet: A Key to the History of Mankind* (New York: Philosophical Library, 1948).

Donnelley, Ignatius, *Atlantis: The Antediluvian World* (New York: Dover Publications, 1976).

Eisler, Riane, *The Power of Partnership* (Novato, California: New World Library, 2003).

———, *Sacred Pleasure* (San Francisco: HarperSanFrancisco, 1995).

Ellwood, Robert, *Theosophy: A Modern Expression of the Wisdom of the Ages* (Wheaton, Illinois: Quest Books, 1986).

[The Book of] Enoch (I Enoch), translated by R. H. Charles (London: Hollen Street Press, 1917).

Ferguson, John, *Encyclopedia of Mysticism* (New York: Crossroad Publishing, 1982).

Fiore, Edith, *Encounters* (New York: Ballantine, 1990).

Flem-Ath, Rand, and Rose Flem-Ath, *When the Sky Fell: In Search of Atlantis* (New York: St. Martin's, 1995).

Fowler, Raymond E., *The Watchers: The Secret Design behind UFO Abduction* (New York: Bantam, 1990).

Frawley, David, *Gods, Sages, and Kings: Vedic Secrets of Ancient Civilization* (Salt Lake City, Utah: Passage Press, 1991).

Freud, Sigmund, *The Future of an Illusion* (New York: Anchor Books, 1964).

Gimbutas, Maria, *The Language of the Goddess* (San Francisco: Harper & Row, 1989).

Goodenough, Ursula, *The Sacred Depths of Nature* (New York: Oxford University Press, 1998).

Gore, Belinda, *Ecstatic Body Postures* (Santa Fe, New Mexico: Bear & Company, 1995).

[The] Gospel of Mary Magdalene, Jean-Yves Leloup, translator (Rochester, Vermont: Inner Traditions, 2001).

Suggested Reading

Green, L. K., *The Astrologer's Manual* (Sebastopol, California: CRCS Publications, 1975).

Green, M. A., *Dying for the Gods* (Charleston, South Carolina: Tempus, 2001).

Greenberg, Joseph, *Language in the Americas* (Stanford, California: Stanford University Press, 1987).

Greer, Steven M., *Disclosure: Military and Government Witnesses Reveal the Greatest Secrets in Modern History* (Largo, Maryland: Crossing Point Publications, 2001).

Guenther, H. V., and L. S. Kawamura, *Mind in Buddhist Psychology* (Emeryville, California: Dharma Publishing, 1975).

Harner, Michael, *The Way of the Shaman* (New York: Harper & Row, 1980).

Hausdorf, Hartwig, *Ancient Skies* (Beabemburg, Switzerland: German Edition, 1998)

———, *The Chinese Roswell* (Boca Raton, Florida: New Paradigm Books, 1998).

Hazelwood, Mark, *Blindsided: Planet X Passes in 2003* (Orlando, Florida: First Publish, 2001).

Hirschberg, S., and T. Hirschberg, *Reflections on Language*, (New York: Oxford University Press, 1999).

Hopkins, Budd, *Intruders* (New York: Ballantine, 1987).

Hozeski, Bruce, *Hildegard von Bingen's Mystical Vision* (Santa Fe, New Mexico: Bear & Company, 1995).

Johanson, Donald, and Blake Edgar, *From Lucy to Language* (New York: Simon & Schuster Editions, 1996).

Kalakaua, David, *The Legends and Myths of Hawaii* (Rutland, Vermont: Charles E. Tuttle Company, 1972).

Kearney, Richard, *Strangers, Gods, and Monsters* (New York: Routledge, 2003).

Klein, Eric, *Crystal Star: A Guide to Ascension* (Livermore, California: Oughten House Publications, 1994).

Klein, Richard, *The Dawn of Human Culture* (New York: John Wiley & Sons, 2002).

Knappert, Jan, *Indian Mythology* (London: The Aquarian Press, 1991).

Knight, Christopher, and Robert Lomas, *The Hiram Key: Pharaohs, Freemasons, and the Discovery of the Secret Scrolls of Jesus* (Rockport, Massachusetts: Element Books Inc., 1998).

Kohlenberger, John R. III, ed., *The NIV Interlinear Hebrew-English Old Testament: Vol. 1/Genesis-Deuteronomy* (Grand Rapids, Michigan: Zondervan Publishing House, 1979).

Korsak, Mary Phil, *At the Start: Genesis Made New* (New York: Doubleday, 1993).

Krapf, Phillip H., *The Contact Has Begun* (Carlsbad, California: Hay House Inc., 1998).

Langley, Noel, *Edgar Cayce on Reincarnation* (New York: Warner Books, 1967).

Leveque, Pierre, *The Birth of Greece* (New York: Harry N. Abrams Inc., 1990).

Mack, John, *Passport to the Cosmos* (New York: Crown Publishers, 1999).

Marciniak, Barbara, *Bringers of the Dawn: Teachings from the Pleiadians* (Santa Fe, New Mexico: Bear & Company, 1992).

Marks, Jonathan, *Human Biodiversity: Genes, Race, and History* (New York: Aldine de Grutyer, 1995).

Marshack, Alexander, *The Roots of Civilization* (New York: McGraw-Hill, 1972).

McDermott, Robert, *The Essential Steiner* (San Francisco: Harper & Row, 1984).

McKnight, Rosalind, *Cosmic Journeys* (Charlottesville, Virginia: Hampton Roads Publishing, 1999).

McMoneagle, Joseph, *Remote Viewing Secrets* (Charlottesville, Virginia: Hampton Roads, 2000).

Mellaart, James, *Catal Huyuk: A Neolithic Town in Anatolia* (New York: Bacon, 1960).

Mercet, Charles, *Alexander the Great* (New York: Harper & Row, 1962).

Michell, John, *New Light on the Mystery of Glastonbury* (Glastonbury, Somerset: Gothic Images Publications, 1990).

Monroe, Robert A., *Far Journeys* (New York: Doubleday, 1985).

Moody, Raymond, *Life After Life* (New York: Bantam Books, 1976).

Morehouse, David, *Psychic Warrior* (New York: St. Martin's Press, 1996).

Narby, Jeremy, *The Cosmic Serpent: DNA and the Origins of Knowledge* (New York: Putnam, 1998).

Newberg, Andrew, Eugene D'Aquili, and Vince Rause, *Why God Won't Go Away: Brain Science & the Biology of Belief* (New York: Ballantine, 2002).

Suggested Reading

Olds, Linda E., *Metaphors of Interrelatedness* (Albany, New York: State University of New York Press, 1992).

O'Leary, Brian, *Reinheriting the Earth* (Ridgeway, California: Brian O'Leary, 2003).

Pagels, Elaine, *The Origin of Satan* (New York: Random House, 1995).

Parrot, Andre, *Tower of Babel* (New York: Philosophical Library, 1955).

[The] Pentateuch: Vol. 1, Genesis, translated by Samson Rafael Hirsch (New York: The Judaic Press, 1971).

Pye, Lloyd, *Everything You Know Is Wrong* (Madeira Beach, Florida: Adamu Press, 1997).

Quan Yin, Amorah, *Pleiadian Perspectives on Human Evolution* (Santa Fe New Mexico: Bear & Company, 1996).

Roberts, J. M., *A Short History of the World* (New York: Oxford University Press, 1997).

Robinson, James M., ed., *The Nag Hammadi Library* (New York: Harper & Row, 1978).

Roland, Paul, *Revelations: Wisdom of the Ages* (Berkeley, California: Ulysses Press, 1995).

Ruderman, David B., *Kabbalah, Magic, and Science* (Cambridge, Massachusetts: Harvard University Press, 1988).

Russell, Walter, *The Universal One* (Waynesboro, Virginia: University of Science and Philosophy, 1974).

Scallion, Gordon-Michael, *Notes from the Cosmos* (Chesterfield, New Hampshire: Matrix Institute, 1997).

Schwartz, Gary, et al., *The Living Energy Universe* (Charlottesville, Virginia: Hampton Roads Publishing, 1999).

[The] Scroll of the War of the Sons of Light against the Sons of Darkness, edited by Yigael Yadin (New York: Oxford University Press, 1962).

Siblerud, Robert, *In the Beginning: Mysteries of Ancient Civilizations,* The Sacred Science Chronicles: Vol. 1 (Wellington, Colorado: Sacred Science Publications, 1999).

———, *Keepers of the Secrets: Unveiling the Mystical Societies* (Wellington, Colorado: Sacred Science Publications, 1999).

Sitchin, Zecharia, *Divine Encounters* (New York: Avon Books, 1995).

———, *Genesis Revisited* (Santa Fe, New Mexico: Bear & Company, 1991).

———, *The Stairway to Heaven* (Santa Fe, New Mexico: Bear & Company, 1992).

———, *The 12th Planet* (New York: Stein and Day, 1976).

———, *The Wars of Gods and Men* (New York: Avon Books, 1985).

Smith, Bruce D., *The Emergence of Agriculture* (New York: W. H. Freeman, 1994).

Spence, Lewis, *The Outlines of Mythology* (New York: Fawcett Publications, 1961).

Sproul, Barbara C., *Primal Myths: Creation Myths around the World* (San Francisco: HarperSanFrancisco, 1991).

Stanford, Craig, *The Ape-Human Continuum and the Quest for Human Nature* (New York: Basic Books, 2001).

Stearn, Jess, *The Search for a Soul* (New York: Doubleday, 1972).

Steiner, Rudolf, *Cosmic Memory* (San Francisco: Harper & Row, 1959).

Stone, Merlin, *When God Was a Woman* (New York: Dial Press, 1976).

Strassman, Rick, *DMT: The Spirit Molecule* (Rochester, Vermont: Park Street Press, 2001).

Suares, Carlo, *The Cipher of Genesis* (York Beach, Maine: Samuel Weiser, 1992).

Swami Prabhavananda and Christopher Isherwood, *Bhagavad-Gita: The Song of God* (New York: Mentor Books, 1954).

Swann, Ingo, *Natural ESP* (San Francisco: J. P. Tarcher, 1991).

———, *Penetration: The Question of Extraterrestrial and Human Telepathy* (Rapid City, South Dakota: The Twiggs Company, 1998).

Sykes, Bryan, *The Seven Daughters of Eve* (New York: Bantam, 2001).

Thompson-Smith, Angela, *Diary of an Abduction* (Charlottesville, Virginia: Hampton Roads Publishing, 2001).

Vallee, Jacques, *Confrontations: A Scientist's Search for Alien Contact* (New York: Random House, 1990).

Velikovsky, Immanuel, *Earth in Upheaval* (New York: Doubleday & Company, 1955).

Von Ward, Paul, *Our Solarian Legacy: Multidimensional Humans in a Self-Learning Universe* (Charlottesville, Virginia: Hampton Roads Publishing, 2001).

Walsch, Neale Donald, *Conversations with God: An Uncommon Dialogue, Books 1, 2 and 3.* Book 1 (New York: Putnam Publishing Group, 1999), Books 2 and 3 (Charlottesville, Virginia: Hampton Road Publishing, 1997 and 1998, respectively).

Suggested Reading

Wise, Charles C. Jr., *The Magian Gospel of Brother Yeshua* (Penn Laird, Virginia: The Magian Press, 1979).

Wilson, Katharina, *The Alien Jigsaw* (Portland, Oregon: Puzzle Publishing, 1993).

Zimmerman, J. E., *Dictionary of Classical Mythology* (New York: Bantam Books, 1972).

Zukav, Gary, *Seat of the Soul* (New York: Fireside, 1990).

Index

Index

Index

About the Author

An independent scholar, author Paul Von Ward brings a cross-cultural perspective and an interdisciplinary approach to his writing. Ordained as a Baptist minister and trained as a psychologist, he served consecutively for three decades as a U.S. naval officer, U.S. diplomat, and international educator. Founder of the nonprofit Delphi International, his multilingual experience in 100 countries combining social and physical sciences with history, religion, and consciousness studies results in an iconoclast's view of human development. This third major book questions conventional cosmologies and describes the "emerging new story" of the universe and the history of *Homo sapiens.*

With graduate degrees in government and psychology from Harvard and Florida State University, his books include *Dismantling the Pyramid: Government by the People* and *Our Solarian Legacy: Multidimensional Humans in a Self-Learning Universe.* His "frontier science/social change" articles reach a worldwide audience, and his lectures and workshops empower individuals. A member of Mensa, the Institute of Noetic Sciences, MUFON, and the Association for Humanistic Psychology, he is active in other professional and cultural groups. He lives and writes in rural Tennessee.

Hampton Roads Publishing Company

. . . for the evolving human spirit

Hampton Roads Publishing Company
publishes books on a variety of subjects,
including metaphysics, health,
visionary fiction, and other related topics.

For a copy of our latest catalog, call toll-free
(800) 766-8009, or send your name and address to:

Hampton Roads Publishing Company, Inc.
1125 Stoney Ridge Road
Charlottesville, VA 22902

e-mail: hrpc@hrpub.com
www.hrpub.com